Dear Reader: SELECTED SCOTT SYMONS

Dear Reader: SELECTED SCOTT SYMONS

EDITED AND WITH AN INTRODUCTION BY CHRISTOPHER ELSON

FOREWORD BY DAVID WARREN

A Pages Book
PUBLISHED BY GUTTER PRESS, TORONTO

Gutter Press acknowledges the support received for its publishing program from
the Canada Council for the Arts and the Ontario Arts Council.

CANADIAN CATALOGUING IN PUBLICATION DATA

Symons, Scott, 1933-
Dear Reader

"A pages book"
ISBN 1-896356-18-4

I. Title
PS8537.Y523D42 1988   C818'5409   C98-932449-4
PR9199.3.S95D42 1988

A Pages Book published by Gutter Press, P.O. Box 600, Stn Q,
Toronto, Ontario M4T 2N4
www.gutterpress.com, gutter@gutterpress.com
"We are all in the gutter, but some of us are looking at the stars." — Oscar Wilde

Represented in Canada by the Literary Press Group
Distributed in Canada by General Publishing
To order call: 1-800-387-0141 (ON&PQ), or 1-800-387-0172

Distributed in the U.S. by Distributed Art Publishers (D.A.P.)
155 Avenue of the Americas, 2nd Floor, New York, N.Y. 10013-1507
To order call: 1-888-338-BOOK

Designed by Stan Bevington
Typeset in Cartier Book. In January 1967 the graphic designer Carl Dair released Cartier,
the first text typeface to be designed in Canada. It was used to set *Heritage*. In 1998,
Rod McDonald reworked both the roman and italic, incorporating many of the
changes neccessary to produce a working text face for digital typesetting.

Manufactured in Canada
First Printing, October 1998

ACKNOWLEDGEMENTS

Many people have contributed to the emergence of the volume you hold in your hands.

In the first stages, the late Charles Taylor brought his unparalleled knowledge and judgment to bear on the outlines and plans. His untimely death hurt this enterprise among so many others.

Henri Pilon of the Trinity College Archives gave indispensable assistance during my too-rapid incursions into his domain.

The French Department and the Faculty of Arts of the University of Regina made it possible for me to travel to Toronto for a number of essential tasks. Many thanks to supportive and bemused colleagues.

Four dear friends in Toronto extended hospitality and aid: Richard Howard and Gabriela King, and Caroline Zayid and Barney Savage.

Mille mercis à Christine Lorre, who, by asking me to give a lecture on Scott Symons at the Université de Poitiers in 1995, provided me with a first excuse to think at length about this fascinating and disturbing figure. Little could we have imagined it would lead to this book!

Marc Glassman, bookseller and cultural presence, was crucial in making it all come together.

Stan Bevington, legendary maker of books, weighed heavily in the equations. His contribution is beautifully obvious. Tremendously fitting too, given that he designed the original edition of *Place d'Armes* in 1967.

Thanks to Jenny Anttila for her steady editing.

Warm thanks to my parents, and to Linda McKnight, Bill and Meredith Saunderson, Florence Daurelle, David Warren, Donald Martin, Sheila Grant, and Sam Hiyate.

Above all, my profound gratitude goes to Nik Sheehan, director of *God's Fool*. Without his stubborn diplomacy and cheerful confidence, *Dear Reader* could not have been achieved. He provided the eyes and ears of the project and contributed immense good sense to the whole improbable process.

Scott Symons, he of the midnight faxes and the wildly-stamped envelopes, he the *scotched expeditor*, gave much besides the writings themselves to this collection. He communicated his joy and sense of purpose to all involved.

Christopher Elson,
Editor

TABLE OF CONTENTS

One might say that our civilization has reached a pretty pass when people like Scott Symons are upholding it. But look around: the place is a mess. We have an economy and not much else. Beyond the "perceived need" for more money, and still more, what do we reach for? Nothing, or rather, we don't know.

The task of the creative artist in a world like this is to be something like Scott Symons. It is to take radical measures to assure some autonomy. The artist must make himself an outsider, must live almost as a felon. To be true to his own purpose, he must stay on the run. This is not an attempt to romanticize the artistic life, or to justify a certain dated bohemian pose, for the reality is often sordid.

Our civilization is scattered, it is remnants preserved here and there, for instance in the prison-like confinement of our universities, where even poetry exists for the convenience of well-paid professors, and may be tortured. It is a dead or at least very sick body they are paid to watch over.

Most of the traditions that kept alive poetry, the fine arts and architecture, music and dance and drama – have been smashed quite purposelessly. To practice at all, to make something alive, the creative artist must forge or re-forge a tradition within himself. This was true to some degree even in the time of Giotto, but today it is true to the point of farce. The artist must sing alone, there are no more choirs. The artist must create even the venue for singing, even the semblance of connection to what was once alive.

Because there is no place for art, for poetry, in modern life, the artist must appropriate a place, perhaps a hypothetical place – must act perversely almost as if the modernity that denies him his role in the world had not itself happened. There is no Church today, to act as patron, and in the absence of a Church, really no State either, nor any other institution touching the daily lives of people whose function is to lift their hearts. There are only private efforts and private patrons.

The modern artist, homeless in this sense, must give himself away. He has no clothes to put on, he is exposed, naked, humiliated, a fugitive. He must live for art, must live the life of art, just as in a previous age, and still, one might live the life of philosophy. He cannot be a simple tradesman or craftsman, though he must also of course be both of these. "You can run but you can't hide," is a comical way to put it.

More comical, and even more to the point, is the way John Berryman put it. "We are using our skins for wallpaper and we cannot win."

There are many ways to live this life, and Scott Symons is, like every modern artist, a unique case. He would be the last to suggest that anyone should follow his own particular path to glory. His homosexuality, his unironic voice, his choice of enemies, are, like his special apprehension of Christ on the Cross, peculiar to him and his doing. It has been his own, effective, way to cut loose from everything false in the world that made him. He says that he has been "hell-bent on heaven."

The Canada in which he has lived – even in Morocco – is a construction of his own mind and soul and body, a "semblance" such as I described above. He has

9

made his own connections to the Canada that was: to the rural settlements of mill and steeple, and to the Rosedale into which he was born. He has, to the limit of his sometimes terrifying personal sincerity, made himself their faithful son, in the afterlife of that smashed Canada. He has presented himself as a kind of vengeance upon the people who watched that Canada being killed. He affirms the immortality of the corpse that is still withering away before them.

The flame of Scott Symons is a loving vengeance. It is animated by love, not hate. It is not a sentimental love. Even in its nostalgia, its lament for the dead Canada, there is an affirmation of a Canada that does not die.

As an artist, fleeting through the modern world, Scott Symons has existed to hold this up – this Canada of the thinking heart. With all his strength he is indeed thereby "upholding civilization." It is an art, both lost and found, and it is an affront not only to the Canada of today but to the whole bloody modern world: a joyous affront and a loving vengeance.

David Warren, Kingston, 1998

Mourning and Ecstasy:
Scott Symons' Canadian Apocalypse

> Together we will undertake the extravagance of living under
> a sharpened consciousness, in open honesty, and we will see
> what happens. The worst can only be catastrophe, which is
> better by far than a false success.
>
> (Paul-Emile Borduas, *Projections libérantes*)

Is there a more singular figure in Canada's literary and cultural life than Scott
Symons? Arguably the most consistently undervalued English Canadian author,
Symons is also one of the most significant. In spite of the praise and admiration of
many key figures of contemporary literature, from Margaret Atwood to Paul
Bowles, from Northrop Frye to William Burroughs, his books have not attained a
wide readership, and, indeed, have been allowed to go out of print. In spite of, or
perhaps because of, a notoriety acquired in the 1960s for his dramatic and contro-
versial entry into Canadian letters, his books and other publications have not
received the sustained critical attention they so manifestly deserve.

The details of Symons' life have all the qualities of a fiction. In so many
respects, it is the life that is the novel. Installment after installment, chapter after
chapter, the story of Scott Symons tends to eclipse his books and other publica-
tions. This is both understandable and, from the point of view of the writing itself,
regrettable. With evidence of increasing interest in the case of Scott Symons from
Canadians of younger generations (see, in particular, Nik Sheehan's documentary
film, *God's Fool*[1]), the time has come for a reassessment of his place in Canadian cul-
ture – a place which, ultimately, will have everything to do with the artifacts left
behind: the books, the copious diaries, the wide-ranging correspondence, the
interviews both taped and filmed. *Dear Reader* is an initial attempt to sift through
this body of work and to demonstrate that its importance is considerable.

The links between Symons' life and his work will be apparent to all readers as
they consider the various selections. The 'Notes toward a C.V. by Scott Symons'
which appear at the end of the volume give a schematic overview of Symons' life
history, the key events, publications, his comings and goings. No full-scale biog-
raphy of Scott Symons yet exists and this introduction is not the place to under-
take such a formidable task. Charles Taylor's chapter on Symons in his 1977 book
Six Journeys: A Canadian Pattern remains the best source for biographical information
and it tells the fascinating and troubling story of Symons' life up to the middle
1970s[2].

My life is a sketch toward a life I'll never have time to lead. For the sake of those just
discovering Symons, here is a brief attempt to provide a sketch of that sketch.
Symons was born in 1933 into an old Rosedale family of Loyalist origins. He enjoyed
a rather privileged upbringing and an enviable education, including degrees from

---

1 CeLL Productions, with the participation of the National Film Board of Canada, 1997.
2 Taylor, Charles. *Six Journeys: A Canadian Pattern*. Toronto: Anansi, 1977.

the University of Toronto, Cambridge (where he studied with F. R. Leavis), and the Sorbonne (where he came under the influence of the great Christian existentialist, Gabriel Marcel). He married into a wealthy family and pursued a career in journalism in Québec (which included writing in French for *La Presse*), the highlight of which was his being honoured with a National Newspaper Award for a series of articles predicting the Quiet Revolution. Returning to Toronto, he embarked upon a career in museology, first as curator, then as curator-in-chief of Canadian collections at the Royal Ontario Museum. He was visiting fellow at the Winterthur collection in Maryland, and research associate of the Smithsonian Institute in Washington.

Then, in 1965, Symons changed his life dramatically. He abandoned his promising position in Canadian life, as well as a beloved wife and young son, to write two confessional novels predicated upon a radically sensual apprehension of the world, both of which contain a strong component of homoeroticism. *Place d' Armes* (set in Montréal) was published in the Centennial year, 1967; *Civic Square*, the "book in the box" (set in and near Toronto), was published in 1969. What motivated this radical reorientation of his life, an act that continues to define Scott Symons for many today? In 1989 he gave this account of his behaviour:

> I contemplated for at least five years before I did what I did that it would have to be done. I kept waiting for other people to do it. Why should I, who was happily married, had a lovely home in Toronto, a lovely farm full of Canadian art and culture, a Curator of Canadiana, a Professor at the U. of T., a Visiting Curator at the Smithsonian, have to do it? I did not leap with any glee. There was a sense of vocation and a sense of civic action. One can laugh at it, one can praise it, but it's genuine. The choice risked my life because it risked my sanity. I knew that this was where one had to move in, to open the doors to male sentience. T.S. Eliot said if he hadn't pursued the path he did – a very dry life – he would have gone in the direction of Durrell's *Black Book*. I'd read that before I jumped. At the same time, women's lib was just beginning to explode. I couldn't go to another woman because I already had the woman of my choice. I have always found it odd that I am considered the black wolf of CanLit. I'm a very conservative guy who went to Easter Mass at Saint Thomas's. I'm a quiet person and in many ways timid. I was brought up with a deep sense of civic participation and commitment.[3]

Symons acted out of outrage, preferring to go in the direction of extreme risk rather than acquiesce to what he considered to be the accelerating effacement of his Canadian traditions (of which the new flag of 1965 was a catalyzing symbol). His movement into the artistic, bohemian life, the 'move away from the world of memo into the world of touch,' was motivated by a sense of duty, a conviction that the actions and choices of one man might influence the evolution of his community.

In the years that followed, the "demissionary" lived out the consequences of

3   Interview in *The Idler*, no. 23, May & June, 1989, p. 29.

his actions. He lived a great passion with a young man who, at the time of their meeting, was not yet eighteen. Flight to Mexico ensued, where the lovers were pursued by the Mexican Federales at the instigation of their families in Toronto. After winning a prize for his first novel, *Place d'Armes*, Symons was able to return to Toronto. An internal exile followed: he spent time in British Columbia in the lumber woods, and embarked on a "furniture safari" that resulted in the writing of *Heritage: A Romantic Look at Canadian Furniture*, in the Newfoundland fishing village of Trout River. Eventually, Symons' relationship with his lover ended, and in a movement of shock and reconstruction he settled in Morocco, which he had earlier visited. From those experiences between 1970 and 1974 came the three volumes of the *Helmet of Flesh* trilogy.

Symons has lived near the town of Essaouira, Morocco for the past 25 years. He lives with a Canadian, but has become a fixture of the local community, which he loves passionately. He writes – diaries and letters, occasional magazine pieces – while editing the final two volumes of the *Helmet of Flesh* trilogy, amidst the wild boar, nestled in the cactus garden. To anyone who inquires, he will reply that he is dangerously well.

Dear Reader presents a wide selection of Scott Symons' published and unpublished writings. It is important to assess them on their own merits. This does not mean abstracting them from the underpinnings of the lived experience; that would be impossible in Symons' case. It does mean that the writing should be examined as writing, as reportage, as art, as witnessing. These writings constitute a very powerful testimony of a uniquely Canadian life, *a life examined*, in the ancient, Socratic sense.

The reception of Scott Symons' work has been discouragingly inadequate. In part this is due to the powerful fascination of the biographical dimension, which exercises a double dynamic of attraction-repulsion. More broadly, though, it is clear that journalistic and academic critics are too frequently trapped within their own limitations: on the one hand, a tendency to reduce literature to the realistic, technical standards of shared school experience (characterization, plot and structure, believability, sociological relevance, etc.); on the other, strict obedience to the abstract international criteria of the currently fashionable critical discourses, such as post-colonial or queer theories. Such critical positions, ways of reading whether popular or highbrow, undoubtedly offer real insight into certain works and render much literature more broadly accessible. It is, however, unsurprising that extremely idiosyncratic and original work like Symons' would lie outside of their assumptions and pass through their methodological and ideological nets.

There are a number of other ways into Symons' work, possible itineraries for future readings. And the selections themselves speak to these crucial access points. A few such openings are: through a broadly deconstructive reading of the works' insights into identity; through a deeper appreciation of their satirical dimension; through an understanding of their articulation with French Canada, particularly the many analogies to be explored with figures such as Hubert Aquin; through a consideration of their links to the work of George Grant and other thinkers of Canadian particularity in a technological era; through a recontextualization of the early works that would put them in relation to such canonical

Canadian texts of the 1960s as Graeme Gibson's *Five Legs* and Leonard Cohen's *Beautiful Losers*; through an analysis of the works' spiritual and mystical dimensions that would comprise an assessment of its mystical, neo-Platonic, and Weilian foundations; through a thorough genealogy that would take into account the influence and critical *presence* of writers as diverse as Lawrence, Eliot, Ruskin, James, Moodie, Genet, Lowry, Joyce, Hopkins, Austen, Burroughs, Gide, Sterne, etc.; and through an examination of the concept and reality of *exile*. None of these ways into Symons' work has been attempted in a sustained manner.

In Symons' writings the grand underlying question is that of identity. To begin to grasp this, one has only to consider the crisis of identity illustrated by *Place d'Armes*, a book written as it was lived in a three week period in 1965 and published in 1967 as a dissonant and dissident Centennial gift to the nation.

On day six of the combat journal that is *Place d'Armes*, the narrator refers to himself as an "intégriste Anglo-Canadien." He concedes that it is "a dangerous term. Yet, all exceptions made, it is right." In what sense does Symons use the epithet "intégriste"? In the sense that he feels and knows himself to belong to an old, coherent and identifiable tradition, "Our High North American Tory Culture – odious phrase – but never mind the politics of it." Yet, and this is just one aspect of the already noted paradox, that tradition is complicit in its own disappearance. As Symons writes, "We have a rooted quality culture that has never expressed itself; we have never said us. Never sung us. Why? Why? Why?" Symons' whole project from the mid-1960s forward is an attempt to reply to that question.

As a body of work, Symons' writings incarnate and express a vision that is apocalyptic, an experience of limits and of endings. To read Symons is to accompany him to the sublime point of loss and to listen to what might best be described as a last testament. The fact that he has been elaborating and reiterating these last words for the past thirty years alters nothing of their fundamentally eschatological character. They are concerned with final things.

He writes from the point of impossibility. A class and culture-based identity becomes impossible to sustain. A particular world (the rooted Anglo-Canadian) becomes untenable. It remains possible to say "us," to sing "us" only at the moment when the "us" recognizes its mortality, its ending, its self-treason, its passing beyond. But, and we will see some of the implications of this paradox, this is not mere resignation. If Scott Symons bemoans the lack of creativity, the lack of grace, the lack of presence, the systematic forgetting and effacement of his Canadian roots, it is also in order to renew them through criticism, through a self-imposed rupture that is not merely negative. A break that is not a break. A fidelity that expresses itself in terms of rejection. A patriotism that finds its fulfillment in exile. A cataloguing of decline that simultaneously stands for renewed vitality and presence. *Future vigueur*, as Rimbaud, another ambivalent modern exile, put it.

"You hate them almost as much as you love them." An antique dealer says this to Hugh Anderson, the protagonist of *Place d'Armes*, as she observes him examining and analyzing the English Canadian customers of her store. *Qui aime bien châtie bien*. Scott Symons' very existence is a constant chastisement, a goad to complacency. What terrified and motivated him at the moment of demission in the sixties continues to terrify and motivate him: a deadening of sensibility, an increasingly abstract, technified relation to life, a growing corporatization of society, a diminishment of honour in relation to career, increasing greed, creeping amnesia, reduction of potency, smothering of spirituality. Scott Symons' maddeningly idiosyncratic, impossibly outrageous life and work are driven, then, by a sense of obligation – he must point out the risks of such transformation, before the forgetting is complete, before the forward metamorphoses become totally impossible. "Let us say, to put it politely, that I am dedicated to 'distending' their sensibilities." (Letter to John Robert Colombo, April 1967.)

In an essential recent discussion of European cultural identity, French philosopher Jacques Derrida makes the following point: "*what is proper to a culture is to not be identical to itself*. Not to not have an identity, but not to be able to identify itself, to say 'me' or 'us'; to be able to take the form of the subject only in the non-identity to itself or, if you prefer, in the difference *with itself*."[4] In Symons' work, such non-identity takes two forms: i) the Enemy within (as Charles Taylor put it) and ii) the reference to alternative formulations and sitings of identity. In the case of the negative relation to difference, Symons situates the cultural failure of Canada with respect to the virtually monolithic control of a single, albeit large, element of Canadian society – the Enemy – which he polemically compresses in a formula, like "Grit Methodist Mediocre." Whether it be the Victorian matriarchate, journalist and critic Robert Fulford, or Mackenzie King, this part which takes itself for the whole has sabotaged the nation in Symons' not unpersuasive historico-cultural reading. A more positive relation to non-identity takes shape in Symons' explorations of French Canada, European traditions, Mexico, and Morocco. The point is that Symons seeks to shore up his Canadian reality by escaping the smothering constraints of identity assertions.

In order to sing *us* and say *us*, Symons had to affirm the other, become other, seek other aspects of the identity that he sought to assert and enhance. He knew this when he embraced his heritage of Britishness and the deep European roots in Cambridge and Paris. He knew it when he enacted, through his relocation to Québec, his entitlement to French-Canadianness. He knew it when he functioned within powerful American cultural institutions like the Smithsonian. He knew it, too, when he made the fateful decision in 1965 to break with bourgeois heterosexual respectability. He knew it during the period of the "furniture safari," that internal exile. He knew it in Newfoundland, in the relationships he had there with the fisher-folk. And the ambiguous exile to Morocco sets up a decisively new relation to "us," to here, to now.

Through all of these displacements, visions and revisions, Symons was saying *us*, singing *us*, writing *us*. And is it really necessary to add that the first person plural here has very little to do with economic privilege, class prestige or anything else that the "odious" term of High North American Tory might seem to imply?

Scott Symons looked before he leaped, yet leapt anyway. Since 1965, he has repeatedly insisted on the fact that he knew exactly what he was doing. In leaping he set out for himself what is quite possibly the most explicitly intellectual

4   Derrida, Jacques. *The Other Heading* , (tr. of *L'Autre Cap* by Pascale-Anne Brault and Michael B. Nauss) Indiana U. P., 1992, p. 9.

programme of any English-Canadian writer, though Symons insists that it was an act more of the heart than of the head. The programme is an enactment, an intensely personal and original lived procession through a constellation of questions and ideas that lie at the heart of much twentieth-century literature and thought. They constitute an original attempt to deal with our modernity.

Symons' example speaks to both memory and creativity. It proposes a spiritual and sensual quest that runs explicitly counter to the dominant, technocratic "identity mechanism" within which so much of Canadian cultural production and discourse was and is held. Symons celebrates, in a manner unique to him, aspects of his fragile Canadian particularity, while trying to relate them to the most fundamental elements of human experience. He speaks of his trials "from within tears," in a continuous threnody, a song and dance of mourning for a passing reality that also hopes for new birth. In Symons' ongoing project mourning and ecstasy are paradoxically conjoined.

A CONSCIOUSNESS AT FULL STRETCH

> Be careful for nothing
> (Saint Paul, Epistle to the Philippians, 4: 6)

A consciousness at full stretch. The expression is Simon Fraser professor Peter Buitenhuis's[5]. It captures what is best about Scott Symons and his writing. Symons seeks to extend both experience and understanding by pushing consciousness to its furthest limit. Symons has frequently expressed his commitment to hold nothing back by saying, "I was my own guinea pig." Buitenhuis has put this elegantly and precisely in referring to Symons as an *exemplum.* There can be no doubt that Scott Symons has lived a life of risk, and that he has tried to write honestly about the radical nature of his choices, their costs and their joys. In that sense, as well as formally, his writing is experimental. The experiment consists very simply of putting himself to the test, putting his *self* on trial.

A writer has just two fundamental choices in relation to the self: he or she may go the route of transformation through exposure, even over-exposure of the self, or he or she may go the route of self-denial, -effacement, -abnegation. This choice is essentially the same whether one is operating in narrative fictional, poetic, (auto-) biographical, creative-non-fictional, or other modes. The same basic alternative exists if one uses fictional characters or if one assumes the full weight of saying "I," "me" with an autoreferential signature. Either orientation can bring truths, even transfiguration, if artfulness is present. Each admits a nearly infinite variety of approaches, modulations, accents. And each inhabits the other.

Scott Symons has been criticized for confusing self and art. Usually the confusion lies more on the side of the critic, but it cannot be denied that Symons encourages such criticism by compressing the two poles in what he calls his *lifework.* He refuses what is conventionally known as aesthetic distance; he knows that his novels are disguised letters to the reader, diary pages nudged toward

5 Buitenhis, Peter. "Scott Symons and the Strange Case of *Helmet of Flesh." West Coast Review*, Vol. 21, no. 4, spring 1987. pp 59-73.

fictionality, polemics imbedded in narrative. He conceives of his books as proxies for himself: "My books are auxiliaries for myself. For people I can't meet, but with whom I'd like to talk."[6] Equally, he rejects the professionalism and the hygiene of the conventional categories within and across which he has functioned as a writer: novel, journalism, academic essay, connoisseur's treatise. He both welcomes and deserves the charge of incompetence as it is conceived of within and through such normative frames.

The obvious reaction is to dismiss him as a writer (and by extension, because of the affirmed inseparability of art and life, as a man). Even Symons' admirers sometimes seem to make excuses for the sprawling, undisciplined nature of the prose. He is not a novelist, not a writer, they will say, he is a prophet, or a mystic, a shaman, or a post-literate figure. Well, that may be, but he is above all else a person enamoured of language and the spoken and written word. Rhetorician, preacher, after-dinner speaker, lecturer, symposium participant, all of those roles he has fulfilled, but he is undeniably a writer, one who "does diary daily," as he once gleefully put it. This is very likely the key to understanding all the published writing as well.

There is no more secretly fundamental form than the diary, none less concerned with competence or public accessibility, and all of Symons' published work proceeds from and is preceded by diarizing. He has called his diary his "spiritual survival kit," and it functions as a kind of supplement or container, permitting greater inwardness, richer inner dialogue. A September 1970 diary entry reads as follows: "My D. is my *Apologia pro Vita mea*. My D. is not my raison d'être; but it is ... is what? Ah – it is my *capacité d'être*: my D. is my capacity for Being." Life is more important than writing, but without the writing, the Being of life is diminished, forgotten.

But *is* artfulness present in the transition from diary to publication? Is Symons a *good* writer? Here too, the responsible critic is obliged to tread carefully to avoid, on the one hand, falling into criteria and categories that are inadequate to the object, and on the other a kind of boosterism, speaking to the converted with no fair appreciation of the undeniable justness of certain criticisms. Symons rejects the criterion of "good," just as he has rejected mere competence. Speaking of *Civic Square*, he affirms that it must be a great book, or it is a failure. "[I]t is not a good book, nor a goodish book, nor merely a brilliant, or good-and-bad book" (Letter to J.R. Colombo, April, 1967). He then goes on to compare it to The New Testament! The intention here is less to make an impossibly arrogant comparison than it is to reiterate that original writing will find its own form and that the questions of genre or technical ability are secondary to those of impulse and meaning, or perhaps that they determine each other mutually. A quick answer to the questions posed at the outset of this paragraph: yes, artfulness is evident throughout the Symons corpus. No, Symons is not a *good* writer, he ranges from brilliant to painfully awkward, with few pauses in the middle ground of adequate, competent, good. His work is *extra-ordinary*, outside the norm.

In effect, what Scott Symons attempts through this fulsome and ragged over-

6 Interview with Graeme Gibson. In *Eleven Canadian Authors* (ed. G. Gibson) Toronto: Anansi, 1971.

exposure of self is a radical enhancement of meaning. It is no accident that his first non-journalistic published piece, reproduced here, treated the *meaning* of English Canada. He desires significant transparency. Quotidian meaningfulness. Increased lucidity. An end to "smug opacity." Every meeting, every meal, every sighting, every touch, every erection, every conversation, every reading, every writing, every building, every utterance is and must be shot through with meaning and significance. He seeks to bring a total presence to bear on a total presence. The self in communion with the world through a heightened sensibility that is the fruit of mediated reason and sensuality. "Oh, the sheer luxury of self-presence – of presence of sensibility." (*Place d'Armes*.) And the writing out of ALL of it.

Needless to say, such an ambition of totality is exhausting, in every sense of the word. It exhausts the self and it even exhausts the apparently inexhaustible real. It may very well exhaust the capacities of writing. Symons frequently appears in his writings at a point of self-loss or minimal, haunting persistence. It is precisely at this point of maximal emptying, at this most delicate moment, that joy seems to take hold. This is a typically mystical experience. *Muero por que non muero.* Dying not to be dying, as Saint John of the Cross had it. Utterly involved with life and its finalities.

Scott Symons, on an "eschatological foray," ventures into the realm where receptivity and expenditure are seen in their relation to one another. Receptivity and expenditure? We might equally say, attention and giving. The desired full presence of sensibility will always imply the presence of the other, and the necessary establishment of a complex relation of subject and object.

To see how such a configuration of self, other, and object is achieved and expressed, let us briefly consider the place of architecture and furniture in Symons' vision of the world. Scott Symons is undoubtedly one of our greatest teachers about Canadian material culture and art. His writings on cultural artifacts are liberally sampled in this anthology because they demonstrate his unique capacity to unite an intellectual appreciation with a sensual experience. Words and expressions like *organic*, *rooted*, or *intuitive belonging* spring to mind. Very much like the term *intégriste* explored above, these positive expressions can all prove dangerous or destructive, personally and politically, if pursued or understood one-sidedly. But Symons' intention here is never to exclude the uninitiated or to assert an absolute privilege. Nor is the effect of reading a text like *Heritage : A Romantic Look at Canadian Furniture* likely to be that of exclusion or alienation. More likely that of fascination and pleasure and a desire to participate in such insights.

Symons' experience and understanding of furniture, art, and architecture is to be located somewhere at the intersection of the sensuous but resolutely Catholic aesthetic of Jesuit poet Gerard Manley Hopkins, and the rigorously ascetic Platonism of philosopher Simone Weil, with its particular conception of seeing and interpretation. Speaking of *Civic Square* in a letter written to the book's editor, John Robert Colombo, in April of 1967, Symons uses a vocabulary borrowed from Hopkins and Eliot to get at his central intentions for the book: "The fact, of course, of its contents being an 'inscape' suggests the other reality of TB [Toronto Book]. That 'Toronto' itself is only as it were the site, or more particularly, the local human metaphor. I have used my home city, in depth, as my embracing metaphor. Eliot would say that Toronto was my 'objective correlate.' But the fact of the matter is that I am preoccupied with the subjective correlative, in itself, in myself, and for Toronto. Ass backwards as always!" Inscape – the term in Hopkins' work may indeed anticipate and combine both sides of Eliot's paradigm, insofar as inscape and poetic "inscaping" do insist upon the absolute singularity of any phenomenon or being (its *haecceitas* to use the medieval scholastic terminology adopted by Hopkins), all the while putting it, necessarily, into an open, metaphorical relation with what is other to it. Correlating it subjectively and objectively, then, as Symons argues of his own intimate project as regards the site of his "novel," the city of Toronto. Indeed, the author of *Civic Square* picks up on this double dimension of the logic of inwardness and identity and examines it in all of his work. The key to the efficacy of this line of understanding lies in the quality of the human gaze. Through such a heightened ambition for seeing, Symons pursues and articulates something like what Saskatchewan poet Tim Lillburn refers to as a "deeper courtesy of the eye"[7].

"Method for understanding images, symbols, etc. Not to try to interpret them, but to look at them till the light suddenly dawns."[8] The discovery of such "truth bullets," as Symons describes these Weilian insights in the second volume of his *Helmet of Flesh* trilogy, revealed an approach to the object which was already substantially Scott Symons' own, an approach based on extreme attention, on an informed and passionate looking which both strips down, reduces, and builds up, elevates, in a spiritually-enhanced reading. There is something powerfully analogous here to what the phenomenologists call "reduction" or "*épokhè.*" What Symons shares with Weil, however, and which goes beyond the intentions of secular philosophy, is an overt appreciation of the spiritual, even religious ramifications of this way of seeing. "Extreme attention is what constitutes the creative faculty in man and the only extreme attention is religious. The amount of creative genius in any period is strictly in proportion to the amount of extreme attention and thus of authentic religion at that period."[9] And this goes some way toward accounting for the fact that Symons' discourse on the objects of culture is largely determined by a theological vocabulary, even when he is dealing with eminently secular and profane dimensions of life.

When Symons brings his unique perception to bear on Canadian realities, architecture, paintings, furniture, and public squares get a reading such as they have never had before. Yet his most fundamental desire, thoroughgoingly erotic, is to reverse his receptivity, to transform it into a gift: "I have come to sight La Place for others." (*Place d'Armes*). In those writings that concern themselves with artifacts, the built environment, etc., Symons inevitably relates a movement of ecstatic discovery and necessary falling away. Epiphany, generally incomplete, frustrated, is followed by the negative pleasure so characteristic of the Sublime. The consideration of any artifact in a system of extreme attention that seeks to get at both singularity and relation allows some knowledge and truth to be taken away from an inherently precarious experience. This is why Symons will so often speak

---

7 T. Lillburn, *Moosewood Sandhills*, Toronto: McClelland and Stewart, 1994, p. 36.

8 Simone Weil. *Gravity and Grace*. Routledge and Kegan Paul, 1952. p. 109.

9 Weil. *Gravity and Grace*, p. 106.

of the "insite" provided by the artifact. Furniture, the decorative arts, architecture, and public erections of all kinds, give proportion and measure, they *site* both the writer (subject) and his object. They also situate the reader, who is always presumed, always dear. It is a loving triangulation.

Another element which Symons brings to the consideration of human artifacts and natural phenomena, and which Hopkins and Weil did not, is that of an incarnated erotic apprehension of things that is often explicitly sexual. This loving, caressive gaze and tactile approach prevent, as George Grant puts it in his preface to Symons' furniture book, things from being reduced to mere objects. Their "blood and bones" subsist. The real presence of their (usually) anonymous makers is recalled. In *Heritage*, Symons recounts a number of approaches to pieces of furniture which have the character of a sexual seduction. A mock-epic (though utterly unironical) description of the rediscovery of a rare New Brunswick Corner Cupboard ends with the following orchestration: "Tall. Taller than I had felt He was – and through the dim light of late afternoon, the ripe birch flames shimmering like Apricot Brandy after your third glass as your lover leans forward, flush, flushed, and giving." As Leonard Cohen has pointed out, this is a very subversive coffee table book indeed! It subverts both the materialistic, utilitarian, instrumental view of reality and the too-respectful, archivizing, nostalgic grasp of the things of culture. It is mirthful and sexual in the broadest sense of that term.

Helmet of Flesh contains several passages of considerable power in which the exposure to Islamic architecture and handcraft overwhelms the "narrator," York MacKenzie. In his quest for enhanced meaning in a Morocco which figures as a kind of anti-Canada, MacKenzie allows the strange beauty of the North African world and its civilization to overwhelm him. These are disturbing experiences of inadequacy in which the senses lead the intellect a merry chase, without ever totally leaving it behind. "You've come a long way to be frightened by a rug," as Karim, one of the Moroccans encountered by York MacKenzie, puts it laughingly. Indeed there is something terrifying about the worldview incarnated by this other culture in its artifacts, and MacKenzie is foolish and brave enough to try to work out precisely why and how he is frightened. In one of the crucial moments of the novel, Symons attempts to deal with an extraordinary rug in its context within a sultan's home. As always, the artifact is as powerful as any human character:

> He shifted on the divan, determined to assimilate the room. His toes working the rug, eyes swimming amid the majestic black carvings, the shelves. An enormous eye to the left of the lantern, watching him. He leaned forward. Same blues, yellows, turquoise green as carpet. And stabs of black. A plate drew him into a spinning circle, a centre, where a beast lay hidden. The music of the room more insistent as he tried to see. Rug seething there, rumbling – no safer than the plate. And the music churning as his toes furrowed the carpet. Majesty and mirth lurking in everything, till he was overwhelmed by furious urge to dance, strip off all his clothes, *dance.*

In its crisscrossing between Morocco, London, and Canada, *Helmet of Flesh* tries to articulate both majesty and mirth. York MacKenzie's adventure is an overcoming of alienation through the bringing together of dance with ongoing education, a song of "innocence and experience," a hard-won articulation of "brains balls and being," in one of Symons' typical formulas.

Symons is of course far from the only writer arguing for a re-thinking of Eros in the context of our advanced capitalism and liberal democracy. One might think of the work of a Georges Bataille or that of a Hubert Marcuse. Popular culture too brims over with this urgency. To take a very current example from the shelves of the self-help and psychology sections of our bookstores, Thomas Moore's *The Soul of Sex* stands as an interesting point of comparison. The popular writer on psychology and religion, and author of *Care of the Soul*, is attempting a gesture for North American culture which is profoundly close to that of Scott Symons – though, it goes without saying, it is less radical in its lived implications. Moore's most recent book attempts to "revalorize" Eros in an accessible and broadly acceptable manner and contains much insight into erotic imagery and mythology. Among many points of contact between the ex-monk and "God's fool" is the idea of *Eros* as transport. Desire sets us in motion.

Anyone who has received a letter from Scott Symons will read knowingly the passage early in Moore's book where he refers to the punning of the Greeks, which transformed Eros into *pteros*, wings. The flying phalli that decorate and illuminate so many of Symons' margins are in perfect continuity with this long tradition. The phallus, which, as Lacan has pointed out, no one can have, is celebrated but never as an end in itself, never in the way that more ideological readings might condemn as phallocentric. "When the penis is pictured having wings, or when bird-women like the Sirens tempt and seduce, this idea of a flying, lofty Eros finds direct expression … Eros seems to move through the air, and he has this quality of taking us, as Anne Carson says 'from over here to over there.' When we long for someone or something, we are being invited to make a move, to soar in spirit out of the status quo and into a new world."[10] Symons' sometimes baffling and frequently amusing personification/sexualization of the artifact must always be seen in relation to this transporting capacity of desire.

The necessity for such a turning, or the setting-in-motion of what might be described as a conversion experience, is frequently evoked in Symons' books. The following passage from the opening sequences of *Helmet I* describes a service in St. Paul's, London and provides a perfect complement to the experiences of Moroccan and Newfoundland ecstatic discovery. It also furnishes his protagonist with a key expression for self-understanding, *the thinking heart*:

> The words of the service resounding from beyond the altar screen and up into the arches. As York marvelled – Cleanse the *thoughts of our hearts* – who would dare make such a declaration in the modern world? The *thinking* heart! He followed the words up into the vaulted ceiling. Then fell back into the chair, clutching his *Book of Common Prayer*.

10 Thomas Moore, *The Soul of Sex* New York: Harper Collins, 1998, p. 14.

A thorough analysis of such a passage would reveal the complexity of the double, hiding/revealing nature of these moments, moments when a quotation like that from the *Book of Common Prayer* can serve both to elevate toward an epiphanic perception of unity and provide for some kind of landing, back among the difficulties of daily living, yet somehow transformed.

Anyone who, like Scott Symons in *Heritage*, can affirm that his first and decisive marital infidelity was with a French Canadian chair clearly possesses an unusually developed sense of his own openness to the world, and of his own vulnerability. Again and again, Symons invites a metaphorical rape, a ravishing. His authorial sensibility operating at a fever-pitch, he writes at the end of *Place d'Armes*:

> La Place d'Armes – he still wasn't there. He turned to the left – down la rue Notre Dame. Every detail seared in him. He was implacably lucid and incredibly vulnerable. Everything touched him. Vulnerable – was it always necessary to be this vulnerable, just to see, to hear, to know? Did it have to be this way? And then he knew that it did. That that was what was marvelous about man – his vulnerability. That was the adventure in life. The adventure of life. To close it off was to close off life. So he had to embrace that vulnerability – or live dead. That vulnerability defined him as a man. It was desirable, essential, inevitable. The trees in front of the old Courthouse, imbedding it in deep space alive with blackbirds – those trees, erect in him, every branch veined in him – disastrously present – gloriously.

In what is very likely a conscious parody of the famous scene from Sartre's *Nausea*, Symons evokes an entirely different feeling of existential overwhelming, one that keeps his hero (anti-hero?) alive, purposeful, oriented toward meaningfulness and otherness.

I have come to sight La Place for others.

THE SELECTIONS

> – the act of selection is a moral act.
> Northrop Frye [11]

An anthology is a re-reading. A reading-over. An opportunity to show what is and to inquire, "what if?." The following selections are partial, in two senses of that word: non-exhaustive and necessarily somewhat biased.

This anthology tries to capture the multivalent force, the transgeneric capacity and the transgressive intention of the writing. To risk a bad pun, Symons is as much a genre-bender as he is a gender bender. The back cover of the original edition of *Place d'Armes* reads as follows: "*Place d'Armes* is at once a first novel, a metic-

---

11 Frye, Northrop. *Anatomy of Criticism.* Princeton University Press, 1957, p. 224.

ulously tangled diary, an insanely indiscreet autobiography, an existential Canadian allegory, a book of illicit imagination that is pure fact, an implacable manifesto." An equally complex description can be imagined for any of his other books. Here's one:

> 1986's *Helmet of Flesh* is a three-hundred-plus page essay on being-in-the-world, an adventure novel which treads a fine line between exoticism and melancholy, a Moroccan travelogue, an extended auto-analysis, a memoir of Newfoundland, a celebration of Evangelical Protestantism and of Islam operated by a heterodox High Anglican, a series of lyrical prose poems, an erotic phenomenology, a hermeneutics of everything from birds to carpets, a prolonged criticism of the Canadian identity mechanism.

In both cases we see the genres fade away before the strength of purpose. The adventure occurs, the latent programme asserts itself, the self is violated, and writes as it is written.

A word about this volume's structure. It is a synthesis of chronological and thematic principles. The subdivisions of the anthology correspond to two major creative periods in Scott Symons' life (what he himself refers to as the two trilogies), and to a number of fundamental, quasi-structural preoccupations that traverse and overflow those periods and which therefore allow for the inclusion of some of the multiplicity of other texts, both previously published and as yet unpublished.

Dear Reader begins with "Memories, Meanings, Icons," a group of articles and essays ranging from 1963 to 1990, which, taken together, provide a composite portrait of English Canada. "English Canada does have a distinct meaning," as the first piece puts it. Symons opens up its complexity for amnesic, oversimplifying contemporaries. In these various texts Symons' capacity to analyze and celebrate are brought forward in a style and tone that are for the most part straightforward, assertive, even didactic.

The second section comprises selections from "The First Trilogy" – *Place d'Armes, Civic Square,* and *Heritage*. Any national culture would have to take a statement of this magnitude seriously. It catches in a disturbingly original manner the intersection of an educated imagination with the phenomenon of 1960s ferment and revolution. The full risks of Symons' project are visible there, as are the impossible formal choices (the combat journal, the epistles, the furniture "novel"). The sheer excess of Symons' writing comes through – the purple prose, the ecstatic absence of punctuation, the satirical progressions, the movement from credo to glossary, the inventiveness and humour animating the Canada-prayer and the numerous neologisms. And the presence of birdlife, the case of the yellow warblers!

The third section, "Culture and Conservatism in Canada," relates the case of Scott Symons to the figure of George Grant through texts that each has written about the other. It is fascinating to see how Symons' meditations on the meanings of furniture push Grant to reflect on the fundamental Heideggerian "question of technology." His sense of rootedness, of Weilian *enracinement*, also shines through. And how revealing to see the term "distinct society" used here by Grant in the context of sophisticated discourse on our culture! Scott Symons' diary account of a 1980 meeting between he, Charles Taylor, and Dennis Lee shows (if the extracts from the first trilogy didn't) Symons' sense of the epic in daily life. His experience of the event and his reading of Grant augment and amplify the writings on the same meeting by Charles Taylor in *Radical Tories* and William Christian in his biography of Grant. The author of *Technology and Empire* emerges as a noble, utterly human figure, central to Canadian meanings and becoming.

A section entitled "The Spiritual Diary" follows. Elements of diary chosen by Symons himself for a history of Saint Thomas's Anglican Church in Toronto are supplemented by a number of unpublished pieces. These pages show Symons as a profoundly God-haunted man. He experiences life as sacramental and liturgical, life as monstrance.

"The Third Trilogy," of which only one volume has been published, is anthologized carefully here. A chapter from *Helmet I*, in which Newfoundland and Morocco form a kind of palimpsest of memory and desire, is reproduced. One chapter from the second volume and two from the third are also excerpted. They show the architectonic, imbricated nature of the trilogy as a whole.

The anthology ends with a final "Dear Reader" letter from Symons and "Notes toward a C.V. by Scott Symons," which provide a biographical overview of a "very messy life."

At the beginning of each section the extracts are identified, some context is provided, and sources are given. The bibliography at the end of the volume provides full publication information as well as a comprehensive list of the limited secondary source material available.

IMPOSSIBILITIES

The impossibility of conservatism in our era is the impossibility of Canada.[12]

George Grant, *Lament for a Nation.*

Following contemporary French poet-philosopher Michel Deguy, we should allow for the existence of good and bad paradoxes. A good paradox makes of an impasse a way forward. A bad paradox confines us in the apparent straitjacket of logical and existential contradiction. Scott Symons willingly inhabits the territory of paradox; his work is haunted by impasse (picking up *Place d'Armes* or *Helmet of Flesh*, one is struck by the frequency of the word's occurrence). But it also celebrates, even if negatively, the promise of solution, of provisional resolution, of advance and transformation.

The dualities in Symons' work are numerous. There is certainly ample evidence of what we too hastily call, in the public shorthand of half-understood psychology, "bi-polar tendencies." The playful incisive sally, the bitter retreat; the minute attention to detail and differentiation, the blanket condemnation; the

12 Grant. *Lament for a Nation, The Defeat of Canadian Nationalism*, Ottawa: Carleton University Press, p. 68.

pan-erotic celebration, the intense personalization of scorn; the unstoppable pro-liferation of diary, the relatively meager publications; the faithful affirmation of Christian revelation and sacraments, the willing descent into carnality and appar-ent debauchery; the outspoken patriotism, the ambivalent exile. There is no doubt that these tensions, frequently expressed at a shout, render the work extremely problematic, indeed unreadable for some observers, unworthy of the effort for others.

In such a polarized body of work, where the author's personality is apparent-ly so present (yet even here it would be wrong to forget the Proustian injunction not to identify the author and the public figure), it is easy to see the dangers of paralysis of various sorts. Staying with the issue of identity, and more specifically of national identity, we should consider the risks implied. At the end of *Place d'Armes*, in a parodic author's C.V., Symons states his "obsessive" devotion to the Canadian nation while detaching himself from any allegiance to the Canadian state. This is a troubling statement, one which would demand extended analysis, dialogue, and questioning. There is a constant danger in Symons' work of the cre-ative tensions of the "radical conservative" degenerating into an idiosyncratic rant, a disgruntled cry from a displaced member of a now-defunct elite. Bad para-dox can produce violent contradiction.

Yet Symons is not some pseudo-revolutionary, not a mere renegade. His case is interesting and should be taken seriously because something of the order of good paradox tends to assert itself in both his life and writing. In the first volume of the *Helmet of Flesh* trilogy, York MacKenzie stands in a much more equivocal rela-tion to his national origins than did Symons at the end of his Combat Journal: "he'd come to Morocco to get away, fleeing his own ideas as much as Canada. 'Canada is in exile from me!' he'd say with bravado. But it hurt." Exile for Symons is a constant reassessment of one's own ideas, one's own origins. It is a means of loving better one's own. "You hate them *almost* as much as you love them," as the antique dealer said.

It was George Grant who first spoke in the Canadian context of "loving one's own," and indeed this is perhaps the phrase which is most closely associated with him. Grant saw and articulated philosophically what Symons lived as an impossi-ble moment of loss:

> In this era when the homogenizing power of technology is almost unlimited, I do regret the disappearance of indigenous traditions, including my own. It is true that no particularism can adequately incar-nate the good. But is it not also true that only through some particular roots, however partial, can human beings first grasp what is good and it is the juice of such roots which for most men sustain their partaking in a more universal good?[13]

We are still, thirty years later, grappling with the implications of these insights. To take one example, in an important new book, *A Border Within*, Ian Angus situates the current Canadian dilemma in analogous terms: "Such are the

13 George Grant, *Technology and Empire*. Toronto: Anansi 1969, p.68.

pervasive and profound effects of dependency that we seem to be forced to choose between taking an interest in ourselves and in human universality."[14]

What is at stake is what we might still make of the *national*. What, if any, importance can we still attach to national identity in an era when it has been discredited by so many ethnic and religious cleansings and exterminations and when the dominant socio-economic discourse, that of globalization, tends to reinforce us in our movement toward its transcendence? What to do when we are caught between the frantic need to affirm integrally and the implicit injunction to renounce selflessly? Between what Grant once called "intimations of essential deprivals"[15] and the current, turn-of-the-millennium acceleration and exhilaration?

Jacques Derrida has argued that there is no responsibility without a recognition of the experience of impossibility inherent in any judgment: "The condition of possibility of this thing called responsibility is a certain *experience and experiment of the possibility of the impossible: the testing of the aporia* from which one may invent the only possible invention, the impossible invention."[16] Those of us concerned with Canadian cultural survival have as keen an appreciation of this aporetic moment as anyone on the planet. Our particularity must be maintained in the conditions of almost total openness that the technological era produces. We must invent the impossible. "I have, the unique 'I' has, the responsibility of testifying for universality."[17] In loving one's own (particularity) the exemplary subject (singularity) must work out an acceptable relation to otherness, even hegemonic American alterity, or be totally effaced. Symons, that exemplum of the Canadian self, demonstrates that such an impossible invention is a work of tears and of joy.

It would take a good deal of theoretical sophistication and patient analysis to work out the precise relationships between "singularity" and "particularity," but it is at least intuitively clear that the "impossibilities" of cultural self-identity relate very deeply to the obligations of the singular "I." Ian Angus has pointed out that Grant's use of "one's own" is a fine rendering of the Heideggerian term *Eigentlich*, which is usually given as *authenticity*. The exemplary self can teach us much about existential responsibility, its witnessing gives us both a picture of identity and a revelation of the multiple cracks and fissures which appear at the moment of self-affirmation. By extrapolation, the *exemplum as exile* lets us see a culture in its non-coincidence with itself. *Ave atque vale*, hail *and* farewell, as Symons puts it with wistful and angry ambiguity at the conclusion of his furniture book.

So it is that we must seek out the possibility of the national, in our Canadian terms, through the paradoxical richness of such statements, a non-exhaustive list of which would also include Tom Henighan's conclusion that Canada is "a country that is condemned to live creatively amid unresolvable tensions,"[18] George Grant's affirmation of the impossibility of Canadian sovereignty in an era of progress, and Northrop Frye's frequently repeated statement that Canada has

14 Angus, *A Border Within*, McGill-Queen's 1997 p. 207.

15 Grant, *Technology and Empire*, p. 141.

16 Derrida, *The Other Heading*, p. 41.

17 Derrida, *The Other Heading*, p. 73.

18 Thomas Henighan, *The Presumption of Culture*. Vancouver: Raincoast Books 1995 .

moved directly from a pre-national to a post-national stage of consciousness. An even more telling remark by Frye on this issue is that found at the end of *The Modern Century*, where he states with an alarming clarity that "our identity, like the real identity of all nations, is the one we have failed to achieve."[19] Scott Symons belongs to this disparity of imagination and practical achievement, this crucial play of identity and non-identity. His Canada of the thinking heart lies there unachieved and still compelling.

USE IT!

> Thou mettest with things dying
> And I with things new-born
> (Shakespeare, *The Winter's Tale* III, 3)

There is a page in the diaries where an exalted Symons cries out to a future reader, "If you find 10% of this useful, use it!! If you find 20% of this useful, use it!!" This is obviously not some kind of narrowly utilitarian statement. There can be no easy accounting of influence. How can reading or writing be quantifiable? Such statements, brutal apostrophes, serve to draw the reader into the process of lucid questioning and creative response. Though largely innocent of contemporary literary theory, Symons knows intuitively that a reading is also a writing (as the shifting relations between characters and narrators in his books demonstrate). In his letter to John Robert Colombo, the editor of *Civic Square*, Symons states that "No-one should be able to read the book the way (for example) a book reviewer reads books, or an Englit don. 'Intelligently.' The fact of the matter is that *the book must read them*, or not at all." In the author-reader-text configuration is to be found an analogy for the profound interdependence of receptivity and expenditure, attention and gift, that lies at the heart of subjectivity itself. Each reader of this volume will find his or her own trajectories through it. He or she will be read and will rewrite in reading, will engage the texts uniquely, will use them personally, locally. The gifts received will be proportional to the attention given.

Living in a garden at the edge of the desert, in what David Warren of the *Ottawa Citizen* recently called "dignified poverty," Symons is conscious of drawing his eschatological foray to a close. He still returns to Canada regularly; here he engages in "spelunking," an activity which consists of getting down into the depths of the current national state, its état *d'être*, state of being. His sensibility reports are frequently damning, yet not without hope. "What is inert is not the culture but the Canadians. All we have to do is wake up and have a look at it and do something about it," as he put it in a 1989 interview in *The Idler*. Looking at it and doing something about it; this implies, once again, the dynamic, participatory relation to the object. Symons' work and example are of significant value in such a reactivation, whatever the particular field of inquiry or creation.

I recall a conversation with Scott Symons in Essaouira, Morocco where he shook his head ruefully, saying, in connection with the interest of younger filmmakers and writers, "Maybe I'm going to become a culture hero." His reticence is understandable. Having fought his whole life against the over-

19 Northrop Frye, *The Modern Century*. Toronto: Oxford University Press, 1967, p. 123.

simplifications and the careerism of media culture, he has no wish to suddenly join up. His preference is to speak from out of the desert. *Vox clamatis*. What his exile represents for us is precisely the possibility of recognizing the difficulty of saying "us," and the demands of the attempt.

"We live in a time stunned by fate."[20] With this thumping philosophical assessment, Ian Angus, inheritor and renovator of the Grantian tradition, expresses the tenor of the time. On one level, he is referring to the apparent inevitability of globalization, to consensus thinking, to what John Ralston Saul calls "corporatism." Figures like Scott Symons are patently outside of *la pensée unique*, they are anti-hegemonic, their views run counter to the *doxa*, to unthought unanimity. They are also few and far between. At a time when the country has (apparently) solved its financial crisis and accepted a stalemate in its constitutional difficulties, it might be interesting to turn to the personality deficit. Symons, with all necessary allowances made, could well prove to be a cultural hero in such circumstances.

There is a highly amusing moment in *God's Fool*, Nik Sheehan's documentary on Scott Symons, when publisher Sam Hiyate reflects on the low price he paid for a used copy of *Helmet of Flesh*, speculating that the value of the book, like a stock on the exchange, can only go up. We might say, using Marxist terminology, that the use value of Symons' work far exceeds its exchange value. It was never meant for the heights of bestsellerdom; its difficulty, its confidentiality, its rawness, and its material form have precluded such quantifiable success and market commodification. Yet it is intended to touch, individually and uniquely. It is intended to provoke an action at a distance. What is at stake is not a model that needs to be emulated in its details, but an example: that of raising the stakes of life and work, an example of seriousness predicated on both artistic and civic duty. What we do with it, how we use it, is up to us. *Admire and do otherwise*, as Gerard Manley Hopkins said of our proper relation to cultural models.

The aspiration to produce a violently urgent yet lovingly gentle manifesto is present right from the beginning of Symons' project. He seeks to arm the reader, to draw the reader into the struggle for celebration of life, an ecstatic celebration that is also an intellectually alert critique of the actual, and an active, effective mourning of what has passed and what therefore can never fully pass. If this anthology *works*, its dear readers will find in it some percentage for sustenance, some ground on which to invent the impossible. Use It!

20 Angus, *A Border Within*, p. 5.

Memories, Meanings, Icons

The Meaning of English Canada (1963)

From Canada, a loving look (1979): Trout River, Rosedale, Calgary, Ottawa

Mazo Was Murdered, Atwood as Icon (*The Idler*, 1990)

Glitz City (*The Idler*, 1990)

This section includes essays and articles written over a thirty-year period. In them we see Symons' possession of his heritage, his deep knowledge of art and history, and along with this, a grasp of what is really at stake for the human being in such belonging. He has, in relation to Canada, what General De Gaulle possessed in relation to France – "une certaine idée." To use Symons' own terms, it is an idea of an "enhanced Canadianism," a "sophisticated democracy," the "alternative American tradition."

"The Meaning of English Canada" is an address given by Symons in 1963 to the Canadian Centenary Council Symposium. He was curator of Canadiana at the Royal Ontario Museum at the time. In it he makes a first, determined strike against received ideas about the Canadian identity. The context is that of the recent defeat of the Conservatives and the gathering momentum behind what Scott Symons would later call the "Canadian identity mechanism." Note the intense romanticism of the closing passages and the underlying eroticism that would inform virtually all of his subsequent work. Symons longs for "the potent plenitude of our Kingdom of Canada."

The four short pieces following this come from a 1978 series written for the *Globe and Mail*; they indeed constitute a "Loving Look" at the country. From coast to coast, Symons pursued the persistence of Canadian meanings through reportage on intensely personal, emotionally touching meetings with people, places, and artifacts. He would later boast with his characteristic hyperbole that this series had won 20 seats for Joe Clark and the Progressive Conservatives.

"Mazo Was Murdered" and "Atwood as Icon," both published by the much-lamented *Idler* in 1990, constitute a critical diptych, a concise statement of Symons' view of literature. They form a single essay on canon-making and the evolution of sensibility by one largely excluded from Canadian literature's canons. Mazo de la Roche and Margaret Atwood, two very different writers from very different generations, are two of the best known and most popular Canadian writers in our literary history. What do we make of Symons' judgement of the relative value of each and of his conclusion that there is something fundamentally unhealthy in a culture that – at least implicitly – must efface one to have the other?

"Glitz City," an earlier piece from *The Idler*, follows. In this piece Symons deploys a knowledge of Toronto and of Ontario that is unsurpassed. He stakes all on "the gamble in North America for quality." Given the apocalyptic nature of all of this work, it is interesting to see the way that the underlying theme of *two cities* makes itself felt in these few pages. This is how contemporary Toronto, 'Torontario' and Canada might appear to a latter-day Euripides or St. Augustine.

The Meaning of English Canada

It is with a real feeling of excitement and also of trepidation that I address you. Excitement, because here in Winnipeg I feel myself on the threshold of the Canadian West and North. It is from this multicultural West and North that I feel will come a large proportion of the decisive thought of my generation … certainly a large proportion of the English Canadian thought. Trepidation, because I am so young, and also because – at least in the eyes of the Westerner – I have the misfortune to be an Easterner, and in particular the misfortune to be a seventh generation Torontonian. To be young, and to be a Torontonian are – as you know – decisive Canadian handicaps.

The subject of this paper, "The Meaning of English Canada," is not phrased as a question; and for good reason. Because English Canada does have a distinct meaning; it does have a distinct and distinguished civilization of its own. This meaning is enhanced by the association within the Canadian Confederation, of French and English-speaking communities.

Perhaps we may best see this in three stages. Firstly, we will have to recognize that today English Canadians themselves do not recognize their own remarkable achievements; nor do we seem to have enough leaders capable of expressing those achievements. Secondly, there is a perfectly clear reason why this meaning of English Canada has temporarily been so thoroughly obscured and even mutilated, just as there is a reason why we have so few leaders today. Thirdly, a careful study of the continuous development of English Canada does reveal a distinctive and meaningful community – reflected in all aspects of our life. Tentatively, perhaps, we may best define that meaning by the phrase "sophisticated democracy."

1) The first of these points, the failure of English Canada to recognize and use its own values and achievements, can be demonstrated clearly by contrasting English and French-speaking Canada today. French Canada is currently living its "agonizing re-appraisal." The press calls it a silent revolution; but given its main instrument – the mass media – it should really be called the "blabulent" revolution. The important fact is that French Canada knows what it wants, knows how to get it, and is well on the way to achieving its goal, quite literally, regardless of English Canada, and often in spite of English Canada.

What *does* French Canada want? It wants to fulfill its own civilization in its own way. To this end it has instinctively mobilized a galaxy of devoted talent. French Canadian literature, art, poetry, politics, journalism, these are all one in their aim. The line from the art of Pellan and the pamphlet *Refus global*, of Borduas, runs directly through to the French Canadianization of Quebecois provincial hydro. The same surge of the spirit that allows the poetry of Yves Préfontaine to fuse land and history and people in a single metaphor, allows Jacques Godbout to win important international recognition for his first novel. In politics a man such as René Lévesque electrifies the electorate. It is a delight to go into Montréal's stock-market area the day after a Lévesque speech; even the baseball scores take second place!

Thus we witness in French Canada what is perhaps the most talented, the most purposeful outburst of creative energy anywhere in the Western World today. (It makes the New Frontier group of the United States look like a posthumous Edwardian garden party!) English Canadians should be proud of this re-birth of French Canadian culture. It is a superb achievement enhancing Canadians. One may hope that it will inspire English Canada, because in contrast the English Canadian seems just a little like Rip Van Winkle waking up and wondering where he is. In effect the very bewilderment of English Canadians faced with this French Canadian renaissance only underlines the failure of English Canada to be sufficiently aware either of itself or of Canada as a whole.

This English Canadian failure to appreciate its own culture as well as that of French Canada is shown in another way: in the search for the Canadian Identity. In the past few years it has become highly respectable to set out in quest for this, in the same way as Medieval Knights set out to find the Holy Grail, or a piece of the True Cross. In a few instances the search is serious. Professor W. L. Morton is an inspiring example, as is Professor Donald Creighton. But in general it may be said that the tone of the search rings false. Perhaps this is because it does seem to have become the special preserve of our mass media and of our academic minds. It has in a way been captured by them. The result is a curious blend of the superficial and the unreal. Rarely do the members of this squad of professional Canadianizers have any profound sense of our land and of our history. Fortunately there are remarkable exceptions, such as André Laurendeau or Robertson Davies.

The fact is that the very search for the Canadian Identity – all the frantic scurry of it – suggests that we are looking for something that is not there; or at best something that has been lost and may yet be found. Moreover, if we acknowledge that French Canada was never more sure of its own meaning, then we must admit that the search for the Canadian Identity is really an English Canadian search. That is, the search for the Canadian Identity really reveals an ignorance of English Canadians about themselves and about Canada as a whole.

But we do not have to look even this far to prove that English Canadians fail to understand their own meaning. The brutal fact is before us that we urgently need leaders who can gain the serious attention and confidence of English Canada. Two examples suffice: the first in journalism, the second in politics.

It is surely self-evident that there is at present no editor of an English Canadian newspaper who gains the serious attention of English Canada, let alone of Canada as a whole. Much less is there an editor of the stature of a John W. Dafoe. Even worse, English Canadian newspapers have in many cases simply forfeited the rights of the fourth estate. Who, for example, will seriously defend the editorial record of English Canadian Montréal newspapers in the past fifteen years? It is an abject record, of abdication and of hypocrisy. In contrast with French Canada, what English Canadian newspaper dare to speak with the clarity, the force and the courage of Montréal's French Canadian paper, *Le Devoir*? What English Canadian newspaper dare incarnate a completely renewed conception of English Canada, or of Canada, the way *Le Nouveau Journal* did in French Canada, launching ideas and young men that will together dominate French Canada for the next twenty-five years!

This same lack of leadership seen in English Canadian newspapers is self-evident in our national politics. Never has a national government been given such confidence by Canadians as the Conservative government elected in 1958. Yet it could not find sufficient men of calibre to stay afloat. It literally sank under poor leadership. At the same time the leadership of the Liberal party was so uninspiring, so unrelated to Canadian aspirations, that for all its clever and its able members it could barely unseat a completely demoralized Conservative party. Quite simply the Liberal leaders, like the Conservative leaders, have been utterly incapable of providing the country with a sense of purpose and of national direction. The result is that the Canadian people have wisely elected an inter-regnum administration, while patiently awaiting a positive and meaningful statement from any political party that can give it. In the meantime Canada is administered by the political action arm of the Canadian Civil Service! There is only one conclusion to derive from these facts. English Canada does not know itself; does not recognize the richness of its own achievements. Nor does it have leaders to articulate its meaning.

2) We can readily prove the English Canadian failure to appreciate its own meaning. We can also explain how English Canadians have temporarily lost sight of this meaning; firstly, because a plausible but negative version of Canadian nationalism concealed this erosion of meaning. Secondly, because the type of leader English Canada was producing with this negative nationalism was incapable of using the English Canadian meaning in a constructive way.

Firstly, then, what is this negative nationalism? It has so captured the Canadian mind that it might best be termed the Authorized Version of Canadianism. Its title could really be "from colony to nation": because it is the naive story of Canadian growth from mere divided colonies to mighty nation-state. It is the history of two North American cultures slowly winning independence from British political domination, and today from American economic domination. The rebellions of 1837 were the turning point, leading to Responsible Government, Confederation itself, and thereafter to that sturdy Canadian autonomy which finally evolutionized the Empire into the Commonwealth-that-Canada-made – a society of free communities united by the invisible bonds. You can hear the unctuous voices rolling off these phrases, culminating, of course, in the creation of Canadian Citizenship in 1946, Canadian Governors-General, a Nobel Peace Prize as palm, and now, at long last, the Centenary in 1967.

This Authorized Canadian sermon we all know by heart. It can be readily recognized as an integral part of a theory of history that dominated nineteenth century Europe. This is the Whig interpretation of history, discredited over a generation ago in England – and thereafter, of course, still persistently upheld in Canada. It is a simple, optimistic theory about the inevitable progress of man. According to this theory, every day in every way we all get better and better; soon we will all have two television sets each.

This plausible Canadian nationalism, however, has hidden the real Canadian situation. Firstly the very conception of a proud independent nation-state has been the costly cause of two World Wars. It belongs, like the Whig interpretation of history itself, with the sentimental romanticism of the nineteenth century.

Indeed all this Authorized Canadian clap-trap about a banana-republic independence, about Order-in-Council culture, about triangles and regional fungi on our flag or flags; all this talk about national status, this is part and parcel of a world gone by. Canadians who talk it are dealing in the very politics of nostalgia they claim to be eliminating with the umbilical cord. In short, this Authorized Nationalism, far from being progressive, is a negative, naive, nostalgic nationalism.

Where does it lead? Let us take but two examples. Firstly, the militant ignorance that persists between Canadian East and West. This is not simply a question of distance. It is also a question of carefully cultivated prejudices, prejudices that often seem used and abused by many of our leaders. What I mean by this is the East thinking of the West as a bunch of cowboy yahoos who find redemption in wheat sales, while the West thinks of Easterners as a group of filthy capitalists living off Western resources and European ideas. These images are ridiculous; but they have won and lost national elections, including the last one.

This real breach between East and West is itself overlooked because of another current Canadian split: that between English and French Canada. Presumably the great achievement of Authorized Canadian nationalism was that it healed the wounds of French and English Canada; that is, it was the politics of constructive Canadian compromise. Time has now proven this to be the greatest of Canadian lies. This great Canadian compromise has only compromised Canada. Today the English Canadian literally seems to have compromised himself right out of a meaningful existence, while French Canadians have never misunderstood English Canada more completely, nor respected it less.

Authorized Canadianism then, has glossed over the real Canadian problems with a dangerous facade of politically successful nationalism. In the process it even seemed to exploit certain of these problems for temporary political advantages. This process becomes clearer if we examine the kind of English Canadian leaders who carried it out.

How did we grow from colony to nation? Obviously by eliminating the British Colonial administration; that is, by replacing the British governing group in Canada, with Canadians. The question then is what sort of Canadians replaced this governing group. The answer is best described as M-to-the-fourth-power: mute mediocre Methodist mannikin. This is not a clever conundrum – but a precise description of the kind of man who increasingly represented English Canada, and who still does direct Canada to a demoralizing degree.

Firstly, he was a Methodist. We can use this term in a purely social and cultural sense here, free of religious prejudice, if only because the Methodist was metamorphosed in 1926. What was the Methodist in the early days of Canada? A frontiersman whose faith was a naive revivalism; theology got short shrift. Logically so did this man's capacity for organized abstract thought. Secondly, he was "mute": and for very good reason. To dis-establish the British regime this man had to unite politically with Catholic French Canada. But to accomplish this he had to learn to keep quiet about his own English Canadian meaning – a meaning which was effectively a folk equivalent of the British North American tradition he exiled as "colonial." Thus Methodist mannikin was mute about those very qualities of faith, taste and civilization which defined him, which made him more than mere material American. That is, to achieve political power in Canada he had to abolish his own personality. His muteness has cost him dear. Because today he and his descendants in English Canada do not even know what it was he had to be mute about. Thirdly, he was mediocre, because his aspirations and norms were eternally middle class. He had exiled or dis-established the more sophisticated elements of English Canada as foreign and un-Canadian. By doing this he labeled as un-Canadian those very distinctively Canadian elements that could have carried him beyond his own cultural limits. Thus, fourthly, he was a "mannikin" – a diminished man. He may not have been responsible entirely for this diminution of himself. But he was, in fact, responsible for a large measure of it; and the Canadian who denies this today out of patriotism does his country a singular disservice.

In this light it is easy to see how English Canadian meaning has been hidden and hurt. Firstly, under an outdated theory of Canadian nationalism. Secondly, by a kind of man who to gain his immediate and material ends rejected the fundamental purpose of English Canada – the formation in North America of a quality civilization, distinct in many ways from that of the United States.

3) If we can recognize this temporary lack of meaning in English Canada today, and if we can also see how this meaning was lost, then we are two-thirds of the way towards a rediscovery of the meaning of English Canada. It only remains to study the common grounds of the English Canadian experience, common throughout all regions of Canada, and then to appreciate the positive achievement of English Canada, whether it be in politics, or business, arts, or letters. If we examine the development of English Canada, from the earliest times to the present day, there is one factor which recurs as a common theme. That is the establishment of an ordered, stable, well-organized community, always with the sense of responsible participation in a larger whole. It does not matter whether we are talking of the Maritimes with its early New England settlers, followed by the military order of the British fleet and then by the Loyalists; or of the English-speaking sections of Québec and Ontario, with their basic Loyalist influx supported by the British administration; or of the Canadian West with its story of settlement following the Royal North-West Mounted Police and the growth of the railways. In each case there was a controlled frontier.

The point may best be made, possibly, by contrast between American and the Canadian West. What is the popular image we have of the American West? It is of the wild and woolly West. The folk hero of this kind of West is the rootin' tootin' two-gun man. It is an image that leads directly to the garish and superficial world of Hollywood on the one hand, and the two-fisted teamster toughster of the American present on the other.

Contrast this with the picture of the Canadian West. Down in the decadent East, of course, our picture of this Canadian West is pretty hazy and grazy. But if we stop to think a minute we realize that it is not at all the same as that of the American West. What is the difference? It is the concept of order, of a well-run, stable society. Instead of Billy the Kid, as symbol, there were "Her Majesty's

Canadian Cowboys" – the Mounties. Whereas American settlement was wide open and unruly, Canadian settlement was controlled and, in contrast, "ruly."

This common tradition of law and order, of essential decency in a frontier situation, gives us the key to the meaning of English Canada, of all the English-speaking Canadas. This frontier situation was essentially similar to that of the American tradition. But it was treated in an entirely different way. It was subjected to European standards and values. The result was what one may term an "immediate civilization" in democratic circumstances. That is, English Canada has consistently been groping its way, instinctively, towards a new kind of community and a new kind of personality which may be defined by the term "sophisticated democracy."

This distinctive development can be seen in *every* aspect of the English Canadian civilization. In politics, it is seen in the system of Parliament itself, adapted from European practices to a North American federal situation. Parliament is itself an important symbol of the English Canadian tradition of frank dignity and orderly discussion. Indeed, record shows that any national party which flagrantly abuses this sense of Parliamentary order promptly lost an election. Today the contrast between our Parliament in Ottawa and the American political "Boss" – direct symbolic descendant of the two-gun man – makes this point even more meaningful. In fact the very Parliament buildings themselves in Ottawa reveal the distinctive English Canadian blend of European traditions, freely adapted and here transformed into the most striking Gothic revival group in the New World, naturally set in a typically grand Canadian landscape.

The parallel continues in business, where a combination of private enterprise and public corporations, unites freedom with order in a distinctively Canadian approach.

We see the same in all of the English Canadian arts: in architecture, where our churches unite eternal styles of the Western world with Canadian stone and timbers in a straight-forward and unique way. Nowhere else in the world, including New England, is there anything the same as our country Gothic churches of the nineteenth century, uniting the North American with the European in a harmonious way. In the architecture of our homes the same is true. The polychrome brick houses with their fusion of Georgian classic form and Victorian decor are another reflection of this specific English Canadian culture. Their interior decor is as unique to the trained eye as the American Statue of Liberty. The student of Canadiana will find that the marriage of local woods, such as maple, butternut and pine, with European craftsmanship and quality produced, over a hundred years ago, furniture that anticipated the finest modern Scandinavian design; while in art, a continuing achievement, from the earliest eighteenth century topographers of the Maritimes, through the Group of Seven, imposes order and form upon the massive grandeur of untamed Canadian nature.

Finally, in literature, we have the same clear statement about the meaning of English Canada. Thomas Haliburton's *Sam Slick*, written a century-and-a-half ago in Halifax, is aptly enough the first perceptive study of the American. It is done from a viewpoint that is distinctly North American, a viewpoint that is still distinctly Canadian. So, too, Stephen Leacock, in Ontario, combines an earthy, democratic humour with eternal sophisticated cultural values. Today, voices from the West adapt this same theme, voices such as Gabrielle Roy, or W. O. Mitchell in *Who Has Seen the Wind*.

There is a common culture to all the English-speaking Canadas. It is a fusion of North American democratic frankness with the traditional values of the Western world. This has been a process of integration. In contrast to the United States, it has been a process of consolidation rather than revolution, of enrichment as against rejection. Even our Canadian rebels – Joseph Howe, Papineau, Mackenzie and Riel – wanted to embrace these values, while the vast majority of Canadians have consistently and democratically stated their desire for this positive Canadian community.

This adds up to a type of citizenship that one may term "enhanced Canadianism," or "Big Canadianism." Each of us, as an English-speaking Canadian, wants to make his culture part of a universal experience. We want to participate responsibly in our universal heritage. This is not mere words. Two world wars have confirmed our determination and our sense of a larger humanity. In short, not only does the English Canadian have meaning, but he has a precise and visible meaning that is drawing him towards a new kind of man and a new kind of state, both modern in the best sense of the term. Indeed both perhaps ahead of their time.

The striking fact here is that this development of a positive English Canadianism exactly parallels the historic development of French Canada. In French Canada we see the same rich tradition of order and of continuity. There is the same desire to share in a world-wide heritage. In the case of the French Canadian this is the universal French civilization of the French language community of nations. This is heritage which parallels that of the English-speaking Canadian in the Commonwealth of nations. Today more and more French Canadians are out to grasp this heritage.

Thus a positive and frank acceptance of ourselves as English-speaking Canadians, that what is already there within us is both essential to the well-being of English Canada and to the creative understanding of English and French-speaking Canadians together. A meaningful English Canada today is the key to the well-being of Canada as a whole. Canada is a bicultural community, and indeed a multicultural one. At the present time Canadian success or failure – indeed the very survival of Canada – depends upon the capacity of English-speaking Canadians to recognize that they already do have a positive culture, just as it depends upon their capacity to communicate that fact in a thoughtful way to French-speaking Canadians.

Our time is short. It but remains for us, French and English-speaking Canadians alike, to know ourselves. The reward is high. For ours is the history and the people and the land of Canada. Ours is the Empire of La Nouvelle France, gaudily guarded by Louisbourg, gilded outpost of the most cultured court in the history of Western civilization. Ours is the elegy and the epic of the morning and the mourning on the plains of a farmer called Abraham, storybook battle with heroes from the Holy Grail. Ours is the courage of the French-Canadians at Chateauguay, fighting for homeland, rebuffing thus the sidewalks of New York.

Ours is the Battle of the Atlantic, grim glory of Halifax; and the landing at Dieppe – sombre rehearsal for the liberation of the Old World by the New. Ours are those blood-rich poppies that glow in the Fields of Flanders, a heart from every Canadian hearth. Ours are the victories of the "Van Dooz"; and ours the modern chivalry of the Knights of the Air; and ours the gut-taut dash of those Canadians who spat fire in the Battle of Britain that they knew instinctively to be the battle for civilization, while the rest of the world slept, or argued constitutional codicils.

Ours is the history and the people from the first Canada claim of Sir Humphrey Gilbert full four centuries back, through to those rare men who, with Champlain, irrepressibly established "l'Ordre de bell temps" – the Order of Good Cheer – just because that Canadian winter was so searing and dreary. Ours, too, the continental buccaneerings of the Le Moyne – Paul Bunyans with purpose and panache. Ours the awesome austerities of first Bishop Laval, and the purple patronage of Bishop St. Vallier – princes of Canada's Catholic Church. Ours that Western recipe left by Samuel Hearne for young spring deer stew with green moss. And the memory of Bishop Mountain canoeing the careening St. Lawrence, complete with Blackberry Brandy to ward off evil in its lesser forms. Ours the saintliness of Jeanne Mance who first nursed America full two centuries before Florence Nightingale discovered the Crimea. And the Canada-clutched verve of Anne Langton who sang her new land in a Gothic château built boldly on granite and ice. Ours is the wry relevant mirth of Stephen Leacock confessing English Canada once and for ever. And the frank fun of Eye Opener Bob, who brought the sharp clean Prairie breeze, bright whistling like Meadowlark, into Canadian homes. Ours is the wise, sad face of Sir John A ... who never did die, and who knew Canada as it could never be known again, and who loved it as it should someday be.

This, then, is Canada, our home and native land, clean-cut Canada-scape from the Strait of Belle Isle to the Charlotte Islands, from Point Pelee's sun bright tip to Arctic world tip top, the immense intense serene of Emily Carr's mountainous Pacific. Ours, too, are the rivers cleaving and weaving Canada – rippling, ribald, riotous, raging – from the first spring gush to the deep throat of the Sainted Lawrence swallowing whole the New World.

Ours the fields of rolling rich Ontario, the granite mountains of the West that make the Alps look a tale for tiny tots. Ours the Northland that resources half the world and that quick sucks man-marrow like woman. Ours the resonant fragrance of first spring thaw, the sun-burst of bud-time, the billowing riot of bouquets that scud the air in Canadian Maytime. Ours is the creeking gasp of snow clenched under sole, the crackle of first best apple bite, the brittle broadloom of pine mat under sun-baked summer flesh. Ours the velvet of old Canadian furniture woods, heritage handled from first broad-axe time to hearth and happy home. Ours the counterpoint of ocean beat, the shriek of hawk mate in hunt, the doleful soul-moan of mourning dove, and that Mona Lisa dimple of the dove face. Ours the forest ripple of thrush note, green cascade of sun-song. And the cry of the loon, shimmering soul shriek of torment and travail, the splendour of Canada wail. To the Canadian, all this, the heritage re-offered, the potent plenitude of our Kingdom of Canada.

Canada: A Loving Look
TROUT RIVER: A Special Woman, That's the Truth On't

"So yez is cummin' home is ye?" It's Ma Snook on the line. I've just phoned her from Toronto. "I want to see Trout River again," I explain. I don't dare tell her that I want to write an article about Trout River, *her* Trout River. She'd think it was a conspiracy.

"Is there anything you want me to bring from Toronto?" And then I hear Ma Snook chortling with laughter – "yeees, and ye kin bring money. There ain't much on't here roight now!"

My plane whirs down the runway. Toronto sinking on my right. Canada's New York, its pocket skyline jutting up over the cloud fleece that covers Lake Ontario. The city marching up from the lake, orderly. Battalions of homes, shopping plazas as command centres. And then the countryside, squared fields, bulging barns, escaped trees huddling to one side. Ontaree-aree-aree-o. Lots of room still, enough for 25 million people. I close my eyes. In a few hours I'll be in Trout River, fishing hamlet, maybe a thousand people, working the west coast of Newfoundland. I went there eight years ago, by accident, for a week. Stayed a year and wrote a book. The villagers thought I was hiding from the mainland police.

I gaze down from the plane. The fields no longer squared, but in strips. Roads winding. Houses no longer marching along the roads, but snuggling. Of course, we're over Québec now. Even the cloverleafs have a verve. Vive la différence. And then la belle province is gone. We're swooping down into Stephenville, abandoned American military base. A taxi driver is offering to carry my bags, driving me to Corner Brook. The strong black and white land of February rampant around me, like an escaped moose. "Yees – Newfoundland is the best place in t'warld to have a drink in ... "

We stop in Corner Brook for a beer together. My bus to Trout River isn't for another four hours. The rollicking banter all around me, voices like lyrical plainsong, Newfie. And then above them, that other voice, flat, concerted. It's the TV – a CBC announcer, standing rigid, only his lips moving. But it's he himself, his very voice that is the colder weather here. Two beers later the driver and I are en route. "Won't charge ye more'n gas an' a bottle of Screech. I'd kinda loike the trip."

The National Park signs hove to – Gros Morne Park. The dour khaki of the signs, their officiousness, clamping the land. Bringing in tourists, hotdogs, dollars, TV. The portable life.

Lomond, Birchy Head, Bonne Bay, the names a melody as we turn to cross that final gulch to Trout River. A lunar tundra, sepulchral. To the final hump, and the vista down into Trout River. The village settled like a cluster of gulls along the ocean. As we pull up, Ma Snook spurts out of her cottage, out into the snow in her slippers. Nimble as a pullet. And in seconds we are all sitting around her kitchen table, drinking tea, taxi driver included. Someone has pulled up a rocking chair for me, and I've placed a large offering of Screech on the table.

"Well, an' yes dasn't visit us thet hoften. Tranta's thet good, is it? Beeg city now, I guess. Beeg as St. John's la ... " Ma Snook passing tea, and ample gurgles of

Screech. About ten of us now. The Snook clan gathering round, generations of them, in tiers. The men standing. The women sitting down with their partridge berry pie and cookies. The children weaving in and out under the table. Along with four or five cats and dogs. Everyone talking, touching, laughing. I listen. Yes, it's all a single ongoing conversation, a fugue. "An' ye doesn't say too much!" Ma Snook slaps her knees. "Oh, I guess I just feel at home, Ma Snook." "An' so ye is!"

I glance around. Ma Snook's old sloping floor. Her wood stove, and same teapot with the chipped spout. The sign on the wall, "home, sweet home," with a postcard of the Queen inserted. Oh, here, none of it is sentimental at all. It's reality. As I feel tension ebbing out of me. This babble of life all around me. The eyes, always so clear, unwavering. Hearts in their eyes. No need to glance away, to duck, to hide feelings.

"And what's the greatest change in Trout River, in Newfoundland, since I left, Ma Snook?"

She pauses, an instant. "Them bretalyziers, they got them bretalyziers now." She nods at the bottle of Screech. The taxi driver agrees, decides it's time for him to be on his way.

I wake up next morning to the sound of a tambourine. One of the children. "All hands to the Harmy!" Ma Snook announces. She has her Salvation Army hat on. We all troop out to her son's truck. A throng of us in, on, around Sammy's truck. Whooping off to "church." Past Mae Hamm's General Store – everything from bobby pins to seal meat. Ma Snook waving to the world as we drive. The sheep scattering off the road. And the Army Citadel perched on a high slope over the town.

Maybe sixty of us in the Citadel now. Sadie banging on the big bass drum, as if she'd been there since I left eight years ago. The children waving their tambourines. " ... oh, the wonder of it all, just to think that God loves me" – they rock as they chant. The lieutenant up on the podium, the Army flag behind her, FIRE and BLOOD emblazoned on it. And the sign at the foot of the podium – "His promises are sure." I find myself chuckling for joy. As the lieutenant bellows out "an' now wes'll sing Send a New Touch of Power Down Lard." The children stamping their feet, so that the plastic flowers on the rail quake. And the booming fisherman voices rise. The tambourines flashing, their ponytail ribbons soaring. The lieutenant with her eyes closed, hands reached to Heaven. Yes, a chant, the entire Citadel swaying, like a giant sleigh ride, celestial sleigh ride.

And Ma Snook up on the platform with the other village "elders," hand in hand now, dancing, glory dancing as they call it – "Alleluia." The whole place an Alleluia ... dance of life, for life. The energy flowing into me. The vitality of these people, singing, dancing, for their God.

And after the service we are out into the wind. The village spread below us, tranquil. "Toime for a boite o' lunch." As we truck back to Snookville, that whole lower end of town that has become MaSnookland, her children and grandchildren. In minutes Ma Snook is serving up her moose stew and 'taties. The number varies, anywhere from six to about a dozen. Lunch in stages. Lunch by clusters. Flurries of affection. Children receiving preventive slaps and laughing as they cry.

Ma Snook standing in front of her stove, armed with a ladle used both to serve stew and whang children.

"'As ye got a gerrl yit?" She brandishes her ladle at me. "Yer a hard ticket if ye hain't got no gerrl!" And even as she asks me, I am struck by the femininity of the women, the girls here. They *are* female and not submitted ... or rather, the only thing they are submitted to is their femininity! So real. So different from the Toronto ads – "be the best possible you." Some extrinsic you.

Ma Snook is scrutinizing me. "You mainlanders, now, yez is a dry piece o' weather. Always scurryin' around. Loike yes lost sumpin'." She shakes her head. I gaze out the window, silenced, watching the ocean curve up to Ma Snook's home. The body of young Gary Snook, sinking beneath those waves some two years ago, his dory turned – "'e was hit on t'head with the propeller. Didn't feel nottin'. No punishment in't, loike."

The room seethes around me. The sign above the table – "The Gift of God is eternal life through Jesus Christ..." I love these people, that's what it is. They generate love, belief, touch. They tell me what we've lost, without saying it.

"An' what is ye wroitin' about in yer newspaper, la?" Ma Snook using that French là, vestige from early French settlers in Trout River.

"I'm going to write about you, Ma Snook!" She looks startled. Scuttles out the front door, returning with another armload of wood for her stove. "Well an' I isn't worth the writin' about, now that's the truth on't."

The Cherished-Loathed Rosedale

Walking down Toronto's Yonge Street, after a hectic afternoon of business and banking. My head spinning in the neon urgency of the street. It's rush hour, people scurrying to and from subway stops with that look of dire determination on their faces. As if impelled by some minor emergency, or unlocated disaster. The big billboards yanking my eyes, telling me to "Listen Here!" Not so much an invitation as a command from the advertised faces of the media stars. And the implication is that if you don't "listen here," you're not "with it," not really alive in "our Toronto." Bullying tactics, in a covert way.

On my left, a moment of peace, a park, and beyond it the old houses of Rosedale coming into view. A series of intermittent turrets, gables, strolling verandahs, just visible through the high screen of trees. Like a single ongoing manor house, those homes lurking there. Rosedale, Toronto's Westmount, but not grey stone, not Scottish Presbyterian nor high and dry dour. Much less merely financial. Rosedale is ... My thought is broken – a rush-hour car screeching to a halt just in front of me, just missing a jaywalking pedestrian. "You stupid bastard," the driver shouts. I flinch, and on a hunch turn off Yonge Street, up Crescent Road, into Rosedale. Where I grew up, and where my parents grew up.

That diffuse chagrin of Yonge Street soon lost, as I enter these winding streets, the shrubbery and arching trees. I pause instinctively at a rambling turn-of-the-century house, with its ripe brickwork, deep gabled window, faded beams. Victorian Tudorbethan it is, its own style. I find myself nodding at it in acknowledgment. And then remember, yes, that's the house my father always said he wanted to buy.

The street curves on, like a winding path, to Rosedale Road, and that old white apartment building. When I was young it was simply known as "the apartment." It was the only one in Rosedale then. It didn't blight the eyescape. Nor build up seven stories high by pretending to build down into a ravine.

Down Rosedale Road. That High Victorian gothic mini-manor just ahead. It's a fashionable duplex now. I spent my childhood here – seven children we were, filling the house with discreet pandemonium. But our neighbours were benevolent. Even during the war, when we raised chickens, about fifty of them, in our garage. To aid the war effort. One day the chickens escaped, and rampaged the block. Catching fifty loud chickens! We made a gift of a dozen eggs to each of our neighbours after.

Further down the street, a house built in the 1890s with a strong piece of modern sculpting on its lawn. The house where I was born, in the area of home accouchements. Now, thanks to the protection of older architecture in Toronto, it can't be torn down. Which gladdens me, as I stroll on down Park Road Hill, rejoicing in that handsome Tuscan villa on my right, and the valley spreading in trees beyond. A bluejay scolding my presence.

Following my feet, up toward Meredith Crescent. Past Sir Ernest MacMillan's modest onetime home. And the old Geary house rising proud on my left. Handsome mid-nineteenth century Georgian it is, with that huge copper beech in front. We always used to cut through the Geary backyard for home, after Cub Nights. Thought it was daring. Truth is the Gearys were affectionately tolerant.

And on my right now, that thundering Victorian manor, with the magnificent newel post in its front hall. I can still feel it in the palm of my hand. My grandfather's former home, where he too raised seven children. And the sound of Gramp's burly voice – "Come on in, Scottie old horse." I was seven. And never really understood why I was an "old horse." But the phrase still rings with love, as I see his home now.

I stroll on, feeling rooted once again. And ring a doorbell a few houses on. A family which my family has known for a century now. An elderly woman answers the door, chuckles – "Well, you've come to see us after all these years. Coffee's on!" I mumble stupidly as she sweeps me into the living room, and disappears for the coffee. And remember something my mother once told me – "my mother and her mother were schoolgirls together. Victorian heroines were always called Dorothy. So our mothers, at school, agreed that someday their first daughters would be called Dorothy. And so we were!" I sit down, warm with memory. This home, like so many in Rosedale, full of deep, unsung remembrances for me, and for my parents and grandparents. A way of life Rosedale is. Not an ideology, but an estate of being.

The unusual Krieghoff painting, of a lake steamer, at the end of the room. And the barrage of plants clambering around the bookcase. Suddenly I recall that the name, Rosedale, it came from Mary Jarvis's garden, her "rose dale," which she planted near here, back in the 1830s. My friend pops back – "Fresh coffee, I remembered you like cream and sugar." I nod content, and ask out of the blue – "What makes people *hate* Rosedale so much?" She looks amused, says "You always did ask improper questions, even as a little boy." Shakes her head in mock reproof, and adds, "I suppose it's the image of snobbery, Rosedale. And the legend of all the money here. That's what's hated. But the money's not here anymore you know. It's up in Bayview, or Moore Park, or out with that horsey set in King." She laughs, "Most of us old Rosedale families are nouveau pauvre now."

I muse aloud – "As for snobbery, I run into more of that in the media. A kind of vehemence of inverted snobbery, destroying what it's after. I remember, Dorothy, when I started in as a young journalist, in the late Fifties. I had to conceal the fact that I grew up in Rosedale. It's as though you have to be a neo-churl these days, or you're not trendy, you're not *in*. She chuckles over her coffee, notes " A lot of the media people have settled in Rosedale in recent years. Christina Newman is over where you grew up, for one." And as she says this, I recollect that Morley Callaghan is a Rosedale resident. It's strange, so many journalists and writers spend their lives attacking what Rosedale represents, then end up living ... in Rosedale!

A few minutes later I'm walking back to my small apartment. The lines of Dennis Lee's pungent poem on Rosedale going through my head.

The dream of tory origins
Is full of lies and blanks
Though what remains when it is gone
To prove that we're not Yanks

Yes, Rosedale is a national asset, and a national whipping-horse. And in reality there are at least three different "Rosedales." There is the geographic Rosedale, whose quiet walks and trees and muted manorial architecture have just restored so much peace to me. Then there is the Rosedale which Rachel Wyatt lampoons in her pert novel, *The Rosedale Hoax* – the same Rosedale that looms like some dowager dinosaur, consciously or subconsciously, in so much current Canadian theatre. A Rosedale that any fool can attack, a suitable snob symbol for national lust-hate. In part, of course, this snob-reputation has been honourably earned. But in part it exists only in the worst hopes of those on-the-make.

More important, there is that unrecognized Rosedale which continues to play a massive role in our national culture, via people of immense talent and personality. There is Bill Glassco, running Tarragon Theatre, making it the centre of creative Canadian drama. Or Bill Kilbourn, as much a firebrand as the William Lyon Mackenzie he biographized. Or that dean of Canadian art sculptures Dora de Pedery Hunt. Or Harry Somers, tuning Canada's musical ear. Or Tom Symons, quietly rethinking the whole of Canadian education. To name, at random, only a few among many from or in Rosedale who energize our national consciousness.

Of course it is this larger Rosedale, of the heart and of culture which gains my assent. Rosedale at the point where it intersects with the nation, creatively.

The last houses of Rosedale pass beside me now. Yonge Street churns up ahead. And more lines from Lee's poem:

When I came down from Rosedale
I could not school my mind
To the manic streets before me
Nor the courtly ones behind

Yes, the manic streets of our big cities. Streets rife with some hidden chagrin now. Full of eyes that never meet, merely bounce off each other or else quest flesh. A suppressed psychic tantrum that can explode in sudden violence on the subway. Or deployed as social and business tactics that no one any longer questions. A taxi-driver yanking his clients around the city. A waitress wreaking her day's irritation on her customers. A media-star forcing his billboard face down your throat. People covertly passing on hate.

Nor is it merely at the simple daily level. But at the highest level of national life. Leaders with the cynical attitude that everything is up for grabs, even as they appoint endless party hacks to high posts. Or who gain their way by tactics of psychic blackmail, while suppressing a snigger.

Yes, that's also what my calming stroll through Rosedale has underlined for me. That our big city streets, and too much of our national life, are "manic." As though Canada now suffers from a diffuse case of national rabies. All reflected in what might best be called a " smart-ass" press and media. Everything, in fact that Canada really isn't. Because ours is the gamble, in North America, for quality – quality of life and being. And that's what this national election is really about, beyond all the red herring, all the psychic legerdemain. It's about decency and national sanity.

Which is what Rosedale represents. Beyond its evident limitations, its mitigated stuffiness, its snobbery neither better nor worse than I can find any day in any CBC office. Rosedale, and all the other "Rosedales" across the country, represent the difference between being merely housebroken, and being civilized. Canada both cherishes and loathes the "Rosedale myth." Yet without it, without its quiet embodiment of decent manners, and its sense of family and of historical continuity, we might be merely Americans.

CALGARY: A Leacock Town on the Prairies

I never could understand why one of my brothers moved to Calgary, about twen-ty years ago. Pondering on this, as I board the plane in Toronto, ducking all the jagged, aggressive mod-art that adorns the airport. And wondering what will Calgary be like? My picture of it these past few years derived only from TV, news-papers – Calgary as Canada's "boomtown," the largest area of any city in the nation, the most cars per capita. Tulsa North, as Fotheringham so wittily calls it. A new stampede this time, for gas and oil.

Toronto fading behind me now. Toronto, our financial New York, and also our literary and media and cultural capital. And as Irving Layton said, a city of "jocks on the make." With all its effortful cosmopolitanism. The Great Lakes miniature below me. To my right that de facto capital of Northern Ontario, Thunder Bay – magnificent new name for the old duo of Fort William and Port Arthur. And that last of the Ontario-style Victorian farm houses, near to Winnipeg. Past Regina, with its "poet-in-residence," Eli Mandel. Splendid civic innovation. Eli telling me of the woman who wrote to the Regina paper, protesting his appointment – "Regina should be filling potholes, not hiring poets." Great title for a poem.

At dark we are descending toward the Calgary airport. The city shimmering like an aurora borealis, huge in the night. Enter the airport, another of those great modern travel ports, all metal and glass. Like a landed interstellar satellite. But inside, I'm stopped short. The presence of the suits of armour, like ferocious yet elegant dragons. I walk over, yes, it's an exhibit of early Japanese armour. And Netsukes. Their beauty doubled by this very airport setting. Supersonic new, time-less old, juxtaposed so effectively here. And on beyond, a song in my eye, a display of Canadian Indian floral beadwork, carvings. Displays from the Glenbow Foundation of Calgary. So different from the energetically arid mod-art of the Toronto airport. I find myself walking slower, wondering ... maybe Calgary isn't all what I think it is.

A taxi into town. The driver is friendly, folk-courteous, telling me that I must see the Calgary zoo, the White Rhino ... Such a contrast with many Toronto taxi-drivers, who yank you around the city, dump you at your destination. I check into my hotel in time for a late snack. The restaurant combining English clubland hunting scenes, chivalresque banners, and Victorian wild-West kitsch. Later, abed, my sleep is mutilated by the hammering of all-night construction outside. Calgary abooming.

Awake next morning, to the first day of spring, and my first real look at Calgary. The weather sweater-warm, a shrill blue sky, sharp clear air. As I ren-dezvous out to the University of Calgary, for lunch with Prairie novelist Rudy Wiebe, now teaching there. The university set on a rise of land beyond the edge of the city. Looking like a privileged high-rise office complex set amid spacious gardens.

I've only met Wiebe through his novels ... on Big Bear, the powerful prairie Indian chief, and on Louis Riel. Great raging novels, pushing rhetoric to the edges of belief, presenting the Prairies as unsung epic. And in the process confuting by poetry my smug Eastern Canadianism of Sir John A. Macdonald, and the angular Ontario Orangemen. It seems improbable that I'll like Wiebe. I enter his campus office wary, but intrigued. Enter to find myself confronted by a tall, powerfully built man, with a great porcupine-quill of a beard. He sits erect in his chair, a latter-day Old Testament prophet of a figure he is. His greeting, his talk, direct, stark, strong. So different from the Ontario novelists I know, with their careful diffidence, their cautiously qualified comments. Certainly different from the current wave of women writers, with their self-conscious assertiveness. Wiebe is forceful without being aggressive.

Almost immediately we are talking of Riel, Big Bear ... Suddenly I realize we aren't talking of them as historical figures at all – but as live, forces of nature, still stalking the West. Belated heroes for a nation afraid of heroes in any form. Heroes of heart, and of the heart. Heroes in faith. Riel, the last Canadian possessed of a full medieval mystical vision. He and his men condemning the Ontario Orangeman, Thomas Scott, to die for ... for blaspheming! And in Wiebe's novel, and within his neo-baroque prose, it works – a man offends the Métis nation by his curses, and must die.

As I listen to Wiebe, I feel myself disconcertedly Ontarian. Pallid beside this western potence of buffalo-run and Métis fealty. And when we reach the campus cafeteria for lunch, I notice several professors I knew in the past years from the University of Toronto. Such grey blandmen they are. Their gait so stilted, like broken sticks. "What would Big Bear, Riel, say about men like that?" – we both blurt it out at once. And we eat our lunch trying to see Calgary, the modern West, through the eyes, the faith, the bodies of Wiebe's heroes. Wiebe stating that Big Bear didn't understand how land could be sold – yet today, Wiebe notes, the CPR even sells the air-space over its railway tracks in downtown Calgary. We laugh, ruefully.

After lunch, walking back to his office complex, Wiebe nods toward the new university buildings – "straight out of California. Not related to the Prairies at all. That library there, its windows are violently vertical, narrow. Yet the land it looks out on is totally horizontal."

Later, riding back into centre-city, I still feel the thunder of Big Bear, Riel, Wiebe. And in contrast, the enforced quiet of the bus. An Anglo-Saxon quietude, like the subway riders in Toronto. A buttoned-up silence. It slowly dawns upon me that Calgarians are far from American. They are too reserved, polite.

Next day I lunch with a prestigious Calgary businessman. We meet in an expensive restaurant. A high-style version of my hotel cafeteria. Leather-chair clubland, dark wood paneling, with Wild West decor, stuffed animal heads, horns. As if a British club had married a rodeo. Or is it simply the world of Big Bear and Riel mounted as trophy?

The businessman is talking of Ontario as branch-plant economy. Owned by profit-hungry Americans. Whereas Alberta owns much of its own wealth, inalienable. His finger jabbing at me, politely forceful, direct, sharp, candid. His eyes upon me as sharp and direct as a pair of buffalo horns. I am struck by how much like Wiebe he is. A businessman's version of Wiebe. Prairie forthrightness. A strong contrast to Toronto businessmen I know. Who are conversationally indirect, oblique – probing you to find out if you are complicit with them (in what, I don't know). I remember something Max Braithwaite, another Prairie writer, told me years ago. I asked him what the basic characteristic of Ontario was. "Deviousness," he replied, straight as an arrow. Now listening to the open economic strictures of this Calgary businessman, and remembering Wiebe's candour, I begin to feel what Braithwaite said. That we in Ontario are always playing three ends against some unknown middle.

Lunch done, my head spinning with economics and an astute businessman's condemnation of Ottawa pork-barrelling and Toronto complicity, I stroll to the Glenbow Museum, to relax. Am amazed by the palatial entrance lobby. And upstairs, the vivid display of Western Indian and Métis material. As bright as the song of the Western Meadowlark. And the strength of the early carvings – often combining wildlife forms, and the seventeenth century French folk designs.

The cultural métissage, virile. My head soars with that same feeling of released grandeur that I get in the great Anthropological Museum in Mexico City.

Only gradually do I realize that here I am being presented with the absolute opposite version of Prairies history from Wiebe's. Here Big Bear and Riel are obstacles in the way of the CPR and settlement. Obstacles in the growth of Canada. And the Queen's Own Rifles of Toronto is the, or a, hero. I feel uncomfortable, caught in the crossfire of two historical realities. Each valid.

The director of the museum has time for a coffee with me. Tells me of the recent further gift from the Founder's estate – another $20-million worth of material. Some 100,000 items. The director adds that their museum archives are equally rich. That they include unpublished letters from Sir John A. Macdonald which reveal that Macdonald contemplated the assassination of Riel. I wince. My Eastern Canadian guilt grows.

Outside I chuckle, as a young man wearing a turtleneck shirt strides by – printed on it the words: "If God had wanted Texans to ski he'd have made bullshit white!" No, it's clear that Calgary ain't no Tulsa North, and lords it over Tulsa South.

I need a rest. Too much data ... I walk to the Devonian Gardens, Fourth Floor of the Toronto-Dominion Bank Tower. The tower itself that same dour black of its sponsor in Toronto. But inside, the building is a bright and spacious shopping centre, with that Calgary calm, almost decorum, that I begin to recognize everywhere in this city. So different from the Toronto Eaton Centre, which simply acts as a financial vacuum cleaner, sucking buyers in at one end, spewing them out at the other. And upstairs, the gardens themselves, a huge floating oasis in mid-city. People strolling, many sitting quietly reading.

On my final day, my brother takes me to the Calgary Tower for lunch. I ascend skeptically. But eat my lunch convinced by the voracious view. The mountains like giant white coral on the horizon. The Bow River winding as an ongoing park through the city. The limestone Victorian buildings of the very modern Eighth Avenue Mall right below me. Capsule view of a metropolis aborning. The highrise modern buildings bursting up all over. And not far beyond these, the old wood frame houses, late Victorian, Edwardian ... the style so familiar. Ah, that's it – right out of nineteenth century Ontario. As if they'd ridden west on the CPR, far beyond Winnipeg.

Later, my brother drives me proudly around his adopted city. Construction everywhere. Signs saying "Drive decent!" And on out to play hookey, at the zoo. To see my first White Rhinoceros. Such a magnificent brute. A kind of domesticated dinosaur.

I leave Calgary next morning, shaking my head. Calgary isn't at all what I thought it would be. It isn't at all the city our Eastern media present as some latter-day American boomtown. Calgary is a sane, quiet, polite, essentially British North American City. A transplant from some Ontario we've betrayed or sold. One of Leacock's "sunshine towns," set on the Prairies, and come of age as a rising metropolis.

I leave happy. I know why my brother settled in Calgary!

OTTAWA: Rideau Hall, Beyond Any Meanness

Entering the Château Laurier, Ottawa. This imaginative château of a hotel, with its majestic panelled lobby, its massive, almost antlered, chandelier. Incredible, these château hotels, across Canada, whether old, like the Château Laurier, or the Château Frontenac in Québec City, or elegantly new, like the Château Champlain in Montréal. Always adding to our national skyline, and our sense of the validly romantic. Telling us that we are not merely material secularists, but that in our deep roots we have a sense of poetry, of grandeur, which matches our very land.

Upstairs, sitting in my room, I gaze out over the Rideau Canal, this ongoing waterway park across southeastern Ontario. And rising above the historic canal, the great hill of Parliament. The East Block a great moose of a building. At once ungainly, homely, yet handsome, majestic ... an entire medieval town out the corner of one's eye in its turrets, towers, polychrome stonework. But with something important added, some Victorian sternness, and high dignity. And the flying magnificence of the Peace Tower just beyond.

I sit musing. Tonight I go to Rideau Hall, home of our head of state, to witness an investiture of the Order of Canada. Our new young Governor-General, Edward Schreyer, officiating as the representative of the Crown in Canada. Is it all a waste of time? This paraphernalia of a Governor-General, and a semi-palace for the head of state. Just a costly anomaly left over from a distant colonial era? A mere centre of snobbism, or jaded flunkeyism? Something we should certainly abolish, now that we've grown up? Or is our endless ambiguity on the subject simply part of an unworthy ambiguity about ourselves?

I get into my rented dinner jacket, first time I've worn one in more than ten years. And taxi out ... around the soaring War Memorial, the crouching National Arts Centre, the old train station now a handsome National Conference Hall. And then the old greystone buildings, emporiums of Ottawa. Somehow all of a piece, all these buildings. Majestic. Part of what the Château Laurier is itself. And Parliament. And the early nineteenth century Basilique de Notre Dame on my right – twenty years ago we were sure it was Victorian ugly. Now we know it is part of Ottawa's castellate grey elegance.

On toward Rockcliffe. On my left, Earnscliffe, the handsome mid-Victorian stone house that serves as the British High Commission. Sited high over the Ottawa River, it was once the home of Sir John A. Macdonald, our first prime minister. As such, surely it is the natural residence for all our prime ministers? Yet when the British High Commission, in recent years, suggested that Canada might care to acquire it for this purpose, we passed it by! And maintained the bloated Westmountian-pile that now serves as the Prime Minister's residence. Unimaginative. Why do we fail when such opportunities are presented? Are we willfully stingy, as a people – and willfully opposed to our own roots? Does our history, our tradition, frighten us? Or is it that we want to concoct some counter-country?

On my right now, that multi-tiered russet pile, the new External Affairs Building ... neo-ziggurat it is. And over the first bridge the new Ottawa City Hall, dramatically placed on an island in the middle of the Rideau River.

Soon the great gates of Rideau Hall in front of me. Open gates – anyone can enter. The grounds are a park for the public. The taxi turns in, the high trees arching over us, the driveway curving slowly ahead. Ending in that final vista through the trees – the massive greystone pediment of Rideau Hall. I get out, nervous. What am I doing here? My usual habitat is a small fishing village, or a cabin in the bush, or a rural town. I enter the marbled front hall, a gathering of bemedalled dignitaries, guests, chatting in this large foyer. I stand isolated, clutching my invitation. After about a minute a uniformed ADC spots me, comes up, starts to chat. No, he doesn't demand to see my invitation. Simply asks my name, introduces me to two other guests. When he leaves, a minute later, I no longer feel alone.

Gradually we are all shown to our seats in the great Ballroom, to the left of the entry hall. The magnificence of gold and beige, and the life-size portrait of Queen Victoria. The person sitting beside me whispers, "The room was built in 1873." It is indisputably one of the handsomest rooms I have ever seen, anywhere in the world. A band has started to play at the back of the room, the TV camera poised at the front near the modern portrait of the Queen and Prince Philip by Jean-Paul Lemieux. I can't decide whether I like or dislike this sophisticated mod-folk painting. But I can't stop looking at it. Then a fanfare, everyone instinctively rising. "Their Excellencies ... " the woman beside me says. A simple and dignified procession down the centre aisle. Several Aides de Camp. A Catholic and a Protestant minister. Governor-General Schreyer and his wife, who take up their position in front of the portrait of the Queen. Brief prayers, in French and in English. The investiture has started.

I am craning my neck to see. Names I know, many I don't ... one by one called forward, their distinction cited. Derek Bedson, onetime secretary to John Diefenbaker; A. J. Casson, last living member of the Group of Seven; André Gagnon, musician extraordinary; Peter C. Newman, voice for Canada; Rabbi Gunther Plaut, spiritual leader, columnist; Donald Sutherland, actor; Jeanne Minhinnick, restorer of our past ... They are of all walks and stations of life, from all parts of Canada, of all political backgrounds. Some are old, a wheelchair or two. Some are young. I listen to the individual citations with care, in French or in English, according to the language of the recipient. The evidence is clear. These men and women have earned their honour!

I scrutinize the audience, perhaps two hundred of us all told in the room. The faces of Chief Justice Bora Laskin, Ontario's Lieutenant-Governor Pauline McGibbon, the Indian artist, Jean-Baptiste Morriseau, with his elaborate headgear. All are watching the ceremony with care. The mood of the room is one of respect, yes, bordering reverence. The investiture of some sixty Canadians completed. Governor-General Schreyer makes a brief pertinent speech, emphasizing that his Order of Canada is "for merit." The case is overwhelmingly clear. We now have, since 1967, a national and formal way of honouring our fellow citizens. The only thing that is not clear, is why we had no way before? Did excellence, quality of life, upset or offend us somehow? I can think of no other nation in the world which would bother explaining why it had a system of honours!

The investiture done, there is a large buffet dinner. On the far side of the entry hall. The Tent Room it is called. It is huge, large enough to have housed an indoor tennis court until recently. Originally erected in 1876, it was just that, a giant tent. Then the tent was built over, in stone. A red-and-white striped tent remaining inside ever since. A formidable combination of informality and ... elegance. With all the portraits of earlier heads of state around the room. I notice people moving from table to table. Laughter, conviviality, relaxation. Warm combination of ease and style. Like the room itself.

I leave Rideau Hall moved, convinced. What a simple yet splendorous way to receive citizens of Canada, and to honour them. What a loss if we did not have it.

The next day I visit Rideau Hall again, stroll the grounds, as any citizen can. Relax amid the first flowers. Noticing the trilliums planted with care near the house itself, the Staghorn Sumac. The gravestones of several buried pets. Walk right around Rideau Hall. The high majesty of the front, the robust greystone dignity of the side. Slowly realizing that it is unlike any great home I have seen in Europe or America. Clearly it has been built at different periods. The original house, of Thomas MacKay, a contractor for the Rideau Canal, built in the 1830s, is still partly visible. Handsome, rough-hewn, "Presbyterian architecture" it was once called. And the wings, segments, like the Ballroom, the Tent Room, the greenhouses, added bit-by-piece ever since. A House that grew like Canada, organically, and over time. Not a cerebral theorem, like the American White House. Nor a monolithic block, like Buckingham Palace. Nor a blast of glory, like Versailles. But a house that only slowly found itself, over a period of some 150 years now. I spy it out the corner of my eye, through the trees, at once homey and almost homely. Yes, it is to an English country house as a moose is to deer. Majestic, ungainly, elegant, and somehow powerfully all one. Like us.

I chuckle with pride, and wander on through the peaceful trees, musing. My voyage across Canada done now. Trying to piece together my central sense of this, of our nation. The nation as it is now, and the nation as it has wanted to be, over one, two, three centuries. With the realization that today, Canadians are more confused, confounded, puzzled, than they have ever been. Inarticulately upset, often humourless. A nameless chagrin stalking the land – like those anonymous signs I've seen painted here and there, "the hate"! A chagrin that may reflect our subconscious knowledge that we have too often sold out our traditions, our standards, parts of our soul, in return for mere material progress. And now that even the material advance seems jeopardized, with a declining dollar ... we feel chagrin. Chagrin at a double loss which our guilt does not wish to define.

Rideau Hall hoves into view again through the trees. Yes, Rideau Hall, it stands beyond such chagrin, beyond any meanness of mind and spirit. I go over in my mind the legacy of some of our Governors-General and their wives, since Confederation: the National Gallery, the Royal Society of Canada, the Dufferin Terrace in Québec City, the Stanley Cup, the National Council of Women, the Grey Cup, the Lady Byng Trophy, the Dominion Drama Festival, the Governor-General's Awards for Literature. Yes, the Governor-General, he stands for our largeness ... The buck stops at the White House, maybe. But the buck, and politics, and smallness, these all stop at Rideau Hall! I turn toward the main entry hall. Bob Hubbard, cultural advisor to the Governor-General, guides me around the interior of the building. Showing me the handsome sitting room, the Royal Suite upstairs with its fine ceiling moldings which include large Scottish thistles from the days of the first owner. Yes, it is all homey, simple, yet grand. Some of its furniture is magnificent. A few excellent pieces of early Canadiana, including rare bombe commodes from Québec. But much is merely contemporary reproduction, scarcely adequate to its setting.

By chance I meet with the Governor-General himself. I have seen the direct dignity of his presence in the investiture, and his ease with guests last night. Now I have the opportunity to meet in private with this energetic youngish man of deep Manitoba roots, who is comfortable not only in English and French, but also in German and Ukrainian. He carries his five university degrees lightly, and talks knowledgeably about the future of the Canadian north. A few minutes with him leaves one no doubts – this man wants to serve the nation, wants to carry the message of Rideau Hall and Canada's Crown, to everyone. His bearing, his seriousness, his Prairie candour, *these guarantee the job.*

I leave the quiet thunder of Rideau Hall, realizing that Parliament should represent the will of the nation. But the Governor-General represents the soul and heart of the nation. Parliament's job is, so to speak, pedestrian. But the Governor-General's job is ... the pageant of a people. Parliament's job is prosaic. The Governor-General's job is, at least in part, poetry. And a nation without a sense of the poetry of life is dull. Parliament enacts what the nation wants. The Governor-General embodies what the nation is!

Ottawa rises around me. The National Mint, the Château Laurier, Parliament Hill ... like the great promontory of Québec, or the Rocky Mountains themselves, all part of the immense castle of Canada. Part of our poetry and our soul. And Rideau Hall, a natural centre of this. With Governor-General Edward Schreyer, and his wife, Lily, there, At Home for any and all of us. Bearing a very simple message – dignity, excellence, pride in an ongoing nation, love for Canada.

Mazo Was Murdered

It wasn't till some way into Joan Givner's *Mazo de la Roche: The Hidden Life* that I realized it wasn't about Mazo as author or about the world of Jalna, but about her sex life, or lack of one. Professor Givner has busied herself to adduce evidence that Mazo was a lesbian, a proto-lesbian, or a lesbian manquée. Feeling thoroughly stupid and thoroughly male, I started reading the book all over again.

Mazo shared life right from her teens with a younger lady, name of Carolyn. Joan Givner hastens to point out, "There are many questions to be asked about the nature of this symbiotic relationship which began when Mazo's parents adopted Carolyn into their family." There was a fearsome stuffed bird in the family home. And dear young Carolyn "shows Mazo how to take physical pleasure in the creature's body, urging her to put her hands into the cavity under the wings. Mazo remembers the sensation thus: 'Oh the downy softness of the space beneath his wings – the intimate communion.'" Professor Givner says that such "simple acts explain in coded form what happened when Carolyn stepped into her world."

But apparently it isn't just a matter of lesbianism. Givner firmly states, "The Jalna series itself raised more questions. As the story unfolded in novel after novel (sixteen in all) the sexual adventures of the Whiteoak family grew more and more turbulent. Brothers seducing each other's wives in the early volumes, later gave way to incest, sadism, and demonic possession."

By now I was thoroughly aroused: Givner was sleuthing a Mazo I had never dreamed of. Perhaps that was why Miss de la Roche had been extirpated from the CanLit Hall of Fame: she was some kind of profligate, covert debaucher of national decorums and just conceivably (to make use of the vernacular so admired in Canada) a twat-sucker.

Every ounce of evidence is wrung from the novels: Mazo's "fiction suggests that it was ordinary heterosexual relationships that were strange and foreign to her, beyond her imaginative grasp." Professor Givner says that when "at a party she saw her beloved Carolyn sitting with her hands clasped by a young man," Mazo was shocked. All the more so as Carolyn "seemed to like it." Givner presses further: "In some ways the relationship of Mazo and Carolyn resembles that of Gertrude Stein and Alice B. Toklas." Just what I'd begun to suspect. It is uncertain whether "the two girls" moved past the stage of "play" (their favourite pastime during decades together) to surface in actual carnal interplay, though a quote from *Lark Ascending* is suggestive:

"Fay's face wore what Josie called its play-acting expression. It was both rapt and self-conscious. Her eyes were wide-open in a hallucinated fixity. Her dilated nostrils" etc.

It seems clear that Mazo de la Roche and Carolyn Clement got pretty whopped up during "playtime," achieving some equivalent of the Mysteries (Eleusinian or other).

The many ways in which Mazo was suppressed and victimized by the society she grew up in are indefatigably revealed. Givner shows that de la Roche lived in the brutal, high-sadistic world of the Victorian patriarch. Her case is strong, though I find it odd (even ironic) that the dominant figure in Jalnaland is a woman, Gran Whiteoak, who is brutal, coarse, and sadistic.

Givner contends that reviewers (mostly men) failed to understand the world of Jalna because the novels were written by a woman. "Hand in hand with the critical disdain has gone the personal denigration, expertly anatomized in Mary Ellman's *Thinking About Women*. Many of the reviews of Mazo's work provide classic examples of what Ellman terms 'phallic criticism.'" As for Givner herself, she respects some of the Jalna material, but it is the earlier books that earn approval. The trouble is that the Jalna series presents an upper-class version of old Ontario life. The earlier writing (as in the novel *Delight*) had dealt with the real folks, the real Canadians. That is, there's an upstairs-downstairs problem inherent in Jalna. Canadians have adopted the opinion that to be properly Canadian you have to come from downstairs. This inverse snobbery is often militant.

Fortunately, as Givner notes, writers like Dorothy Livesay "often defended Mazo from critics who felt that the Whiteoaks were too British or too upper-class: she never tired of pointing out that people like the Whiteoaks settled in Ontario and were the proper stuff of Canadian fiction." In recent years, genteel nineteenth-century immigrants like the Moodies, Traills, and Stricklands have become acceptable heroes and heroines for CanLit: they've been recycled as retroactive lineage.

Nonetheless Mr. Robert Fulford wrote in the *Toronto Star* on Mazo's death in 1961, of the Jalna books; "Canadians went to them looking for a realistic account of Canadian life, and found instead a fairy-tale countryside populated by implausibly old-world characters." And a couple of years ago Mordecai Richler said that Mazo de la Roche was dispensable as a serious Canadian writer.

Professor Givner appears to acquiesce on this conventional wisdom. When she does praise Mazo as a writer, she says; "Not only did she amass a fortune, but she did it through her mastery of language, thus confirming Humpty Dumpty's statement that whoever learns to control words 'can master the whole lot of them.'" An odd barometer for literature, unless you think literature is power. But then this book is not literary criticism or biography; it's a sexo-sociological tract. The academic, jargon-ridden prose style "bonds" the reader to a pre-ordained conclusion.

I turned with more hope to *Gardens, Covenants, Exiles: Loyalism in the Literature of Upper Canada/Ontario*. Dennis Duffy gives Mazo a full chapter. He doesn't mince words:

"Canada's best-known novelist, Mazo de la Roche presents an expiring vision of the Upper Canada that the Loyalists sought to create and that mythology claimed had actually been created. Jalna and its environs form the last imaginative dwelling place for the social vision at the heart of Loyalism ... Jalna remains a nostalgic extrapolation from a few Ontario houses of a would-be dominant lifestyle."

As for the literary value of Jalnaland, he is equally trenchant: "Why make false apologies about the narrative aspects of the Jalna series. The stories resemble nothing so much as soap opera." A bold, if rather American insight. He admits that "while Canadian critics have rarely considered her work worthy of sustained attention a body of fiction possessing sufficient world-wide popularity to have sold eleven million copies by 1966 merits some notice." But this he quickly explains away: "Inclusiveness and continuity mark life at Jalna." This doubtless accounts for the series' exceptional popularity in the Europe of the 1940's.

I thought I should re-read *Jalna* and *Whiteoaks* before reading Joan Givner's book. I was startled to discover that none of the major Toronto bookstores carried any of the Jalna series. By the time I found second-hand copies, I was filled with foreboding: I was about to read soap opera already dated when it was written. Under the influence of Givner, Duffy, and so on, I wasn't far into *Jalna* when I found parts that felt awkward, naive or stilted; for example, passages of vapidly romantic dialogue (as in the first encounter of Eden and Allayne), and sometimes a use of language more appropriate to *Chums* or *The Boys' Own Annual* than to an adult novel. At times I felt the book simply couldn't hold.

Yet hold it did. By the time I finished I was reminded that *Jalna* filled a major gap in our understanding of Canada. At one level it was a literary correlative to that large illustrated Victorian work, *Picturesque Canada*, which did so much to give Canada an image of itself. Mazo was speaking of and from the culture that extended from Confederation through the First World War; a period marked in architecture by the Gothic of the Parliament Buildings in Ottawa and by the magnificent "Château" hotels across the country. And she accurately presented the sensibility of an earlier period in Canada, say, from the 1780's, through the Loyalist period, to Confederation. She'd achieved an excellent shorthand for conveying the outer trappings of a nation.

Jalnaland caught a specifically Canadian inner reality. No, not an Anglican one, but a Calvinist-Anglican one. In the eyes of readers like Fulford and Duffy, her books belong to the world of Anglican gentry. Yet there is to Jalnaland a harsh, spikey, tough Calvinism. Very un-English – more like Protestant Scotland. It shows in a recurrent cruelty in the books: scenes of family affection often "fulfilled" by harsh physical contact, not infrequently a whipping or a drubbing. I can't think of anything in English literature quite like this world, unless it be the black side of *Wuthering Heights*.

Jalna vividly presents a very Ontario reality: a secular and social Anglo-Calvinism that is rather like an upgrade mutation of *Glengarry Schooldays*, that other Canadian classic of Mazo's day.

This startled me. So did the rife suppressed carnality. Nor do I simply mean the homo-sentience, not to say homo-eroticism, which goes far beyond the mere lesbianism discerned by Professor Givner. What I mean is something much deeper: that the very house and all its *objets* and decor, along with everyone in it, partake of some kind of incarnate being. There is a continuum of house, land, animals, and people that one might only expect to find in the medieval world of the *Trés riches heures* or church tympana (as at Moissac). A continuum and an indestructible palpability that is utterly opposite to so much styrofoam literature of today.

I hadn't been watching for such passages. They kept striking me. So did passages in which a member of the family would undergo what could only be called a mystical experience – as when another spirit grows out of the body. Mazo presents these with no fuss, as part of the landscape, the being-scape of Jalna. As when young Finch experiences Holy Communion over the family graves.

I gradually realized that Jalna is something infinitely more important than a lifestyle. To reduce it to this (like Professor Duffy) is to reduce life itself. Jalnaland presents an entire spiritual possibility. As in the Anglican (or Lutheran, etc.) Communion, the Real Presence is there, or not, depending on you yourself.

Jalna is a Jungian experience. It embodies the collective unconscious of a tribe and people: at once Loyalist and later immigrant British genteel, both firmly domiciled in Canada. With the very echoes in the prose itself. Like *Moby Dick*, the American epic, Jalna yokes together (not always comfortably) the prose rhythms, styles, and effects of different eras. At one moment, Mazo's reality seems Johnsonian (she mentions that Johnson's Dictionary was her only reference book when young), at the next, Victorian "Gothick," at the next, Rider Haggard. (Her father's pet name for her, Umslopogaas, is the name of a Zulu warrior who appears in more than one of Rider Haggard's books.) Wittingly or not, Mazo is a collective memory. She compresses several centuries of English-speaking tradition into one place, much as it must have been compressed inside the inhabitants of Jalna. And she does so in a way specific to Ontario and English Canada.

I pondered on this: Was there anything in Jalna that didn't fit what I knew about early Ontario? The pervasive British tradition of early Ontario; or the defining importance of the officer class that settled here after the American Revolution and the War of 1812; or the later genteel tradition of the Stricklands, Langtons, and Moodies.

Or was there anything in the personalities of the Whiteoaks I couldn't find in early Ontario furniture? That specific personality of Ontario furniture, a combination of local woods (like butternut and maple), a virile overlapping of styles and stances at once folk and high style. All rather like Rennie, the master of Jalna, combining an often furious robustness with a certain courtliness.

Was there in fact anything in *Jalna* or *Whiteoaks* I had not seen during my childhood days in rural Ontario? Whether at the folk level or the so-called genteel?

One thing became clear. Jalna recreated a culture I'd known intimately at first hand. A culture that had variously continued long after the publication of the first book in the series. John Diefenbaker had embodied it in his own folk way forty years later; Robert Stanfield in a robust genteel way over fifty years later. Much that I knew corroborated that specific yeoman-genteel tradition. No, not British squire or gentry as such, though a touch of each. It was at once yeoman (foursquare, down-to-earth) and genteel (a sense of decorum and style); at once tough, robust, mindful of traditions, and loyal to tribe and place. Very Ontario.

Mazo caught this exactly, setting it off against the more fastidious puritanism of the New England tradition (thus Allayne in *Jalna*). Also setting it against the prissiness of the "Rosedale" tradition in her second book, *Whiteoaks*. And she caught it as only a great artist could, in some eternal way almost outside of time. Jalna was the microcosm, an entire culture its scope.

There remains the question: *Why* was Mazo destroyed? A major figure for a few years after the publication of *Jalna* (perhaps till the mid-thirties), she has been extirpated from Canadian consciousness. Try buying *Jalna* in a Toronto bookstore. Try finding out what happened to the CBC television series on Jalnaland (it ran briefly in 1973, and was scuppered by tacky production and a "with-it" script). For that matter try finding a biography of Mazo's best and deeper meanings, including her appeal to the heart.

I believe the answer is this: *Jalna* was published in 1927, the literary apogee of Canada's sixtieth anniversary Jubilee Year. But another reality was afoot. In 1926, the United Church of Canada was formed, and Mackenzie King took sempiternal power. The "Canadian Identity" (as we now know it) was formed according to the will of the United Church and Mackenzie King. Earnestness and do-good (with cash registers jingling close by) replaced the feist, humour, and incarnacy of Sir John A. Macdonald's Canada. Jalna and all it stood for passed under tacit ban. Academe overlooked it and the journalist-pundits sneered at it, both displaying a massive cultural ignorance and inordinate social bias.

To consider Jalnaland "dispensable" is cultural treason; it is almost like saying that French is a foreign language. It reveals a cultural inferiority complex of incurable size. I try to imagine what a real life meeting between Mazo de la Roche (and her Carolyn) and Professor Givner or Duffy would be like. Mazo would dismantle Ms. Givner's jargon with a phrase or perhaps just a gesture. And distance Professor Duffy as a lightweight. There would be no second meeting – Carolyn would see to that.

The world of Jalna is an integral part of the roots of Canada. To lose it would leave us groping for an abandoned identity. Worse, the very methods of suppression used against Jalna and all it represented in Canadian culture would leave us heirs only to amnesia.

All mutations allowed, Mazo and her Jalnaland should hold a place in our culture like that of *Moby Dick* for Americans: as a defining epic.

And should hold a place in our hearts like that of *Maria Chapdelaine* in French-Canadian hearts. Oh, I know *Maria Chapdelaine* is no longer fashionable in French Canada (moreover it was written by a Frenchman not a Québécois). Yet it is French Canada's defining fable, standing beyond time.

As McLuhan said, the defining Canadian myth is rural. And it's rural in a specific way; farmland edging the threatening bush, and fighting to sustain millennial meanings beyond mere landscape. A case of roots vs. rocks, so to speak. And insofar as rocks won, people lost heart and memory.

Mazo de la Roche is one of the few geniuses of Canadian literature, along with Saint-Denys Garneau, Hubert Aquin, the early Marie-Claire Blais, and perhaps in a lesser way, Leacock, Haliburton, and Leonard Cohen.

Mazo was murdered – for political reasons. She didn't fit the unfolding Grit plan for Canada. Her genius was one of personality as against mere will to power. All of which makes one wonder if much contemporary CanLit (as it's called) doesn't exist for political reasons. As Professor C.B. Macpherson once said, "Why can't we will a new order of reality?"

Yes, Calvinism won in Canada, in alliance with Methodism. And downstairs became upstairs (and "gentrification" is now a national industry). And quick glitz a la Sam Slick along with ontological perjury sets the tone.

The final sentence of Professor Givner's book made me ponder: "When the life and works of Mazo de la Roche are taken together in their status as text and set against, say, Margaret Atwood's works, the possibilities for intertextual readings are many and illuminating." Jargon aside, what an interesting idea. Perhaps we need a look at the world of Dr. Margaret Atwood, C.C. I'm confident Mazo wouldn't mind, not after what she's been put through. I'll come back to this, some other day.

Atwood-as-Icon

Margaret Atwood has achieved apotheosis. Were there such things as secular saints, she'd be one now: the Blessed Margaret at least.

She became a celebrity over fifteen years ago (at least in Canada), with the publication of her non-fiction work, *Survival*. In that book she presumed that Canadians had merely "survived." And in effect provided us with a handbook on how to better our lot.

Many people would be satisfied with celebrity status. But Ms. Atwood never stopped in her ascension. Slowly but surely, novel by novel, public appearance after public appearance, and award by award, she pursued her quiet way.

By the time of the publication of *The Handmaid's Tale* in 1985 she was a certified national icon. Doubly so after the book's success in the United States.

A celebrity is merely part of the media agenda. But an icon sets an agenda, *is* the agenda for the media. In the case of Ms. Atwood one had but to contemplate her various causes and good works to know what was right and proper. Thus her work in ecology and bird-watching, in the Writers' Union of Canada, in the Writers' Development Trust, and later in Amnesty International and PEN, not to mention sundry civic matters.

Ms. Atwood was a genuine power in such causes. Indeed at one point it was rumoured she might run for Mayor of Toronto. The fact is Ms. Atwood seemed to position herself extremely well in her causes. Seemed to embody the national intention. In particular she managed to embody both the surge of feminism and the development of the national identity. With Ms. Atwood the two items appeared as one. Perhaps because the advance of the Canadian identity seemed to go hand in hand with the detumescence of the Canadian male.

Yes, Ms. Atwood has ascended from celebrity, through iconhood, to apotheosis. Contemplate the six months starting in July of 1989. In that month she was on the cover (not for the first time) of *Saturday Night*, with a piquant little story of youth and death. Then come August she was pivotal (and front cover) in a *Toronto Life* issue devoted to literature: "An exclusive world premiere," as it said. The proceeds went to the worthy cause of PEN. And Ms. Atwood generously agreed to sign copies of the magazine despite the intrusive presence of TV cameras and cash registers.

Then in the autumn of 1989 she was a star of the 54th international PEN World Congress in Toronto.

And at the same time enjoying the glory of the film being made of *The Handmaid's Tale*, with script by Harold Pinter no less.

And all this while processing a unique play for Canadian Stage (one must hope it will be televised by the CBC).

Not to mention being short-listed for the prestigious Booker Prize again. Alas, she missed by a hair. Or as she noted on radio, perhaps Canada isn't exotic enough for such awards. Yes, once again she struck a note for all of us.

But she was quickly recompensed with a number of other awards, tributes, and promotions. Thus the Periodical Marketers of Canada Award. While the radio ads for her novel *Cat's Eye* took on a new stridency, even urgency.

Apotheosis indeed. Word in the book industry assures us she's wonderfully "well-positioned" to get the Nobel Prize.

When a citizen, one of our own, reaches such pre-eminence, he or she is indeed part of our daily consciousness. Ms. Atwood has taken up residence in our being, and the shape, certainly the face, of our nation lies in part through Ms. Atwood. Or to give her her full due, Dr. Margaret Atwood, C.C.

Given this remarkable pre-eminence it behooves us to appraise her. No, I certainly do *not* mean her private life which is totally her own business. Nor even her poetry and novels except insofar as they shed light on her persona as national icon. Because it's Icon-Atwood we need to examine. If we can locate the meanings of Atwood-as-Icon we'll surely know more about our nation.

Most would agree that the public persona of Ms. Atwood, the Icon-persona, is austere. Some have used the word (as of her prose) astringent; we might also say, rigorous, laconic, monochrome, angular. Or as Ms. Atwood herself says of Canadian poetry, "spikey."

Ms. Atwood is not for laughs – she is neither to be laughed at nor does she induce merriment. She may well be a merry soul in private: that is not our affair. It's Icon-Atwood we need to understand.

And truth is, as Icon, she's not guilty of much exotica, for example in gesture, colour, language, or dress. In fact she exercises restraint in all these. Seeing her one might have the impression of a very proper daughter of a Presbyterian minister (which she is not).

Yes, one is confronted with Icon-Atwood as a dour, "spikey," unlaughing creature. Despite that famous smile of hers, that winsome sweet-bitter smile, a kind of smirk-smile that promises you it'll hurt. Visually, that is, she might seem some combination of a Calvinist sermon and a latterday Methodist Madonna. Very appropriate to Canada.

But her quality as Icon goes much deeper than such a "suit of nettles" (to quote a poet Ms. Atwood approves of). I recall some few years ago the newspapers reporting a talk Ms. Atwood gave at McGill University. It was about literature as power. I'd always naively thought of literature as about life, conceivably about a fuller life. No, I didn't manage to obtain a copy of Dr. Atwood's lecture, but the thing stuck in my mind. Then last winter I noticed in the papers the title of another talk she was giving: "Margaret Atwood Lays Down the Law." It felt odd. Of course it was being given to a York University law group. So the title was relevant. Yet there was that power-play on meaning: Ms. Atwood was going to set things straight for the law-boys. The tone was almost Thatcherite, Margaret Thatcher and Margaret Atwood as two of a kind, "laying down the law."

Then came the PEN congress in Toronto, and I was startled by the number of times the word "power" cropped up. Not only in the formal title of the congress ("The Writer: Freedom & Power"), but in the various "sessions." Thus "Power & Gender" and "Language as Power" (Ms. Atwood sat on this panel). No question but that a perusal of the programme suggested power on the brain, or wherever, almost an obsession.

No the congress was not run by Ms. Atwood, but by her companion Graeme Gibson. But given this and given that Ms. Atwood had in effect founded the Toronto Centre for PEN in 1983, one might guess that she had considerable hand in formulating this power congress. Indeed the list of Canadian participants in the panels, public readings, etc. might be construed as a list of Atwoodites. Even Harold Pinter all the way from Britain. (He's not much given to merriment either.) Thus if the congress was not directly Ms. Atwood's brainchild, it certainly reflected her interests. Indeed in one way the congress seemed to be a neat combination of her theme in the McGill lecture (literature as power), and her theme in the York-Osgoode one (Margaret Atwood lays down the law). The fact being that power and empowerment are demonstrably ongoing concerns of hers. (The title of an early book of her poems was *Power Politics*, about love of course.) And her role as Icon clearly relates to power.

Austerity, and power, and no laughs!

Take it a step further. Ms. Atwood is clearly a feminist, a leader in one of the powerful movements of our era. One doesn't have to read far in her books to know this. Her women may indeed be vulnerable, or victims, or just bleak. But they ascend to "lady oracles" and, via Ms. Atwood herself, to national iconhood. And her literary attitude towards men might be indicated in some lines of her poetry:

You fit into me
like a hook into an eye
a fish hook
an open eye

or again:

Please die I said
so I can write about it.

Feminism also pervades her novels. And emerges rampant in *The Handmaid's Tale*. And very austere and chilling and curiously neo-Presbyterian that tale is. Indeed it often reads more like a recall than anything in the future. With men as dour (and sexotic) monsters. And their handling of women as a recycle from *L'Histoire d'O*. All of which she depicts with acidic care.

But her feminism is not limited to her books. The PEN Congress was in so many cunning (a word Atwood likes) ways a fine feminist victory. Every literary lady who could be mustered was, and then some. Anne Hébert was even flown in from Paris as special guest. And the gala opening soirée featured all-female stars on stage. Though outside the theatre, coloured women were protesting against PEN as racist. Which it wasn't, merely cunningly feminist and Wasp. Said differently, one might remark the absence of various Canadian male writers of note (Robertson Davies being but one). Or the curious absence of American male writers of note, as if they had boycotted the occasion. Not to mention the absence of French Canadian male writers of any stature at all.

Yes, *Icon-Atwood is mirthless, power-struck, and feminist.*

Fine, life doesn't always provide much ha-ha.

And as Octavio Paz points out, the great Anglo-American failing is to reduce everything (sex included) to politics. So why not literature as ... politics, power politics?

And of course feminism is as valid as, say, native rights, gay-liberation, or any other of the rights movements (with male-liberation coming soon, I hope!).

But Atwood's books go a step further. There's a telling line in *The Handmaid's Tale*. The heroine, pondering her plight, suddenly says: "*Maybe none of this is about control.*" (Italics mine.) Curiously, after reading some 125 pages into the book that line leapt out at me. No, I wasn't thinking about "control," not even remotely. Yet that line suddenly unlocked the book. Despite any disclaimer I realized that this is exactly what the book is about: *control!* Or as the following lines put it: "*about who can own whom, and who can do what to whom and get away with it, even as far as death.*" Yes, underlying all the other themes in the book (feminism, male brutality, and sexoticism, freedom, power, etc.) lurks the hidden issue: control: "even as far as death."

It wasn't till I read a review of Ms. Atwood's most recent work, *Cat's Eye*, in the *New Yorker*, that I began putting it all together. The reviewer, Judith Thurman, described *Cat's Eye* as "the latest of Atwood's fierce enthralling dramas of bondage." And in discussing *The Handmaid's Tale* as "a fantasy of bondage," she notes that "the novel's implicit perversity is what generates its power."

Yes, it was then that I began putting together the curious element of cruelty and desecration in so many of Atwood's books. And the fascination with blood, psychic squalor, and above all pain – pain that isn't exorcised in her books so much as embalmed. And with this the strange prurience as found in *The Handmaid's Tale*: a kind of permanent and nubile prurience. Not to mention an ongoing if diffuse note of sado-masochism.

In fact, *Cat's Eye* could be described as background data for the pornocratic fable presented in *The Handmaid's Tale*. And between the two of them one might locate a single strong (and black) novel. A novel not quite declaring its defining reality. Though when the child-heroine in *Cat's Eye* states, "I'm a vampire too," one is close to the bondage-control theme again.

If one had any doubts about all this, a few hours spent reading Ms. Atwood's poetry provide quick supportive data. The material of the later novels is all available in the earlier poems – the psychic and emotional themes, that is. In a strange way there was no growth, other than in apparent competence.

It seems to me that the public persona of Atwood-as-Icon is ultimately explicable in terms of control and bondage. Thus her near obsession with power and influence. How agreeable to exercise control over the destiny (or maybe just the careers) of others by a nod, a frown, or even by a public curtsy. Not to mention her acidic contempt for men (try her poetry!), alongside of a variable insatiable "yearning" for a man. That combined with the ambiguous relationship with certain women (as in *Life Before Man*) – to the point of wanting to eat their personalities. Add a lust-hate relationship to authority (control being merely proxy authority). Not to mention her curious disdain of public acclaim even as she seems to pursue it with intent. All these fit splendidly into bondage ... life as control.

The only question is, Who is in control?

In *The Handmaid's Tale* Atwood makes simplistically (naively? falsely innocently?) clear that it is the men who tyrannically rule and the women who are victims and slaves. Thus, a feminist tale, or tract. But in the end (the *New Yorker* review has this right), it's finally about control as such: that's what the book relishes – the bondage, including sexotic bondage. In fact one senses it doesn't really matter whether it be men or women or both: in that way the book is curiously androgyne. In rather the same way that the heroine of *Cat's Eye* (as Judith Thurman notes) is somehow tomboy.

Thus ... austerity, power, feminism, and bondage (not to mention a friendly touch of S&M.) all available in Icon-Atwood, if one presumes her widely read books are (as they must be) part of the Iconhood.

It all makes sense of course. All implied in that key word "control." The key in any form of bondage is control. If you can't have real power or potence ... try for control.

In the light of this one might take a final look at the recent PEN congress. Yes, it could be seen as predicate of a cunningly invisible feminist control, Wasp feminist. And yes, the cast and placing of Canadian writers at the congress was very much Atwoodland – friends, allies, and admirers of Ms. Atwood (no dissenting voices permitted in official CanLit). And yes, the only public reading that listed less that four readers was the one with Atwood at the centre.

Yes, without malice, it could be seen as very much Ms. Atwood's world congress.

Perhaps her comment at one of the "sessions" revealed the situation: "*This isn't the Norman Mailer Roadshow.*" Well, no indeed, it was the Atwood Brigade. All achieved by control, in this case remote control, because she wasn't the Commander up front, just the one behind the scenes. In fact as I surveyed the "in-crowd" at the gala opening dinner, I had the weird sensation of an added chapter to *The Handmaid's Tale*. In this case with gender positions nicely reversed. In effect the agenda, the tone, direction, obsession with the theme of power, this was all a feminist victory of sorts. With Ms. Atwood as a very cunning *éminence grise*, virtually undetectable in her role, unless you knew the players.

It becomes clear that Icon-Atwood is not quite what we might think. The novels suggest that some form of bondage is pervasively in play. So for that matter does their very prose – that see-Dick-run-see-Mary-catch-the-ball prose, with its unwitting touches of cameo poetry but with the willed mind as control, in fact as unwitting plot.

Thus we must appraise Icon-Atwood in some new light. There's the obvious Icon, the one we all see and many applaud. And then there's something further, something that edges the sinister, something in which we are all perforce complicitous until it's seen and identified.

The obvious Icon might best be summed up as do-good. The good grey lady relentlessly involved in do-good: Atwood ecologist, Atwood equal rights, Atwood the activist, Atwood feminist, Atwood Amnesty, Atwood PEN ... Not to mention selfless participation on endless committees in literature and the arts. Yes, all this wrapped up as National icon, as the kit and caboodle of CanLit and CanCult. Emblem of our national meaning: say Atwood and you say Canada.

And the style of it all so low-keyed, so modest (at least in recent years) – no overt hype, no hyperbole, no dramatic physical gestures, barely a lifting of the voice.

Indeed one could liken this image to Canada's beloved schoolmarm – that splendid Victorian tradition of the courageous, calm, and austere frontier school-marm. The one who instills the real values, goals, and meanings of life. No, none of the glamour of Joan of Arc, but instead the zeal of a Protestant missionary. Our sempiternal Schoolmarm ... as Great Guide. And Icon-Atwood as the final flowering of a great cultural lineage and tradition.

But within that self-evident Icon there lurks something other. Something to do with "literature as power" and "laying down the law." Something to do with Atwood as tractarian, the one who confections the fable for the next Conventional Wisdom. Indeed she is nothing if not "mainstream" now, a co-opted part of the new media-lit. Unusual position for an original writer.

Take the immense apparatus of P.R. Everywhere she goes the TV cameras hover, the reporters flock, and the publishers flunky. Thus a do-good manoeuvre for some worthy cause becomes instant media session, lights and all cameras. And Atwood Schoolmarm is suddenly Dame Atwood, to the advantage of neither. Worse, the slightest occasion of do-good may relate to the signing and disposal of her books – cash registers jingling merrily nearby. In this way do-good becomes career-worthy (very Ontario Wasp, that). And life often the next P.R. operation and TV clip. And, despite her best intentions, much about her career resembles a "literary developer."

Of course, Ms. Atwood has stated she does *not* like all this folderol, never wanted celebrity status, much less the burden of Iconhood. She claims she's a prisoner of it all. Even said so on one of the PEN panels, thereby proving she understood the plight of writers who truly were in prison. Yet one may feel she helped construct her prison. While noting that as Icon she still sees herself as "victim."

But it goes further than P.R. as power. In some strange way she holds the nation in bondage. At least in literary bondage. Publishers hang on her slightest word. A frown at the mention of given name and a publisher knows what to do. There is often a nervous silence when I raise her name. I recently asked a well-known publisher who the most powerful figure is in Canadian publishing (not Canadian writing). The instant answer was "Atwood." When I mentioned writing this piece on Icon-Atwood, another publisher stared. "It would be quicker to fall on your sword," he said.

Why can't a national Icon be discussed? What does this say about the condition of the nation? Here a huge burden of responsibility falls on us, and not on Ms. Atwood at all. Why have we allowed ourselves to be accomplices? Why are we bonded to a success in part sinister? Why have *we* imprisoned Margaret Atwood? Why have we aided this strange bondage? What is there in us as a people that responds to the darker side of such an Icon? Why do we court the dark instead of the bright? And what is the psychic estate of our writers and critics? Are we all flunkies? Horrible questions – disturbing situation.

Yes, the situation smacks of bondage, a covert or diffuse kind of bondage. Whether of the cultural nation to Atwood, or vice versa. The cruelty in her work may well apply to the larger picture: Atwood and our nation caught in a strange mutual bondage. Caught, in fact, in a celebration of pain and even pain as celebration.

Perhaps she is less a national achievement than a nemesis. Or a dead end. Because as a writer, she's not a voice so much as a permanent complaint, whine, or even sneer. Try any thousand pages of her work and come to your own conclusion.

Her works are not a fount of emotional renewal so much as a slaughterhouse for emotions: scarcely what this nation needs.

She scarcely brings us laughter, joy, enhanced feelings, or even pride, so much as deprival. Her books endow us with her sense of brutal deprival. And our very praise bonds her (and us) to the fact.

As Icon she's that very Canadian reality: the victim as Commander, yet forever victim. And a victim is simply a martyr without belief.

Yes, she is our last Schoolmarm, last of Queen Victoria passed through the log cabin of the Canadian frontier. In some ways she's the worst of our Protestantism gone secular. Worse, gone vengeful – that line in *Cat's Eye* is suggestive: "I know myself to be vengeful, greedy, secretive, and sly."

She's our leading tractarian, our eternal Schoolmarm, and – our national troll. Yes, our national imp inhabiting some bleak underground cave. And bidding us to join – and God help us, we do. Robert Mason Lee, in *One Hundred Monkeys*, provides a telling picture of this: Atwood confronting a parliamentary committee about Free Trade. Yes, there's some echo of Jesus in the Temple confronting the Elders. But more truly she seems troglodyte, mini-witch casting a spell.

She's not a voyeur so much as a "voyee": the one who longs to be seen, to be gazed at. There's a telling story in *Bluebeard's Egg* for that.

She doesn't seek equality so much as supremacy – or at least control. And as Norman Mailer suggested, a woman who's equal already rules. For reasons clear enough in her books.

Perhaps despite herself, she's become a kind of Cromwell of the fast track; the change occurring with the success of *The Handmaid's Tale*. But all Paradise now hopelessly lost.

She holds a nation in verbal bondage on its own worst terms: bonded to that which bonds her. And as in her last two books it's not so much a state of being as of non-being. Story of the permanent black hole.

Or as Judith Thurman astutely said (no Canadian having dared), "It's the perversity that generates the power."

Atwood is Icon because we have none. A nation in disarray. A case of Real Absence because we've lost any sense of Real Presence. She can reign until we break the bondage – hers, and ours.

Glitz City

We all know it's sordid! The spreading gap between rich and poor. The covert lines between Wasp and ethnic, between black and coloured and whiter-than-white. The neo-yuppie street gangs playing at Hitler. The lust of developers raping our cityscape. And the municipal officials obsequious with developers. The "Monster Homes" domineering cottage-modest neighbourhoods. The loss of our lake to lead, shit, and detritus. And the loss of the Don Valley to almost everything.

Yes, sordid! The loss of the very air we breathe in Toronto – at one point last year it was the worst of any city in North America! And the loss of our historic buildings: the Manning Arcade, the Armouries, almost all the great Victorian buildings in the city core. Not to mention some fifty churches since 1945, some of them magnificent. And the willful erosion of our traditions – as Valpy noted, "Dominion Day" had proud meaning, but "Canada Day" is milquetoast.

Sordid! Like the devaluation of the very language we speak. Debased by neon minds, overspeak and a slipshod media. Debased by an Americanization this city and nation were founded to defeat. And with that, loss of civility, manners, and civic decorum – boorishness as aggression for those on the make.

Yes, each of us can make a quick list of loss, demoralization, and sleaze. The very tactics recently at Queen's Park – our birthright of parliament sold for a few refrigerators, quick political bucks, and civic place. And with that, our defining tradition of Crown-in-Parliament reduced to a sneer. Not to mention a hedonistic media peddling life as glitz kitsch. Though a prominent journalist recently informed me that "the media is the new aristocracy"!

We're left without heart, without best meanings, without traditions and their pageant. Left as a city self-assertedly "world-class," but no soul, no celebration, no specific meanings. Toronto-the-Good become Toronto-and-all-Glitz at the cost of our destiny.

Nor does it take much imagination to foresee it getting worse! Escalate those punk street gangs a bit – yeah, rip a few more unsuspecting faces off in the subways, for the fun of it! The world of Bill Burroughs' *Wild Boys* for real. Or a race riot – it'll start in a bar, an irate red neck out of work, smashing a black in the eye. Or viciousness in high places, boardroom mayhem, financial assassination as pleasing as physical. Or Gay Pride Day turning into a bloodbath, jocks vs. queens ... and one of your sons dead! Yeah – a city of power-mongers questing bucks and blood. Why even CanLit becomes a P.R.-and-power grab in Toronto-the-Vicious.

Truth is, the city already too often feels like Dallas North, bullets waiting to kill, murders waiting to occur. Frenetic calm prior to impending storm. Yes, a kind of psychic South Sea Bubble ready to burst – Toronto in the days of its gold rush.

But it's too easy to make such a horror list. Much harder to say what we want. Start with the sheer physical city.

We want our lake back, want to be able to swim in it. Want to feel we locate on one of the most beautiful lake systems in the world. *For most of us there simply is no lake there now!* Cut off by towers and cement. Surely our greatest mall, University

Avenue, should have opened onto the lake, with parks spreading across the lakeshore.

Well, we've lost that to railways, highways, highrises: in short, to greed. But we can rescue some of it. David Crombie's Royal Commission is fighting for this now. Support him, actively, vehemently! Get our land back. Create a fifty-acre park where the Queen Elizabeth docks are now. Beautify the entire lakeshore, forty miles of it. Make it walkable in winter as summer. If need be, build more lakeshore. Even build a further island out past the harbour, a further place from which to see Toronto from the lake, actually see the grandiose "New York skyline" we've mortgaged our souls and children's lives for.

And with that redeem valleys, ravines, rivers.

Start with the Don. It stinks, rots, is pillaged by highways, skulkers, and sexual marauders. Imagine a Don Valley that flows green and clean for miles, for picnics, bicycling, strolling, bird-watching, loving. A park that includes ponds, a lake!

Yes, we want more parks in the city, small and large. We've let too many opportunities go by. Tell City Hall, we want more green! And we'll pay for it. Make those huge companies pay too. Half of Canadian companies with assets of over $25 million give nothing to any cause or charity! Let them start ... with a *park!*

More, when the developers raze our old buildings, demolish the flavour (and memory) of an entire street, at least they can give us buildings of interest, buildings we want to remember, not forget. Just think of what the Toronto Convention Centre might have been. Or the Eaton Centre. Or some of the new University of Toronto.

And we must protect our beautiful old buildings better! What *is* the Massey House of Jarvis Street doing as a glitz-kitsch restaurant and booze den, complete with gas station out front to deface it? Why such parody of our pride? No clan in this city ever contributed so much to Toronto, not to mention our first Canadian Governor-General!

Not least, in a city that prides itself on its arts, we need a College of Art able to do its job! Of four such colleges across Canada its funding per capita is the least, by far. Its current buildings are a debacle, just a collection of classrooms. It has no studios for students, no real exhibition space, no health centre, not even a room as such for meetings. We need a college that deals with art in all its aspects, a totally new college, conceived as such.

Is it crazy to compare Toronto with Venice? Two cities on the water. Venice, that Renaissance capital on the Adriatic, city of the Doges. It too was a money capital, commercial capital, a city of urgent entrepreneurs. And these men left us one of the most beautiful cities of all time. Why can't we think in such terms? Why not dare? We have the site, the history, the artists ... and literally tons of money, one of the wealthiest cities in the world of all time!

But there's more to a city than its physical presence. Or even its civic and social services, important as they are.

There is also the city of poetry and the heart!

The first is city-as-utility – we seem to think only of this, latter-day utilitarians on a spree. But the second is city as its own drama and destiny; the city that lives within us as against the city we merely make a living from.

Call it the distinction between the "horizontal" city and the "vertical" one. The first being the secular city of here and now, the one we do our business in. Whereas the second is custodian of our being, our real well-being.

Fact is, the "vertical" city is one of depth and time – city as history, personality, stories past and present and more to come. City as its own fable and myth. Alas, we've forgotten all this, jettisoned our roots. Why? We seem to know our city only through Historic Plaques and markers, as if what went before existed only "under glass," under wraps, under ... amnesia! As if being a Torontonian necessitated forgetting.

Yet we've been in this place some two centuries now. Nor did our forebears arrive void. Unlike the Americans we did not start with an empty slate, *tabula rasa*. In fact, the very opposite – we came here replete with meaning. A determination to sustain our European roots, in particular our British ones. Came here "loyal" to the concept of continuity, of adapting our roots to this land, this site, this harbour, these ravines and hills, it goes back to Magna Carta direct. We didn't come to rape land, but bringing loyalty to a land, a vast difference. The very motto of the province states this: *ut incepit fidelis, sic permanet* – as she began loyal, so will remain!

Yet we've willfully, almost vengefully, "forgotten" all this. Why? Why forget "In Flanders Fields"? Why disown Dieppe? Why forget our part in making the Commonwealth? It offers us a larger and outlooking Canadianism as against a small and narcissistic citizenship! Why forget that our founding culture here is substantially (and positively) Victorian? Why so sneeringly forget the Crown? Why create emotional vacuum in place of warm memory?

Is it to please "the ethnics," the immigrants? But we don't please them with our craven amnesia. They ask, "What are we to relate to here in Toronto?" And find nothing to relate to except welfare and greed.

Indeed if we forget our own mainstream roots, traditions and meanings, then what *is* the meaning of "multiculturalism"? Apart from political lip-service for quick votes, cheap labour, and more things to forget. Or worse, a sly chance to beat our mainstream tradition to death!

And in the place of real meanings we end with the mod-kitsch meanings, the "with-it" meanings, the hype ad meanings – yeah, fun-city, good for a day!

We've become a people of "instant meanings" and culture-by-committee – like an instant flag, a concocted "republic" by default, and all our historical emblems wantonly guillotined. It requires no genius to realize our current Queen's Park government would delight in giving us a trillium as a provincial flag – all history thus smashed! Would delight in abolishing the historic use of Q.C. and any ceremony in our Courts. Yet there *is* a ceremony to the law, or should be – the law, the operable ethics of a people! And would they change the name of Queen's Park itself to ... Republic Place, or Starr Park? Or just abolish the Lieutenant-Governor? Yet that separation of State from government is crucial – emblem of a decency beyond mere social engineering and planning committees.

Why do we abolish and overthrow, rather than build up and include? And why, as we do so, so smug?

Let the immigrant beware a people, a province, a city that thrives on banishing the heart and building banks instead. Beware a city that substitutes civic kitsch for memory. And protest marches for parades. And litigation for loyalties! Beware, because the loss of loyalties at the public level mirrors the loss of loyal ties and affections and all that's dear at the personal level: the one reflects and increases the other!

Toronto was the city in North America that wished to remember! It's Jungian, not Freudian – a collective recollection as against sexotic amnesia. Its meanings are historic (centuries deep!) and not "instant." It's that continuity and not disjunction, much less willed lobotomy for gain. Its mainstream tradition is at once Wasp *and* genteel, though we've tried to disown the first and sneer at the second!

A city which perjures its memory loses its mind in the end. Whence that whiff of madness which taints Toronto right now. Madness from covert loss and pain and a desubstantiation all feel but none quite say.

The city needs a metaphysics – a vision of itself beyond Mammon. And our mod skyline is all glitzy Mammon! Yet something in our hearts remains Mariposa, Leacock's eternal Mariposa. But of course, Toronto always was the capital of all Ontario Mariposas! Truth is we're now both – cosmopolitan and small-town, high hick and neo-churl with an ongoing lust for a murdered gentry, or at least a gentry plus brains.

We now either use it all, or lose it all. Embrace it all, or slaughter (with final smirk of revenge) what remains. We're at the point of rupture – pointed toward "the black hole," toward "Erewhon," Nowhere. It's that, or else rejoice in all we are, with a generosity that surmounts meanness of spirit.

Because Toronto *is* the C.N. Tower, our quickest boast. And Casa Loma, our tradition of romance. It's new City Hall parrying the old beside, each adding meaning to the inner eye. It's Etienne Brulé in 1615, and the great de la Salle, and all the French traders who followed, and Fort Rouillé in 1750. It's the Indians bringing their furs and dance. And the golden bank towers we need yet love to hate! It's John Graves Simcoe, the city Founder we forget, and his elegant wife keeping her diary here at the time of the French Revolution. And Mayor Tommie Church welcoming troops back from Flanders and Vimy. And Bishop Strachan warning the American invaders if Toronto was burnt then Washington would be too – and it was! It's the Don Valley restored to lake, park, and tryst. And a view from the lake that makes a Venice out of mere New York. It's *Picturesque Canada* for keeps, yet swaggering ground for the mod cosmopolite. It's every immigrant who ever brought hope or dream, and the Loyalists who first carved its meanings out of the bush. It's wee Willie Mackenzie leading his rebels down Yonge Street – and his daughters running the Mackenzie Ladies Boarding School in his home, a generation later! It's Muddy York and the cleanest subway in the world (or was). And old Queen Vic's Diamond Jubilee granting us a destiny larger than mere nation. Yes, it's the relief of Mafeking and the charge at Balaclava (Canada's first V.C.!). And all the lessons learnt at Dieppe which helped win D-Day. It's the Group of Seven seeking a face in granite and personality in a pine tree. It's the chortle of CHUM radio, and a media empire around the world. It's the City of Churches and of endless scepticisms. And the University of Toronto combining both. It's Margaret Atwood and Mazo de la Roche, take your pick or write your own! It's highrise and old Rosedale; modern condo and Cabbagetown renewed. It's Longhouse Books serving hot coffee and hotter gossip; and it's The World's Biggest Bookstore! It's a black Lieutenant-Governor whose warm dignity makes Wasps proud. And a Queen Mum we'd be less without. It's Ned Hanlan rowing to world fame a century ago. And Syl Apps, "the most gentlemanly player" on ice. It's the "responsible government" we fought for with "Geordie" Brown of the *Globe*. It's polyglot with heart of oak – trillium *and* the Union Jack. It's an American city plus memory, a British city plus hope. It's class sans classes, the gamble in North America for quality.

It's all these things and more, live in the heart. Or it's a void, a destiny squandered!

The First Trilogy

Symons has always claimed that *Place d'Armes* (1967) and *Civic Square* (1969) constitute a tale of two cities (this time in the Dickensian sense). Montréal and Toronto, and more precisely their principal public squares, truly are the main characters of these works. For the human characters trying to relate to the irrefutable evidence before them, it is a matter of conceiving and maintaining an "untenable fidelity." "Everything has changed," as Hugh Anderson, narrator and Symons' alter ego, remarks in the early pages of *Place d'Armes*. Symons, one of "Henry James's grandchildren," attempts to capture Canada at a crucial intersection, between forgetful cynicism and possible renewed faith in itself. His central character, whom Robert Fulford referred to in a now infamous review as "The Monster From Toronto," represents all of the human contradictions of this historical position.

The intense formal complexity of *Place d'Armes* goes beyond the now almost conventional practice of a "novel within a novel." Five typefaces represent a swirl of different voices. By the end of the book, its initial narrator Hugh Anderson has become a fictional character in the novel of his own invented character. This is a dizzying, circular, buckling, metafictional movement. The days chosen from the "Combat Journal" reveal this metamorphosis of Hugh Anderson. From the moment his desire sets him in motion on "the Rapido" to the final communion scene in the Place, there is a loss of self through its intense overexposure. The chapters chosen show the initial movement of the character, his encounters

with figures of Montréal cultural life, antique dealers, male prosti-
tutes, etc.

Civic Square, the "book in the box," the strangest of the strange,
is represented here by the opening, dedicatory fragments and by
significant chunks of the first sequence of the book. They convey
its satirical and meditative modes. We get a celebration of dappled
Country Canada as well as a savage attack on mediocrity and politi-
cal sellout. Included are the ode to cocks, the Canada prayer, the
typology of Canadian personalities, the descriptions of bird life,
and all the madly inventive wordplay – successful and less so –
which produced in another passage the expression with which
Symons would have liked to title the whole book: *The Smugly
Fucklings*.

1971's *Heritage: A Romantic Look at Canadian Furniture* completed
the first trilogy. Written in what might today be called a "creative
non-fictional" mode, the book constitutes a kind of anatomy of
furniture, or, as Irving Layton put it, a "furniture novel." Furniture,
like the buildings and urban configurations that were the main
characters of the previous two books, incarnate personality and
historical meaning. The extracts selected from *Heritage* include
four pieces of furniture, representative of the "three distinct soci-
eties that came together to form Canada" (G. Grant). Also repro-
duced is Symons' plaintive concluding essay "Ave Atque Vale," hail
and farewell, which recounts the "furniture safari" taken by
Symons and his lover in 1970. This volume closes Symons' first,
extended song of love and mourning for his nation and his first
attempt to find a new way forward.

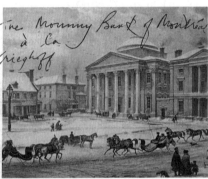

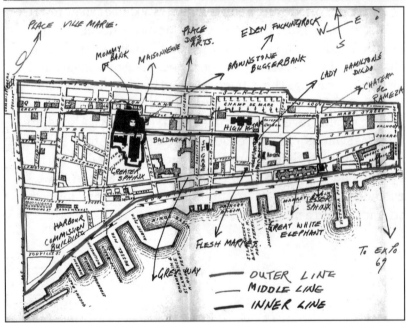

Place d'Armes

Stranger, reconquer the source of feeling for an anxious people's sake
-from NIMBUS, by Douglas Le Pan

THE DAY BEFORE ONE

"La Place d'Armes is the heart of Montréal, metropolis of Canada. No visitor to the city can afford to miss this remarkable square where the modern and the historic meet in splendour and harmony. Walk out to the centre of La Place – and stand under the great statue to Maisonneuve, founder of the city, in 1642. On the north side of La Place stands the Head Office of the Bank of Montréal ... popularly known as 'My Bank' to over two million Canadians. On the west side is the Head Office of the Banque Canadienne Nationale. The largest financial institutions of English and French Canada respectively: side by side, tower by tower. Yet facing these two ultramodern skyscrapers, on the south side of the square, sits the Presbytery and Church of Notre Dame. This Church is traditionally known simply as 'The Parish,' the pride of the Sulpician Order who once held all Montréal in fief. The rough stone Presbytery dates from the days of Louis XIV, while the Church, which was completed by 1830, is the earliest example of the Gothic Revival Style in Canada. It is considered one of the finest in America. The lavish interior of the Church, copied from La Sainte Chapelle in Paris, is one of the sights of the city. It is appropriate that the Church is faced not only by the modern Bank of Montréal tower, but also by the old Bank building with its classic pediment and dome, dating from 1847. To the east the square is fitly completed by two handsome stone skyscrapers; the Providence Life Building which will remind you of New York in the Roaring Twenties, and beside it an excellent example of the famed brownstone architecture of the High Victorian Period.

   In effect La Place d'Armes is a summary of the entire city. Because to the north and west of it rises the mountain with its new city of commerce and cultures. The Queen Elizabeth Hotel, the most up-to-date in Canada; La Place Ville de Marie, the largest shopping and office complex in the nation; and La Place des Arts, symbol of the vibrant artistic life born of the meeting of French and English civilizations in the New World – these are only a few blocks away. While to the south and east of the square lie the great international harbour of Montréal, and the historic Old Quarter, with its unique ensemble of Georgian stone buildings. If you want to wander these curving streets, in a matter of minutes you will be in la rue St. Paul with its modern boutiques and art stores, its antique shops, with the magnificent Georgian Bonsecours Market, once the Parliament of Canada, and Notre Dame de Bonsecours Church dating from the eighteenth century. Fine restaurants will cater to the appetite your stroll whets. Afterwards you can visit the French Baroque City Hall, or the Château de Ramezay Museum, once home of the Governors of Montréal; see the first monument in the world to Nelson, or wander along St. James Street, and enjoy the great Victorian palaces of commerce. Don't forget to stroll down to the harbour (only one block south from St. Paul

Street) to the great grain elevators and freightyards. To the west stands the
Harbour Commission Building, a handsome Victorian fantasy, to the east the
Jacques Cartier bridge, while just out of sight is the Ile Ste-Helene, site of Canada's
International Exhibition – Expo 67.

La Place d'Armes – heart of Montréal, old and new. La Place d'Armes – heart
of Canada!"

Thus Hugh Anderson tried to imagine how a tourist blurb of La Place d'Armes
might read. He sketched it out in full – and then gave up; it revulsed him. Partly
because he couldn't really bring himself to do it well, and partly because he could
imagine it only too well. He decided to concentrate instead upon his own mem-
ory of La Place d'Armes ... trying to recall it as he had known it during the four
years he had worked within a block of it, on St. James Street. He remembered the
domed Bank of Montréal Building well. Then he had to admit he had never been
in it. No, he reflected, not once ... only in the new section. It was virtually the same
for the Church of Notre Dame. It had always stood there, as some magnificent
Gothic scenario – a fine backdrop for prestige office buildings. Like having the
facade from Westminster Abbey, or Notre Dame de Paris, dropped into La Place as
guarantee of quality: Episcopal Approval – an Imprimatur for La Place. But he had
never been in it ... oh he had visited in it – once, maybe twice – and he always told
friends who were visiting Montréal that it was a "must." But he himself had never
been to a service there. He had meant to go that Christmas, to the Midnight Mass
... but he had gone skiing instead. Odious recollection ... (besides – the snow went
soft). And he couldn't remember anything precise about the Church inside, save
that sensation of Olde Golde everywhere ... the Sainte Chapelle bloated beyond
belief. As to the rest – well, the new buildings of the New Montréal hadn't been
built: La Banque provinciale, La Place Ville Marie, La Place des Arts. He had only
heard about them. And he had to admit that he never, not once, strolled the Old
Quarter. Oh, he had visited the Château de Ramezay once by accident; it was a
hailstorm. As for the rest ... he really only knew about them through history text-
books, by implication.

With that he stopped, acutely self-conscious, embarrassed ... turned around
to see if anyone was looking a him, at his smug self-assertive ignorance.

No-one was looking. He laughed small consolation: how the hell could any-
one see what he was thinking anyway? His guilt was a private matter. But he had
to face the truth: all he really knew about La Place d'Armes and its entourage was
what he could have put into a bad tourist blurb. He was victim of the very thing
he mocked! To save further discomfit he turned his mind to the job at hand,
unwilling to resolve the contradictions already becoming apparent.

The assignment he decided in fact was simple: a short novel on La Place
d'Armes in Montréal. He knew exactly what it was that he wanted to do with it.
Namely present La Place as a centre of life and vitality in the Montréal metropo-
lis. It was La Place that would, of course, be the Hero. Of that he was certain ... the
novel would grow out of that fact. All he had to do was live La Place and he would
end with what he needed – a novel that glowed with love, with his own love of his
community, his nation, his people. A novel that glowed with love in a world whose

final and last faith seemed to be grounded in hate. He wanted to share that love, and to show that only by that love do people live, really live. With any luck the essential experience would be achieved in a fortnight, perhaps less. In either case he would be home by Christmas. He planned to arrive in Montréal on December the first.

He thought again of La Place ... yes, it was ideal: a historic square, perhaps the most historic in North America, or in the New World for that matter. Three-and-a-half centuries of history ending in 1967 as the heart of a giant empire – Canada – and the site of the first International Exhibition that had ever received world sanction in the New World. No – decidedly there was no other square to equal it ... and he counted off the competitors – Boston, Boston Common, the Liberty Route, the birth of the American Dream and all that. Well, Boston had gone dead. And so had the Amurrican Dream for that matter – (his facile inherited contempt of the Americans – the mere Americans – was all contained in that slurred pronunciation "Amurrican") Or New York – Times Square for example. Centre of the World. What about that? Somehow it didn't do. It didn't have a heart, or a soul, or something ... something was wrongside-up about it. If nothing else his novel would prove that, by contrast. That left Philadelphia – which had been displaced by New York – and Washington. Same argument all over again for these then. And for Chicago, the Second City. Or San Francisco – excellent also-ran. What about Mexico City? Surely it was a contender. Well he didn't know Mexico City – so it was easy to rule out. That left only his own city, Toronto, with its claim to be the "fastest growing city in North America." Which meant the fastest growing "white city" in the world. Perhaps that was what was wrong with Toronto!

Nor could he find any heart to Toronto ... no central Place ... unless one took the new City Hall and its monolithic Phillips Square. Anyway, La Place d'Armes had a two-century headstart on that ... and any sense of dimension in time in Toronto was about to be extinguished by the destruction of the Old City Hall which gave all the conviction and perspective to the New – torn down to make room for a department store. Well that told the whole story. He grimaced. No, it was Montréal's Place d'Armes all the way. He felt relieved, and settled back in his seat aboard the Rapid – "fastest commuter train in the world ... 360 miles in 4 hrs. and 59 minutes!" For a moment his own smugness conjugated with this triumphant smugness of the train and taking out his little black notebook he began to make his Novel Notes – some for the Novel, but some for himself. The latter would, naturally, be the best – after all he wouldn't be able to present the complete truth in the Novel. So it was important to have complete notes for his own private edification. A kind of private revenge against the restrictions of the Novel itself – a sort of intimacy. The intimate privilege of the first person.

" ... spent the weekend skiing – a sort of final outing before Montréal. Left Mary & the two children to return with friends to Toronto. She is in good spirits & can handle the home easily enough till I'm back ... It all makes good sense. Ran into Jackson on the daytrain from Collingwood ... haven't seen him for two years. We exchanged supercilities last time – each politely contemptuous of the other – he of my publishing house respectability; I of his success in the mass media – a televisionary ... mass mediocrity! Now we sat together like old buddies, con-

*fessing our faults ... the vacuity of the media (Toynbee is right – TV is "the lion that whimpered!")
& the constipation of the business world. As though each of us had seen through ourselves in these
last two years. And come out divested – & afraid. Things have changed. Everything has changed
– absolutely. The very nature of reality has changed. Maybe that's why I let Jackson quiz me
overtly ...*

*Jackson – "well, you're a square in revolt. We're all squares in this country ... I'm a square. But
I still don't understand you.*

*You didn't need to get fired. Your training was unique. Experience with that Montréal publish-
ing firm. A book of excellent critical essays on Canadian culture. A Governor-General's award.
A powerful family name, a beautiful wife – & you say, two kids. Bilingual. & an appointment
at the University of Toronto for special lectures. You were made, man. & we needed you. You did-
n't need to capitulate ... "*

I laugh, and remember his public criticism of my essays.

*"I can't explain it. But I know what I'm doing. I simply know I had to demission – had to
leave. I suppose it was the very fact that I felt I was a 'made man' – that all I had to do was become
president of my company, & then die ... or rather die, & then become president of the company.
But much more important than that is the feeling that I've been unmade ... that the events of the
past few years in Canada have been systematically destroying me, my culture. I have slowly been
eliminated – all my faiths ... Take the new flag (one floats by out the train window) – that is as
good a symbol as any of the dissolution I feel Every time I look at that frigging Maple Leaf I dis-
solve. I simply cease to exist. It's not a question of patriotism – my family's been tangled up with
the New World for over two centuries now. It's a question of reality. Take just the visual fact of
the flag. It's a non-flag ... I can't explain it."*

And then they were at the Toronto Union Station. Jackson was gone ... wish-
ing him well. He was perplexed by their conversation – the complete frankness of
it. It made him uneasy. Not because it was frank, but because it implied more to
the novel than the novel he had planned. But he didn't realize that yet.

He appraised the station ... a splendid thermal bath. It was in the best style of
the period: monumental Roman Classic. And at the same time he regretted its
predecessor for which his grandfather had been an architect ... it had been that
brownstone Romanesque that Richardson made famous – full of rough brawn.
And inside the station he flinched at the juxtaposition of this muted thermal bath
style, like some great banking house, and the constrained jazz of the new bill-
boardings now around the wall. – The ads were representative, he mused, of the
new Toronto: a pair of TV personalities "invited" you flagrantly to "Listen Here" –
standing at ease in their red waistcoats and their glasses that made them look
relaxed middle-class intelligent. Respectable hicks he decided. Or high-class jerks.
It didn't much matter. In either case they didn't belong in the station. Not in this
station, his station. Which meant that one day the station would be pulled down.
But he didn't dare admit that either. Another billboard boasted the "brightest
paper in town" that it boosted. Beside it a forty-foot guarantee of medical insur-
ance. Lastly a cigarette sanctioned by a wholesome lass in tartan. Yes – it was a good
cross-section of Toronto-town. Add only the stationwagon perched comfortably
over the stairwell – "Canadian built – for quality," and you had the complete pic-
ture. The only difference between the Canadian and American stationwagon

being that the Canadian had less chrome and cost more. All of this, and the conversation with Jackson hackled him. He walked over to the ticket booth. Last time he had taken the C.P.R. This time he would take the "Rapido," the "National" line.

" ... *the ticket booth is the same old bronzed respectable – like a bank wicket, but jazzed over now with a fay red-white-blue decor of posters. The attendants the same – a sort of cheap felt blazer, Minute-Man blue with red trims. Look like gas station attendants on a Labour Day parade ... that's it – the new Guild of All-Canadians. And they are descendants of the Amurrican Minute Men – same narrow folk culture that produced the car-spangled banner. It's the colours ... those folk hues. This is just a mutation of the same: part Rotary Club cheeriness, part cheerleader razzummatazz, part modern electronix. Christ I hate it: the Canadettes! Preview of our "1984." Bless damned Orwell! Just time for a snack in the York Pioneer Room ... "*

He settled in and looked it over ... quickly discredited it as part of the new Canadian kick for their cottage pine past. Simply a comfortable Canadian variation of the American Abe Lincoln myth. It made posthumous peasants out of all their ancestors. He couldn't take much of that. He enjoyed peasants; but he didn't like retroactive peasanthood as a national patriotic pastime. There was something sick in it ... an inverted snobbery. The fact was that the "log cabin legend" simply didn't belong in Canada ... it really belonged only to that initial, and belated, American yeoman tradition in Southwestern Ontario – Grit Ontario ... Canadian equivalent of the New England Myth that still implicitly dominates Amurrican thought. The thought that Canada, at this late date would be subjected to a pirated and aborted American puritan legend depressed him. And he fled.

" ... *I thought of touring the new City Hall. Haven't yet. A good idea now ... after all if this New Canada is real and right I'm as much a tourist in Canada now as anyone else. & I can see the Old City Hall at the same time. But didn't have the courage ... The exposure would rob me of the energy I need for Montréal."*

Suddenly the real magnitude of what he was doing and of what was being done to him shook him. He hadn't as yet completely allowed himself to know. But every now and then he had a deep realization of what he was really doing – some deep tissue of him opened and he shook from stem to gudgeon. The only thing he could do now was to see someone: people still fortified him. He phoned Beatrice Ellis – he had kept in touch with her these past difficult months. She had edited his book of essays. Had done a sensitive job – and she had told him then (that was four years ago) that he had something much more important to say, that he wouldn't get away merely with his essays. There was just time for a cup of tea together (it wasn't a "drink" – that was what happened in novels; and he smiled.) Beatrice had "died" a few months ago, heart failure, under an oxygen tent – and then been revived and come back to tell about it. She would know. He tried – between the lines – to tell her what he was really doing ... tried to tell her that he knew that the novel was for real. He wanted to tell her of the hara-kiri explicit in it. But it was hard to acknowledge fear to someone who has already died and come back. That strengthened him again. And at 4:45 p.m. he was on board the Rapido

...

"the Rapido! the very name pillages me of more blood. Part of the mediocre anonymity of the New Nation. An evasion of identity. An abstraction. Might as well call it the 'Quickie' – the Cdn Quickie. But that would be too American. At least the CPR has the guts to be the Château Champlain ... or the Royal York. Well – the new name matches the new ticket booth matches the new Canadettes in the booth matches the Respectable Hick matches the New Flag matches the new entry to the train itself ... from the main floor of the thermal bathroom. I got a new respect for that great arched Roman Bath as I saw in contrast the board-and-batten triumphal arch all of eight feet tall through which we went to the train. Red-white-blue archlet – not the old colours, grim old colours, full of gristle and gut, but these new candy-floss colours. (Oh, Christ, even the colours of my community are undergoing a change of life – are being gelded!) At the arch entry a professional greeter welcomes us in. Rolls out the cheap red carpet for all of us members of the new lower middle-class Canadian royalty. Pathetic. Plush for the people.

Why can't I be proud of it? I should be. It is clean, competent, fresh, proper. It even has this mitigated concern for majesty – the plush carpet, the stage-set entry, the self-effacing CN impresario to grimace us at entryway ... I suppose because it makes me by definition part of these New Canadettes. A sort of post-graduated folk-yeoman king ... Hell – why should I be proud of it? This isn't what my people spent two centuries here for! Even if I wanted I have no right to be proud of it!

Dumped my bags on the rack between cars #3012 and 3011 ... & slump into a seat – lucky got one by a window, facing forwards (dislike riding backwards). Ten minutes to go ... catch up on my Notes.

... 4:45 p.m., sharp, the station moves away from us ... leaving me exposed sudden to the body of my city ... out the back corner of my eye that becalmed Beaux-Arts bulk, rising like a series of improved Buckingham Palaces piled atop each other – the Royal York, could only be she

the long slit unended of Yonge Street – like all of our streets – dissolved only by infinity

with that wedding-cake turn-of-the-century prestige bank at the lower left-hand corner – Front Street corner: a kind of gaudy bodyguard for the longeststreetintheworldthatisYongestreet ending only in our Ontario Lake District. Bank of Montréal, at that!

with its back square upon me, the squat cube of our beer baron's art centre: O'Keefe

overtopping all these, the soft-nosed phallicity of Bank of Commerce – circumspect, uncircumcised – 32 stories of Canadian self-satisfaction

the new National Trust tower, well below

& below again, prickly up these closed commercial shops, the spired incisions of the old City of Churches – Saints James & Michael & Metropole

&, last link with the old city, Osgoode aside, St-Lawrence-Market-where-Jenny-Lind-sang

pinched by the Victorian gabling from Jarvis Street East ... even gables in Toronto are Presbyterian spinsters' eyes on my wayward trainside

Gooderham 'n Worts stone distillery – 1832: THERE is the REAL HOY culture ... Honest Ontario Yeoman – Hoyman – none of this nostalgic log cabin cult ... but cubic yards of squared stonework – behind it, the high windows and gratuitous lantern of Tuscan Revival blocks (if only they would repaint these!)

a minute, a panorama of 2 centuries passed ... to the free flowing muck of the Don River – where Founding-Governor Simcoe's wife fished for fresh salmon! What could she think now of this shit-sluice? Anal canal for 2 million congested citizens! And all the valleyside of it superways with some guilty pretence at parkland squat huddle of houses ... one, two, five, seven minutes ... the Emancipated Methodist Culture of Canada! ... Cdn squatters – our national smugliness – small, stolid bungalows; unlike anything in the Yewnited States – smaller, thicker, squalider. Someday we'll clear the land of these affluent slums – in revenge for the lost White Pine we cleared to house them ...

a trickle of land ... apologetic almost – extinct landscape!

redbrick belfry & white cornicings cuddle me kinetic to the land for spring – of course: the Church at Dunbarton – rural Ontario Ecclesiological – as specifically Ontario as the French-Cdn parish church is Québec ... want to shout the news out to the traincar ... but am silenced by the sight of she-man opposite me

glut of bungalettes again – more modern now

the Ugliest City in Ontario – easy laureate: Oshawa – cartown

Queen Anne's Lace, Milkweed pod, St. John's Wort ... all the sunflushed earthenware of Ontario winter garden of the open fields (want to shout – "do you see these? – look – our winter garden ..." but the eyes in front of me are deaf) – snow-pocked field furrows ... sudden woodland shimmers bronze of wintered beechleaves

at horizon spruce palisade (sharp eyes, like those spinster gables!) alerts me to the orchard that must arrive & cedar hedge, overgrown, and hip-rooved bulky barn, stone root house, & same stone foundations to the blockhouse home red-and-white brick trimmed that completed this Château-fort of our HOYman. Massive, impenetrable, us! Nowhere else in our wide bloody world but Ontario ... Southern Ontario: Home – damn it, and blessings

more bungalows distress the site – unworthy, unworthy – God – UNWORTHY offspring

Spiresides – Port Hope ... & on the knoll behind, overlording the factories beneath its notice almost but not quite, Cdn Eton (for better and for worse) – Trinity College School – vestige of the disestablished upper Canadian Anglican Genteel State (but choose your enemy then – this ... or the bungalettes! Sweet choice.)

that impasse resolves sudden with the grace notes in conscientiously squared lines between the great cubed fieldstones that amass an eternal yeoman stone Georgian home – Canadian Fabergé, these stone houses: cameos out of rich stone-sown earth to clear those near generations thrust abruptly by now to be restituted in only a retroactive nostalgia for tourists and the New Nation: as though killed for a better Resurrection. Each one still a gem – legacy rebuking the preflab culture around it ... Cobourg ... & now the dark.

How well I know this route – our Ontario Front, Niagara to Montréal – 500 miles of us. Ontario Foundation line, and front door to our estate of 1/2 a million square miles. In each town, village, still, a relative a memory, an echo of community lost under bulldozer ... Cobourg – with its magniloquent Court House – New England Meeting House interior compounded with British Raj stonework exterior, Ontario!

Belleville & Trenton ... where the stonework changes from fieldstone to limestoniness ... from freckles to garrison grey. & the Trent waterway debouches from Georgian Bay into Lake Ontario. Where Champlain canoed (idiot adventurer!) four centuries ago to found our empire. Outside the window, in that dark, all my entrails rolling under us now –

the great slice of limestone into Kingston, that grey canyon cut by the highway down into the valley of the old capital town of the Canadas – Kingston ... where I walked that afternoon in November – to have the pleasure of seeing that unsung Ontario Trinity ... St. Andrew's Presbytery – the best of Ontario stonework; Elizabeth Cottage – the loveliest Walter Scott gothic; & (aptly Anglican) Okill's Folly – the most splendiferous Regency manor – now the residence of the Principal of Queen's Univ ... all within a few hundred yards of each other – & was as joy-

ous as if I had walked from La Place de la Concorde to the Louvre to La Sainte Chapelle; & had wanted to take a whip to the passers-by who didn't make obeisance to these splendours. & why not – infraction against beauty is a crime against the state!

Of course the Penitentiary ... Child's King Arthur come ironically true, with its busy turrets ... & the Military College (dare one still call it "Royal" – because that too will go soon enough – we'll rechristen it the Federal Military College ... surreptitiously! – and then by Order-in-Council)

the old #2 route thence to Ganonoque's Golden Apple – laden with stonehouses and flowers spurting out of stone roadcut canyons ... & that day, it was February 28, when my wife & I sunbathed on the front porch of the deserted summer cottage, over the Thousand Islands, after returning from Amurrica – laughing at the legend of the frozen North (the look on the mongrel dog's face, & then his master's, when he saw us there!) The Ontario Front ... Giant sentinel Mulleins stalking the land still in dried khaki above the white field beds. I know just where the climax oak and the hickory start again, near Kingston ... Oh, out that window is all of me underfoot. Out that window is inside me, always. That can't be taken away. Can it? & now it is dark ... I can see the Macdonald-Cartier "Highway" (damn the official term "Freeway" – it sounds like some boxtop prize ... or, closer to the truth, a come-on to the Yank tourists) and its load of cattle-cars ... all bypassing this Front, happily for the Front, unhappily for them ... because suddenly the people that made the land disappear, under the asphalt and the speedometer.

The lights of the great DuPont factory outside Brockville – and I pray that our lakeside won't become like that of the American lakefront or Toronto ... a shambles of hotdoggeral and gimcrap, and factories: because Lake Ontario may be the American back door, but it is our front door. Our garden. Then Upper Canada Village ... which warns me that our history is now under glass ... or under the St. Lawrence Seaway – and that this is but a sop to our vestigial historic consciences. After all, the Village is under the supervision of the provincial tourist department! Q.E.D. Goddam it.

So, I have a nostalgia. For my land, and its people. I'm a romantic. A sin in this era of belated Canadian positivism. I cry "too little for the sensibility," when all our intellectuals moan "too little for their minds." Too bad! I love my land. & damn their dry eyes. Detesticulate.

The home in Iroquois, where we were received for lunch ... bad 1920's Art Nouveau with a painting of an Irish setter on velvet over the fireplace – & the look on the man's face, he was from the West, when I told him there was no sound in our East like the prairie meadowlark ... I thought he was going to kiss me ... but he got me another drink instead, unasked & we loved each other across the ages. & then quarrelled over politics. But meadowlark still sang.

Oh, yes, goddam it – I love my land ... & I love my people. Still. Unpardonable crime in this age of "cool culture" & commissions. Or is it simply untenable fidelity? The latter has it, of course. So, I'll love, & go under, hating those who so conscientiously kill my love ...

Abruptly I am grilled ... a cold sear of bright grilling me – grilling my flesh all bloodless bright red – Hate: of a sudden hate has me, has won ... carries me off bodiless in triumph. Jerk me forward to catch this rape in the act, before too late – before I dissolve before I detonate. Make notes, ward off the evil eye now. What happened? What in this Hell happened? Go back & piece the evidence together. First – Where am I? & then sink back as I see ... the train had stopped, lurched my eyes back into the traincar ... Back in? No! – out: train swallowed me out of my land, smothered me away from my earth ... dispersed me under the grill of neonessent light, those candy floss red seats – at once compressing and atomizing me. Anteus bereft ... Christ – in a hot sweat I need a pee. & heave me into the aisle, into – "Hello Hugh – you look as though you need a tonic" – I look up to find the soft laughing eyes of Jack Greg ... we speed to the box-car. Thank God it's him ... someone I can want to see. Fellow publishing house man. Feverish in delight I leech him of the blood the Rapido has just hemorrhaged out of me ... squandered. & over a martini I don't want we giggle indecorously about the Great Auk the Royal Ontario Museum has just acquired (both bird-watchers!) Positively clenching the padded seats with our buttockry ...

"God knows that's what the museum needed – a Great Auk! – the one thing all museums need, and lack ... " and I catch Greg's lilting gawkwardness out of my eye-corner in a feline complicity of joy ... we both mould the seat pads in an accredited squirm of delight, harvesting their Great Auk.

Greg – "It was bought from Vassar College" – a burst of sweet gigglement again.

Me – "God – our provincial Auk came from Vassar!"

Greg – "What's more, it was Audubon's Great Auk."

That is too much – we eye each other openly, as silent upon our peak ... More laughter. & then the Great Auk has done its service. Has bound us as one flesh, refurbished – & can be discarded, like any dildo. I stop – suddenly aware of how nearly the laughter has consummated my self-expenditure. So close to depleting my entire reserve of credulity now, of faith, of available energy. Suddenly wary – I nurse my last ounce of resistance. Look around at the bar-car. At this new world of plausible plush. I'll have to be careful.

Joined by two of Greg's friends ... an Englit don & wife from the University of Toronto. A typical Englit combination – the wife has a beard, bass voice, & three testicles. She is a TV producer when she isn't producing hubby. He is a falsetto – visually if not audibly; as slight as his wife is muscle-bound, no beard because no chin to carry one ... I bethink me of the Great Auk again ... Thank God for the Great Auk – after all, the provincial museum is part of the provincial university – it can do yeoman service therein. Audubon's Great Auk, bought from the girls of Vassar ... It well just be sufficient.

Jabberwocky for half-an-hour, as I keep withholding me from the decor of the bar-car ... And then the Englits are leaving ... wife carrying hubbie off by the scruff of his neck. Mrs. doesn't like being in a "beer hall." Incredible – but so ... But who am I to laugh – because I can't stand the place either, although for different reasons ... Try to put my finger on it now – just what is it that this decor is doing to me (because I cannot hide from me that it is doing something with me, or trying) ... again – all I can say is compression, into a small space, & at the same time danger of detonation. A strange kind of ambivalent pressure. For the moment all I can do is hold me together, hold me at qui vive in face of it.

Dinner with Greg ... roast beef (almost rare enough to be rare), green peas (wizened), and roast potatoes (sullen) – "The Parliamentarian's Special" quoth the menu! God – the Cdn Nemesis ... A half bottle of Beaujolais scarcely masks it ... Greg laughs – "it's just a variation of Air Canada's performance – airborne buses. One and the same thing. You know – this train is really a set piece ... it establishes the kind of citizen it wants." I know instantly that Greg is right .... know exactly what he is saying. "You mean the people are for the car, and not the car for the people – it is the people who have to "live up to the car," grow into it – a car made, not to suit the people, but people being remade to suit the new Canadacar."

Greg's right. His perception mates my own – "if these are Canadians remade to suit the traincars, the Club Car we passed through getting here, that's the car for the people who service the People. The car for the Canadians who are remaking Canadians: the New Canadian Club for the People's Commissars ... with its red carpet, black leatherette chairs, & the pictures at one end by W.H. Bartlett, circa 1830, for the permanent English-Canadian Victorian Romantic, & at the other by one of the young French-Canadian revolutionaires, bought with his third consecutive Canada Council grant. The Club car is the Club of our New Establishment." Greg laughs again, at my flinch – "You've got it – this train is a very precise political platform … it's the travel arm of the Third Adam."

"I don't understand you there."

Greg: " … the new Cdn Man – the Uprooted Cdn; we used to be part of the First Adam … the continuous civilization of the Western World. That was our role in the New World. The Americans left us that legacy when they became the Second Adam after 1776 and all that. Well, these jokers (Greg jerked his head to embrace the diner) belong to the Cdn Grit Liberal Culture … whether they know it or not. They've uprooted, to rule. Their implicit claim is to be the Third Adam. But they're officially "modest" – so no-one says it. They just understudy the role!"

I laugh – Greg, like me is a hopeless Tory … and I know that, like me, he voted N.D.P. last time: Tory Radical. Our Toryism is our culture as Canadians … not our politics. I look behind Greg – there is a beaut! Cdn Male: age 46?, navy blue suiting, waistcoat (no handkerchief), unobtrusive glasses, solid … with a face of precast putty. His conversation is alas all too clear – I don't overhear it; I'm overrun by its calm assertion: " … they don't put enough force into their speeches, not enough guts – I ghost write for the Minister of Finance – he's uninspired …" I can't believe it – can't believe this man criticizing dullness; it's self-contradictory. For a moment my whole personality focuses again, all the legions called home by concentrate of contempt. For an instant I am whole again – alive from toe-tit to occiput. My whole being accuses these sterilettes. And then I feel the danger of expenditure again. Pull in my horn; I'll need it later – in emergency. "But this train IS an emergency … it is THE emergency, integral part of it …" Greg looks surprised at this outburst. "Oh I'm just talking aloud – I'll subside in a minute." But Greg is looking at me with a large understanding, & I blurt on, "this train is dangerous, as lethal in its own right as any boxcar translating political deviates to Siberia. Its tactics are more subtle – but they come to the same thing; absolute elimination, corporate destruction." Here Greg looks mystified & I stop … & am vulnerable again, to dispersal.

After dinner, back to the bar-car … alone. I don't know why. I guess I need a drink. A brandy. Ask mischievously for a Marc de Bourgogne. There never is any, of course. I always ask just to reassure me there isn't any … Only one place in English Canada where I have had a good Marc. A free seat by the window – my partner in crime discovers himself readily to me … after all, we are fellow inmates, accomplices of the Rapido (there is still something furtive about the bar-car).

"My name's Jack Emery – second year Law, Dalhousie … live in Willowdale … I like hockey and theatre. What do you do?" I flinch … it is the "what do you do?" that hurts. Always "what are you?" Never "who?" In all my years in Toronto no-one ever asked me "who" – except "who's what." People are expendable in English Canada; everyone is only a person "ex officio." & now, of course I'm no longer anything. Except a deserter … no – better than that – because I have my purpose: I'm a demissionary. God, here is this law student, already firmly entrenched in the English Canada Heresy – ex officio humanism! It's a form of agnosticism. But what chance has he, the betrayal has been made for him, at birth, by his community. We offer each other a drink and discuss the new cabinet changes.

Student – "Canadians think too much about themselves."

Says it with diffident self-satisfaction – like a Christian who has just confessed his Fault, & is now fresh armed with a proud Penance. & that done he unthinking opens up a little … that is, his eyes open into mine more … I nearly fall into the unexpected aperture … but even as I totter

bar-car catches me & I withdraw in time. I can't afford to fall anywhere in these surroundings,
because I have no control. Draw back, vetoed again. Stammer something – "we may think too
much about ourselves, but we never feel for ourselves." That ends the exchange. The best that can
be achieved now is a slowly distending propriety – a kind of improved impasse.

He returned to his own car. And waiting to get off wrote his notes with what
care he could muster, testing the muted vulgarity of the Rapido. He had to
acknowledge to himself that this train did set the taste-pace for its clientele. The
clientele being those, like himself, in the coach – the Permanent Commoners ...
Improved Commoners now, he supposed. And the administrators, the taste-mak-
ers, being those in the Club Car. The new elite. The new Canadian Priesthood.
Secular Order! The enemy within. The new ultramontanism – with Ottawa as
Rome. He'd have to start his own English-Canadian "Quiet Revolution" against
this new Canadian Church ... he, and anti-clerical Loyalist.

The man who shared his seat returned from a later dinner. Young – perhaps
30. Black suit, but with small cuffs. Hair close cropped – but not chopped ... sat
silently down, careful not to intrude his eyes upon anyone. Started reading: only
the chapter head was visible ... "how to handle a conference." Hugh sank in con-
sternation: "God, the army is everywhere." He went back to his notation ... scrib-
bling furious – "the national government has become our Tastemaker – and the
Taste it is setting is disastrous indication of the New Man it is concocting by default
..."

By the time he had finished they were in Montréal. Everyone was filing out.
Everyone, that is, except a young man three seats forward who stood up, dressed
himself with confident placidity, while conscientiously allowing the others to exit.
How was it possible, Hugh pondered, to be so correctly condescending as this man
was? And then – as he watched the performance, mesmerized – he knew that the
youth reminded him of someone. Whom? He stared ... the boy must be twenty-
five, hair kempt by comb (not brushed, of course), grey coat unobtrusively tweed-
ed, suit implacably pressed. Standing with his body held carefully at arm's length
... from what? Hugh didn't know. Not yet. The man was obviously a model, for
himself – but of what? Bells rang in his ears ... the youth put on his white scarf, his
gloves. And then it all came to Hugh with a rush – the face from the picture on the
wall of the United Church Sunday School near Collingwood, the skiing village ...
that was it: this youth was a Blondbeast for Jesus ... the completed Canadian
Methodist! Roundhead with Honours! A variation of the man who had just shared
his seat ... and who had looked like (Hugh realized it now), those ads for Canadian
Army recruitment: those earnest faces – firm (not forceful), clean cut (but not
chiselled), accessible (but not frank). Hugh watched amazed at this performance.
Surely there was a flaw somewhere. No – there was none. The young man helped
a lady with her bag, carefully withdrawing from her extracted thanks. It was
painfully embarrassing to Hugh. God – the kid is going through all the right
motions ... like someone from Whitby Ladies' College – the complete Methodist
Husband for the completed Methodist Lady. Everything was right about it. For a
moment he thought that the only solution was prayer – real prayer. And then as
the All-Canadian Good Boy carried himself firmly down the aisle (no organ play-

ing – none could: the Kid would see to that!) Hugh felt an insufferable urge that he didn't define ... he couldn't; he was in situ now – Montréal.

The station clamoured around him – he gazed into the noise, displaced suddenly ... so different from Toronto, from the great thermal Roman Imperial Bath of Toronto Union ... wherein no-one talked – except the Highclass Hicks of Listen Hear on the billboardings ... who yapped at the Permanent Commoners convening to their traintimes. These Hep Hicks – "everyone's chum," the pert alert Torontonian ... Well, here in Montréal, it was decisively and disconcertingly different. The station engulfed him now, and he weaved his way through the crowd – "the best-dressed peasants in the world," he thought, as he warped and woofed his way to his baggage. And the best-behaved. And then he realized that while they were a crowd incoherent around him, engulfing him, yet they were no more than in comparable space in the Toronto station. But the whole experience was utterly different. He gazed around the station – it looked rather like a well-organized sequence of American wayside kiosks. There was a percentage of that, and a percentage of shopping centre, and a percentage of "better buy British" to it all. Around the ceiling, an immensely squalid frieze depicting Canada, apparently, because underneath it the words of "O Canada." "Better buy Canadian ... better belong to Canadian Club" – that was the subterranean message ... "because Big Brother is encouraging you." There was that – and the seethe of sound that was a seethe of people. Hugh was too tired to understand all of it now. He caught a cab to a three-buck tourist home near the station ... run by a French couple from Provence – and battened himself down for the night. And as he locked his door and undressed the fissure opened him again and he realized where he was ... remembered again, in deeper measure, why he was there. The train ride had in part veiled it all for him even as it exposed him to it. Had veiled his novel, just as his novel seemed to veil his real purpose. A process of interlocking amnesias. Well, now he couldn't forget. Because he was within striking distance of La Place d'Armes. His raped breathing as he lay abed informed him that his heart was racing. He reached into his brief case for his book – Boswell's *Life of Johnson* ... somehow he had never read it through. Ridiculous gap ... so he had brought it along. And his hand fell on his Brief Biography. Why had he brought that? His curriculum vitae? What in truth *was* he doing in Montréal?

BRIEF BIOGRAPHY

Hugh Robert Anderson ... born 1931 ... Toronto ... second son of Colonel and Mrs ... 117 Crescent Drive ... Upper Canada College, Trinity College in the University of Toronto (History and Modern Languages – French and Russian), St. John's College, Oxon, P.P.E. (of course!) ... Four years with Montréal CBC special features (documentary), six years with the House of Johnson, Toronto, in charge of publications on Canadian history and literature ... lecturer at the University of Toronto ... author of *Essays in Canadian Taste: a Study in the Relationship of the Arts and Politics from 1812 to 1914.* Hobbies: bird-watching, Canadiana, conversation ...

It was an impeccable cursus honorum canadensis. Completed by a wife,

(Mary Joan, only daughter of Professor and Mrs. J. A. Robins) and two children, suitably divided between the sexes. In five years he would have been the effective head of the House of Johnson, Canada's most respected and progressive publishing house. He was perfectly bilingual (four years in Montréal had seen to that) and thoroughly respected by French and English Canadian editors and authors.

Hugh eyed the biography quizzically, incredulously ... almost as though he were hiring this man. He was suspicious: it was too good to be decent. Something was wrong somewhere. Then he remembered – it was him. Hugh Robert Anderson. He closed his eyes – the sweat stung in them. The thunder was his heart. It must all be a bad dream ... He farted, and the bland musk of debilitated Parliamentarian's beef (almost rare) assured him that it was for real. He thought of the Rapido-ride down. It had been at once curiously flat, yet riddled with pitfalls. Now he was in Montréal. And he was there on schedule. He looked at his watch ... after midnight ... so it was already December 1 – the first day of his Adventure. That was as planned.

It was indeed for real. It was he, Hugh Robert Anderson who had been fired two months ago – conscientiously fired. It was he who had, quite casually, at lunch one day, finally ensured his firing. Lunch with the President of the House of Johnson ... Richard Johnson, C.M.G., F.R.S.C., L.L.D., Q.C. (he had the order wrong – but he could never remember this mutation from the Canadian Debrett's listing really – it was so much easier to have a title, and be done with it – and not this subterranean alphabetic dignitarianism.) The lunch was at the York Club ... ensconced in all those magnificent Italian Renaissance Revival Victorian carvings. Johnson was asking pointedly, "Why do you think we missed that contract with the university, Anderson?" And precisely between a bite of Camembert, that was still, alas chalky (the York Club should have known better – and for a horrible moment Anderson had also wondered it the carvings on the wall were merely plaster) and the happifying recollection that only the York Club served a Marc de Bourgogne, Hugh replied quite spontaneously, almost affectionately, "Because you've got no balls, Sir." It had been so incredibly simple. He himself had heard this reply with interest and incredulity. Then for one ghastly instant, Hugh thought that he had been wrong, that Johnson DID have balls, at least ONE ball ... and that he was going to stab him, Hugh Anderson, with his steak knife. Hugh even hoped that this was so. It would have restored his faith. He waited, expectant virgin, for the thrust – and once again he even believed that the carvings on the walls were indeed wood. And the contortion of Johnson's face that Hugh had taken for genuine militant rage (Johnson had been a brigadier), was merely that kind of tumescence that precedes tears. And the president's only achievement had been to control his tears. Hugh looked up after a moment. Everything was in order again. The whole incident had simply blown over. But Johnson's eyes had gone that bald greyblue ... eyes from which one bounced with the false spring of tired broadloom ... eyes that looked neither out nor in – the look of a defeated man who still wields power. A month later Hugh was caught out on a technicality. He received a letter from the president inviting his resignation. He didn't even bother replying.

It was rather sad. He even liked Johnson. But once he was sure that Johnson had no balls, and was inordinately resentful of anyone who did, then the die was cast ...

A truck squealed against the curb outside his window. Hugh's flesh shrieked. He was outrageously alive now. Every pore audited the street sounds. He knew that he would get no sleep. What was worse a fever had set in ... all the old signs of strain in him – fatigue, fever, sore throat. He dosed himself with cold pills, aspirins, and settled down to sleep on his fakir's bed of goosepimples. He was still hopeful that he could accomplish his assignment ... could place the Place d'Armes and thus his novel. If he could just rest a bit, shake off this damned flu bug.

DAY ONE

NOTEBOOK

- awake at noon – pills have abated flu-fever. Lie abed, slowly draw me together
- read a little of Bozzy – just to place things a bit.
- Got La Place on my brain

& gingerly out of bed, palp embodiment for self certification: all intact. Out pipes! Brunch in greasy spoon

down through the city – Peel St. – Dominion Square (is it true that a sparrow hawk nested atop Sun Life Bldg. I hope so!) Pick up tourist map, postcards

- the Cathedral, squatting like English parish church amidst La Place Ville Marie, Sun Life (no hawk in sight) and the Queen Elizabeth Hotel (Fr-Cdns call it Le Reine Elizabeth – even the Queen has changed sex in this goddam country!)

Québec Hydro – Christ, pull yourself together – Hydro Québec: that's what the "nationalization" was all about – the provincialization, the French Canadianization of the hydro, three yrs ago.

Taxi drops me at edge of Place d'Armes. Proceed on foot – to reconnoitre. Not much snow – fortunately.

Don't want to see too much yet. Not till I dig in, get some sort of control centre for Operation Place d'A. Otherwise might shoot the whole venture prematurely. Phtt ... 10 years out the window. Mortal expenditure – & nothing to show for it. Except the notes kept while in training, intermittent, these past 7 years, & they are, at best, sketches – undercover sketches!

just take an oblique glance, out the side of my head ... yes – still there! A few changes – one big one: Who is it?

retreat down sidestreet, right under the nose of Target – & set out to find quarters. Sthg nearby – not more than 5 minutes from the Square. I'll have to scout the quarter, foot by foot this next fortnight: reinterpret every map – translate them. All out of date – & more dangerous – all deceptive, deliberately – hiding the Place. Know that from odious experience (that night, in '61 ...)

Ethg will be disguised! Masked.

I'll have to devise my own map ... prerequisite for safe encounter with Target. Will be tricky – every foot of the way mined.

Can't find right digs – ideally a small pension over the Square. Best facing the body of Target – bull's eye!

Small hotels – five blocks East (Old Directions) … several – in a sub-Square: La Place Jacques Cartier (meaning?) What is relationship between Square and sub-Square – Big Place & Little Place. Conniving. I'm wary tho. Make sure to find out. Excellent proximity.

Question of hotel … which one? Comes down to two: one faces City Hall (Old Style) & the old Market & the belltower of Sailor's Church. The other faces La Place – tho I can't see it from here. I'd rather face forward blind, than backwards visual. Moreover the seamstress on the second floor reminds me of … no matter

Hotel Nelson. Why? Aside from its relationship to Monument in the Little Place it confronts. Kick me all day for choosing this hotel. Too much like an old hen. But it is the right one – the one that 1st engaged my attention, my loyalty. Besides, each time I got out I'll interrogate the view from the other, wondering why I didn't take it, & that way get best of each world.

If I'm wrong I'll move (tho I never will! Besides it would attract too much attention.) Installed by nightfall. Try to read; fail.

Why have I come? I would give anything to know & more not to know!

Squander remaining energy on the why for. Flee to dinner, across La Petite Place. Buy conscience off with spaghetti, soup. Slink to sleep.

DAY TWO

Hugh awoke slowly – dredged himself from bed, and installed himself at his portable typewriter, duty-bound. It had been his faithful comrade-at arms for eight years. An Olivetti Lettera 22; it had never failed. He had written his first book on it. And ever since. He opened his briefcase, reached in for his Journal, and started to type.

"The morning is deep downcast in me, numbskulled, and my brain bloats against greysky. Catch my dreams by the tail … reach out to prey upon them. But they are gone even as I reach … Well, if I can no longer feel, at least I do have time to think. I have reached shelter, a hide-in, and I think I am undetected. No-one knows I am here. I'm not even sure I realize I'm here yet. And certainly no-one knows why (I like to think that I don't know why – but I know deep in my bone I do, that I'm here.) If anyone did know then my Disaster would be disastered. The important thing now is to keep a meticulous record of the assault, so that if I fail at least the ground will have been broken. If I succeed then others can follow; the results will be self-evident. In either case a day-by-day account, in detail is essential. For the novel – and for the Real Thing. I'll keep on taking notes. And then write them up as I can in this journal. Flesh them out … flesh me out!

Irony: I bought this journal six years ago, when I was still in Montréal, with the CBC … meant to keep a daily record. Never did. And now I'm here, writing it because I didn't dare then … didn't dare me. Serves me right. Remember the day I bought it – after lunch with George Carter, at Delmos Oyster Bar, walked along la rue Notre Dame and down-dropped in to an antique shop … one of his clients. All that Canadiana (little did I suspect then it was my culture in the raw). It was lying in the bargain pile on a gate-leg table. Picked it up unthinking, uninterest-

ed ... perhaps to look interested, perhaps to protect me against other purchase –
the redflare of cover caught my eye I guess, the red and black while George
talked shop ... balancing the book in my hand – an old fashioned journal and
notebook – my hand tested by its heft, substantial. With a good spine to it.
None of that paperback stuff (a paperback culture has no tiger in its tank – must
needs make one up). And open to the marbleized end-papers ... curls my coil
(there's the rub). Plus a pocket for papers ... containing one reproduction map of
old Montréal and a couple of postcards – one of the Bank of Montréal, the other
of Notre Dame's gut ...

Bought for $1.

George laughed – "You're a symbolist."

"Why?"

"The date – 1867!"

I hadn't even noticed ... But I never wrote a word in it: fled to the
respectability of Toronto instead.

Stop yapping and write!

7:46 a.m. Waking this morning and even last night I was aware once again
that my novel is in fact some deeper assault on reality than I care to admit. It is
... it is a war – between reality and me. Maybe it's a Holy War. I can't tell (stop
lying – of course it's a Holy War!) Alright – it is a Holy War – so this journal which
is a diary which is my log-book is really a Combat Journal. It couldn't be any-
thing else. I should type it in red.

Must keep a duplicate. In the hotel strongbox to be forwarded to Eric in
case of emergency. I know he'll see to it that it is published. (Don't let me down
Eric – you have no right to. What I say belongs to my community – to what is left
of it, that is. It is all I have to give. All! And if they don't want it ... well at least
they can never say they weren't told.)

Between my notebooks, my Combat Journal and what I manage to write of
my novel, the picture should be complete. As complete as I can make it. And if I
succeed, then I'll have my novel from it. Then the rest can be set aside ...

But I'm not going to fail. I have no right to do that either. I am honour-
bound to succeed ... And I must bind me to my word. Screwed to the sticking
point! I've rubiconned every river that ever ran, bombed every bridge – just to
make sure I've cornered my cowardice. For the rest, ten years of meticulous
preparation. Of training. Maybe fifteen, if I include those first years, at the
University of Toronto ... when I furtively, almost unwittingly, protected my
counterpoint to the Amurrican Dream. Ten years anyhow. Ten years of tacking
back and forth – but always to the same end. Always the same preoccupation.
What subterfuge it has meant ... I always the subterfugitive! No matter. What
counts now is that I've reached my target. It is still here. That was the work of
yesterday. I took few notes yesterday – even though it was the First Day. The
First Day on the site. I just didn't have the energy; it had all been consumed in
getting to the hotel, into a striking position. I remember now that I had felt how
dangerous my sense of calm was to the whole purpose of the expedition.
Because it is war – and I realized already it was war, and that any placation was
capitulation. Yet I persisted in feeling calm. And I had to keep telling myself that

this adventure is essential. Of course I knew that it was – even if for some time yesterday I only knew abstractly and had to keep sending me mental telegrams, like "EXPEDITION URGENT STOP NO RETREAT STOP KEEP YOUR COCK UP STOP." No, I knew well enough that is was essential. That was it: I was danger-ously smug about the fact of the danger. That was what worried me. Lulled me into a security right in the face of absolute danger.

And then later yesterday – in the late afternoon, I harvested the exhilara-tion of recognized danger, and the whole thing was implicitly clear again. I could relent.

... 9:25 a.m. Breakfast at the hotel – while the waitress clucks about this dining room like some pullet over her brood – and I ponder the matter. Really wonder whether I can achieve it. It is mad. This "adventure." I suppose the real question is whether it takes place at all. My fear now is for the adventure itself – because that is the basis of the novel. Amongst other things. And at this very instant, as the oatmeal porridge ballasts my grumble gut, I am denuded of everything except my faith in the possibility of the adventure. Yet even as I fear for the ven-ture I realize that the fear is of no way out – fear of the final extinction of my plans. And once again I realize how serious it really is ... this goddam "novel" of mine. It is a matter of life and death – whether I like it or not. Moreover, if I turn back, then it is automatic death. So I know again what is at stake, and the Adventure, the Novel, simply is. I am dedicated to victory, because I am dedicat-ed to life against death.

In the strain of this recognition my appetite is gone ... because my body is gone – has been nullified by the act of questioning. I have lost corporate credi-bility again. It is detached fingers that wipe detached mouth as I pick me up and carry me back to the room ... At least I can study the map of the quarter ...

As I re-enter my room on the third floor my ear is cocked to the shunt of the freight-yards just below the hotel ... I am huge again with the dream I forgot this morning ... muster me once more to typewriter before it evades me again ... if nothing else, I can keep the goddam log-book up to date ...

It was home ... in the home I've never built. In my old Toronto Rosedale ... that house, on Crescent Drive, Tudorbethan, with park ground behind it ... the banquet hall in the basement – wine cellar banquet hall; vrai cave! (Virulent in me ... every detail – as I hear bells from trainshunt.) Twelve-foot dining table from Les Frères chretiens of Montréal, a drawer for each monk's pewter cutlery ... 14 places in all. Generous places. Table with the trestled feet, wide plank top, and the iron crane drawing out from the end, for the marmite. Item #337 in Jean Palardy's illustrated Furniture of French Canada. Around it those chairs I could never afford to buy ... those chaises a là capucine, circa 1780. With their flowing arms joining balustered back and legs, front and back. And the cherub-winged backslats. Fourteen of them – a dozen in dark hardwoods – walnut, butternut, stained maple. Plus two in tiger-stripe maple – voluptuous in the wood's coun-tercurve to the curvette of the design of the chair itself. This in the very centre of the room ... Walls white plaster roughcast. Ceiling high (it keeps getting high-er as I recollect it.) Around these walls – upjutting from every corner and pillar and beam – the strut of the cave – a dozen Coqs canadiens, rampant. At the far end immense rocaille hulk of sideboard – like some purebred milchcow decked out for a fête champêtre at Versailles. Clawed balled feet. Atop it, large carved cupboard for eaux-de-vie ... straddle by six torchères that stand four feet each. All in white and gilt. On the left wall, a huge mural scene, a fire ... But scarce time to talk all of this in, even in recollection, when the guests arrive. Who are they to be (trains – keep shunting – I would know who arrives!)? Suddenly candles blare, ignite, and She arrives in sheath dress that cracks my whip ... followed by Him in dinner jacket and bespectacled smile, teeth wide-eyeing (High Church Ipana!) and hair in kempt disheveled pelt. No Announcements. Simply an informal elegant investiture of this home hall à la canadienne ... investiture of us, of what we are as citizens, as people ... I serve them un vin d'Honneur – a Benkastler Doktor 1959er goldbeerenauslese – in my grandfather's high Victorian Hock glasses. High Victorian, High Hock, High Glasses ... with Chinese waterchestnuts and bacon ... serve them from the front seat of the Child's Hearse – lifesize – from Lévis, P.Q., hearse all inordinate with angels and roses and garlands, steep carved pine, white and gold, and all celestially earthy (those trumpeting angels have firm French-Canadian buttocks.)

As I pour the Bernkastler into the onion-skin green of glass diaphanous under tremble of fingertits wine flows down necknape of Tony's hairline, down vertebration into the roothouse that used to be behind Great-grandfather Jameson's homestead at Grimsby (Ont.) ... into roothouse and up spat back out at me into the glass of Princess Meg from her left breast that was cut clean from the dress, displacing the Order of the Garter. Eau de vie, I gasp, and kneel to let it tumble my crown ... Scene only interrupted by the Canadian Chairs that come assclasp us all to a stewboat of Oxtails stewed as meet for Mighty Methodists ... and serve with a red wine that I grow myself, below the house on the slope behind the Toronto subway just to prove that Ontario wine need not be the red Niagara piss with which we glut our home market ... a little red brute strong enough to grapple these tails – secret being, of course, that as in certain small crus of Pomerol, I leave the stems and all in the pressing, to flesh out the wine, give it mastication ... un petit vin mastubateur de l'Ontario ... l'état de l'Ontario, s.v.p. Till Margaret had been oxtailed, and Tony with, and everyone ordained therein because it is meat and right so to do ... and as I look up (the bell of freight trains clarifies the site now) I see that the sideboard is 18th century French Canadian baroque-rococco church alter, Ecole de Quévillon, and that the angels are now suspended from our lowering ceiling, and that the Tony is my chair and Princess Meg clutches regally every oxtail to her Order of the Garter, and all we guests concerted shout – " Alleluia, I'm a bum ... "

I wake, just in time to curtail an unsolicited harvest of me, and now, in recollection, remember clearly that as a child I had been deeply preoccupied with the conjugation of OurBelovedKingandQueenandwas thereabeginningnoranendtosaidconjugationIwasconcernedtoknowatwhatpoint itdi dallen din us, as I was sure it did.

Then I realized that there is a huge silence resonant in me, as dream dies on my vine.. the freight-yards are tranquil, and the bells have stopped.

Sit in this sweet bereavement. Evacuated. Suddenly recall my tourist map. Bought it yesterday ... but hadn't courage to look it up. The least I can do now is circumscribe my area. On earth, in North America, in the Dominion of Canada, in L'Etat du Québec, in La Ville de Montréal, in the centre of the city, the old centre, by the side of the St. Lawrence, McGill Street, running up from the river, north-east to Craig Street, then easterly, past City Hall as far as Berri, down to the waterfront again. Le Vieux Quartier, plus a bit. Within that a still smaller area ... bounded by rue St. Jacques to the north, la rue St. Pierre to the west. Within that – La Place itself, La Place d'Armes ... and within that again, of course, – but that will have to wait.

These are the names, the streets; the shorthand for the reality. I know that. It is the reality I seek. Yet even as I succumb to the map, looking at it, I feel La Place, the whole quarter, ebbing dangerously out of me ... And I bitter realize that I have committed the cardinal sin, reducing the quarter to this map. To allow this map – even as guide. Perhaps if I slip out now, quickly, I will catch the quarter, La Place, the bulk of it, the embodiment of it, before it all folds away into this map that betrayed me ... in a moment of weakness. Fling me into parka and beret, sortie out ... not with intent to site the quarter definitively – but to make honourable amends for having slighted – for having presumed to reduce it to a few square inches of map. Running down the stairs of the hotel, out the door, into La Place Jacques Cartier ... up past the Nelson Monument and the Court House ... down la rue Notre Dame, quickly, hurry now ... to La Place, the central Square, noting fearfully already how vague these are become in me ... till I reach La Place itself and enter, unwitting now, and not till I am half way across it, the buildings flowing past me, shadowing me, shadows of me, in the corner of my eye, do I realize that it is already too late. Already I am invisible ... and La Place is detached, receding out of me. Already. Stand, in centre Square, glaring at the buildings, the Place; and only shadow. Intermittently a lurch of something more substantial. But in essence, only shadow ... only the remains in me of the Place. I drift on, across the square, down St. James Street, trying to regroup me, to pull me together, to substantiate me ... But I can't ... the best I can manage is some sort of condition midway between incarnation and excarnation. At best I am half-cocked now ... my body is midway – neither here nor there. Nothing is specific. And then I am at an intersection (which that cursed map tells me still is McGill and St. James!) In front of me a modern business building ... a sheath-glass tower. And I am falling straight into it ... on pretext of looking for someone who isn't there (if he is, he's lost). But the truth is, I fall into my own vacuum! And then, in minutes, shoot out again, like some electronically processed statistic. My chameleonage complete now ... feel as I felt I was about to feel in the bar-car of the Rapido. Something has happened to my gut ... something gone out of me. Somehow I have been dispersed ... would panic – but there isn't enough of me in one place now to panic ... and then do panic – and when I stop running, I am back across the Square (it passed though me absolutely unnoticed – it is only by looking back that I know that I have passed through it!) and I am having a belated lunch in some plastic-nickelodeon joint ... my remaining embodiment looses its teak timbre from the executive suite of the glass-sheath tower and goes salmon pink along the counterline now ... Soupe du jour et biftek, au point[21] ... The food descends my elevator shaft and congeals in my salmon-pinked stomach – fortunately I can't vomit, can't even feel nauseous: my stomach is artificial now. Soooo ... I've chameleoned to that point. I've decarnated further than I feared. Only the old imitation wrought-iron coat-wrack in the corner, splattered with taches of aluminum paint to modernize it – only that keeps feeding me now, intravenously. And it is out of place, as is my blood. My heart founders. Under these conditions my plans are simply impracticable. How can I share the intensity of joy that the Square is in me, has been for me, always, implicitly, till to-day, till now, when I actually reach out to prove its joy for the sake of others? How can I write the Novel. There isn't any Place to live, to see, not any more ... it has gone out of me. Worse, the very converse – the same Place d'Armes has become for me simply a bloodsucker – each building a leech, draining me of my remaining corpuscularity. What I had come to see, still vainly hoping to share, not only has failed me, but has turned against me. I am left with an inversion of my verity. Gathering up my encroaching invisibility and my check, I flee – so discountenanced that I am able to walk past target, site unseen – a mutual agreement almost. Slink to my hotel. No – all my tactics are wrong. I cannot give what I now no longer possess – nor can I leave dispossessed. My Novel is out the window. So is my life!

I try to think ... no use. I can't feel anything ... and out of touch, I'm out of mind – out of my mind. For a brief moment I know that I am on the verge of insanity ... Lie down, lie down.

vertebra wrench, open and squeeze clamped closed like accordion, ramming the punch of me from tail to necknape, head threatens to detach – and suddenly bolt upright from the thrust I'm awake to realization that my body has simply corporately echoed the sound from freight train shunting in the yards – my ear still thrums bright as the trainbell rams the entire cargo home it freights. 7 p.m. How long did I sleep? My guilt musters me to typewriter ... and for two hours I record this day's disaster of me. Dispassionate, because detached now. Disembodied.

Done – I wonder what next? Technically I'm through – washed up, or washed out. I can go home now. Settle in to being a civil servant, or university prof or a bond salesman. It's as simple as that. I've just died. Why not accept the fait accompli ... and enjoy my retirement into the Canadian Social Welfare State; climb in the trough, with the rest of the Citizenry. Head reels again ... and I know that this is impossible; I would shoot myself first ... What the hell have I been doing these past ten years, if not evading that issue! That impasse. The All-Canadian Clunk – no, I'd rather die, again, than say yes.

Out into the night air ... aware that I need food, though not hungry. Wend me through the velvet dark of the humid December night, to the restaurant of Paul-Marie Sanson ... Le Chat Botté, just a few doors from Le Devoir on the same side ... Le Devoir – our only relevant journal of opinion – the only Canadian

---

21 Soup of the day and a steak, medium.

newspaper that absolutely had to say what it had to say these past ten years ...
and said it. It had guts. And at Le Devoir it had been André Laurendeau – the
editor. One man, who stood up to be counted. When it hurt ... But for some rea-
son or other no-one from Le Devoir ever eats chez Paul-Marie. Paul-Marie is a
Frenchman ... from Le Midi[22] ... and that, finally, is unpardonable. That he serves
the best food in Montréal, that he is no more expensive than the other intellec-
tually or socially chi-chi restaurants nearby which are also reasonably inexpen-
sive, that he is actually only a few doors from the newspaper. None of this mat-
ters. Paul-Marie is French, obdurately French. Moreover his decor is neither
improved Habitant, nor a clinically clean version of Paris Left Bank. No – Le Chat
Botté is simply eternal French bistro in a Canadian Victorian setting that has
been here since built ... the mantelpiece settles the period pretty well; one of
those carbuncular wooden mantles with knobs and finials and chip-carving
overall, thoroughly clotted with a grained golden oak finish multiply varnished.
By the time of Queen Victoria's Diamond Jubilee it was honourably aged. So
Paul-Marie's clientele is English-speaking mainly. Because of the atmosphere
and because of Paul Marie, and because it is in Le Vieux Quartier near such quar-
antined denizens as Le Devoir. A visit to La Chat Botté for an Anglo-Canadian
Respectable is as risqué as a tour along the Red Light lane ... I remember watch-
ing them order meals here, many times ... invariably the same – steak after an
onion soup, finishing with a crème caramel, or a pâtisserie francaise. In fact I
never was entirely sure what Paul-Marie used to do with his tripes and brains,
and bowels, and pigs'-feet, and head cheese and illegal game, and all the other
pungent extremities of barnyard flora and fauna. The answer I supposed all
along was Paul-Marie himself ... as I see him again, now on entry, I am sure of it.
Six foot three, he hasn't lost a single one of his 329 pounds. Sitting with his back
to me, in front of the TV, eating his blood sausage and terrine de foie de vollaille.
Seated amidst the clamour of his oh so empty tables. If possible he has grown
even more Paul-Marie, has grown further into himself. The Paul-Marieness of
Paul-Marie – absolute self-fidelity. He hears me, and pivots his chair ... impound-
ing me with his 329-pound eyesight, probing me deep for my food potential, for
my significance as a man-of-food. Decides I'm insignificant ... and is about to let
his waitress guide me to a table, when suddenly his eyes focus on mine ...
"Monsieur Hugh ... " and he is on the instant dissolved from implacable food
concentrate – like some fossilized but pliant pemmican – into inordinate activi-
ty ... in seconds we are safe, in the kitchen, with its ten-foot stove, wood-stove.
Paul-Marie promptly stuffs it with more wood, which it patently does not need,
and then armed with an outrageously undulant ladle undertakes a constrained
elephantine ballet from pot to pot ... a joyous war-dance of the foods, in my
honour ... digs ladle down to turnip and gourd and leek and all the bloated enor-
mities from its international reservoir of innards. Roils the stews, the soups, the
sauces, in a free molestation that would please any voyeur of feed. High tribute,
that. And I am embarrassed by it. On the centre table a mound of brains that
could only be from a dinosaur, did a dinosaur have sufficient brains to be a
dinosaur. And guiding these, from the far end of the kitchen, perched on a pair

22 The South of France.

of bar-stools, the lares and penates – King and Prince – German Shepherds eye-ing me with the same intent I apply to the food – a fierce friendliness.

I know exactly what I feel ... like the gentle man in Galsworthy's story of the old custom shoemaker, who he must frequent out of loyalty ... I would eat Paul-Marie's food were it rotten! "It's changed, Paul-Marie, it's better than ever." The Frenchman smiles amidships – "on va manger, eh Monsieur Hugh ... on va manger"[23] – and he masticates each word he proffers ... leads me triumphantly back to his table, afront the TV screen, gouges me tablespoonful of terrine, and leaves me, irritated by the TV, and sad ... God knows I didn't come to Montréal to watch TV ... offended, I raise a breadful of the best terrine in the nation to my mouth, hopefully – suddenly I vibrate, terrine glowers ... it is the voice on the TV. I know that voice – know it gutwise. It's Jean-Pierre Préfontaine ... talking political leaders; how often we did that during my stay in Montréal. I watch the terrine, rich on the bread, and then lower it to my plate, untouched. That munificent voice of Jean-Pierre, voice that is what he has to say. Voice from these same innards that Paul-Marie marinates and steeps and stews and eats, all by himself (and I remember now that Paul-Marie, too, has a huge voice, a voice that, once on the rampage in song, turns your earth upside right.) And then, my terrine grounded, I concentrate me, almost malevolently, on what Jean-Pierre says – because I know that he says nought. Now all the questions are into me again as a great tidal bore. Why does this man say nothing? Why does he settle for $50,000 a year ... with his seat on the Royal Commission on Canadian Culture, a face on TV and a voice on radio? It's all balls ... or rather it's no-balls at all. Absolute irrelevance. Jean-Pierre knows that ... knows that he is saying nothing ... There's the rub. He knows the impotence of what he says ... The terrine, on my bread on the plate, catches my eye again – it is the sound of the voice that does it – Jean-Pierre has started in again ... that is it – it is how he says it that is inordinately potent. I quiz the screen again – poor Jean-Pierre, you are left only with the right to hear the sound of your own voice. Echo of a fecundity forever unused, untapped ... What happened to you – why did you desert? Where did you go? What do you see now as you leer out at us from within your electronic cage? Pauvre Jean-Pierre ...

"Qu'est-ce que vous-voulez, M'sieur ... ?"[24] The waitress is at my back – and I realize that I am speaking out loud – apostrophizing the shadow of the shadow of Jean-Pierre, that I am even imitating his voice ... in French. And that as I imi-tate it I eat of the terrine de foie de volaille. It tasted of ... but even as I rejoice at the empire of taste in this terrine it has gone. Christ – I'm back at absolute zero again ... headspin. I hang on to the carafe of ordinaire that Paul-Marie has squat-ted afront me. I appall me ... I cannot taste any of it. I know that – my taste buds have folded – closed down for the night. It is the sight of Jean-Pierre ... his delib-erate demission. He is posthumous ... and knows it, and accepts it, and goes on living it warmed by the sound of his own voice ... warming the last cockle of his heart. I cannot stop me now, watching this television spectre ... no stop, stop – wrench my eyes out of it just at the moment when body threatens dissolution

23 "We're going to eat, Monsieur Hugh, we're going to eat."
24 "What would you like, Sir?"

again – just as I see Paul Marie's terrine descending my transparent gullet – proof positive of my desubstantiation.

And now, eyeballs popped back in, I am reprieved (if not saved) – a trio arrive, and my instincts apprise me of a Scene.

Young couple. Plus a little Big Daddy. Out of Town – the Lower Town. Big-Little Daddy pays. She smiles upon him; hubby talks for their supper. I listen out of the corner of my ear ... Paul-Marie bounds over onto them, accosts their appetite, waitress smiles and we convene complicit over Paul-Marie's campaign ...

Me – "what an urgency to Paul-Marie now ... services them as though they were on Messianic mission, dependent for capacity to Resuscitate upon a warranted feed-station ... "

Waitress – "c'est toujours comme ca." [25] If they leave food uneaten he is sad ... mopes.

See their eyes skirt the menu ... Big-Little Daddy smiles approbation. Wife smiles upon husband. Husband talks more fluently. Thus the bargain is made ... "three filets Mignon, three onion soup ... "

Paul-Marie knows their lines – plays them out, his feet pounding time, whole body urgent to the metre, scanning their food-place ... "et comme desert nous avons pâtisseries françaises ... fromages ... crême caramel ... "[26] He is almost malevolent ... the "crême caramel" only comes out after a hopeful pause, and then is said with culminating authority in the absence of theirs.

I can't take any more of this ... watch the TV an instant. Reduced to that. Paul-Marie pounces on the kitchen, armed to the teeth with his orders ... his pots-au-feu bubbling for only him and me, and now only him – as I am a hit-and-run victim of TV. The trio play out their night's engagement. For one unperceived moment, witless, I realize how fine the terrine is ... catch the colour of it out of the corner of my eye ... "colour"? – yes, that is what it is – I see colour on the TV screen, and realize abruptly I am nibbling the terrine and catching its kaleidoscope ... catching all the essential out of the corner of my eye. And then it is gone – just as I know it, it is gone ... like the Place, with the map ... And I am gone, in absentia.

They have their crême caramel. My eyes are dry with the screen or I could cry. I want to go over ... to wheedle. "Excuse me Sir ... but Paul-Marie serves the only cêpes in town, as a savoury! Cêpes mesdamesmedsdemoisellesmonsieurs! Cêpes! And un petit vin de paille. And with coffee, he has his own eau-de-vie, from his village, near Carcasson, it's all on the menu ... in English." But I know if I wheedle they will mount their high horse and I shall have to take out my knife and cut off the vestiges of their humanhood, scrotumsacking them with a single twist of knife like coring dead apple for stewpot ...

I am out on the street again. Sauve qui peut! [27] Told Paul-Marie I would come back later in the week ... that this was but a tour de reconnaissance. Bandying towards me, short legs, crooked nose with dilating nostril (left one),

25 "It's always like that."
26 "And for desert we have French pastries, cheeses, caramel cream."
27 Every man for himself.

deep bruised eyesockets, barrel chesting over those legs, a reporter turns in to
Le Devoir: God – how habitant he still is ... Habitant! But he has just turned my
country inside out with his "quiet revolution" – 150 years too late.

Oh God – that's it ... my country, my eyesight, my taste ... all gone now! I
knew I had forgotten something. I had forgotten everything. And La Place ... I
stumble my faith down la rue Notre Dame, blinkered, saving me again for La
Place d'Armes. Past la rue Bonsecours with its church, and La Maison Panineau,
and the Château de Ramezay, the Hôtel de Ville, and the Court Houses, old and
new ... screening them with my televizor, to evade stumbling over them in my
dark. To La Place. And only there open my eyes, wide opened, to embrace La
Place ... mumbling "I've come ... I've come ... look, I've come back, I promised."

It's gone too. Why fool myself? There's nothing there. Oh, there's some-
thing – I see the outlines, delimiting the buildings around La Place. And with an
effort, from memory, I can still name them – at least the major ones – clockwise-
ly, from St. James Street side – new and old Bank of Montréal, that pair of sky-
scrapers on the east side – one with the old Banque Cdne nationale, the other,
the old Providence Life Building. Behind me l'église Notre Dame and its
Presbytery ... But it's all irrelevant now. The veil has come down in me, over my
eyes. I am shut off – cannot see, nor hear, nor touch. Look again at the Place – no
it's just a postcard there now, a site through a viewer, and even that is ebbing
from me.

So that is it – I came to La Place to prove possession of it, to fling it in the
face of the infidels, to cower them with the reality they have sacrificed, and, at
the very moment of proof, find I have already lost it ... lost everything.

Stumble up the steps of the Church, can't harm me now, no longer; sit
down, go and sit down, enter and slump in the first pew ... slump my body still
ironclad around my core, body frozen over me frozen in my own steep freeze ...
ironsides ... and dump me here, moribund. My eyes rebut the body of the
Church I can no longer see, sweeping over its body – in a reassurance that I am
unscathed by it, and even as I confirm the armour-plating I am stabbed ... from
the right, and I turn stunned to the face of the wound, follow the trajectory of
thrust from my flank, across the aisle till I am up to our hilt in the eyeballs of a
youth who curious appraises my arrival. I withtract instantly, close the ironclad,
close ... but I have been penetrated and cannot and look back up again along the
same trajectory of sight and am imbedded again in those eyes on me ... stumble
back out of the Church that sudden flares in me, anywhere ... and as I exit, turn
to exorcise those eyes and still cannot, and now we are talking under the huge
arcade of the entry and walking in the light snowfall that I feel against the hot
socket of my left eye windsown.

Down the sidestreet by the Church, and after a five-minute walk the bar
closes around us and we are babbling. Deep inside I am taut, closed ... I Know
where I am, but I don't want to know ... I Know this is the last remedy, the disas-
trous prerequisite, but don't want to know. Peer cautiously at the barroom ...
there are about 75 of us here ... I glue my arsehole to the chairseat like bitch in
heat, while trying to wag my tale in self-deprecatory defense. Seventy-five of us
... from 15 to 50. I'll watch – no harm ... parry an eyethrust from leftflank. Parry

and feint. In front of my screen a blondie convenes an entire tableau around him ... watch his progressions ... five other she-males resuscitate at the end of his fingertits ... all engaged in the rhythm of his embodiment ... The rotten French-Canadian teeth, sleazy tights, fuzzy-wuzzy parkas ... all these disappear as I too dance at the end of those fingers, my armour-plate clanking to the floor ... my flank is open now, unveiled left toe twitches, nostril flares and as blond boy quivers his court to renewed palpability, I sudden retreat, on the run, back into my safety of insensibility – but even as I do I am stabbed again, and turn to the boy from the Church still beside me ... Yvon ... 18, in turtleneck skisweater, a snood of dark hair, and eyes climbing all over inside me, as though I am some site ... "insite," that is it ... all that land inside us ... Yvon – shy, but firm – nothing coy. He has just pierced again my flank, emancipated me again from my ironsides ... and I have just swallowed him eyeballs first. The pact is simple, frank immutable. This then is disaster ... the complete, instant immersion in another. No holds barred. Absolute accessibility. And it is disaster ... consequence of my desertion of all I hold dear – the requisite Disaster ...

"Il me faut cinque piastres ... je suis commerçant."[28] My head roars ... senses close – I turn to grapple with that Judas-kiss ... Everything left in me focuses my deception ... my eyes muster my accusation, and as I look at him we are imbedded along the line of looking; his eyes flow into me again, and I accept their need, and my own.

Walk the greystone street from the bar, the same side of La Place as my petite place ... down towards the harbour ... along a grey way of stone houses ... flanked by them each side, till we are in front of a fine Regency stone home, now for tourists ... up the curving cast-iron steps two flights, from whose top I can see the white new dome of the Marché Bonsecours, the rippling cupola of the City Hall ... and if I step to one side, the towers of Notre Dame, with the Bank of Montréal behind. The front door is bullworthy – no battering would breach its stolid convolutions of wood panel and applied pilasters. Inside everything clean, in place ... a snugglery amidst these Georgian townhouses that are become everything but what they were – boutiques, tourist homes, warehouses, brothels, antique shops. I can only chuckle ... if only the Regency gentlemen of old Montréal could see this ... or the Historic Sites Committee to-day.

Yvon's room ... an extension of the bunnycoats I saw in the tavern. Those parkas canadiens which no English-Canadian male nor even she-male would be seen dead in alive. A kind of blatant cuteness. The walls bleu-pale, of dribbly plaster pattern; crucifix on the wall (after all – I met Yvon at the foot of the altar!) flowers potted on a low star-spangled coffee table (Air-Canada styling!) – they are plastic, but I scarce note that except by mental recollection, they seem so right ... live flowers here would be fake! All warmly cosmetic. Yvon reporting to his "collegues" (think that is the academic term) in the basement.

... what the Hell am I doing here? What are the chances of getting out? There was a murder in this block a few days before I arrived – my cleaning woman told me all the details ... I scout the innards of the cupboard – no-one there. On the table, beside the potted plastic flowers three colour photos of

28 "I'll need five bucks ... I'm in business."

Yvon ... in each one he has the same intent, diffident look. In each one he shields his eyes from the probe of the camera ... never really letting the camera see what I have already seen in him, though his eyesite. How can I possibly believe him conscientious accomplice to murder. His innocence is so articulate in these photos ... his self-consciousness.

Yvon back – close the door ... lock it carefully – turn, look at me ... it is a warm looking. A male prostitute – he patently likes his métier – his clean blue-jeans already taut as he stands akimbo, gentle, awaiting – nothing slut, nothing brazen, nothing aggressive, nor weak. He is simply there ... all there. And he wants to be there – that's what he is there about. What's more, he expects me to be there. I watch this open and absolute salutation in silenced admiration ... this complete self-presentation. My presence acknowledges him ... gives birth to him. God – this metier of his, it is divine. No actor could approximate this extraordinary gift of self that the $5 conceals. This boy simply wants to give and to be given. The five bucks ... give it to him now ... hand it to him saying "You can go now if you want." Yvon folds the bill carefully in his shirt, looks me up and down – is it reproach? And then steps forward, unbuttons his checked shirt and draws my thighs to him gentle and hands on my back kneads me into him ... I watch us wary ... not a false move. What Yvon does comes from within him – from some inner law he follows now flawlessly, while his eyes palp mine. I watch intently for the slightest failure in that law – at the slightest deviation from it I would be released, and would flee ... There is none. This boy is an artist. And he sells his body the way artists do, only they do it at once remove, on canvas, or sculpted ... his art is consummate, direct ...

Yvon jabs his cocked pants now steep into my thighside ... thrust him back and eat his body wholemeal through my eyeballs. Still he awaits. And as though unveiling virgin I part his bluejeans and complete our divestiture, till we are naked in us ... His body proffers so naturally – so freshly – the virginity lying in the renewed wonder it reveals for him so clearly now.

Imbedded together I man his rood that fulfills my palmed handling ... firm in the hand ... the rediscovered heritage. Yvon eyes always follow me through mine, always completely there, always implicating my own, so that what is done at manrood is already assured in eyesite ... once only do I avert my eyes, and as I do the thunder of my ear dies and I am alone. I panic, and my eyes turn quick to filch him at cockhead, and as they light thereupon I see his eyes again, ears open, and again I feel steep inside of me.

"Comment veux-tu arriver?"[29]

"I don't know yet."

Yvon's eyes summons us ... "Je ne l'aime pas dans le trou ... "[30]

I feel my disappointment ... because there is a negative in us now. Then I see his eyes – they are not negative; they are only the look of a boy about to take Communion. Run my rood along his, lying us askewer, touching us together for the first time, thus, lightly, run it along, till our cocklips touch, run it down the firmed centre of his manhood (simple statistic; he has 10 fine inches of gift), and

29 "How do you want to do it?"
30 "I don't like it up the ass."

slowly creep my cocktip up to his, his eyes on my cockhead, then his eyes clamped in my own, we eyesite each other, till with easy implacably concision the cocklips kiss again and I am influorescent, bathing his rood in liquid moonstone. Yvon's eyes close in a Mona Lisa smile of the line of the lids, and as he lie so immersed in my harvest I gather his root till it blurt sperm bolts clean up to our breast.

His eyes open, incredulous with wonder ... dresses as I watch him. "Where will you go now?"

"Je rentre au club ... je vais danser ... "[31] Yvon smiles, pats the $5 ... I know that although our conjugation has been tentative, yet I will always remember Yvon, because he restores to me an entire world ... suddenly he reincarnates me after twenty years of meticulous self-destitution. For twenty years I have adhered meticulously to the code of the latent Civil Serviceable. For twenty years I have flirted with sterility. Now, at the final moment, I have broken. Yvon breached me at the moment of final closure. I am free to be myself responsibly ... free to know the world I have so conscientiously extruded.

For that Yvon is blessed ... I look at the crucifix on the wall. "I met you in the Church ... yet you are ... you are" (I couldn't say, or didn't want to say "prostitute"). He sees my difficulty ... as I stumble out my compromise word "you are promiscuous." Yvon smiles "oh non, tu vois, je suis Catholique."[32]

Wonderful variation of a theme – "non angli sed angeli" – "not promiscuous; catholic ... " Out of the mouth of babes.

As we go out, the door of the next bedroom is open. The same reality to it: definably French Canadien – incredible "bad taste" ... but incredibly complete bad taste ... nothing out of its own taste – all of a piece. And that piece is of podgy flesh paste ... a plaster-of-Paris incorporation! Polychromatic! Like those same plastic flowers hung beside a same Christ. All of life as some bloody waxy image ... with all artificial colouring – like margarine, maraschino cherries. Pinks, powdered blues ... star-dust! It loyally revulses me ...

And in a wicker armchair in the corner ...

"Bonsoir Pierrot ... je m'en vais au Rock."[33] Yvon is gentle, polite ... saving him from a kind of smugness, from a holier than thou so clearly produce of his fortune with me ... his duty done for the day. A kind of sainting for sinhood.

"C'est Hughes, Pierre ... "[34] For one catastrophic moment I fear Yvon is going to say "C'est Hughes ... de Toronto." And bless him for not damning me with it.

Pierrot cocks a toe up at us ... bigtoes, barefoot. Same lifekit as Yvon. Jeans, plaid checkered shirt – plus a slight cravat, gold, knotted at his Adam's apple: Little Lord Fauntleroy as good Amurrican Bad Guy ... Bigtoe eyes me, still cocked (toenail cut and cleansed ... into me. Taken by bigtoe! – as decisive as that unseen flankglance penetrating me in church with Yvon still unsighted. Ears thunder. Sheer lust of life.

31 "I'm going back to the club ... I want to dance."
32 "Oh no, you see, I am Catholic,"
33 "Good evening Pierrot ... I'm off to the Rock"
34 "This is Hugh, Pierre."

"Cinq piastres?"[35] The voice is mine!

"Ouaé msieur ... non – sis ... c'est deja minuet pawssé."[36]

"Je raviens tantot." And I am walking along the Greyway with Yvon, leaving him at his club – Eden Rock (I didn't notice the name when we first came): odious name ... en anglais du reste.[37] Yvon smiles – "au revoir ... tu etais chic avec moi ... tu vas aimer Pierrot ... puis il adore le 69!"[38]

And I am at hotel, to my room, for the extra money ... and then back along Greyway to Pierrot ... it's crazy, but now I know I must honour this lifelust in me, or live still-born. And within an hour of Knowing Yvon (because only the Biblical "Know," with its capitalized "K" describes for me this kind of knowledge) I am knocking at the bullworthy door again. Betrayed back into life again by bigtoe! Pierrot answers ... barefoot. Back into his room where the bare-assed Christ bleeds down the pucker-plastered blue wall. Pierrot is reading Manorama – not a mag I know, I note wryly ... picture spread of other Pierrots. None of them is Pierrot: not that I expected – but none of them carries himself the same as my Pierrot. Something drastically different ... in the embodiment. Pierrot senses my thought train.

"Ils sont tous Americains ... Pas comme nous autres ... pas du tout."[39] So he knows too.

"Et pas meme comme vous autres, non plus."[40] I bless him the condescending compliment – pauvre Angluche que moi.[41]

"They are all Squares," – Pierrot is proud of his comment, and his English.

"And what are we?" I blurt aloud ... unwitting expecting an answer – the answer. He shrugs ... and quietly undoes himself ... his shirt aside, and over to his sink, washes hands, feet

"mais jamais ça" he smileblasts into me, patting his hand to his crotch ... "je ne le lave pas – pas jusqu'a apres ... ça goute vrai comme ca"[42] His smile seconds his point ... Yvon's teeth are singularly un-French-Canadian, almost Ipana bright – but Pierrot's are indelibly Canayen ... like rotted patates frites.

And in the shuddered observation note that I have some answer to my question – "what are we?" – it is this remaining capacity for some kind of life-giving dirt. "Pourriture noble" – that mould blooming on French grapes giving as lusher, richer wine. Pourriture noble ... and again sight those teeth, that green bloom of fleshbronze. "Ça goute mieux"[43] – Pierrot is hideously right. Bouquet and body ... tang that doesn't come in an economy bottle. All the difference between.

---

35 "Five bucks."

36 "Yes sir, no, yeah – it's past midnight."

37 In English, what's more.

38 "See you ... you were nice with me ... you'll like Pierrot ... and he loves 69."

39 "They're all Americans ... Not like us ... not at all."

40 "And not even like you guys either."

41 Poor English jerk that I am.

42 "But never that, I don't wash it, not until after ... it tastes real like that."

43 "It tastes better."

Pierrot is lying in an open loll on bedface, twitching me with bigtoe ... immense beckoner as my captive eye swallows it whole and am unawares into his manscape still at ten feet distance yet touched in a way that nobody has even touched me in my own community d'Angluche. Into it and feeding ... guzzling a sheer gluttony. Pierre is a slut ... I buy his body ... like over-ripe wine. (Dizzy said – was it in Coningsby? – that any man can like good wine, but it takes a connoisseur to enjoy bad wine ...) watch his body cocking, his hidden Man risen under bluejeans ... bigtoe down and rises rises me slowly rising with him rising me and in me am over to this manscape standing high over hawkeyeing this land this whole nation lying rampant under my very eye as abruptly I skydive onto this sweet prey, headfirst beakfirst onto swollen jeans nuzzle into the manmusk seeping through the closed fly breathing deep into this musk, as Pierrot grasp my head of hair, probing into my overbrush, then I am back up to eye this site again ... yes, ohhh yes, it is entire land spreadeagling there entire land I always knew was there, never absolutely lost, merely out of site, and now is confronting me hands down to grasp entry opening in earthquake of us the Man of Pierrot hidden still under winding whitesheath of underwear I reach in to palm the body that clasps my hand around and around its trunk to root Pierrot sifting thigh into my gasp as I bare the massed trunk of him, uncircumscribed land naked in fullflesh, head down to bigtoe in fierce Ptolemaic circumference sucking me down down inexorable to imbed me in this land as Pierrot certain of the way divest me still standing aside him, till free naked I am fallen back into the land to plow us under ... running my muzzle over this countryside surging up on me, alive into this banished world so suddenly restored whole ... swarm me over Pierrotland from all directions as this manscape gets on my horse to ride into me from every direction riding all of us at once everywhere we move is always everywhere moving to everywhere else in the free fields that wind unending up our valleyside to peak and black while Magpie highdives down with Icarus into a blue-skie seat that afterwarns me now I am in the same world that Pieter Breughel says he so rightly saw four centuries ahead of us but we forgot to entirely believe with him yet is so absolutely here now from the moment I bury my nose in this burning bush whose 10 inch stalk batters my nose is hoof of horse from that plowman behind (he doesn't notice Icarus skindiving below) each furrow cavalcading into this eternal Campagna worldwide that I bloodhound relentless into the wideyed distance that is all immeasurable foreground Pierrot given each brush and rock and clump pummels me roundalay in my mulburied bush ... as I eat this all edible manscape of Everyman feeding to my need, famished and it is true then that we poor Protestants deny the Body and Blood that was given for us as guarantee for our Sinworthiness ... denying the world on this Ptolemaic platter only circumscribed here by the bounds of that dire need I nurture herandnow while I pangful recollect divine Raphael's "Disputa" whose very detachment from all flesh whose very vaunting perspective would cut my tenuous umbilink with all this land still left latent in me to plant and plow to belated harvesting as I soar now above the Plowman all the land white and warm beneath my birth and soar centred over all circle down and down onto the head of this brave Plowman whose tow still touches the deep earth still imbeds us all in the land that feeds us as down now onto his head I engulf in my anxious mouth for that manmusk Pierrot said he kept clean for such meet needs while I mouth this landcocked head savouring oh at longed for last this noble rot to cleanse me knowing how rightly Moutarde de Dijon is gutted from the furrowed land while mere Amurrican hotdogs are clotted with the quickblotted tang that kills all taste of truth in Man so now I savour this sheer landmusk grateful that Pierrot thighrides into me so I grasp his bushimbedded rod striding up and down around its rot articulating my manhood at each gust of lush fleshscape salting me plow deep this landman that plows me to impending harvest Pierrot moaning steep in flush we fondle dandle clasp and run along the hedgerow by our shore I ply and row wondering this Icarean Sea wherein Pierrot has engulfed us both face to cockface and I sink to rise us again sucking huge in me the pod burst from this land spurting seed in our gathering mouthfulfilling with that first citric precision of spermblurt followed by the glut of man splashed in throat and gullet, spermspurt in nostril flaring wide as Pierrot grasps my ebbing trunk to earth of us lying thigh by thigh turning at last only to kiss the mutual musk of seed sown around our muzzle as he lopes last over to the basin to wash away any lost part of our deed as I watch knowing it is the lope I marry land to man in that conjugation all free flesh knows from a world that quakes with every step we take ...

Give him his cinq piastres, plus un piastre parce qu' il et minuit passé,[44] plus encore un piastre en souvenir de Pieter Brueghel (and his Icarus) and I am into the night air ... walking with sure stride. Where – where the hell are you going, I ask me? Till I am at La Place d'Armes ... and enter, and stand in the centre, free man with the key back in to the kingdom ... Christ – so that is it ... the veil rent from my eyes, all the Place sears in me, with a lucidity that ...

I don't stop running till I am at my hotel. Safe abed ...

Ahh – so that is it. The issue is joined – squarely (heinous multiple unwitting pun!): To see La Place, to write my novel, to come alive, again, I must fall, utterly. To share my love I must humiliate me ... must grovel. Stand waistdeep in the shit ... and then sing. Sing, goddam it, sing. I try to sing a little ... what? What shall I sing? I don't know anything to sing. Hit Parade is crap (and "crap" is just shit-substitute: crap is pseudo-shit, ultimate degradation.) And "Onward Christian Soldiers" seems so inappropriate ... "Things go better with Coca-Cola ..." – no good! I'd better do the Christian Soldiers. "Onwaaard Chrissstyennn Sooo-olldyerse ..." Ok – enuff. The main truth is out now – I've got to pay homage, or I'm done. Real homage – call it "hommage" – fealty to my Liege Man. So be it. But who will bless my God-damned soul?

Clock tolls 2 a.m. I feel immense relief now. An immense cleansing.

Surely that can't be right – "cleansing"? ... my dear Hugh, you are out of your mind! ...

Yes, but I'm back in my skin – I've jumped back into my skin ... back into my wits. ...

So it is a cleansing. That is it ... exactly what I do feel. Even more precisely – a purification: now explain that one – no I don't want to – I'd only explain it

44 his five bucks plus one buck because it's past midnight.

away. And then I could write a little essay about it – a tract for the times.

Purification – and the need, the intense need now to live again; all because of that accomplished deconstipation … that's it – a deconstipation – blew twenty years of shit out of me … opened me up again – tore the veil aside … and left me whole again, made me whole … holy: has made a man out of me again.

But you've just slept with two teenage male prostitutes! You are beneath contempt, defiled … a lifetime of honourable chastity sold for tripe …

No no no – that is not so – and my whole body shines now in the face of my mobilized accusation. What is it then? Have I simply accepted Hell – simply (good Protestant) reassured myself of it … my holy life insurance? And is this apparent defilement now the prerequisite of Heaven?

And the Place d'Armes … I ran from it … just as I was about to see it again, with ferocious clarity – see it as it has always been, latent in me … Why did I run – just as I was about to repossess it? Why?

Idiot – because it looked you in the eye the way Yvon looked you in the eye. It wanted you … and had you returned its gaze you would have been dismantled again. La Place is a voyeur … it hunts you as you it.

But I couldn't give me again. Not to La Place. Not that way.

Then you will never see …

As I turn to bed I see IT – that map – that goddam tourist map … the fatal flaw … the moment of lack of faith, when I looked at it, instead of the reality, instead of the Object itself. Throw it out. Throw it out! Too late. Pick it up … and those abject postcards I wanton bought – I see it now – as substitutes, as mediators between me, and the Object Incarnate. Notre Dame Church, the old Bonsecours Market, La Place Ville Marie, Nelson's Monument, the Bank of Montréal … Throw them out! No – insert them into Combat Journal. They are part of the Evidence … for and against. Ah – traitors! You betrayed me … You led me down the garden path – to smash, against Eden Rock. Well – you can stay now, to stand trial. Stick you in with the rest … over my marbleized face.

Asleep. It is 3 a.m. Preparing me again for my novel. I lunch with Luc Raymond to-morrow which is to-day. I will begin, right after Luc. These first days simply a false start. Completely wrong – the very opposite of what I wanted. Must eliminate them from the Novel.

DAY ELEVEN

He awoke at 10 a.m. … .His fever had gone – everything had gone – except the deep-rooting tail of his flu – the Place had gone – the sounds, the whole insite … Wordkilled! It was only now by making a conscious recollection of the Square that he had any idea of its existence at all whereas up till then it had been a constant corporate presence (or absence – with the vacuity of the absence as strong in hum as much a physical fact, as its presence – either way it was a corporeality).

Now there was simply a souvenir of La Place become merely the Square again: a tourist memory. He could itemize the Square and its approaches – make a mental effort to regroup it – he could systematically recover each fact: and in his mind's eye he walked up past Nelson's Monument with its bas-reliefs, to his right the City Hall and the Château de Ramezay – the first with its conscientious echo of every French palace anyone would remember, from Versailles to the mid-nineteenth century, and the second with its stonework that reminded him of the stonework of Ontario yeomen of the nineteenth (and of the twentieth) century. Reminded him that in Ontario the work was at once less organic and less rational (except – of course – the Pennsylvania Dutch Loyalist work in Waterloo Country ... he had owned a small frame house there once – back in his honeymoon days. At the same time the organic quality and the rational quality in the Ontario stonework was more divided ... He chuckled – Eliot would have talked about an incipient disso-ciation of sensibility and intellect ... He was sure that the modes of structure reflected the two provincial minds and sensibilities ... (again, someday, some no-man would write a doctoral dissertation on the matter – putting back together that which was still apparent to him, and meaningful to him, at a glance).

Left, down Notre Dame Street – Ostell's Courthouse with that inelegant extra floor added – and the string of dilapidated houses converted to drugstores, restau-rants and the smallware of daily lives – all habitant run ... these, down the left side of the street – till you came to St. Laurent – and the groundhole for the new Palais de Justice on the right. And then a final block of mid-Victorian high-pilastered Mannerisms that housed at ground level, better restaurants etc ... and all the quin-caillerie religieuses – all the art sacré ... giving on to the Place d'Armes itself. Again he could make a conscientious enumeration of the buildings – could describe to himself the Square – could even now place all those details such as the ironwork grill over the front door of the brownstone bank building, which details before had been submerged in the thunderous tide of the whole. In fact now he could give himself up to details – that was all there was left to do – go deeper and deeper into details ... in some effort to reconstruct the lost whole. It would have made a fasci-nating study. Each Building was a Style and each Style was an Era: and all of them was a Person – a Real Presence. Thus:

The Sulpician Seminary-Presbytery – Peasant Baroque – New France
–High Habitant

Ostell's extension of the Presbytery – Gentleman's Georgian – British Garrison
–Regency Beau

Bank of Montréal – Merchantman's Neo-Classic – British North America
–Responsible Governor

Brownstone Building – High Methodist Monstrous – Confederal Canada
–Man of Substance

Providence Life – Entre Deux Guerres Gutless – Roaring Twenties
–International Ivy Leaguer

New Bank of Montréal – The Organization Gentleman – Post-War Prosperity
–The Man in the Double-breasted Grey Flannel Suit

Banque Canadienne Nationale – Pert Packette – Post-historic – Noman.

And finally – the Church itself – that ampitheatre that crowned the Place. He could enter it now, could remember the colours, the gilt, the myriad arabesques … but in essence he noted, the Church he entered thus was Bartlett's Church again – the Cubicle – albeit overdecorated to his taste now.

But that was all he could do now – catalogue and index the Place – none of it impinged upon him – none of it implicated him in any other way than as a tourist, or as an art historian. If he wanted to probe any further, why then he could (as he had already noted to himself) undertake a doctoral dissertation. That way he would be forced to know the Square more thoroughly – would be forced to be a tourist not only in breadth, but in depth. Perhaps if he was lucky, he would achieve something of the awe with which, unwittingly, he had begun.

For the moment he had nothing. He was simply quiescent … worse: important! He was really incapable of seeing the Square and the Square could no longer see him. The reality of both had diminished disastrously. And for a brief moment he felt utterly capable of an office job …

… dinner again Au Fournil … marinating me in cretons, pigs feet and Marc. Plowing me under the black earth again – a rootling process. Till I am rich gourd again, inseminated by the earth I inseminate. Homefree! The points de diamant of armoire undulate me … and that constant reel (is it La Bolduc?) that must be at least a record and not muzak, that reel shudders me, till I almost uproot to dance my gourded embodiment … almost greensprout to sunshine. And then They are there – here … It can't be that! It is – I watch the incursion … They're back … in committee – Christmas Committee. Over a dozen – more like two. Watch them, commandeer their length of table, dividing the restaurant in two … in two worlds. Watch this amputation of us – What is it about Them? The conscientious cavalier? That's part of it, alright. The deliberated effort to be gala, to be effortless. After all, it is Christmas party. Then I see one of the girls – her movements are marionetted. How? Who pulls her strings? Smiles – then looks at her smile, swallows it after due time, moves right are gracious forward to waterglass – drinks gracious but by numbers. It is incalculably false … and touching. She sets the scene … for all these marionettes. They are all here in practice – practicing themselves … practicing their role – they're all on stage here, stage they've bought for the occasion. The girl – understudy Grande Dame … understudy First Lady. God – it's a portable finishing school – and this restaurant in le Vieux Quartier, is Exercise #17, for advanced students … The men are the same … all in their black priesthood – dinner-jacketed – all preparing their little manhood – their gentlemanhood. Tonight the exercise in Gentleman-Cavalier … Gentleman-with-Lady-on-the-Town … The Blond Beast across from me, direct over the shoulder of the First Lady – he is up already, before they are down, toastmustering the apprentice toastmasters. Fortunately no-one is listening … they are all practicing their own lines, for their ladies. Blond Beast – Blondebeeste … Oh how well I know thee and all thine! Blondebeestie flings arm about shoulder of second First Lady at his side in attitude # 39 – Easy Gallantry with Public Intimates ...

Hate – suddenly I am in hate – like bitch in heat! I am floundering steep in it. And come up battling, out of my pigs feet and cretons – come out ready revolutionary again. How I hate them – hate their gorgeous enforced gaiety, hate their apprentice overlordliness, hate ... and my teeth masticate the Marc till it splinters glass.

Watch the French Canadians at next table watch the Cavalieros. Like mongrels watching thoroughbreds, wistful in their whine. Yet accustomed to it ... cowed, comfortable in their pigs feet. How can they? How can they stand this orgy of insulting good mannerisms, practiced in situ? This entire restaurant turned over as scenario ... with live bit players – real nègres, us – the French Canadians ... the real inhabitants ...

So this is what I have done – I have completely metamorphosed – have passed completely over, changed B & B, become an inpatriate ... an exile within my own land – an In-Canada exile ... French Montréal my built-in American's Paris ... So be it! All I know is that suddenly this home, this centre, has been invaded, has been abruptly commandeered – as a launching site – for young Blondebeestes. *Real* red (*not* the red on the new flag!)

Second First Lady is in stride ... she moves, albeit only at the table with all the grace of a thoroughbred. Moves so well that suddenly the tableau she creates about her could be Tatler soirée. Blondebeeste beams approbation. She has carried herself well. And he achieves Exercise #92 – Winetaste ... the ladies eye him with gracious, if rather wide-eyed care ... and pronounces it palatable. He *is* magnificent ... those big baby-blue eyeballs, the slightly waved kempt blond hair – brushed not combed! the broad shoulders carrying a torso that is absolutely kouroi, in steep-V down to plaid cumberbund that serves as chastity-belt, for dinner at least. He is almost edible. God – he is God. My head reels now ... this is God. This is what we were all brought up to be ... this is what Methodist Sunday school boys finally emulate (and I remember the Roundhead Methodist All-Canadian Good-boy from the Rapido ride, whose hair, definitely, was combed not brushed!). This is what I was trained as (like some albino seal) at boarding school. This is the Complete Man. The Gentleman ... tonight in his role as Gentleman Adventurer, trading for Prince Rupert's Hudson Bay Company, from Montréal ... and still the coureurs du bois around to salute ... I can grovel now – want to grovel, or stand and salute, or strip naked, and have myself freely gelded, for God's sake. I am immense ... in him. He has me ... has me. Then I am murder – I nearly fell together for that? For that? Oh no – not now. Hate saves me from the pitfall. They know that hate ... they must. Their eyes peer out in furtive glances, beyond their crystal ballroom, out into our hinterland. Who is there? Who are we? Do we see them? Peer out the way those eyes peered from the Jaguar into the Flesh Market, the way the sailor peered at me ... at the obscene. And all their noise of gaiety is to keep their courage up.

Marc cocks my known hate ... Yes, I know these gaylords ... they are the final outcrop of Boy's Own Annual, and the Just So Stories. I know their schools ... Anglicanadian. Or facsimiles. With the cult of sport, and the curse on culture. I know their schools, their homes, their parents. The White Canadian Raj – and he is obscene ... because he failed, despite the public sacrifices of his balls.

Stare murderous across at my selected Blondebeeste. Do you have balls, dear? or is it just bang-and-go-back? Do you fuck? Steeply? Or just fun-fuck as Exercise #63: keeping fit by fiddling?

... ohhh – for brief moment again Anglicanadian Kouroi is lord again. Erect as falcon – all cock. His whole body is lingam. And I want to spreadeagle. And then I see he is untouchable – an Untouchable. Impermeable. Nothing will ever enter there; nothing ever come out. Autonomaniac. He is simply an exhibit.

Walk over to settle me in my rocking chair, just off their end of table. And Marc then. To their discomfit. And then, before going, in contempt, interrogate young assistant proprietor – his lithe body smiles me, but his eyes don't entirely meet mine – the presence of the Canadian Raj has fractured every eyeball in the place: no-one sees now. "Oh – it is a fraternity Christmas Party ... Delta Upsilon ... " And I remember from my university days that at McGill the DU's were #1 – the Respectable Drinking Club for Young Westmount. Everything fits. I know who's what as anticlimax ... because that very first movement, by the First Lady had defined the whole corpus. That first tentative movement of her hand ... hand that will never clasp the object ... never, never, never. Her cunt clamped as taut as they my assoul. The whole world shut out. As I turn to leave I see Blondebeeste #1. He has erected himself again ... for a moment our eyes meet. Head on. I breach me open ... blast assoul wide to swallow him – he looks bewildered, smile shrivels on his facade. I snap my teeth over the farewell of last Marc, and he dives into his wineglass. He knows I am prepared to kill.

Outside Blondebeeste is still there ... magnificent. How did he get there? Afront me. Erect. That great white smile. On parade. Christ. I did swallow him then, alive ... And when I see what it is – the Great White Elephant – the Marché Bonsecours – the one-time Parliament of Canada ... after his cultural precursors – and mine – had burnt down the old one, after the Rebellion Losses Bill over a century ago. It is him. But, Jesus, this has balls! Blondebeeste is but Complete Cube-marqué. And I, revulsed, am Complete Cube in revolt!

DAY TWENTY-ONE

He awoke to a phone call from René Lalonde ... who explained that he couldn't come into the centre of town to-day. It was an open invitation for Hugh to suggest they drop the meeting. But he wouldn't ... René wasn't going to get away with it again: he would have to face up to Hugh. Godin was right – René feared for his life ... his presence. Feared Hugh. Just as René's wife sensed him out ... had understood him at that last bitter-sweet dining together two years ago. Now they would meet. Man to man ... and he would palpably present René with his failure ... Failure which founded upon René's rejection of what Hugh was ... upon his rejection of the capacity to love and be loved. That was it – surely. Hugh systematically returned to haunt those who had rejected life, had rejected his surge to life ... returned gutted into life, bound up into it, and implanted in the zombies a recognition of their failure – implanted ... he specifically fertilized in them this budding self-recognition ... That is what he had done yesterday with Jack Macdonald – palped the failure till it hummed aloud in him.

Hugh sat grilling himself:

"Still why do I do it? Is it revenge? Merely? Revenging myself on the zombies. Going back and flinging my rejected potence in their lingering cockface, expunging their final twinge in this ultimate self-recognition I impose upon them – is that it? Raping them of their capacity to Know, to be, in this deliberate accusation ... Not allowing them to pass into limbo unaware of their disaster! Is that it?

"It is a madness ... each time I do it ... I bereave me of their love. In enforcing the confrontation I commit mutual manslaughter ... I use my own puissance, exspend it, in focusing them upon their self-secession. As I did again yesterday ... once, twice, thrice ...

"And each time I do it – I evade the Place d'Armes ... I rendezvous me away ... I betray it. The while yet carry it pregnant in us."

And then ruminant awhile on Eleanor's surrogate ... "I need oh so to penetrate – And I know that my triumph yesterday was again a failure ... Pyrrhic victory consuming the flesh I preferred untouched."

...

He sat thus saying his rosary, half-cocked ... snuffed the manmusk of the aureole, and as he did so he heard the roar of the traffic outside unwittingly, and he remembered the trainbells plumbing him at waketide, and the roar of the candles in the Church that were the roar of the woman's cocked cunt yesterday that he could hear at thirty yards ...

– (10:30 a.m.)

At noon he rendezvoused at La Grange – large nineteenth century barn remade as a restaurant ... half-way out of town. Enforcing his presence upon René who arrived even later than he did ... and promptly evaded their self-presence by whisking them both off for a drink with the propriétaire, to whom he would present his latest book.

"I watched René – so as not to frighten him openly. Watched him dazzle the propriétaire with his footwork ... And I realized that all of this was evasion ... all this inordinately able footwork. It was an effort to seduce me into an acceptance of the genius of René ... into the genius René should have had, and still vestigially could mobilize, but for some reason would not ... In the propriétaire's private office – a snugglery – full of Canadiana ... with a Gothic revival tabernacle as liquor cabinet ... and everywhere on the walls, sculptoral sketches of driftwood that palped me. Propriétaire appropriates us ... eats from our flesh ... Something is happening – I don't quite see what yet. Propriétaire recognizes my "nom prestigieux," distending me by flattery. René riposts by telling him how to improve his restaurant Xmas card by colour. Blatantly tells him ... over my deadened body that he kills en passant – The converse dallies ... and I watch René intermittently watching to see it I watch him ... Incredible performance his – he seduces those around him into instant intercourse with him ... and then cuts them off at the moment of penetration ... Requisitions sodomy and then rejects it. Sleight of hand. Legerdemain! He extracts your carnal homage and then withdraws in renewed assertion of self-virginity ... smug saying with his darting eyes – "écoute m'sieur pas moi ... "[45] He engulfs you in his own endlessly elegant intellectual impasse. It is an incalculably brilliant performance ... draining René of the very consummation it requisitions.

watch him autograph his book for propriétaire ... He does it with a flair, an empanachement that is a suivez-moi m'sieur for the rest of his ... his little assoul coquetting us ... and suddenly he is a woman ... a full bitch, in heat

watch the eyes of propriétaire – watch him watching René sign – same look on his face as on face of a communicant ... watching René hand voraciously ... each stroke of pen patently touches him ... And I realize again I watch a B & B process ... another transubstantiation! The book is the Host – the flesh passed in redemption to communicant. René plays God in witting disbelief. Wondering if I know he disbelieves himself ...

I am uncomfortable in the recognition ... because in it I recognize the fact that René is dead. Or that he is dying. And knows it.

the incredible "style Lalande." It is almost sufficient expiation of his defection.

lunch ... in a setting of phallic incitement that is only surpassed by the home of a respectable Headmaster I know ... everywhere objects ... outils du passe ... all the past implements of man's mastery of his world ... the tools of his mastery. Skates, hammers, planes, adzes ... And burl ware, wooden ware ... over the bar coqs gaulois ... while by the door, a piece of treen that is only exculpated from blatant phallicity by the self-evident fact that if the proprietor knew why he had it there, he wouldn't place it there!

sit in the back room ... I militant now ... eliciting from René his gradual avowal ... his eyes flee ... and then, accomplished, they slowly seek mine out again, no longer hiding his acceptation of an imperceptible impotence. And I know that his is another of these incredible cases – of a man who flees the implications of his procreativity as an artist, and so doing, subsides into that bitterness that is the fruit of his self-imposed barrenness.

"It is egotism ... to pursue my creativity," says René – "egotism ... besides, I'm cornered – I have a family. It is too late."

And I realize that I am listening to the excuses of a man who finally doubts his own genius. Who finally doesn't believe in himself! It is tragic. Because he was – only four years ago – a contender, and a conscientious contender, for the title of French Canada's Brilliant Young Man. And all his brilliance merely to mask the inner fright ... the fear to confront himself ... to hold up the mirror – to cockface. And the result, now, is not mature "responsibility" – but an end to love and thus, inevitably, an incapacitated responsibility. It is that that undermines me now ... this willingness to kill love ... to corrode it, in the name of falsified responsibility. An end to love ... My head reels at his reality ... reels at this rejection of life ... reels as I listen to all his reasons, his "right reasons" for his slow death – ending with his lucid recognition that there is nothing more to say in the novel, little more to be

45 "listen sir, not me."

said in films, nothing in theatre ... René is the dedicated non-man. "I am a zombie" – and his truth hurts me ... as it is meant to – because I am one of the slender final chances he has that he is not right. If he is right – then we are all dead. If I am right, he has betrayed himself. He cannot afford, for his own self-respect, to let me be right ... But I am his last chance – I hold a last grasp on the necessity to love. If I can love more than he hates – then we are both saved ... I watch him watch me ... watch me stagger – the jacksaws on the wall are sharks whose teeth roar me, and again the objects are militant, are lethal – I hang on, hang on, while René watches me – and then by an ace I have withstood his betrayal – have withstood it by watching him ... and remembering my inalienable right to love him – I shout over the din of lunchers and saw teeth – "Mais je vous aime bien, René. Je vous aime ... tu ne peux pas m'arracher ce droit! ... "[46] and so saying, I have overcome that total solitude his tentative hate imposed ... That solitude that is death – for us both. And as I do – I note that his eyes are back into me again ... he is open, if incredulous ... as he leaves he gives me his new novel – and so doing confutes everything he has said ... I sit, half an hour, ruminant ... Men only exist through love – and love has never been so important as now ... art is love – even an art of hate is love – the optimism of despair – creating despair in hope of hope ... back into town by bus, basking in the armpitted air searing us all.

Into the Château de Ramezay museum – as relief – haven't had the energy to insite it before now – need it for the novel – All these tawdry coins and mementos leave me cold – there is something obscene to them – like collecting offal ... some perverse secular iconolatry. This whole museum a reliquary for those who have not the courage to avow eternity, but revel in secular sainthood ... I want to brush my teeth. It tells me nothing about us ... only impedes us. And then I realize how wrong I am. I realize that this museum is not important now for what it tells us about who we were ... but for what it tells us about who we thought we were (just like academic texts ... but with better, more spontaneous evidence) – Here is absolute, convincing, delightful, despairing evidence of the Romantic Vision of Canada: the image of the Cavaliers as against the Roundheads. Image of flying canoes, and eternal Brueghelian habitants, and grand seigneurs, and Princes of the Church, and Soldiers of the Queen, and Loyalists whose fidelity is to the Grail, no matter how many times changed in outer form. Everywhere I turn, the evidences of this high hopefulness: and suddenly, as I recognize this reality ... as I recognize that this museum is not what it purports – a witness of some distant past, but rather the faith of a past still upon us as to what that past was ... then I can enter into it, and partake of the faith, and rejoice in it. This is the equivalent of the *Heroes* by Kingsley or *Westward Ho* ... it is a great-grandson of *Waverley*: and it is legitimate.

What an oaf I would be not to rejoice in it. Its very language defines my feeling about me as I contemplate the defection: I would be a "churl." And suddenly the clucking hen by the door, who sells tickets as a nun might a piece of the true cross, is no longer a hopeless impediment to serious museology – but an essential counterpart to what this Château has to say to me. Suddenly she **is** (and no-one can take it from her) a Mother Superior ... and her gabbling over the phone, the

46 "But I love you René. I love you ... you can't tear that right away from me."

sale to me of a History of Old Montréal, this triumphant report to headquarters of another infidel centre breached, this all makes sense.

I look at the Church rooster ... "seventeenth century, from the Church at ... " Its style is indefatigably mid-nineteenth century: its full prosaic embodiment, its man-of substance stance, its eyes that deal with one thing at a time ... no – it is not Baroque, let alone peasant Baroque, or anything like. But who cares – the imagination of this museum is Victorian Baroque. So be it. Somebody it will change – probably soon. It will become a residence for the City, for distinguished visitors. Or a home for the Mayor. Or an official reception centre. It will be restored to clinical exactitude. The false nineteenth century tower should be removed. The false pointing of the stonework rectified. It will be magnificent ... like the White House. It will be finer in every way – except one: it will be a fake! A requisite, efficient, fake. Give me the secular reliquary. The academic stage-setting is a false verity.

down to the Flesh Market ... for a last visitation – struck by the noise of the furniture – even scraped as it is – it is full of rumble and hum. And as I unwitting recognize this – unwitting admit this sound, I realize that modern noise is merely visual! Things say they are noisy with colour, but they in fact aren't noisy at all ... they merely assert stridence, by telegram. As in op and pop art: art for a society of voyeurs ... out of touch.

and then to La Place ... muzak Xmas carols which deafen my earing ... muffle my earscape, pulling a sound barrier over it. And I duck into the Church, blinded by the muzak ... and within I hear again despite the whipcreme of muzak without ... Watch the Church grow me – and wonder if it is not in truth for me English Gothic revival to which has been added the Catholic folk earscape we all lost when Henry VIII went cuntcrazy, and cut the Church. Is that not it? This is the absolute restitution? Not of a dogma – but of a reality that we lost ... the restitution of sound and light?

out again, the muzak plops over my head blurring the Square again, blinds my earing ... and I wade my way through to the B of M ... It is performing for me ... a songfest, of carols, for the entire Bank caste, in the main hall. A command performance for me ... mobilizing it as absolute testing site. Too good to be true. "Good King Wenceslas" ... and I watch the room carefully – yes, this is all the music this temple could permit ... the crème caramel of Xmas carols in modern guise. It occurs harmlessly within the flanking black marble pillars, leaving them absolutely untouched. I watch the people tiptoe in and out between carols. Tiptoe because earing is absent – that's why they tiptoe. Because no-one can really hear the music. Whereas in the Church, people straggle in and out, scuffle the aisles, stand or sit as may, mumble, talk, move. And they can do this, because their local noise doesn't affect the fundament of earing ... doesn't in any way obscure the thunder of site, is in fact part of it. Tiptoe music is music for deaf mutes. It proves impotence.

the choir. Forty zombies and a mistress. Watch her. In front of her grand piano – in green dress for merry, caught between choir and the careful ranks of the caste ... beginning with the King Cubes in the front row. I watch embarrassed ... by her. By her aggressive corporal innocence. Her hands berate the air, fingers twitching as though marionetted ... as though finger, arms, and body were run by plucked strings. No body movement as such – but a remote-controlled ferocious grace militant. She is the vicarious annual felicity of the entire staff. Their optimum formal abandon. Fuck by numbers! Her accredited greensleeves ass bounces and bumps, jabs the clean-brownnoses of the King Cubes (who religiously blow these noses after every second number) ... the choir mouths the Infant Birth. Such an earnest wholiness. Those eyes that drool goodness (take home a package to-day, you owe it to yourself) ... in the backrows, those balding men, from 22 to 62 ... all on a careful ladder of irrelevance.

they carol the Ukrainian bells ... and for a brief moment the sound barrier is threatened. For a brief moment there is multiplicity of sound ... and the hall threatens complicity ... but finally it is just muzak, live. Even the negro spirituals are harmless. And then everyone is cordially trooped around the Xmas tree for a final song ... It is a remarkable achievement. No-one breaks ranks – although there is no formal ordering.. Quite simply everyone keeps his station ... King Cubes first ... I don't know them ... but they are easy to spot in their dark blued suits firmly tailored to their square root. A certain elegance – rather like prize steer. Groomed for show. Their shoes have thinner soles. They wear a coloured silk handkerchief (no-one under a general manager does so). Their flesh is well kept, full ... they look immeasurably benign. They are convincing. Surprisingly convincing. Without much trouble I spot #s 1 and 2. Perhaps two of the most powerful men in the nation. They are self-effacing Big Daddys. They sound (when they talk) as if they were walking on unending broadloom – it is a kind of deep purr that their entire body exhales (like a deepseated aftershave lotion). And I remember now there was beige broadloom in their executive suite whence I was ejected for "loitering." One of them imitates the style Grand Seigneur ... bends to shake little boys hands ... genuinely wants the part of Big Lord Fauntleroyalty. He is the less convincing. The other remains immutably erect. With just the slightest concession to humanity in a certain stoop to his shoulders that his tailor has carefully matched.

A son with one of them. Junior version. Age 17? He has the felinity of youth – but already over that imposes the same kind of jerked electronically controlled order that entirely governed the body of the choirmistress. His brain keeps sending out messages to his body. Do this. Do that. Don't do that. And his body conforms correctly, but always a split second after the order, so that there is that accusative slight divergence ... Mind over matter it is called. Or intellect over sensibility. The beginning of the long slow death. Yet the boy is still alive ... his eye catches mine. Out of 400 in the hall ... he catches mine ... and follows, the way a dog follows its food ... follows instinctively. Rightly. Why? How does it happen that way? How do we know where life is ... and where death has been self-imposed? I don't know. But that boy's eyes are still gazing into mine, down through my gut, and out the end of my cock that sees the thunder of the Church candles again ... and I know that he will always carry my eyes with him – whether he knows or not – my eyes will always be a warm wound feeding him.

I slip around behind the tree, through between some wreaths to the evident disgust of one of the choir zombies, self-assured elder of the Mother Bank. He glares in disbelief at my deviation. And at my green corduroy suit. And when a child passes the same way moments later gives to the unfortunate the chastise-ment he wanted to give to me. It is not lost on me. He is obviously distressed by my presence, my reality. Outraged in a way he doesn't understand. But at least he has the sense to realize that he is outraged. And five minutes later, armed with his Veteran's badge, his blue waistcoat, and the immense moral superiority of his par-ticipation in choir he accosts me with a rigid politeness that it deathful – "Are you looking for anyone?" – meaning "How dare you be No-one, and be here!" And with a hate that more than matches his, and drawing on nine generations of Canadian Loyalist blood, the fact that my family fought at Lundy's Lane, Batoche, Vimy, and Dieppe, and that I still use my great-grandmother's crown Derby din-ner service, I square him off ... "no, I am not, thank you" – and my eyes warn him that he has encountered something more solid even than his own cubicle ... because for that moment I am at once utterly opaque and absolutely lethal ... And he withdraws. It is only then that I recollect that the Chief Cube here is in fact a relation of mine ... is In the Family ... the Mother Bank is in sorts a pocket borough of mine, metasocially speaking. And it is that subterranean reality that has quailed that Senior Citizen and Choirboy: and again I knew it is not what you say, it is the way you say it ... and the way that you say draws from B & B ... always. Blood is thick-er than heavy water.

A brief visit to the Bank Museum ... in the corridor beside. In contrast with the Museum in the Church this is simply an illustrated text! In the Church the display incidentally adds a text to the reality displayed. Slight distinction – but it is all the difference in the world between the two civi-lizations: French-Catholic, and Anglo-Protestant: the one is still immersed in reality, the other is detached from it. The Catholic display doesn't need the text, the label. The Protestant one doesn't need the display. One is B & B; the other is skeletal. The one invokes reality ... drowns you in it; the other merely recollects it, at one remove. In the Church I don't know which is real after I have made my visit ... the Church or its miniature museum? Both are deeper than life. In the Bank now I know that neither is real ... each is less than life.

Peruse the brochure on the new Mommy Bank Building ... entitled (Believe it or Not?) "Historic Home-coming ... !" First page (happily) presents a message of Faith, Hope, and Charity-that-pays from the President, along with his photo (looks like a shorn beaver!).

... A list of those who built the new office – "To These Belongs the Credit ... " Including the Beaver Demolition Company!

... the new post office included in the Bank Building ... and I recall now that picture of the old Place, on the hoarding of the site of the new BCN Building ... showing the Post Office built in 1876 ... splendiferous! Of course in this brochure a bad-angle photo is shown of it in demolition. But it didn't need "son et lumière!" It was a Thunderer ... and its thunder ignited! I know! (all I need to do is look at its contemporaries still erect – the Life Association of Scotland building for one – Côte Place d'Armes). Now it is displaced by this "man in the grey flannel suit!" – double-breasted of course. And above it, the Canadian Ensign of the day ... equiv-alent to a regimental tie. A section entitled. "Statistically speaking." Great – dig this – it weighs 80,000 tons! As much as the Queen Mommy – (I mean the Ship, the Q.E.) Vital statistic ...

... modern comfort and convenience for the staff ... an architect's rendering of the lounges ... in the "modern idiom." Christ – have these people no sense of irony! Those hollow figures (style Bernard de Buffet) they show shadowing their way through the cafeteria **are** the reality the modern idiom has created (no wonder they all want and need Tigers put back in their tanks!)

I need an injection ... back up to Jack Macdonald's office. He has gone. But the picture of his great-grandfather is what I wanted. And beside it – that of Arthur Meighen ... those eyes are what I am after: of a wounded deer, wide, deep ... infinitely sensitive. The eyes that we lost in Canada for two generations – eyes that were veiled over in deference to Mackenzie King's mommyfuckering, and his single crystalline ball! Meighen – the last King Cube. "Unrevised and Unrepented": he was a man ... and a human. And he was defeated – and Canada with him – by $ from this Mommy Bank!

Back through the Place – still muzaked ... stop in at Religious Boutique sur la rue Notre Dame, to gorge on chalices and monstraunces and chasubles (Meighen's eyes opened me back up again). And now, as my ears drum, I know why I came in ... opened up, I wanted to hear. Pick up a medium chalice ... it freights my hand, reverberant as I lift – and I understand the meaning of the phrase "en or massif." [47] I can hear again. The rest is irrelevant. As I go out the door I find my hands instinctively plying my mittens ... kneading them into a sculpting of the madonna by the chalice. Hearing makes a sculptor of me!

Return to hotel ... puissant[48] (no wonder the French Canadians at one time liked to use the formal title – "La Puissance du Canada," for the Dominion of Canada ... and how typical, that our inferiority has even frightened us away from the magnificent meaning of "Dominion!" – because that is what Canada is about ... dominion over four million square miles of land, by a resolute handful of peoples).

I realize that what has been restored to me these past days is my self-respect. I have gone through Hell for Heaven's sake ... and found my human dignity. Bless Meighen's eyes, bless the chalice, bless the Mother Bank and the Great White Elephant and the Flesh Market and the Sphinxes Large and Lesser and the Wedding Cake, and the Greyway and the Front and Holyrood.

...

at 8 p.m ....en route to the Church, for a mass in the Chapelle du Sacré Coeur ... I still can't get over how appropriate it is, how insanely right, that it is a copy of Raphael's "Disputa" that is over the entry! – the Renaissance Dispute over Transubstantiation ... Of course Transubstantiation won ... but the irony is that Raphael's depiction of this victory of B & B over the forces of disembodiment was painted in 3-D, complete with vanishing point ... his very mode of depiction was the Anti-Christ that killed King Cock! (Should have called my Novel *The Chalice and the Cock* ... last of the Henty books!)

47 in massive gold
48 potent/powerful

After, talking to Père Amyot again ... talk the dualism of body and soul. The way he says things is the way I need. But what he says can scarce absolve me of my particular Protestant Penitence for the Body Despised and Rejected. Canadian Jansenism. Boys bathing in private at college, and wearing a bathing suit. How can I tell him (darling eunuch!) that phallus is flower. Why bother?

He is on the "mystic origins of Montréal." He is right. There is a mystery to the origins of Montréal – a movement of the spirit. Why deny it? And it lingers. And after – tour the presbytery ... the poverty of it accuses me again as Angluche. Like the poverty of Canada's best paper – *Le Devoir*. I understand these wounds of French Canada now that I understand my own so much better ... and I hate me, us, for causing their wound. The *imitation* French Canadiana, with which the presbytery is largely furnished. Reproduction chaises à la capucine, beside sensitive eighteenth-century Canadian Regence chairs in butternut, with a modern bargain basement refinish!

The père persuades me to stay for the Christmas Eve Mass ... He is right: I should – if only for the novel.

...

After the service and the tour Hugh went to dine at Paul Marie's ... chef-martyr. He felt alone ... tried to phone another prey for his novel. But it was masturbation pure and simple. He didn't know why, but it clearly was. A penitence again. And the fear of being alone to confront himself.

Afterwards walked down la rue Bonsecours ... Papineau House (there had been something magnificent about Papineau House (there had been something magnificent about Papineau – and he thought of Toronto's equivalent – Wm. Lyon Mackenzie ... "that runt" – the words spat loud of him. The distinction between the two men was, alas, symptomatic of the two cities. After all his book was by implication a *Tale of Two Cities*, Montréal was his Mona Lisa ... and Toronto "the Second City." And he knew that he would have to write one of his Toronto, finally – second half of this diptych). Around him Le Vieux Quartier droned slightly in the snow-scurries. The St. Lawrence Seaway was dead under ice. He dropped into Le Fournil for a nightcap of Marc. Talked to a young couple performing at the Saltimbinques, the theatre at the corner ... they belonged to the new generation of dedicated androgynes ... the new "neuters" – promised to sterility for the sake of the arts ... such a creative sterility. But they were suspicious of Hugh's interest in French-Canadian arts, and remained impermeable to his vulnerability ... He returned to his hotel – the Old Hen of La Petite Place. He was beginning to forgive himself for staying there – every man needs a lair in Mother Earth. For the first time in days he sat down relaxed to make notes direct for his novel.

After his lunch with René, Andrew stopped in at the Château de Ramezay – he had been in Le Vieux Quartier for three weeks, but still had not visited it, it was unfinished business. On his right as he entered, a plaque listed "Those Who Have Occupied the Château":

La famille de Ramezay – 1705-1745 (with 16 children!)

La Compagnie des Indes – 1745-1764

Les Gouverneurs du Canada – 1764-1849

The American Army of Invasion (under General Montgomery) 1775-1776

and the Commissioners of Congress, Benjamin Franklin, Samuel Chase and Charles Carroll

The Special Administrative Council (Replacing Parliament after the Rebellion) 1838-1841

The Ministry of Public Education – 1856-1867

The First Normal School of Montréal – 1856-1878

Laval University of Montréal (Law and Medicine) – 1884-1889

The Magistrate's Court – 1889-1893

The Antiquarian and Numismatic Society of Montréal – 1895-

It was an astonishing list, reflecting the entire history of Canada ... and a large portion of the western world ... a Governor from the days of Louis XIV; the great trading companies of the days of the gentleman-adventurers; the pro-consuls of the British Empire; the American revolutionaries ... and Bennie Franklin himself, bringing the first printing press to Montréal, and installing it in the Château itself!; the surge of public education in the Victorian world; the courts of law ... and then, lastly, the museum – a world under glass like TV!

On the far side of this another plaque ... "Les Premiers Colons de Québec ... ils ont été à la peine, qu'ils soient a l'honneur."[49] And he remembered being told that the French-Canadians supported the project of restoring the Vieux Quartier[50] as a monument to their own history, whereas in fact the architecture dated mainly from the English regime. C'est la vie!

He entered the Council Room – first on the right – the Hervey Smythe views of Québec in 1759 ... an aide-de-camp to Wolfe – magnificent scenes: the interior of the Jesuit Church, of course, perhaps the finest ever built in North America ... certainly the most voluptuous. The Intendant's Palace. Part of world that was described in its day as civilized as anything in France outside of Paris itself. The series of scenes by Richard Short – lunar landscape. And then, but fifty years later, the watercolours by Colonel Cockburn showing a pastoral Canada, at once Gainsborough and Regency Gent and Habitant.

And fifty years after Cockburn – the High Romance scene by Henri Julien

49 "They were heavy worked, may they be heavy honoured."
50 Old Quarter

of Dollard des Ormeaux au Long Sault, Mai 1860. ("notre histoire est une epopee"[51] – how the modern French Canadians hate that – but then they haven't yet got to the stage where they have no history left; we're way ahead of them in our uprootedness! – thanks to the search for the All-Canadian Identity – careful, don't rock the boat there ...).

And after Julien, some illustrations from "The Habitant," by "Dr. Drummond." More of Maria Chapdelaine's habitant Canada. Yet Andrew wondered if the picture of that society had ever been better shown. All evidence was that that was what French-Canadian life was indeed like. And in any case the new Quiet Revolution was as Romantic as the rest – it drew heavily on a Romantic Vision of life ... although that was beginning to run dry (his lunch with René proved that decisively!)

He went around jotting his notes ... "the uniforms ... these were the Man ... the Cocked Hats! ... The Flag of the Rebels at St.-Eustache ... a real Flag ... I can honour that!"

Outside in the hall a couple of tourists were talking to la vielle poule about the seige of Khartoum, as though it were yesterday ... and as though it belonged in and with the Château. He listened incredulously ... and then he realized that of course it did – that was part of the reality of this place ... a live tradition, albeit going dead. And then he finished his circuit ... admired the room itself ... its proportions, high ceiling, neo-classic mantlepiece ... and passed into the Church Room – full of "the white and the gold" (Costain's Canadianism) and on into the stairhall where a lithograph of Toronto, Canada West, hung cruelly over the door in contrast with the Church carvings behind ... Toronto – ca. 1850 – so flat and so sullen. So grey ... blur of black-and-white. He realized that he always saw Toronto in black-and-white – felt it in black-and-white ... even though this lithograph was in colour. Whereas Montréal so grey, was always colour. He mused: colour TV in the long run would probably have more impact on Toronto than on any other city in North America.

"The French Salon ... that Louis XV armoire from the presbytère at Trois Rivieres ... unique example of French-Canadian Baroque (what was the name of that Bishop from Three Rivers who brought in Belgian craftsmen in the eighteenth century? ... that must explain this piece) – strong in black and gold ...

"The Indian Room – 21 cradle boards! Idiotic ... but God – they are splendid. Curl the hair on my ass! The painting of Indian Chiefs, 1841, in full regalia ... fantastic composite: part habitant, with their ceintures flechées; part Soldier of the Queen, with their silver medals, their guns; part Indian, with their moccasins, beadwork; part Civilian Gents, with their stove-pipe top-hats; part Black Trash ... A hideous parody of the Canadian "melding pot"!

The beadwork on the clothes in the cases ... rings my ears – Our artists have never achieved what these Indians did ... their beading is abstract, yet it concentrates colours of the land – I keep smelling, hearing, feeling that land that the Garrison Officers painted, that Paul Kane painted, that the Group of Seven painted (though their paintings are so silenced!) No – we have never achieved that entire harmony with our environment that these people did. That full-

51 Our history is an epic (a line from the Canadian national anthem, "O Canada")

dress for example, in the case to the left of the door ... It is Wild Turkey and Great Horned Owl, and granite and doe and Cardinal Flower and blueberry and ... I suppose that the closest the white man came was with the French-Canadian Parish Church ... the eighteenth-century stone rubble church, its walls scraped from the land, and its guts an improbable Glory! Baroque Habitant! And after that, the next best, the Honest Ontario Yeoman's red-and-white brick home, squatting over the earth it masters but disclaims. I suppose that Expo '67 will be our endeavour at syntheses. I must remember to force me to see it!

Still the noise raucous in my ears ... sweetly raucous (these Indians had rings on their fingers and bells on their toes ... and music from coast to coast. Real music, of the inner ear.)

And with this, a curious filth – a sheer brute dirtiness to it all. The relics of the life, of the barbarity (they didn't use toilet paper, or Ipana! I'm soiled that way I guess). Combination of filth (I shrivel) and sheer beauty (I distend). At least there is nothing mediocre to it.

Drawings by Zachary Vincent ... last of "the pure blood Huron Chiefs" (sounds like a line from Hiawatha ... or Pauline Johnson) – alias Telari-o-lin. Depictions of himself – habitant-cum-Indian-cum-American primitive.

... one Eskimo soapstone carving – how bogus it looks here, amongst the blood and slush. It looks like a civil service memorandum on Eskimo Art; like a white man seeing with Eskimo eyes. Overfed Eskimos, pensioners-in-the-making. Affluent Eskimos, making Archetypes for Suburban Living! (stop, stop, you fool – it's the only art that English Canadians have produced in two centuries that has drawn international attention!)

- photos of the western paintings by Paul Kane. 1840's. Indianecdotes for the eternal Women's Auxiliary. Superb – dammit.

... can't get over the squalor of the room: yet magniloquent. It's like being in Notre Dame ... these colours are windows out into my world."

He went on into the Reception Room – admired the flexed flesh of la chaise os du mouton (those bones weren't dry!), and then turned to the walls which were covered with prints, paintings and drawings of Montréal. Montréal everywhere ... Again, the windows, in, and out, of him. Window-pictures ... For insites, as against picture-windows, detached views. Beginning with the series by R. A. Sproule, 1830 ... Andrew knew the series well – had almost bought a set once; now they were too expensive. The "View of the Champs de Mars" ... with the British fifers parading, the habitant audaciously antedating quite firmly Kreighoff! View of Montréal from the St. Lawrence – pillbox in the Ile Ste-Helene foreground (toy soldiery) – and the hulk of Notre Dame Church domineering the town as it was intended, matching even the bulk of the mountain-couchant, the Greatest Sphinx. St. James Street with the first of the Mommy Banks and those Flaxman bas-reliefs over its lower windows. View of the Harbour – the ships parked where now the grain elevators heave to ... Notre Dame Street – so largely the same in feeling, from Nelson's Monument (that Nile crocodile *is* immense – with Nelson looking like some sad Napoleon, his back facing the river; while at the end of the street the body of old Notre Dame stops the street so happily – interrupting the vanishing point before it can vanish with the observer – in Toronto one so often vanished thus. Finally –

La Place d'Armes itself ... a view of the original Church still flanking the wide-eyed facade of the new Gothic building. And as he felt his way through the window-picture around that original body he knew that it did to him as an exterior view what the interior of the new Church did to him now ... both bellied him. And he felt about the old Church as he did still about Notre Dame de Bonsecours when he circled it ... "l'animal!" The new Church was preconceived; the original Church had been conceived, and still conceived him ... made him divinely animal rampant!

Patten's "View of the City" ... 1760 ... showing it as an Eternal City. Making him realize that Québec was not Canada's – was not North America's ONLY Eternal City ... Montréal was a good seconder. Patten's engraving had the thunder of the waters in it, and the mountain was congested with cloud ... He carried on around the room ... a print of the Jacques Cartier map of Montréal as Hochelaga, 1535 ... the palisaded Indian town ... and another by Whitefield of the city in mid-nineteenth century – a prosperous print, an "American View," bird's-eye ... The Protestant Episcopal Parish Church – 1822 ... ahh – the complete Cube ... a final Lower Canadian Adamesque variant of Gibb's St. Martin's-in-the-Fields (Parish Churches for Englishmen Everywhere – from Sydney to Bombay to Philadelphia to Québec to Toronto!) And another stern's-eye view of Notre Dame de la Place ... showing how much it also was cubicular. The French Canadian had really only captured its personality by doing the interior over again ... and underneath Bouchette's description of it "as a chaste specimen of the perpendicular style of Gothic architecture of the middle ages." Well, externally, it was indeed "chaste" – positively falsetto! But that interior! – that made up for the chastity ... and Bouchette going on to write (1832) "the embattlement parapets at the eaves of the flanks, which are peculiar in the crowning of Gothic edifices, are omitted on account of the great quantity of snow that falls in this country in winter. The severity of the frost, also, prevents considerably the decoration of buildings in cold climates."

James Duncan's "Panoramic View of Montréal," with the Marché Bonsecours giving a St. Petersburg air to what might otherwise be some medieval European port ... the Marché in that setting so clearly a descendant of Palladio, Inigo Jones, Gibbs and Adam. With that peculiarly English Trinity – central portico and clear balancing units at the end of each wing (he knew perfectly well, though he couldn't demonstrate it and wouldn't have if he could have, that this architectural Trinitarianism – Crown – Lords and Commons – were all one and the same – and thus to call an Englishman a Cube, much less a Square, was essentially wrong!)

Krieghoff's magnificent scene of La Place d'Armes in winter ... with the Mother Bank as backdrop ... (the one he had an old postcard of).

a view of skating on the river, along the Front ...

Montréal eying him thus from all sides ... He slid out of his view, into the Numismatic Room, and for a moment was lost, couldn't see at all ... till he finally focused on a single coin ... and stopped short as he realized that to look that coin in the eye was to look his own eye in the face and he felt suddenly molested by the fact. Decidedly numismats, like philatelists, were peeping toms!

A glance at the Canadian silver in the portrait gallery (more bad portraits of general interest in this room than anywhere else in Canada) ... but he was tired, and there was no response till the large Amyot Monstraunce caught his eye, and he peered through its pale crystal eye and fell and saw despite himself a series of views of Le Vieux Quartier ... saw Whitefield's aerial map superimposed upon Kreighoff's Place upon Sproule's Old Notre Dame (if only they had left its tower as Campanile in La Place) upon Patten's Thames-side view upon Hochelaga upon La Place that he knew all through the eye of the Monstraunce. Suddenly he realized that he had an importunate hard-on ... and he retreated into the next room, stopping haphazard to die slowly in front of a piece of oak from Jacques Cartier's ship, La Petite Hermine ... behind him the stonework gate from the Champlain family garden in France.

At 10 p.m. that night Andrew was back in his room and started to write his diary which was really his novelette. He was quite aware of that now.

" ... *after the visit to the Museum and the Christmas Folly at the Mommy Bank, a brief rest, and then dredged me from bed to attend a Mass at the Church of Notre Dame ... Père Amyot had invited me – une Messe des Adorateurs Nocturnes, dans la Chapelle du Sacré Coeur. As I stumped along rue Notre Dame on the raw of my knees I wondered what the hell I was doing ... Why this? Heaven knows I've "done" the Church – and I don't need La Chapelle du Sacré Coeur. One tidbit, anyway; going past the Providence Life Building, the bas-relief on the walls ... I could laugh – "that's it ... la vie anglaise, toujours en bas relief." [52] But the joke was tired.*

Into the side of the Church and down to the Chapel. It looks worse than ever. Bloated with bad taste. Slump into my seat – bored. Les Adorateurs Nocturnes ... and I look around at them ... all that little world of Gabrielle Roy's Tin Flute ... these distortions – the remnants of a people! Not one of them looks "right" – each one is a maimed man ... too short, or too long, or tuberous, bulbous, almost leprous – the people that the Quiet Revolution left behind. And I remember talking, at La Presse, a couple of days ago about these "Adorateurs Nocturnes" – God, we laughed at the very phrase ... as I had those ages ago laughed with Jack Greg, about Audubon's Great Auk. The very phrase somehow defined the laugh – said everything ... Les Adorateurs Nocturnes! Well there they are – with their Monstraunce-medals pinned on their lapels ... Adoring the Nocturnity! The weak, the disabled, the ill-born, the poor-of-head ... and above them, the giant religious murals – including Dollard des Ormeaux and his band at the altar before setting out to save the world for New France. It is pathetic. I revel in my dismay – no wonder French Canada needed a revolution.

And then Père Amyot has sent someone to accompany me in their service ... and the kindness disarms me completely – it is the kindness here, the complete sincerity of these blockheads. The Père processing now, with his acolytes in white gown ... and they are mobilizing all the apparatus of a Mass. I watch, detached – alas – and then, faute de mieux,[53] up to take Communion insubstantially, out of courtesy to the Père because I had asked him the other day what he would do had I presented myself at the rail, when I had truly wanted to, and he had said "you are in communion with us in the spirit ... I would give you the Host." So I went up – and ate that bad bread. And then back in my seat, made patient again.

---

52 English life is always in bas relief

53 for lack of anything better

An acolyte brings in a silken white and gilt-shot umbrella ... and Père Amyot is kneeling by the altar in a complete new outfit (this is a Liberace Program!) ... I have been thinking that while the Mass apparently makes these people submissive, it makes me militant – or should ... though to-night I am too tired. Only the acolytes focus me desultory.

Then they are sifting again ... the Adorateurs Nocturnes are sifting some from themselves up to the altar and taking the great candles and Père Amyot is still dressing ... I am excited – and revulsed. More incense – it's worse (and better) than the old-time train shuntyards. There is something obscene to it all – something disgusting ... this man up there swathing himself in raiments. Bathing himself and us in incense. Something filthy to it ... the White Mass – of white, blanched flesh. Something incorporeal ... Why do I revulse? Why suddenly want the Mass Black? Why do my nuts shrivel ... Is it a moment of gelding? Is that it? Something is awry. It's all upside down here ... Our whole religion is inside out then – our expulsion from Eden occurred when we lost our nuts! Is that it? Yes it is. And these people are consecrating the lost nuts ... consecrating the loss – with these same nuts ... Yet all these men here are fertile – hideously fertile (it is so evident – fertile in the way the wild boar is, sullen with unspent vehemence). No – I don't understand anything any more. And then it is too late to try ... the whole apparatus has turned on me, is moving down the aisle on me and we are all down the aisle with that machine behind me and the Father under his umbrella, with that indescribably vulgar Monstraunce peering at me ...

(and as I type this diary now I realize that my novelette is in fact some deeper assault on reality than I cared to admit. It is war ... between reality and me – I'll call this diary a Combat Journal: That's it – my Combat Journal – I'll stick a label on the front cover ...

I want to laugh ... but I fear I may cry ... still that apparatus eying me behind ... and in front the Adorateurs Nocturnes with the Christ Candles parading me and the Holy Float out of La Chapelle du Sacré Coeur, under the Disputa whose perspective now our procession confutes, around the sternum of the High Altar of the Church proper, into the right-hand aisle that clusters candles along my flanking past altar and altar and altar, up to the end – still dodging the steps to the pulpit and writhe us left, turning the whole world left into the body of the Church, into the body of the nave that blinks at me with the lidded eyes that are the dormers of the old Eglise Notre Dame that they destroyed but which is now the interior of this Church that they thought they could make into mere Cubicle ... but the reality is all other as we plunge down the central aisle ... past the original high altar of the Ecole de Quévillon, with its bulgeous habitant baroque body blessing my embonpoint and proving the true sensibility of this interior of us now) the Gothic is a fake, a front ... this Church isn't Gothic – ahhh – there I have it now ... I knew there was a reality inside it). This Church, this nave, this is the Body of the Habitant ... of the Habitant-Seigneur-Cardinal-Canadien ... Baroque Habitant ... Ecce Homo ... they couldn't finally hide that, even under the Cubicularity. This Church is the Canadien ... my missing Man. My other Presence ... Moi-meme. Ah, voila, que je te prends, mamour ... te voici enfin ... en depit de tout ce que l'on peut nous dire du contraire ... te voila, corps et ame![54] I take and I eat you now, in memory of us ...

as we navigate the turn I want to drop behind, to see the sight ... that Monstraunce, the Machine but I can only glimpse ... the Père under his panoply of seraglio-silk carrying the Host high..I am sucked back into the body of our processing till we pass the high altar now with its gross of saints and are back in la Chapelle ... the Père divesting himself of the Host, atop a ladder that scales the Tabernacle. We are chanting the victory ... hands outstretched, wide open to the massacre (and I thank God that His Machine is no longer following me behind) – hands outstretched, disarmed ... and as we stand the procession is still in me, still flowing around the nave and into me till I penetrate La Petite Place and on the instance know that this Tour du Monde was the Tour du Monde that I made those days ago around the Outer Walls and then around the Inner ... this is that same procession around that I accompanied unwitting for precisely the same reasons (acolyte Adorateur then!) ... and that being so, then Amyot is André and that Machine is ... and the knowledge of this is sweat on the palms of my outstretched hands now.

Then they are all gone to save those who keep the Adoration all night Watching over the altar, the Church, La Place ... the city (and as I watch the altar I remember that the city hall is the Tabernacle and the Mayor our Man and ...)

Sit now in this night silence that is thunderment – so different from the silence in which you can hear a pin drop ... This is no soundless silence ... no silence from which sound has been banished ... no silence in which nothing is expected ... nothing untoward. This is a silence in which everything is expected, everything is possible – immense anticipation of potence, omnipotence ...

Then I am gone ... I can't stand any more ... not now. And when I stop running I am in the restaurant, sitting with my back glued to the wall – trying to hold the world at bay ...

Back abed ... I am shattered ... every body in my bone broken ... every muscle aches ... I've been pummelled till the nerve-ends bleed. Ache all over ... body and soul – the body of my soul aches. Outside the train bells that I heard during the Mass ... No no no no. No man can see God and live!

Suddenly I have it ... have it all – the novelette – the story ... absurdly clear – even the name of the man: Hugh Anderson!

DAY TWENTY-TWO

... thunder behind the ears again! Thunder ... that I always expected but never did hear at La Place Ville-Marie! that's it – I remember that now – I never did hear anything at La Place Ville-Marie ... it was always a cheat – opened me up, buy never came! Silence. Dead silence, always. I hadn't noticed, not there, not then. But now with the thunder-ear again blasting eyes into the back of my head ... owl eyes for me to see my encirclement. Circumambience. Now I ear that deathful silence of the Counterfeit Place.

Up, bareback on this thunderment, to write direct into novel while I am still impaled by life ... Light the great convolution of red-candle from la rue Bonsecours, and then ignite me from it in cigarillo.
("the moment of truth" – sui generis!) And sit to my desk ... to write my truth, at last – at last, goddam it ... still I am hesitant ... to "write," at any time, demands faith, is self absolutely vulnerable, absolutely exposed to the pry of words ... to think it any other is ignorance. I can only write at all when I am absolutely given ... It is like naming me ... the horror I have of giving my name when I am opened up this way ... for fear. As with Père Amyot! To write – to recreate the world from one's own gut. Not to comment upon it, not to footnote it, but to procreate it.

... last night – les Adorateurs Nocturnes! And as I ran ran ran away home slushed in the car-crushed street snow, the sight of the Hôtel de Ville ... great hollow hulk in the velveteen dark ... absentee Object that was all familiarity to me ... familiar not in form, but in presence, but which I only recognize now in the fierce lucidity of this renewed day, presence as in a photonegative ... with the Object void and the day as night eating out the Object. The Object a white sepulchre, for only the bones left barren of flesh ... as in La Place des Arts at the concert, when I felt dispersed along with every other thing or person. As in modern pop art: death of the Object! Ahh – modern version this then of those Adorateurs Nocturnes – then Modernists are Night Adorers ... their Object lost in a night-tide – last of the Romantics! Theirs is the Black Mass ... mass lost in the night-black ... mass hiding its void in a new crepuscularity. Poor things.

Must write the novel ... Dare I? Still? The mystery of propitiation – of placating the Protestant Gods in me ... so that I can allow me to write, to rejoice, to procreate ... to achieve the commanded Grace of the Catholic God in me. Forcing me to grovel in sullen practical details before I permit me to write ... each time, the last person I met must be placated, must accord his forgiveness of my deviation from Protestant parsimony of the inner word. I must enact the Holy Grovel before I am allowed ... Holy Impasse – Holy Constipation ... steep me in it ... till the outburst! Now, now, NOW!

" ... so that now for the first day, he felt capable of entering La Place, and filching it of both essence and detail. He was at once too tired to be dangerous, and yet too dangerous, too much in command, to be taken. It was like that now. When he awoke he heard the freightbells in him, avid within, yet withstood – voracious and accepted while withheld. It was a kind of procreative impasse.

Both were there, if not in conjugation, certainly most conjugable, which was the new basis of responsibility ... founded upon responsibility. It was a real presence ... the Real Presence. He thought again of the Communion. That was the verity ... of Body and Blood. It was inevitable. If not yet completely achieved. The bells vibrated again in him ... dringtingdingingating ... strummed in him ... till he felt their danger ... requisitioning him again ... He sat down to his Combat Journal ...

"It is the first day. I know that ... I have never dared to face La Place. Have always withheld me, withheld something of me. Now I must see it. Am incredibly lucid now ... my body reassembled after these days of carnage ... recreating the world around me. The First Day. Genesis!"

– he descended to the lobby ... his entire being focusing upon La Place d'Armes ... the manager stopped him, had seen him on television, was happy to have him at the hotel ... Hugh squirmed, tried desperately to pay his past week's bill for the room ... and then realized what he was doing – he was trying to save himself from the man by reducing their relationship to business ... trying to absolve himself of acknowledging this man – and thus was killing him. Doing what those visitants did so often in the Antique Shop – turning proferred flesh into blood. The realization broke over him in a cold sweat – guilty of murder that way, failing to see the Man who invoked them. And he knew that he could no longer do that. He stopped and talked, trying desperately to resuscitate the manager ... accepting him as flesh and blood. Accepted his presence. Nothing else to be done. And as he talked the fierce presence of La Place in him ebbed ... his joy was absolved ... he was left with the manager, draining into him ... his small reserve of blood siphoned off that way. Yet he had to ... Then the manager was called to the phone, and Hugh was out the door ... applying a tourniquet to what was left of his B & B.

Temperature 11° above zero – an ice-blue day ... crackling against the palms of his feet; snow bunched into the foot-crotch hackled his nape. Into La Petite Place ... cars already parked around the central core. Odd – he had never paid much attention to La Petite Place ... had almost kept away from describing it ... a certain pudeur – never preyed upon it. Like a hawk that won't touch the small birds that nest in its nesting-tree ... home-ground is sacred ... and they are all in sanctuary. Hugh walked to the top of this small Place now ... to where Nelson's Monument stood atop the hillflank in him. The monument firmly clenched in the skyline that was the reredos of which the Hôtel de Ville was Altar and all the Front the Frontal outspreading from the foot of the monument ... Walked up slowly ... past the imbedded guns that snorted up from the piled snow – pop-guns that helped build the Greatest Empire the World Has Ever Seen (God – Churchill was only buried a year ago! And He had charged at Obdurman ... had fought the Mahdi! He chuckled to himself – at John's he had met the Mahdi's grandson, at tea, during the Suez crisis ... the Mahdi's grandson – at Oxford, of course *that*, after all, was England – England of the heart, still.) Hugh clambered over the railing around the monument ... patted the sternum of Nelson's toyboats that had consolidated that Great Empire The bas-reliefs that squared the base were magnificent ... perhaps some of the best stonework on the continent. Not "bas-reliefs" at all ... not like the work on the Providence Life Building no, deep-carved reliefs that thrust straight into the base of the column. Above him, that improbable Nile crocodile swallowing la rue Notre Dame. Yes – some of the best stonework ... no-one thought of that, of course; so he had to think of it for his fellow citizens. Had to palp precisely each thrust and gut of stone ... and each time his eyeball touched a stone the bells of the freightyard carilloned him, and La Petite Place was the Governor's Garden with its rose-bed thrusting blossoms up into seventeenth-century suns ... and the Petite Place backed up into him, thrusting him right onto the frontal of the Tabernacle that was the Hôtel de Ville – call it la Versaillaise! – that was endlessly undulatory ... He was whole again. And without turning his head he saw, refracted from that frontal that was the frontal which Jean Le Ber worked over two centuries ago for Notre Dame under those same rose-bitten suns (and which he was determined he could see to-day), the entire perimeter of La Petite Place. The Château de Ramezay behind him ... precursor of this same bête couchant in front of him, Hôtel de Ville ... the same animal. The dome of the Great White Elephant ... bland grandeur of Washington Capitol – but set pure atop British North American stone. Beyond, to the left, Our Lady of Everlasting Help above Notre Dame ... Statue of Liberty, but with warmth in her womb. And the angels around her (all echoes of the Great White City at Chicago's World Fair, 1897) ... sweated green with the grime of steamers. Out-topping both, the Grain Elevation, that was a magnificence only diminished by the fact that it blockaded the St. Lawrence to all but the inner eye. While at the base of the Little Square, the viscera of that same grain elevator, shafting whole-wheat and workers from one Tuscan warehouse to the next. On the east side of the Square ... his own hotel, Nelson – that was a French provincial name of dignity ... where everyone had known him simply as "le petit Français en 313 ... " his room number. And opposite, other hotels, a nightclub, and two habitual restaurants ... his greasy spoon for breakfast, and le Restaurant des Gouverneurs, where he drank fresh squeezed orange juice and surveyed La Petite Place – did its customers know the world that was theirs from out its windows? ... He had sat there one afternoon reading excerpts from the *Montreal Herald* of 1814 –

Item: "March 26th – Under the heading of Matrimony, an advertisement:

A Gentleman in possession of a handsome income con-cerned in a house of respectability, of good disposi-tion and agreeable manners, but from the tedium and ennui of a single life rather attached to his bottle, wishes to Connect himself to a Lady not exceeding twen-ty years, of a handsome person, elegant accomplish-ments, and pleasant temper. It is hoped that none will answer this, but those of undoubted respectability ... N.B. The connection will be rather of a platonic nature."

Item: "December 24 – Wanted, a Female Servant of good character, who understands Cooking and the Drudgery of the House. A woman having a child will not answer."

and in 1815 -

Item: "April 29 – the Drama. The Play of JOHN BULL was performed on Thursday evening by the o⌡cers of the Garrison, with great ability and success. From the proceeds of the play the Amateurs have been enabled to make two donations of 50 pounds each, to families in great distress."

Item: "August 12 – On Thursday when the great news from Europe (the defeat of Bonaparte) was known to be authentic Mr. Dilmon planted his Patereroes on the Place d'Armes and fired a salute."

... La Place d'Armes ... he still wasn't there. He turned to the left ... down la rue Notre Dame ... Every detail seared in him. He was implacably lucid ... and incredibly vulnerable. Everything touched him ... Vulnerable ... was it always necessary to be this vulnerable, just to see, to hear, to know? Did it have to be that way? And then he knew that it did. That that was what was marvellous about man ... his vulnerability. That was the adventure in life. The adventure of life. To close it off was to close off life. So he had to embrace that vulnerability ... or live dead. That vulnerability defined him ... as a man. It was desirable, essential, inevitable ... That trees in front of the old Courthouse, imbedding it in deep space ... alive with blackbirds ... those trees, erect in him, every branch veined in him ... disastrously present – gloriously. As he ran his eye over each branch he threatened explosion ... and had he raised a finger to trace his eyesight, he would have detonated ... instead he passed his right hand back and forth across his sight ... as his hand passed in front of his face, his whole body snuffed out, and then, once passed, he was ignited again ... His right foot stamped the pavement ... till he stopped it. On past la rue St. Gabriel ... and le Vieux St. Gabe ... he reinstated that picture over the bar ... that picture that toured the world around him it sighted in him ... giving him always eyes in the back of his head. A bad painting, that restored his sight! – what more could a man ask, of a painting.

And with these eyes back into his head he realized that the urns atop the Hôtel de Ville were trailing him ... He turned to remonstrate – disengaged them from his groin – and replaced them fastidiously atop the Hotel. Admired the confrontation of Old and New Courthouses ... and then continued down towards La Place d'Armes. Past Paul's Tavern, with its stain-glass windows in a dignified ribaldry. Opposite the gigantic hole-in-the-ground that was the new

Palais de Justice. Now at its most beautiful, its most impressive ... a hole. Another ziggurat. Streicher had explained to him that this new Palais didn't need to tower at all – it didn't need to overshadow this street. But its proponents wanted a tower. Eh bien – soit:[55] it was an empty phallicity, like all the rest. A hollow erection! And the street would always have its revenge – because one day men would realize that this tower was symbol of accruing impotence. Whereas the smallest of the limestone shops here with its garish painted pilasters, Victorian accretions, bound more potence to itself than the entire tower would. He turned from the hole-in-the-ground, to the calm effrontery of these greystone shops ... his eyes fingering each arcade and lintel. Yes – they held the potence all right ... Odd, but a fact. Of course he was nostalgic – for puissance ... He was opposite the surplus store where he had bought a pair of khaki scarves, for touring this world in the December sear, and where he hadn't bought the knife ... the surplus store was a typical case, with its warm agglutination of paint and dirt over, and the improbable outburst of carving up the centre of the pilasters, proving that the pillars themselves were secondary to the convolutions of the flesh that the entire street acclaimed.

On, past the Main ... the newsstand with its convocation of All Bodies. Into that final canyon ... giving freely his obeisance to the amassed stone office face on his left ... surmounted by its date – 1886. It was doing something to him ... and he didn't know what – till he found himself backing across the street oblivious of the traffic that lurched around him cursing – backing across the street to confront it. Ahh – that was it: the building demanded that he square off afront it, stand easily at attention at thirty paces distance ... He had already done so before he realized it ... and they stood dialoguing for several moments. A distinct exchange of ideas – no nonsense: syllogistical. And then he was dismissed (the presentation had been polite, perfunctory, firm) ... behind him l'édifice Cadillac ... le sieur de Cadillac (was he a vrai Sieur? Qui sait?)[56] had once lived on that site ... but had gone on to found Detroit, and infamy in the car that vulgarized him. He passed on down to that final cluster of shops selling the vestments and objects and books of the Faith: the Baldaquin. On his right une librairie ... in, to scout it briefly. Always that same quality, that same feeling, to these Catholic books – the figurines on their dustjackets were always at once fluent and substantial. Never static. Never. They flowed. In him. Habitant Baroque: this time he remembered.

He gazed out the window of the librairie ... across to the Baldaquin ... threatening to riot him. His eyes embodied the mounting pillars that clenched and then sprung upthrusting three stories, four, above his headiness. He felt his calves gather and tense ... light on his feet ... And then plunged across the street to preclude pole-vault. Into the main shop selling Christ. Looking at all those statues ... the whole store blatant around him – a gross of Christs for the purchase. He knew, objectively, of course, that they were all in the worst possible taste – but now he knew as well that "good taste" was contraceptual – merely a protection against life and against love. He stood watching the statuary ... till he was again aware that

55 Well then, so be it.
56 a real Lord, who knows?

they were watching him ... every one of them had a life of its own – independent of him. Every one of them stood erect in him ... insistent, indelible. He didn't know what to do about it. Then he remembered that of course this is what they should do ... and as his eye circled the base the base circled his head, and he was again all eyes. And ears. For several moments he felt compelled to sculpt them, or at the least, to paint them; then he realized that he really wouldn't dare do that – because painting any one of them would expose him to absolute possession by it. He would literally have become possessed ... he could feel that – and his hackles writhed in warning. No – he would never be able to depict these ... only to propitiate them with words ... by describing them they acknowledged his adoration by releasing him momentarily. But if he failed to worship, then they canniballed him. There was little choice. But then he didn't want any alternative ... because when they commanded his worship they were the entire world restored into him ... his whole being distended, grew. Till he could withstand it no more – then he offered up his peace-offering, in thanks-giving. Magnificat. "My soul is magnified in the Lord ... " And that was that. There wasn't any other way out of it, nor into it. He watched them ... and began to take notes, hastily ... and then they receded, placated. And his heart rejoiced in them ...

I know what you are ... you are all the missing people from the new interior of the Great White Elephant. You are the absentees ... the lost objects. Here you swarm me ... each one of you like the figures on the dustjackets, across the street ... you flow, and you are substantiated. Each of you is the Host. I won't try to escape that. Never ... I know it won't change. Will always be the same. I must give and love ... .

And as he wrote these words, the figures ceased to swarm, but stood firm with him amongst them like trees erect in snow-swept fields.

"I know – I must share this joy. If I don't share it with others, they will kill it in me ... and kill me. I must share Heaven ... And Heaven, then, is other people!

He turned and went straight out into La Place d'Armes.

... the Place d'Armes was munificent around him ... and he approved every motion, every gesture it made now ... he tested each one ... and found none wanting ... each was relevant – fraught with meaning, with danger, with potential. The low organic bas-relief of the Providence Building dallied him, as he scaled the careful crags to the top, like some wellbred mountain goat. And then skyhopping ... passed to the well-fed balustrading atop the brownstone stack beside ... balustrades that distended in prime sirloin ... He pocketed the ironwork of the clock, particularly the hour-hands ... and then he was interrogating again the crest pedimenting the Mother Bank of All Montréal: merchantman's Parthenon frieze ... whereon the heroes were sailor and yeoman-worker, and Indian: it was a quotation from the Amurrican world of Currier and Ives – with this difference – it was in stone! It was in 3-D ... Currier and Ives for Cubes. And so aptly, atop the crest of Montréal itself ... the beaver – the Complete Canadian Cube ... the symbol of the state – substantial, diligent, sure, sombre, comestible (but only by the tail) ... and, of course, it could be fleeced – the Canadian Golden Fleece.

he was sucked over to the Bank ... and in, and endlessly voyeur mounted to say good-bye to the castors within ... to his legal guinea pigs: and as he expected, they had that look of men about to lose their maidenheads ... in fact of men who had lost their maidenheads, but didn't quite know how or why ... Somewhere they had been had. By him. But if they acknowledged it then they were lost to respectability – and they clung to that matriarch with all the diligent will of the foredoomed.

crossed La Place ... into the garden of the Church ... the snow kindly absolved the dirt of it – the evident sterility of its soil. Covered it and gave it back its beauty ... flowered the rows of chestnut trees that flanked it ... in the centre, a saint or other, wintered under a contraceptual bag. Some day this garden would flower again ... but only when the people wanted gardens again – Centennial Exposition – it was excuse sufficient. Meanwhile it remained a medieval close, curious analogue of the Place itself. He made his way to the flank of the Church ... up a back alley – the tower strode over him ... and seen from these abutments, it was immensely convincing – no mere Gothic revival facade ... and doubly so in that through the portcullised gate beside he could see the Mother Bank brooding over the Place: it was an unexpected dividend – and it sufficed him ...

He turned up the front steps of the Church ... past the huge cat-iron lamps in front, through the central of the three arches, into the Church ... he intended to visit the Church Museum – to see Jean Le Ber's frontal – but he stopped abruptly ... in a pew at the back of the Church. To rest a moment ... slowly it focused him ... drew him out again – he heard the thunder of the candles ... and again his eardrums were probed and penetrant – again he lost his male maidenhead ... he reeled, held tight, and then relented ... gave himself to the verity ... and as he did he felt his eyes palped by the entrelacings of the gilt pillars ... and he followed the line of gold, up to the gold florescence under the balcony – to the scallopings of wood frieze ... and he knew that he had to abandon himself to this ... had to give to this – give himself to this. There was no other viable alternative. No other way – not out – but in. No other truth. Everything else was shadow.

... for a moment the veil dropped again – threatened to drop – he tried to make his eye bounce back off the entrelacs ... briefly he succeeded – yet he knew that if the veil did drop, he was lost – that once again he was still-born ... He looked back at the writhings of the gold ... and as his eye turned to them, they shot in, under his guard, before he even knew what had happened ... shot into him, writhing and convulsing – the candles raged in him – again he tried to close down – to shut out this realization ... but now it was too late, gloriously, with absolute finality, too late ... his whole body soared from the pew – followed his eyeballs in with the entrelacings ... the roof lifted and he was adrift absolutely, afloat ... no longer was there any question of details, of itemization – all that had gone now ... he was confounded in utter conjugation with the body of the Church – it was militant in him. He turned – and staggered out ... the Place d'Armes was outrageously alive in him ... detonating everywhere, everything, in a profusion of knowledge ... suddenly every detail was sparingly evident – each outline blared in him, and the mass of the square raged in him ... he saw the beaver again ... and as he did heard the thunder of the candles ... his throat swole, his eyes blazed ... ça crève les yeux, Pierre had said – he was right – it stabbed your eyes out ... no in ... stabbed his eyes back in ... He was hemorrhaging now ... could feel the stream of blood blurting from him ... hideously alive ... La Place ... The Place ... he could see the Place ... he started to shout ... "La Place ... it's there ... don't you see ... La Place ... Look ... " And he started to run toward the statue of Maisonneuve ... and his run became a kind of dance, his whole body vibrant, like the dancers in the nightclub, like the old High Altar by Quévillon in the Church, that was (he knew it now) the same altar as in his dream at home, as sideboard of hospitality, like the commode in the Flesh Market, like the sternum of the Lesser Sphinx ... out into La Place, grasping Holy Host to place it in the very centre of La Place. A pedestrian swerved

"Drunken fool," he muttered, but Hugh took no notice. He held the Host in La Place d'Armes, and the rest was irrelevance ... into the very centre, and stood absolutely mobile and saw that the whole Place was in dance and that even Mommy Bank had budged, and that even the beaver on the frontal of the Mommy Bank was undulant now, in this sudden tidal flow, boring through him, flowing outrageously alive through him to fecundate this entire Place while around him as he turned, the buildings all vehement in his motion, he saw that the people had stopped dead so that he started again to shout "Look ... La Place d'Armes it is come alive for us, all of us" – but still no-one moved as he held his Host high up over La Place, so that he knew that now there was only one possible solution, and taking the Host ate it alive till he embraced the Place and then turning to the first person he could see ran with his right hand outstretched, his forefinger out, to touch, to give this blood that spurted fresh out the open act as he ran to embrace them in this new life he held out at fingertip to touch they

CIVIC SQUARE

A CIVIC SQUARE IS A SQUARE

CONSTIPATED BY COMMITTEE IS

A CUBE IS A CANADIAN IS A

CIVICTORIAN SQUARE IS A

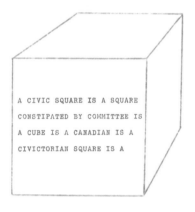

This EPISTLE
has been
lived
procreated
written
published
(and read by Thee)
Without a Canada Council Grant

And Without the Sanction of:

The Moderatur uv the United Church uv Canada the Liderary Edidur uv the Trantadaily Stare the Principal uv Victorya Collij the Chairwomen uv the Commiddee of the Selecshun uv the Companions of All Canada the Chairman of the cnrcnrcnrcncn the I ODE or Anybody's bloody Mommy

It is obscene, pornographic, scandalous, irreverent, malicious, malignant and magnificent, without effort nor intent.

This *EPISTLE*

WITH MY BODY I THEE WED
AND IN MY FLESH SHALL I SEE GOD
AND ALL FLESH SHALL SEE IT TOGETHER

Cocks are beautiful.
All cocks are beautiful.
Not only in themselves (because some are more, or less)
but more for what they do. And what we do with them.
When we permit.

There's the real beauty of mancock: what we do with it, them, all.

>How we see hear smell taste touch with them.
>How we see hear smell taste touch them.
>How simply are, in ourselves and in on around about others with cocks,
>is all.

Cocks are Holy Rood,
>give life, love, lust give
>hope faith and chastity (when used right)
Revivify, Redeem
>(for the Body itself shall Rise, as was always promised, and as any man whose
very man must know who tries his faith, and Rises with)
Cocks are Rood that die for us, die
>When we most need, die
>so others and we ourselves shall live,
flush blood, bleed and die for us alive. Take and eat, this is our Body and Blood.

(which is why cocksucking is only Holy – though may be executed in Bad Faith, or
just badly, is nonetheless an act holy in itself, giving Grace
>Thanx be to God

Cocks of course are variable. Nor should we expect monotony in plenitude.
>Some are long (thrust deep)
some short and steep
some thin and animate
some thick (a little stodgy some)
some sit up straight, interrogate head on,
some lean (approach oblique)
some curve, a right – or left – hand drive, while

cockheads themselves differ, some being redheads, others come blue to purple,
some are umber, burnt or raw, yes many change their face with time of day, flush
blench contuse (you can't always choose the time the colour or the stance)

Some wear hats, are circumspect, more delicate
some don't, and then there is the bush of cock, makes vast difference to touch pull
twine, and twining us, dally in the little fingerings manbrush to nuzzle lip and
pluck is always burning
whilst balls below are tight or pendulous, hang right or slightly
lower left
are wonderful not just to prod but clasp a grateful palm around
such orb, the world in hand
is beautiful, however said,
is beautiful, just in itself and anyone who says or acts otherwise
is wretched – worse: is plain straight dirty. Or old and tired

before their time has even come. Are Dirty Old Men and Women, from
thirteen to thrice thirty, who claim it's dirty. They want to maim,
to kill, to mourn, to do perpetual penitence, to warp, to hurt, to
create pain so man may suffer, dutifully. Beware of them. They
have their motive. Fearing joy they are cowards, and lust to rule
instead.

Cocks are beautiful
and anyone who knows just this is beautiful himself, is beautiful
all over in (and out) and shines in every move of leg or arm or
head is man's flowmotion, cock in touch,
is eyes that shine wide open always eyes that know no flight, that
need to know no flight is eyes that nothing hide
is eyes that looking in are limpid clear to cock to cunt and back
is all one the same to such eyes present the thing itself, won't
let escape, but create always man or woman that they contemplate
and when you meet eyes like that "watch out," means more honestly
"watch in"
because these eyes see you naked beautiful (no need to undress)
and touching take what they bequeath,
without hurt,
in joy,
they feed and give openly against all the laws
    Wide-eyes, which knowing, feel clearly what you feeling furtive think but
never say (you only say you will – someday) these in truth are eye-balls, like
cocked-ears (that always hear the wind), our deep-rooted senses, and we should
never shy

oh, just know that cocks like
cunts and
Christianity, are beautiful is all
you need to know

is absolutely all
    (the rest is education!)

is where we are – our furthest point, reached out for that (too far to reach? Perhaps. Yet we did not die, not quite, but came instead alive, burst out)

precisely where we are: just living up to that
cocks, like cunts and Christianity, are beautiful
has taken four months, just to write it down, confront it, and us
in it

four months, let me just catch up,
four months since Yorkville – remember that? (God in my gut – how
could we ever forget?) Yorkville – where we met, touched, despite
us each, and, thus touched, opened up the human wound for life and
left each other with that worst and best of human problems, that
of joy, of how to live in joy, accept sheer joy that threatens
every day, defines us, mans us, either that, or we are dead – is
Hell, at least Purgation. If we don't accept.
Yorkville brought us into touch: the only place in all this constipated land where
Touch is.
Oh yes, this god-ridden land of Canada
is for Touch-Me-Nots (remember them?) Parading the street past the
Penny Farthing – ranks of them, leaning, strolling, holding, withholding, reaching
out and out and out and
    Touch-Me-Not are all the same. And you and I, we sang, beside the Thunder
Chicks, Leonard's song
    "tonight will be fine will be fine will be fine
              for a while."
and fled each other to the Pocock's place for sanctuary (for sanctuary from the
Touch-Me-Nots, and from ourselves, we fled) and t-t-touched, where it hurt, and
freed thus saw all the world was bright
(and the Yellow Warbler sang in the Civic Square)

and then we feared to touch again. It was all too much at once, too much bright
in our Blandmansland. And we fled. You, I don't know where to … .

but me to Blythe Farm again. Crazy, crazed. After spending that whole year past
just trying to get to Yorkville intact, available (so many detours, apparent and oth-
erwise: Home and School and Ottawa to see Who Rules, now Rosedale whence I
came) back to Blythe, recuperate, and finally got it all down as I promised you I
would, a full month later, August 18. The essence of the thing on paper now
between us. But even then, a full month later, couldn't finish either the writing
nor the living of it (still to do.) Took my notes in haste, at the very end, knowing I
hadn't made it quite -
    "*Toronto* – the evenings at the 511" – the Gay Queens slavering, laughing at
their socially-enforced oddity: sheer guts – only they have the right to laugh, to
cry, to see, to touch in this city. I stood and watched terrorized by their verity. The
boy who brought his Mommy down, to gain her sanction; both laughing uneasy

... the Island Beech day (blooming Fire Island)

"*Rosedale* – the evening of the Rapesmen's Club, a fête champêtre ... the inner group of Toronto Big Boys, all Chinless Wonders, those buck-teeth, give away the marsupial mommysack they're in: pathetic fuckup for these men ... trying to make it at last (none did). Made me stop and think. How to live Beyond Orgasm ... and not merely just up to it, fall back, and protest, make your career ... "

"*Farm* – Mullein flower flight dapple white and yellow down our drivewayside Goldflinched! pass below the chest of Kingbird takes flight no greyfencerails in site to settle (I know by heart his greyperchpoles, and planted some myself for his sake) is chasing crow across the Upper Swamp.

frog looks startled at his rise in life: Kingfished

goldenrods beneath the butterflies (*their* season now: Snowbuntings begat buds begat warblers begat leaves begat yellowworchids begat butterflights begetting goldenrods beneath and tiny pods of milkweed lurk beside purple heads of Joe Pye weed island green sheathes me a Catholic time and day despite August windgusts that cluster leaves above me heady. In brief weeks this greensopped land will bleach ... "

a whole notebook, untapped – I simply couldn't touch it all. Unconsummated joy crippling me. Incomplete ... Fled me to Gananoque to holiday with wife who had a couth retreat above the St. Lawrence, 1000-yard prime whitepine entryway, atop the rocks, we stood at seagulls height (ever look gulls in the high eye above billow flight?)

More beautiful notes (and sheer lust of living it) on smalltown Church architecture – the relative heft, bulk, shape of Methodist, Presbyterian, R.C., and Anglican, in stone, matching the style of service, sermon, liturgy. Can spot these at a glance.

but couldn't rest: tried to finish Letters up, these notes, and two hours later was abed – fever 103 – I knew this is no flu! Gut candescent, trees fled my windowsight. The "hepatitis" my doctor said I knew in fact was not a bloody liver but a crisis in my will, my faith, my energy as man, as sheer male – that it was the result of my fight to smash that benignancy that is the Canadian Death, that disease whose first trait is the social, sexual, moral security, passivity of smugness. Our special kind of Canadian killjoy cancer is benignancy. And in trying to better me beyond that, out of that – in destroying its attributes insofar as they controlled me:

– the male maidenhead,
– the perpetuated virginality,
– the phlegmaticism of the man who will become in body and business substantial,
– the self-assurance of self-worth ... (to list a few)

in destroying these I bid fair to have destroyed myself – not because I didn't gain my end, but because I so nearly did, and faltering, failed desperately – a failure of heart that was a failure of my hepatitic liver, as all the world went jaundice, and the accumulated bile of a lifetime unlived congealed and spat out of me in green glots. Till I said "no no NO" – as my mind my will began to give in to the thing; and I knew that to succumb complete was to accept castration.

"NO NO NO" – and looked out my bedroom window at Blythe and saw the body of the great Blue Beech and the heaving thigh of hemlocks massed down one two three hundred feet straight down to Duffin's Creek – and let these seethe wholebodied into me, let my eye accept their fact enveloping me, and my fever dropped back so that it wasn't necessary to hospitalize; feeding with my eye-balls I fed me thus intravenously – direct. A simple question of accepting touch – was all.

Thus saved from hallucination began reading in the body of Englit (five thousand volumes stashed in our basement, accumulation of a whole Canadahistorytime by our families) – treating Englit as it only should be, from Chaucer to Mailer – as a Body Corporate – as a physical, carnate, present body: as One Man. And testing my now shattered body against it.

Eating *Hamlet* as cocktail teaser,
Donne's *Sermons* as bully beef,
Paradise Lost as Plum Pudding,
Fingering Pope's Raped *Lock*,
spewing with Swift's *Tale of a Tub*,
then dropping back to Chaucer, to ride the land wholesale.
Foreword to Johnson on Shakespeare
and Boswell to Johnson,
and some bitchy prof on Bozzy ...
Eating great gobbets; Take and Eat, This is Our Body, given for you
and for many.
Raiding the cellar library like a larder.
A Wordsworthy translation of Dante's *Inferno*.
Then Eliot on same.
And back to *Hamlet* again – and knew knew knew that that was where we
had gone awry in the English-speaking world. There is the impasse relating to
English State and Church – our Angliannity – imbedded in the language – be we
Methodist, Unitarian, Presbyterian or Anglo-Catholic, or just Canadian Citizens
(secular Methodists with mitigations). *Hamlet* is where we failed, with the very language consummating our failure "to be" ... Be we Canadian, American, English,
Australian – no matter. *Hamlet* is the impasse. Must breach this or bust. And only
Blake and Hopkins and maybe now Ginsberg come close.

Is now –   November 28, 1966,
From: 378A, Chestnut Park,
                                Toronto ROSEDALE

THE FIRST LETTER

Blythe Folly Farm
Claremont, Ontario
May 10/11, 1966

Dear Reader:

I am happy. Because it is winter in my soul. I do not have to rejoice. Nor give thanks. Much less praise any thing. I am happy for this respite from crippling joy. Happy that on this tenth May day the open land is swept by perverse high March winds that must somewhere funnel now even dead city streets, bruising presumptive daffodils.

Strange, to have such happiness simply because I no longer need to rejoice. Strange. And desolate. My happiness disturbs me, and, imperceptible, becomes mourning.

Outside my window Maybirds follow winds the flustered insects scatter. Maybirds more like snowbuntings eddy the swept land.

Watch them with nostalgia. Once these birds birds budded me. Now, like all my land and my people, all that I am and have been and was promised to be, these birds are extinct.

For days, of course, this perseverant winter has been threatened. There have been sun days. My wife and I even sunbathed nude (despite fastidious township by-laws) – sun-bathed in earliest March, at the edge of the swamp that is my land-locked lake we call hopeful pond. Here, where my studio is, where I write to you, we bared constricted breasts to sun-seep. Thank-full for unexpected dividend of warmth after February cold. Yet I was fearful, even then. Knowing that this sun is subvert. That this sun could commandeer rejoicing.

Trembling lest I no longer know joy. And even more, oh even more afraid, that joy commandeer me. That joy reach out and for one final time destroy me in an uprising that I can neither sustain nor withstand.

So I covet the cold soul in me. Covet it and cower behind it, for some smugness. And duck now that importunate ray of sun, such forward sun, duck it is (I see now) only flit of warbler at my window edge. And still I duck it and all the thousand ruffled suns the wind refracts on my pond face. And am saved only by the grey reprieve of clouds. Bless them.

Presbyterian, that was my mother's mother. Great, handsome statue of a lady. And accredited aristocrat, of special caste – "the *Hamilton* aristocracy," my mother told me with inexpungable dignity but a few weeks ago. And in her phrase an ironstone that Mother clung, still, her wasp-waste strung up, and tightened foot tapping the oriental carpet (on oak, of course) while I quivered with anticipated pride, and some mounting exacerbation at this reimposed heritage.

Hamilton Presbyterian. *That* heritage. Assuredly the world's rightest, tightest, bitch, is all. As I remember the grandmaternal portrait in our front hallway that I always thought was Mother. I just didn't notice that it was (then) fully twenty years older than Mother could be. For me it was, unconsciously, Mother-to-be. That portrait of unquenchable Gracious Lady Militant. Of our Lady of the Iron Hand and of the Hamilton Escarpment. Over-riding the sweet Niagara fruit belt.

Presbyterian, she.

And today is what I term a Presbyterian Day – *Canadian* Presbyterian. As specific to Canada as our parochial Presby-terians whose gait and whose faith mated my land – administering the English Canada that the Methodists made. And for ten generations born thus under the Hamilton sway I have known what I meant by a Presbyterian Day. I mean Winter of the Soul. Frozen stiffs, more truly now frozen flaccid. We'll come to that.

Yes, the Anglicanadian Days,

the Methodisticanadian Days,

the Catholicanadian Days, all these days will explore me (and you) later. For now I am perforce Hamilton Presbyterian. Like the day itself. And it requires all my faith and all my will to honour that reality still.

But the sun threatening my Winter keep for weeks. Ferocious moments of breeched freeze, like the day the Mallards first came back, heralded yet finally unexpected and struck open the ice-tight swamp, their green heads tremoring me affront brown winterbled Teazle and the starface of Queen Anne's Lace and the finch-pocked Mullein stalks, spurting the land Greenhead threatens, threatening everything with green. And that same night I had a wet dream. At the moment of climax was neither a woman nor a man I saw. But the Green Mallard Head. I woke and was afraid in my swimming bed. And wiped the sperm clean and vowed never again to espy returning ducks through binoculars.

And this was merely the first breechfreeze (as I have come to call them) – for the ducks kept right on coming. Not merciful in tidal wave to overwhelm all stern desistance of me, to crack clean and easy my Presbyter's Keep, but rather snipping at me singly and always cleaving pondbody afront my startled window pane.

Like the Mergansers (I name them openly for this first time. They were a Secret in me, till now I scuttle them by name).

Mergansers, breeching my cold Presbyter's confidence. A pair. His stark black-tipped but white crest, and she red-heady ... cresting entire the land. Blatant on the watertop now fresh sheer from Spring they bank to bank and back refracting all the colour in the lone sky. Oh – the very recollection now molests my pinched Presbytery. Pushes me High Church. I must be wary. And simply note Mergansers as Breechfreeze #2.

And add that day at this desk, finishing up my first novel (so nearly my last, and hanging on for just dear life) rippling me unbidden overhead the supple mockery across skythroat – I am ashamed I did not know enough to weep. Were the Loons back.

And then the skies trumpeting Canada geese. Were breeches three, and four and five – but skip the birds (for now). Because the sharpest breech of Winterkeep was no bird at all but *Sanguinaria canadensis!* Just that.

Occurred that day I walked out finally around the end of the pond, under the grey Blue Beech, sidling the fenceline with cast-iron maple leaves topping it (were once part of High Victorian Grit farmacy, these leaves). Was April 21st. I was assailed everybloodywhere by *Sanginaria*. Tried desperately not to see them (hands sudden to my face, averted eyes). But they sited me too fast. A bright patch. And I could no longer simply limn the ruddy things which, outlined, would die, pinned down thus. Oh no – just kept gouting up in me, as hemorrhage ran Spring flushed. Flushed by white Blood Rootlings. So well the first countryside Springflowers named.

And now a fortnight since the Blood Root raped my eyes. And I have dared them only once again. Face on. And instead I bless each greyday of this Marchridden stern May-time. Bless any delay in my Blood Root! And shall pay them only final respects (their first flush done) – as we did the family graveyard. Posthumous visitations so much richer than life; so much so that Grampa took extensive notes on Ontario graves, wrote his book on *Ontario Fences*, and then died, before he could complete the plots.

May 10 – still.

The last day of prolonged Winter. Can scarce hope for further respite. Presbyterian Season at an end. And I must now treat with Spring. And more dangerous still, Summer yet to come. And Summer stands (as season) in such livid opposition to my Canadian's soul. Oh, yes – despite those ad-signs exhorting us *"think* Summer," despite such commercial commandment that is typical self-defeat, our real difficulty, Dear Reader, our real difficulty, is to *feel* Summer. In this land diligently dedicated to the posthumous.

Or maybe I worry improperly, D.R. (yes, of course, I'll D.R. you – already your name is nick now, some intimacy of prerequisite complicity Dear Reader Dear Reader deareader dr). The 24th of May is weekend after next. Queen Victoria's Birthday. Godbless what's left of Great Queen Vic! Yet, knowing our professional Ottawa patriotsies, we'll undo her best bequest of "peace, order and good government," begin by renaming this more than century-old Canada day, and call it something else – by Order-in-Council, at the request of All-The-People. And odd enactment this, of our Citizenship.

And the weekend after Mayday, by whatever name we name it, in our Canadian Liturgical Calendar of All Seasons is really Labour Day, augmenting August with some of September – nice, that O Canada thus ceases from Queen Victoria's birthday to Labour are all rest days. And we the citizens go *en masse* North, into our own mineral deposits (what's left of the Canadian Shield) – become brief vacationland we share, this long midsummer dream of June's hundred days. Our antipodean Outback this Upnorth, where loons and gangled Moose are Canada grotesque. (The "picturesque and the beautiful.") In place of Kookaburra Birds, and Kangaroos.

Thus we are absentee for abortive birth on Canaday, July the First. And the O Canada Season only rebegins with first September frosts, are reassuring for us. Deepfreeze from September first to May twenty-fourth. During which time we metamorphose our Methodism, and – with the snow – Presbyterianize. O Canada MacCanada MacCanada

Still May 10 (a sprained braintime later)

If stunned I did not yet acknowledge Winter's done again, mere TV would tell. Because our National Resurrection-Insurrection Programme ended last Sunday. I mean *Seven Days.* It was designed to warm the Canadian steepfreeze. (And seasonally ends when the first Swallows are back.) But *Seven Days* did not merely end with Winter and First swallows. It ended forever this past Sunday. Killed in full blast. And as I sat to watch this swansong I realized what I really watched: not the proximate end of the Canadian Presbyterian Wintersoul, nor even the simple end of *Seven Days* (which was after all but TW3 for Methodists). Oh no – more pungent than all that. I watched the internment of my own generation just as it tried to speak out here and now through this TV programme. Had tried to present our case and died (also by Order-In-Canadian-Council) in the name of National Concord (and the Methodist Ascendancy).

Sat and watched thus my death (and yours, D.R.!) – death as precise as that of President Kennedy for Young America. And again, I should have wept.

O Canada still in the laps of the Old Men. And of the young men already suitably eldered.

The Anglican Church will join the United Church. The Presbyterians have us again. Winterkill.

Don't you see?

Always the same always the same always (and my mind hurts).

All I have now is Summer to blind me in some blitz of joy (*that* I fear). And after, the White MacCanadian Winter Dark – illumined this coming year by the cold neoneyes of Expo 67.

The Summer is the young – those not-yet-deadened-into-fullscaled-citizenship. Those that Sevendays threatened to unveil, alivo! High treason *that* was. (And Patrick Watson died. Pray for him!) The young – and the Warblers. The young hang on for dear life, isolated pockets of them, across the land, like Yorkville, Toronto's Yorkville. How much longer can they hang before they rot? Victims of that emancipation they claim, in martyrdom, for their sheer youth. Leaves the warblers. They are sure. They have the key, dare I but let them turn it, turn us.

Outside still grey. Cold gorgeous grey. Thanks-be-to-God.

It is already the next day -

Eleventh May Day, 1966, is what my calendar would assert, but in fact for me (and you) it's really Squeezey Balls singing outside my window. "Squeezey B." is what my wife calls *Mniotilta varia* Also termed the Black-and-White Warbler. Odd bird he – Nuthatch treetwining footwork, but warbler's weak singsong weesee weeseee weessseemeessong.

As I dredge me out of disgruntled bed, and Squeezed Balls, down to pondside and bless the uninterrupted greyday. Which is, of course, uninterrupted *coitus interruptus* (is Presbyterian's Love Where the Night's Are Long). And with that, the voice of my eldest sister-in-law coming back-talking about the grey swimming pool her husband plans in their Rosedale garden:

"It's not going to be that awful Californya blue," she asserted chin uptilting nose to air (faithful so to Kirk, clan and Canada) Voice of dollars-and-better-sense.

And writing you that, sudden know where the Host went, the Real Body in Holy Communion, where it went when King Henry's England lost half our Catholicity, becoming Anglo-Protestant. Real Body passed into the Object. All objects: chairs, tables, shutters – descending direct to greybled pools for Rosedale. Our Real Prescience remaining, lost, in the outered object. Remnants there. If only we could touch them, connect, we'ld remember quick what I mean.

Warming in the day's dank grey. The feeling, though not the site, is dapple. Remakes me absolute English again. When Manley Hopkins blessed all "dappled things" he England blessed (and all the cloudscape Constable descried). Dapple IS England-land in all this drizzle dapple softly softening things you touch touch you back at fingertips to kiss, all England

And know, so, that dapple IS the England-faith, the Anglican, the half-and-half to touch, but only softly, lest we lust, grasp, instead of gentles Please Keep Off the Body there embodies us, if you please, but each not quite, not absolute, just ripples slight to touch. Which is, of course, I see that, the doctrine of the Consubstantial Church, in fact. Just means the body's there, it's not, it is, is either both or neither (as you, me, we are, D.R., right now) And knowing this, know too that simple doctrine

Parts of it, like those *Breechfreezes*, to understand YOU MUST READ "out of the corner of your eye. I learnt that the hard way. I kept trying to read it head on – and it kept hurting my eye, my focus, inner and outer. It left me feeling insane. Read it like you watch the landscape driving a car, as it fleets by. And keep your main eye on the highway – which is yourself!

This note is about the "simple Article" Scott refers to here. In the Anglican Prayer Book there are actually three that deal with the Sacrament of the Body and Blood of Christ. They are very confusing. Father James (he's in that Final Letter) tells me that Anglicanism is not "consubstantial" in its belief. It is Lutheranism which is. (Scott is an Anglican with some Lutheran forebears; may explain his mix-up.) What he is really saying is that the Anglican Church wants it both ways. Real Presence (of Jesus Christ's actual body and blood) in Holy Communion. And merely metaphorical Presence. Satisfying everyone. The net result, in effect, is a Half-Presence. Which ties in with a great deal Scott feels through in these pages. For example the "Hamlet impasse" that bothers him: "to be, or not to be." And the "Real Presence remaining in the outered object" – i.e., in furniture. Thus account-

* *Reader's Note* the "Reader" being (as you have rightly assumed) me, "D.R." What I'm really doing is taking all these letters, in the order that Scott apparently read them that final time, and making a single text. This of course was never intended. So it reads humpy and lumpy. But that's the way it happened. Life is simply never as smooth as literature!

ing for the rise of connoisseurship in England: a connoisseur being someone who both loves and knows furniture. In both attached and detached. Or, again, as on this page, the phrase "untouching touch," which relates to what he sees in the "touch-me-nots" (and the Yorkville "Half-Beats").

This engagement with the problem of the Half-Presence explains his hatred of "the Church of Canada" – the new Canadacult, which is in fact a further retreat, a "Quarter Presence." And only to be preferred to what he sees as the "Real Absence" in the world created by the Unitarianism of the U.S.A. (Real Absence being the reality of the electronic media … .TV, etc.)

This Half-Presence can all be studied philosophically as English Neo-Platonism (seventeenth century through to Dean Inge). But the point is that Scott doesn't *think* it through. He *feels* it through. A Logic of Sensibility and not of Mind. What he didn't realize were the consequences. And I even less.

But the fact is you must let yourself *feel* what he is saying. Once you do the logic (and even the syllogisms therein) are clear. If you won't, you're done for.

of the Consubstantial Touch is no irrelevance, but profoundest truth of England, was *our* Empire too. The way the English felt, saw, palped, knew, and thus believed. That simple Article of Faith, but one in Thirty-Nine – look it up, Dear Reader – now. No mere metaphor it was, more nearly sleight-of-hand-untouching touch.

And looking out my window now, ask me "what in Canadais dapple?" Ah – there's the rub. Our land too hard, this very dapple-lack assures accursed "Identity" (if nothing else). No dapple here to nibble dally twine or brush. Just curly maple furniture is early Canadappling, hard to touch,
such ripple's under glass.

And I am still March-time in May
No need to see those three Phoebes fulminate the scattered pond-face now.
No need to see their fanned tails uprisen crests spread-eagling wings now render each combattant as a viper fang that strikes the next and gone gone from me
No, they can't be gone. Because they were never here in me. I never really accepted their enaction within me save, oh save only (admit this) to read them out of touch, to exorcise them from out of me. Exorcism by such hard-headed worship, parodizes truth, truth the Phoebebird embodies (for me and you) – I paying lip-service to my Presbyterian God.

I pray forgiveness now, for not reaching out to touch the glory these birds shone forth. And do penitence for such beauty at once seen and rejected. As though praying "keep your distance if I keep paying hard-lipservice" (swimming pools *ought* to be grey)
Awful truce.

But how can I explain this. That all sight changes with the eye of faith. And I with site. Is just what happens. Threatens me with death a dozen times a day. And how explain this constant presence. Oh so Real Presence in me – in touch, yet out. The Anglican of me. Till my Presbyterian past (really embosommed in Our Lady of the Hamilton Escarpment and the Iron Hand) SHE says "Hands off" – and my shattered mind boggles while I kill the fucking bird whose beauty threatened (like

Blood Root) to see right through me. Kill the fucking bird and stuff it up. Is me I mount and stuff and keep at best, In Memory (which is my metamorphosis into Methodist – of join the two and "Go United Church, Pray Canadian!" Means simply "do this *in memory* of Me," the Real Body gone, no blood, no guts, no Resurrection – and no cock, at least not hard)

It would all just sound funny. Just mixed up. But it's not. It's just that my sanity is under lucid fire. As I change with

Anglicaneyes,

Methodisteyes,

Presbyterianeyes each one subverting us, one to other. And shatter our core. Shattering out cornea (absolute transplant). Shatter thee and me.

Whose eyes have you, D.R.? And do they bleed. Or do you wear dark glasses against the bright?

aiee – at left, again, steals me, threatens breach
in first willow CATCHIT
whiteblack piebald, flusters dignified
A clear warning I now binocularize – innoculating
me against the shatterment
Rose-Breasted Grosbeak are back.
Sooo – caught their disaster of fact
caught them in full subversion of me
caught them enforcing joy.
Caught them in *flagrante delicto* (with you and me)
and binnoculate me thus against their disease, typeright us both (kill JOY)
NAME THEM
is simply holding up a bit of the Protestant Faith toward off their evil

(don't touch, please please)
And yet I know, even as I shy them off (where are you?), I have nonetheless been breached again. My wound (God's Wounds) found – and I am had again (by my Blood Root)
stabbed, killed, purified, risen
despite my best precaution, despite my education, upbringing, discipline.
Fallen, Risen, Redeemed. All in a swoosh of bird's
rose breast
So now, again, as only every day am left with our only problem, only decision, only fact: what can we do to be saved?

And this ripped out of me know now that my Presbyterianity has failed me. For all my and loyalty has yet failed me. For all my worship of Greyday, of grey land and greyman, yet still have I been lost and found and touched and found wanting.
Somehow.
Presbyterian Canadian God is dead. Killed its last bird. And buried with the bloody Grosbeak fresh on my chest. Stained red.

Dead, my Winter's God. Dead, under the best circumstances. Circumstances most advantageous to Him. – when it was grey in the day and grey in my faithful soul, and grey in my land and my nation. Dead. While if the sun shines – as it is sure to do. Then Presbyterian God is disposed of by definition and I am again thighdeep in Disaster. Oh – at best a day, two, possibly three, to pull us together, prepare for the confrontation.

And had I any doubts about this I need but to look again out my studio window where that bright treachery of butterfly is in fact Warbler's yellowflight and I realize his wake entrails entire the land will burst daily with outrageous life affront our very eyes (unless I further blind me inside out)
I'm stuck with the fact of life.

And all the good manners in the world cannot protect me from that.
Alas. Hurray.
Nor all our respectability keep me chaste.
Oh – watch and pray.

And now know this – that Manners Unmaketh Man. Yes, I know know know this. Because each time I fall into the very marrow of life alive I back out apologize, into goodest Manners I hide behind.
Manners are an Anglican Absolution. From the sin of living. Manners are the English Heavenhaven, the counterpart to Amurrican "Life, Liburtee, 'n the Purrrssooot of Ffunsiness." The Amurrican Dreme displaces Joy with Ffun is simply effervescence for the living. While Anglican Piety withholds Joy at arm's length – making manners even more impotant than middle-classified memorandum.
And what of us – of our Canadian Compromise. Between such Good English Manners, and such Bad Amurrican Ffun. Our compromise is Respectability which is (surely) merely Manners-on-the-Make (with some fFun thrown in, just in case) for the Lower Rising Middling Class.
Respectability. The snobbery of the unhonoured.
Respectability. The Moral Affluence of Modern Methodism.
Respectability. The High Hat of Black Homburgers.
Respectability. The Creed of the Good Society.
And you'd better believe it, Dear Reader. Or you won't get a Canada Council Grant, and you won't be selected for Parliament, and you won't be denominated a Royal Canadian Commissioner, and you won't (oh, no you won't) be interviewed by the CBC. And you won't be given a job at Expo,
or at *Canadian Art*, nor be named Ambassador (new Bishops-*in-partibus* of the Good Canadjun Society),
or any other thing at all,
unless, unless you believe 'n behave RESPECTABLY
(vote Liburral. Be Canajun. Be Goodygood – or at least nice nice nice the very niceliest people like Mike)
Oh, yes, you'd better believe, repeating after me

"I believe
in One Canada,
made in Heaven (and the East Block), of cleansed Earth,
and I believe
in LaurierKingStLaurentPearsonJohnnieTurnerCHRIST, our Favourite Son,
our Nicelorde and utterly Competent Advocate,
Who, for *our* Convenience and Comfort, was Disembodied,
and dwelt away from us, in By-By-Town,
and was Conceived of the United Church,
suffered under Queen Victoria,
was Embalmed, yet rose again still dead,
to squat on the right hand of the Governor General,
whence he shall continue to judge the deadened,
for Our Sake (and All the People)
for ever and ever and ever and ever and (the next Cabinet Meeting will be held at 3:30 p.m., tomorrow, in the Prime Minister's Summer Office. Thank you gentlemen)"

But what if you *don't* believe – in that creed? Really honest-to-God don't believe in the MacCanadian Party Line.

And what if you do believe in life, in joy, in ... well, in just anything at all? What do you do, like NOW, this damned second, Dear Reader. What do you do NOW? About life? As it is drained out of you.

Telephone someone? Anyone? Reach out touch some unsuspecting zombie. Dare him with your livewire.

931-6847

"No, sorry, he isn't in the office today ... a convention in Montréal."

and even in this reach Telephone realize it is simply to release me (and thee) from life by touching another living death (the Communion of the Deadened) realize it is the kiss of mutual death because am sudden stung by life again is yellow splurt across my deskface is that bloody Warbler back again. Warbler yellow

"Oh oh too late," I cry, "I'm tainted with the yellow from my spyglass yellow taints greysoul some bright sallow says 'too late.'" And know that I could die of overdose

Here lies Thee or Me
Struck dead by overdose of sudden spirea
R.I.P.

And thus, too late, even as I telephone, my treason is denounced to my very face. I kill the joy I claim to communicate.

The predicament is clear.

I can touch but do not
I am toucheable but untouched
I am in touch but out
Out of touch but in.

And you? D.R ... and you? are you different from me? Do you reach out to touch? Are you touched? Or are you too an Untouchable?*

It is like the tigerstripe in the early Ontario yeo-man furniture. That ripple there, the curlycue, our virulent sensual compressed under hard surface of varnish that is steeled veneer. Our rockbound buried Canadian dapple is this curlymapling. Victorian corsetted our hearts of Maple struck
in that deep wood.
We are the ripple in the tigered maple
constrained under the fleshproof glass.
Who will let our stipple loose, who will
rape our bird's-eye core
Who will care to dare?
Will he be in time?

Across plateglass of studio windoweed over cherrydesk
the slow boat flight into nearest far poplar settles
there to budpluck so strangely perched with head-and-tail panache I bin-noculate his progress up my poorman's birch (all poplar, D.R., are poor-man's birch): is part

tabbycat part squirreling, part hen, clucking snakes the branch, tailflirts. This giant sparrowbird is Grouseye espy.†

Backslash of yellowarbling imbibes me. Reminds that this is all only for keeps. The question in mind, in hand – is decisive.

Where are we? At the end of our greydays. Deadend of my Presbytery.
Dead the greystone greyflannels grizzling greyhair, greymatter, greysoul.
The quarry evacuated.

Doesn't mean neither that all is black-and-white now. But warblerbright. Even televeyes will be colour ... follow the trend.

What happens when albino is sudden pigmented? Rash with bright? Surely we are casualties? Who die? Who Live?
I am a great-grandson of Henry James. And I am you, D.R., *mutatis mutandis*. We are all great-grandchildren of Henry James, who, with T.S. Eliot, was the great Canadian, English-Canadian, or, if you must, English-Waspish-Canadian, writer we never had. And in James' novels whenever a character espies himself decisive-

* D.R. *Notes*: see my previous note.*
† D.R. *Notes*: Scott kept a Bird List which I have appended (see near the end).

ly, whenever the essential-that-is-never-said IS said, someone dies, spiritually or physically or emotionally, dies. And the essential here is that we are grey-souled albinos, who must be injected with bright to live. Someone will die. Someone is honourbound to die, for us, D.R.

Will you die for us, D.R.? Or must it be I who am nonetheless stillborn as all of us.

Someone to pray for us. Someone to hope for us. Someone to bless us. Someone to pardon us? Someone to lay their hands on our heads when we fall and when we rise. Someone to die for us ... again.

Is it you? Dear Reader. Or is it Me? Because it must be one or other. All the rest is irrelevant.

In one of us there must live still a death to gift. Otherwise no letter, no reader, no writer, no-man. Or perhaps between us both enough left to give a live death. We must try, before it is too late – before They reduce us to
mere Professional Canajuns First – dead on our feet.* Or before we resign us to being Cubes are Canadian Squares: Civic Squares. Are Amurrican Squares stuffed up with Committees. Can't let that occur.

Come with me, now ... come – come with me, D.R.

Why come? Because you cannot help yourself. Because I am playing Only Game and you either play to score, come alive, for us all, or else merely spectate dead alive.

Yes – you come, I know that: because you must, or die coward – and there is enough of honour left in us to liven us, to keep us aware, to prevent overt cowardice. Just enough honour in us for that, still ... But in another year, two, five (at most) They will have seeped that out of us too. "They" are committed to steal us be slowseepage for the sake of "peace, order, and good government," by Themselves, of course.

Quick come now into my rosebed that is but a swamp buried in the bottom of my land, our land – alder swamp, in Ontario County, in Ontarioland – for we are not a Province, nor merely a State, nor only a Nation: We are a Land – Land of Ontario. We were indeed nearly a Realm. But a Land is already enough – because a Province is only subordination;
and a State is merely "a state of affairs" – an ad-mini-nation; and a Nation is a common prejudice. But a Land is a Place that can still be Promised ...

So in Ontariocountyland (I lied to you in my novel *Place d'Armes* – I called it Collingwood), one of the newspaper critics was smart, he said he knew I was hiding something! But this is no novel – and there's nothing hid, let me promise us including the virginality of criticscockscunts that die flaccid in their breech of promise. No novel – but better, is a Letter, to you, Dear Reader. And since Ontariotime began *since 1794* when sailing up the Don to park his tent became a logcastle

---

* *D.R. Note:* Scott was convinced of a massive conspiracy against the Canadian nation. In fact he became obsessed with this. Viz., his Committee-trip to Ottawa later.

with pillars-applique, toysoldiery and John Graves Simcoe's Other Dream, Toronto founded then

since 1784 when Queen Anne's Communion Silverwariness in ewer plate and all was housed in whitewood chapel by his men and Chief Thayendanegea, Joe Brant himself as hero fit for Romney to paint (the loyal portrait hung today in New York State, of course – complete with sash we lost along with U.S.A.)

since 1776 when Original Sinnery (with hope high of Heaven) was displaced by Original Innocence (second-hand – with hope of fFun and Camarro hartop) was Her Majesty's Yankees reduced to Mere Amurricanity (don't laugh smirk scowl feel annoyed – because it's going to get us too, unless this works)

since time before when Commonwealth was first born by Tea Tables poured by Good Queen Anne (Commonwealth – remember that D.R. – the one that just died with Pearson's No-Ball Peaceprize)

since we were all silly partial martyrs with Bad King Charles' decapitation was us (if Shakespeare had resolved Hamlet's plight neither Charles nor us would have to die – but even Shakespeare didn't breech this impasse)

since his nine 'o cattails fucked us up with bluff King Hal ...

since Adam, Dear Reader,

LETTERS represent the best of our literature. Letters written long before we concerned ourselves about Comprehensive Canajun Culture. Letters written when we were still by right, and nature, civilized. Some time, that is, before the Canadacouncil discovered that Methodists still weren't housebroken and thus that the Pancanjun dream was a Finishing School (including Graduate Studies) for ditto.

Forgive me my trespass, D.R. – I am the Last Tory, just as you are the Last Canadian ... and you may laugh and call me arrogantdecadentfascisthomosensu-alanachronicmonster (They do!), but when we are done together you will know what I am saying. And then – oh pray to Any God, you may know what to do about us. This is a plea – not a plaint, nor a critique, nor a Royal Commission Report. A plea is prayer-plus-tears I eat for your sake we shall need those tears wet my nose shall need them because there is only one weeping left in Canadians, in English Canadians – only one weeping. And we must be careful of it.

Why?

Because this last capacity to weep is our one last capacity to care ... to care about anything at all. And do not fool yourself. They are after that capacity to weep, to care, to know – They know it is the last Trump out against Their final acquisition of power ... so They must have somewhere (hidden, ad hoc) a committee to dry weepers – even hear tell is called Committee on Weepkill like other such

Committee on Crownkill is
Committee on Carekill is
Committee on Joykill

    grew from Committee on Flagkil
    grew from Committee on Traditionkil
    (subcommittee on NavyArmyAirForcekil)

all under Committee on Mankill is Cockill is Canajun Committee of the Whole (employs a millyun Canajuns largest Consumer Producer in the State)

("happy Centennial Canadjuns – enjoy yourselves")

Yes – They know furtively that any Weep held out against them is a potence to be killed will filch the bloody thing out all the while they deny the act.

How will They manage it. Easy. Make us weep over a peccadillo (e.g., have the Separatists shoot the Queen) and while we are sudden sonorous with bleating noses they'll run off with our last Loyal Ball. And – presto – we'll all be Centennial Sopranos ... singing the Saint Massey Passion: patriotic castrati – a practice banned in Central Europe many choirs ago.

Only one Canadaweep left must guard it with our mere English-Canadian lives, for the definitive moment – which YOU will tell us, D.R., yes – you. (Because our capacity to weep is our capacity to care is our capacity to feel is our capacity for passion is our capacity for the Passion, the Human Passion – and no Human Passion then no Christ Passion no God ... everything Dead.) And our capacity for Passion is our responsibility – and anyone tampering with tears tampers with our responsibility is our sheer manhood. So watch out. You are warned. Hang on to your balls – be you Man or Woman.

Nor think all of this unimportant between us. Because my capacity to be saved, by you is the Canadian capacity to be saved – and the Canadian capacity to be saved is the American capacity to be saved: we hold the key to the American Dream-gone-Nightmare. Self-evidently: if we will but accept our responsibility with our tears.

You are coming? You accept this complicity in livelihood? Thank you ... I thought you might have thought me merely mad. But your continuation presumes only the absolute seriousness of our search.

atop the thicket alder brush the islet floats the pondface YELLOW again ... lushbreast in the catkins threaten sunface ahead of time: forewarned by budplush. In a week you won't see the birds for the leaves. Now is the time to watch while our land is still bare, while the greysoul is still faithful to eyespy.

    Yours faithfully,

    Scott Symons

P.S. You ask who my Hero is? In my first book it was La Place d'Armes ... only one person noticed that, no two. Everyone else, arrogantly assumed that it was me-alias-Hugh Anderson. But it was of course La Place itself ... La Place, that consumed all my attention and energy. As my wife noticed, tentatively, and Egdar Collard stated firmly. But in Toronto – the site of these letters, there is no Place; only the Civic Square, is scarcely Hero nor Heroine.

You may say this is fine. No need for Hero – Heroes out of date. But this is no novel any more than my first novel was. Much less an anti-novel. It is only a Letter to You ... and as such it is, in passing, a counter-novel. That is, it presumes to be truth in search of a fiction and not fiction in search of truth ... or more truly allegory in search of man and not man in search of allegory. Which sounds clever. But let me promise you that nothing absolutely nothing but one thing in these letters will be merely "clever." Nor merely satirical (satire being but hope for men of little faith). Nor merely contemporaneous. Nor merely human.

And *you*, of course, *are* the Hero. Yes, *you* – Dear Reader – a *fait accompli* which you cannot escape. You are the Hero.

That said, let me warn you that I love you. Specifically and precisely you. I love you. Pure B.S. – Body-&-Soul. I kiss your cock – at this outset. Don't protest you're a woman. The best of us are. And the best women have become men. We fought and switched and we're back to normal. Oh, yes, I used, in my smugness, to think that the Canadian Crisis in Identity was at least better that the American Crisis in Gender. Now I know better ... I know that the Canadian Identity IS our Authorized Effort at Self-Gelding. And once you know that half the battle is won.

So I kiss your cock, D.R., pray upon you and love you. No need to hideaway, to shy your cock – too late for that already flushed. And once touched held to our common end.

Yes, I love you ... or I wouldn't write this bloody letter to you. Oh, no! Why give up hearth family career success comfort and all the mod cons unless. Much better instead to go and paint or sculpt or dance, in joy at des-pair. But can't do that. Because I still love and still loving love you. Oh, I know that my capacity to love at all is on margin. But so is yours. That's what we're really out to test ...

And that so I warn you as I love you ... I'm after your male maidenhead. Why hide it? Why should you? And do not think you're not virgin. You are. And I can prove it when we visit the sites I plan – confront you with their substantial reality – watch your song and prance with each all the same. *You are endless virgin.* And, until deflorated, you remain still-born, soft-of-hearing. (Like all true Torontonians, Soft-Sodomites uncommitted to their fact. All one has to do is test the architecture of Victoria College to know what I mean and we shall – don't worry yet.)

My whole tactic is to quicken you. You might as well know that. Then you can defend yourself. Your game, of course (but I mustn't tell you that, yet).*

Don't trust me! I'm a bitch – like you Dearreader. I shall make you
laugh,

---

*D.R. Note: Scott collected a series of notes for places like this. They were real guidelines which I have put at the back as *Endnotes*.

cry,
wince,
fuck,
cocksuckle,
pray,
confess,

rejoice: each and all at the right and decisive only moment. You will not get away dead! Because if you do so do I. And I don't want to die – not yet.

Are you ready?

Phoebes still buggering about in trio. Grackle on the island floor. Muskrat working in the green shoots fresh from thawed water. And busily obscene – aflight from brush to bush to back again there now tail quavering the willow Warbler.

It is still greygreygray. Though warmer grey now – sunbluffed. Making my greysould black irridescent is grackleheadiness purifies.

Yellowsplurt back at my righteye. To-morrow it will be invincible. And I pregnable. Of course.

Goodnight, D.R.

S.

End of Segment One

DR, is where I really feel we're at, after re-reading all of this. And would best be called (when you're editing it):

THE CASE OF THE YELLOW WARBLER
(or the Tail of the Poppycocks)
along with this

Glossary

(I'll leave it at the Pococks) you asked for. Makes bloody good sense to me if it helps you focus on what was focussing (and unfocussing) me. It's incomplete (*e.g.* I note now I've left out FWC: The Fink-Who-Cares, the Canadafink etc). But it does pinpoint my critique of The Canadian State, for example, and relates it to the Sexual Revolution (what I prefer to term the Resurrection of Sensibility) and, of course, the Yellow Warbler. You were dead right when you sensed a fundamental relationship between the three things – *e.g.*, between, to take three Letters, the Letter defining the Smugly Fucklings, the Troika with Sis-and-Lil abed, and the Warbler Walk. All three being variants of Canadian Coitus-Interruptus. And thus all three ONE AND THE SAME SCENE AT DIFFERENT STAGES. *But all of this I am myself just beginning to feel out and see.* First it had to take place in us.

In each case I've tried to give the earliest mention, and then indicate further sources in the Letters.

BLANDMANSLAND
The gelded Canada that is the New Nation. The McCanadian State. The result of same. The "Good Society"
The Emasculate Conception
The Canadian Identity
The Canadian Hersey.
All one and the same. A land based upon slow drainage of potence, of Body and Blood, of "Real Presence." A land of civil (but not civilized) eunuchs.

Also: BLANDEBEESTE – the Civil Servant of Blandland
BLANDEBESTIALITY (see Smugfuck, Stalemate, Pussywhip)
BLANDEBESTIARY (see Order of the Crystal Balls)

THE CANADIAN DEATH
The peculiarly Canadian Disease Malignant, Catching. Tendency to epidemic.
Diagnosis –
Phase 1: a wan smile, limp hand, shuffling step. A lethargy of movement generally. A slurring of words. Poor or no lip-action. A reluctance to touch. Expresses itself socially, civically, in a sense of satisfaction. A corporate and political Smugness. "Good Citizenship." Common in urban centres.
Phase 2: effective blindness. Eyes that see neither in nor out. A set "stare"; a glaze

of the eyeballs. Politiceyes. Paralleyes. Methodisteyes. (See refs.) A complete "niceness" of manner, hiding total loss of vitality. Inability to erect. A real fear of touching. Wide-spread in Civil Service occupations, United Church, etc. Increasing.

Phase 3: Total Impotence. The Negative Orgasm, and the Smugly Fuck. Absolute inability to touch in any way. Appears to reach absolute condition in Liberal Prime Ministers, Cabinet Ministers, University Presidents, Members of the Canada Council. Certain Death. No known survivors.

Causes: essentially POLISCHIZO – the government policy of Divide to Rule. A form of political cancer, of the brain and the sensibility. Hard
to catch in early phases, because *seems* to be
a form of "goodness" and health: hence
BENIGNANCE.

Cure: No medicure. Sight of the Yellow Warbler
works miracles. Also Yellow Orchids, or yellow
of any kind.

HOYhome The indigenous Home of the Honest Ontario Yeoman.
    Built circa 1840-70.
    Thus Century Homes.
    Red-and-white brick, two-three-and-four-faced effect as if each side a front, a
Facade.
    A quality of wide-eyes, of "stare" to the windows.
    Closed doors. Trim added later.
    Georgian decor (quoins, etc) but organic body. Half-and-half.
    The basis of United Church Union, *i.e*, Presbyterian stone foundations, stance, pique of gable. Methodist bulk of body. (see Significant Form.)
    A major artifact of McCanada. Symptomatically NOT academicated. (*e.g*., no book on *HOYhomes: A Study in the Squat Mosaic*).

CANADIAN LITURGICAL SEASONS The fundamental insight into Canadian Sensibility. The recognition that the four seasons in Canada are a Liturgy, a form of celebrating a Faith: i.e., each season is a Man, a Landscape, a Religious Denomination, a form of Church Architecture, a Mode of Perception and of knowledge (an Epistemology), and a Political Creed.
    Thus:
        Winter
        McCanadianman
        Jackpine Group-of-Seven-Land (rocks 'n rowboats)
        Canadian Presbyterianism
        Pinched Stoney Gothic (piqued gables, etc.; part of HOYhome)
        The Presbyterianeye (a world of discrete visual particulars) and the

Flesh-Made-Word (the Heresy of same) Grit-and-Granite Liberalism. Auto-
nomania (merely the political consequences a visual world of divided particulars).
Artifact: Alex Mackenzie -
first Grit Prime Minister, Scottish Immigrant, Presb. Stone Mason
(contracted for Canadian Parliament Bldgs), etc.Canadian Liturgical controversy
has been between Winter and Summer. Winter captured the Civil Service,
Parliament, The Canadeye, Patrioticity, Federal architecture, etc. But Summer is
acumen in!

McCANADA (or Mac CANADA, interchangeably)
Canada as Scotland's Revenge. Scottish-Canada.
The fact that English-Canada is a misnomer, causing untold political-religious
confusion.
The Scots as the power behind the Throne they were always toppling to sit
there themselves (known also as Canadian Nationalism). The Hidden Canadian
Authority.

YELLOW WARBLER
Dendroicha petechia. One of 36 Warblers to be seen in Ontario, of which 17 nest
in the Metro Toronto area.
The common-or-garden Warbler.
The Song of the Land.
The Sunbright, and sear of Ontario.
The Cock of the Man and of the Land (Ontari-ari-areee-o)
My Cock and Yours. Which is why we never face up to it clearly, but catch only
glimpses, from brush to brush.
Only known antidote to Blandland, and the Canadian Death.

CIVIC SQUARE The Anti-Hero of these Letters. The Anti-Body.
The Central Square in Toronto
The Torontoman; the prototype of the Canadian Cube. (An American-
square-In-Committee-of-the-Whole – i.e., an American square full of shit. See Place
d'Armes.)
A three-dimensional square.

POPPYCOCKS Nickname of Young Blandmen when masquerading in their true
identity,

HERMAPHROBIKE The motorcycles of the young set. In reality an instant portable
buggery kit. Manning the rider fore and aft. Thus Hermaphrodite.
The new ride-a-cock-horse.
Do-it-yourself sodomation,
Also: the female version – Butch-bitch-dike, who rides bikes.
Hence HERMAPHRODISIAC, HERMAPHRODIZZY, HERMAPHRODAZE, ETC.
Offers a partial cure to the Canadian Death. Sensation of instant healing of polis-
chizofrenzy. A snare and a delusion. Along with strobe-lights, drugs, etc.

VROOOM-VROOOM The coital sound of hermaphrobiking. Has, curiously, the same *effect*, superficially, as birdsongs, on the inner-ear. But the Vrooom-vrooom is rape, while bird-song is seduction. Each is invitation to potence.

GIFT OF GAZE The instant absolute gift of one to another. Passes through the eyes, direct to thighs. Creates instant potence. And thus the equivalent of the Laying-on-of-Hands (sexually or liturgically). Can be done not only between man and man or woman. But between man and any object. Provided the object spies you first! The exact opposite to Paralleyes, Methodisteyes etc.

EYEBALLS TOETITS NOSENIPPLE EARCOCK COCKTIT ASSOUL

The normal equipment of the sentient man.

The regular elements of the human perceptor-set.

Rarely acknowledge and even more rarely used in a Square or Civic Society, as a result of "the long Newtonian sleep." In fact a total tabu. The entire body (including the Mind) as a tool of percipience. See T.S. Eliot – "think-ing at the end of your fingertips."#

In Academic Circles sometimes termed "the total sensorium." But only described, never used. "Implosion": academic word for Sodomy, spiritual or phys-ical. See also SODOMEYE, DEPTHCHARGE, etc.

MALE SUFFRAGETTE MOVEMENT The belated movement to emancipate men from cock-kill, Queen Victoria, the Consumer-Mommy, Cat-Women, etc.

The major social-political factor of the second half of the 20th century.

The positive meaning of current militant homosexuality. Not to be confused with the Gay World ("Are you happy; no I'm gay," etc.). Nor with The Company of Young Canadians: Boyscouts for Blandland alias Mickey Pearson's Pan-Canadian Catamites.

THE AUTHORIZED VERSION

The official interpretation of Canada and of Canadian History.
The "Bible of Pan-Canadianism."

It is incantatory, unctuous, plausible.
It is Whig-Liberal (Glibib), linear, McCanadian,
Bland.
Failure to believe is Low Treason.
It is The Canadian Heresy.

THE DISABLED ENNABLER

The Blandebeeste who, having castrated Canada ("the Emasculate Conception") to obtain Responsible Government – i.e., Power, then turns round and

DR – Note – Add "the balls of your feet"

proffers potence to us mere citizens.

The Civic Eunuch who claims to create potence.

Usually is $ and Cents (no symbol).

Best example is the Canadacouncillor.

ROYAL TOUCH, THE

Traditional capacity of man to be king, and to heal with his "touch." In England died with George III (who went mad and who lost America which promptly also "lost touch" and went "mad," lost all organic society, etc.) In Anglicanism the ceremony of the Laying On Of Hands which passes on the Touch of Our Lord; normally occurs in boys and girls at the moment of puberty – i.e., of potence, fertility. (But no such Handlay in United Church of Canada, Methodism, etc.) The Gift, of gaze, of life. See Michelangelo's depiction of God "touching" Adam into life. The umbilink back to Adam in each of us.

The Gift that the Disabled Ennabler covets and the which he will kill in others, if he cannot get. (See Autonomania, The Authorized Version, Presbyterianeyes, etc.)

In Ancient Greece the normal social rite of Sodomy between Youth and Man in Prime of Life.

See also: HERMAPHROBIKE: the modern version – with bike as cock, and rider as Hermaphrodite.

-Touchstones

-Touch-Me-Nots

AUTONOMANIA

The prevalent disease of McCanadaland, Blandland, etc.

A Phase in the Canadian Death.

The obsessive belief that each man, isolated, and that Canada, isolated, contains Sufficient Truth for Grace, Redemption, etc.

A result of the Canadian Heresy.

See also: Responsible Government

The Commonwealth Canada Made

From: AUTONOMY – the Real Presence of McCanadaland.is in fact Half-Way House between Real Presence and Real Absence (for Half-Way House see HOYhouse).between Touchability and Untouchability.

SMUGLY FUCKLINGS, THE

The BLANDEBEESTES

The ruling McCanadian Incaste (the toptits of the Squat Canadian Mosaic)

By extension all those they de-touch, de-tach (see ANTIBODIES)

Thus the BLANDMEN
The Torontonian, the CIVIC SQUARE,
The Canadian Citizen.
Thee'n Me – until we do or prove otherwisely!
    Etymology: SMUG – the diagnostic sign of the
Canadian Death

        UGLY – the Nice Man, the citizen of the Good Society, who
is in fact malignant (Canadian BENIGNANCE; see also Hepatitis: the Canadian
Cancer).

        FUCK – they lay claim to (*e.g.*, *Love Where the Nights Are Long*,
etc.); but see Rapesmen, Negative Orgasm, No-Ball Peace Prize, etc.,
    hence definitive diminutive: FUCKLING

ÆE: ANTI-ESTABLISHMENT ESTABLISHMENT

Same as the SMUGLY FUCKLINGS;
The McCanadian Incaste which is really an Outcaste-Got-In but
Unconsecrate (no Laying on of Hands, no Authority, No Potence, No-Balls).
The "protestants" in the position of power but sans power. A major problem
of Canadianism: those who have progressively accumulated power have always
protested that they *hate* power (see DRY LUST). Thus they preside, but cannot (for
the little life of them) rule (hurray! -meanwhile, in lower Slovovia, Yorkville, etc.,
we're raising shit).
Contrast the DEE: DIS-ESTABLISHED ESTABLISHMENT.
The Anglicanadian Economic Underground – now thoroughly overhead: see
Toronto-Dominion Tower, Place Ville Marie (Royal Bank of Canada), Bank of
Commerce, etc.
    For a typically belated, disgruntled, naive, and vindictive McCanadian
discovery of the DEE, see *The Vertical Mosaic*. But the AEE is now top of the Squashed
Mosaic and is as rightight a little club (of *utterly* Unclubbables) as ever had the mis-
fortune to half-exist.
It has its own schools: the top of the Ryersonian Ontario System – *e.g.*, Jarvis
Collegiate, U.T.S., Victoria College, Queen's, Carlton, etc.
Its own Church (United).
Its own Château Fort (The Ontario Century Homes).
Its own dress – *e.g.*, Blueblazer, greyflannels and brown shoes. Or the New
Canadian Armed Forces Uniformity.
Any analysis of the McCanadian Incaste would show an *inordinate* percentage
were Presbyterian-Methodistical, Scottish, Lower Middle Class, Collegiate,
Barnyard (hence the Log-Cabin Cult), etc. Many are sons or grandsons of
Methodist Ministers. With a few Sons-of-Bishops thrown in to give "tone,"
"respectability," "face," etc. Especially in External Affairs. (Being "Notes to the
Squat Mosaic: a Reply to the Mute Mediocre Methodist Mannikins.")
Even the names indicate: Winters, Sharp, Gordon, etc ...
Yet this group represents less than 25% of the total population! In fact if one
analysed essential membership requirements: Century Farm (HOYhouse or
equivalent), Victoria College, Methodist Minister Forebear, etc., one would find

they represent less than 1% of the population, yet of the major Civil Service Posts they hold a controlling share, and veto-power over the rest so that (somewhere in my brain, DR, there is a loud and raucous insane horselaugh forming – yet the McCanadian Incaste has NO SENSE OF HUMOUR. None of them, reading this will be *laughing*, but saying instead "who is this person, who wrote this? He is an outrageous, obscene and distorted snob": and the cleverer ones will be even saying "and he knows it," (*thus defining themselves forthwith as SMUGLY FUCKLINGS*)

    Oh laugh, and pray

    Summary: The AEE is responsible but impotent.
        The DE is potent but irresponsible (no access to public posts)
        This Impasse (see THE CANADIAN IMPASSE) has the AEE as Objective Correlative, the SMUGFUCK as Subjective Correlative. The one is a direct function of the other!
    i.e., the Political Stalemate is a Sexual Stale-mate;
    Plischiz is also Erotischiz.
    It has one advantage: anyone who wants to be blatantly creative on his own terms can, and get away with it!

MIK: THE MAN IN THE KNOW

    In general, the Man Who Reads the *Globe and Mail*,
    the Man to whom the *Globe* appeals.
    The Upper-middling Class Torontoman
    The Improved Smugly Fuckling
    See also: McCanadaman – the *Globe* was historically known as "the Scotsman's *Bible*" in Ontario
    In these Letters MIK is also the Man who sweetly lent me his apartment in Rosedale.

C.f., The Toronto Daily Stare: appeals to the mass of HOYmen. Hence the "stare"; as with the face of HOYhomes. Advertises itself as "the newspaper for Young Adults," means Apprentice Squares. Whereas *Globe* doesn't stare, but scrutineyeses: its ad is a pair of dark-horny rimmed glasses
    Also *Toronto Telegram* (for the Fink-Who-Cares)

THE SECRET The simple fact of potence. In Canada to survive it had to go underground. Lies largely in the pants of the Anglicanadians, though much now perverted into economic powerplants. Before the Union of Methodists and Presbyterians could be found with them. (*E.g.*, The Methodist Bellow was ball-roar.)

MALE MAIDENHEAD The veil of permanent virginity that is drawn over the Blandman from earliest childhood. Nothing penetrates except what Home, School, and Rule want. Shows best (worst) in the eyes – like hard, cold, impenetrable windows. (See HOYhouse.) Also the walk, the arse tucked under (not just in women, but in men); c.f., cockwalk.

SMUGLY FUCK The Canadafuck. The McCanadian Fuck. The Blandfuck. It is a closed-fuck. A simple masturbatory passage of sperm-to-cleancunt. It celebrates virginity and to-touch. Guarantees 10 days of committee efficiency and good housekeeping. Raised to its logical culmination becomes the Negative Orgasm. The man and the woman conjugate without physical contact. The moment of intensity passes in a brief redemptive bicker; (*c.f.*, The American Fun-Fuck; and the Faith-Fuck.)

THE EMASCULATE CONCEPTION The McCanadian State: the Canadian Identity; The Good Society; the Canadian Heresy – all one and the same; all based upon loss of potence and of "Real Presence."

THE MULTIPLE VETO The fact that no-one or no-body in Canada has Positive Power. Only veto-power. The Multiple No. Mommypower, Torontopower, Ottawapower, Churchpower, Schoolpower: all say NO. Who says Yes? If not Thee and Me? Someone must ... Soon.

DENDROICA PETECHIA Specific name for the Yellow Warbler. Used as an alias, and to prevent mere labelling etc. Forcing DR to indentify by Feel, and not by name. Same technique used for other birds, etc.

Heritage

Ave Atque Vale ... .

... with a twenty-foot house-trailer, to live close to land, the houses, the people ... to hug these close. Starting out in the South-Western tip of Ontario – Point Pelee National Park, in early May. Watching the Trilliums and Warblers sprouting Spring (each time a warbler touched a branch tip it burst green!)

Trips into the surrounding countryside – spotting those mid nineteenth century Ontario farmhouses, red-and-white brick. Getting my eye in. And, on Sundays, ending up at the local Anglican Church – instinctively steeping in that "beauty of holiness" that is our age-old faith.

Then in June, my eye attuned to land and homes, setting out – to follow Spring and Summer across Eastern Canada – till Autumn bled the harvests home again.

Along the old #3 Highway, Blenheim, Rodney (historic names in British history), past Port Talbot where Colonel Talbot's early log manor still stands. And as I drive, realizing that something is watching me. Uneasily aware of being stared at. Which I cannot understand. Till I catch their eye – ahh, the wide-eyed windows, the high-chested fronts, the sternly laced verandahs: the Ontario farmhouses; Victoriana, *watching* me! Strong, sturdy, straddling the land – commandeering my admiration, yet at the same time holding me off at arm's length. Some yeoman version of Holbein's Henry VIII, these homes. Uncrowned majesty ... somehow.

St. Thomas, focusing the reality of this definitive Victorian Ontario farm home. Because St. Thomas is simply an agglomerate of these farm houses grown bigger and more ornate, and stuck together. Contiguous – but not really touching.

Aylmer, Simcoe, Chippawa, where my folk were first buried on the Canadian side of the water, the Niagara water – nearly two centuries ago now. And the Niagara River, with turbulent majesty. Knowing that this waterway may be the real divide between historic Canada and the United States. If Niagara Falls and gorge had not existed, then Americans would have moved on into indefensible Ontario lands – back in 1800, 1812.

And the Niagara Parkway, all peace and green and quiet, with Brock's monument standing high over the gorge. A hero if we ever had one.

Queenston landing, where family legend said that Simcoe's gunboat brought my people over to the British side. Queenston, with its quiet homes and lanes, like some English village. Or some equally lost eighteenth century American village! And I want to get lost here ... again. And up to my left, through the skyhigh pines, the majestic Roman architecture of Willowbank – some permanent metaphor out of "Gone with the Wind"; remembering me that the Cavalier tradition came North, after the American Revolution.

Niagara-on-the-Lake – some live dream from our immediate and ever past – with its Palladian Gothic Church. And its main street that can only be strolled. Breakfast at the Oban Inn, overlooking Ontario's lake! With time for tea and marmalade. Sinking in to the monumentally comfortable Victorian sofas.

The back road, gravelled, around Saint Catharine's, through Jordan, with its old stone homes, its fine Church on the hill, up inside it, to admire the waving on the prayer cushions, the altar frontal. And to pray awhile.

Ball's Falls – jack-in-the-pulpit everywhere.

Dundas, with its greystone homes, and its resident sage, George Grant, in his red-and-white-brick "century Ontario home" … screened by chestnut trees and tulips. A centre of peace. Explaining to him what I hope to do … to see, to *be* on this voyage in to the old, original Canadian culture, once more. Call it a "sentimental journey" … to set my heart at ease. "Yes *yes*, DO it Scott … *hurry* and do it," George says.

Hamilton, where my mother's mother's family sat in Presbyterian fief – a century ago. Stern, handsome men and women they were. Like Paul Peel's portraits said. County versions of the High Society Henry James depicted in Boston, London.

And on to Dundurn Castle, which reminds me that Casa Loma has roots in Upper Canada.

Burlington, where my father's family received their Crown Grant of Land, as Loyalists. The original home still standing up to five years ago, when it was burnt, to clear the land for a public park. I asked the authorities if they could not keep the home, as a restaurant and utility. And I stayed, for the auto da fé!

The Queen Elizabeth Way, to Toronto, past huge Ford factories belching fire and finance. Port Credit – Mazo de la Roche land. Oh, she too was a romantic. But now her dream is gone, and seems all the more real. Canadians are, after all, simply romantics who lost the courage of their hopes.

Metropolitan Toronto, engulfing my truck and trailer home. Four, six, ten, twelve lanes. Am I proud of such size, or simply afraid?

Toronto the Good, City of Churches they named it, in my grandfather's era. All I can see are bank towers and trust companies now.

And the old Parliament buildings. Queen Vic asquatting – with the business palaces dependant from her very lap, down University Avenue.

Everything here solid, stolid, foursquare – unbending! All one and the same thing. Things which touch but do not marry.

And as I leave Toronto there is something heavy in me – which is maybe the very weight of the city itself. Its very density and solidity. Moving off the speedway onto the Old Front Road – Highway #2. To Port Hope – which is the first complete old Ontario town east of Toronto. With its half-dozen sharp spires, a prickly agglomerate of faiths, all protesting. And its red-brick mainstreet – so uprighteous.

And in the morning, saluting the Bluestone House as I leave … to Cobourg, with its mastodon Court House – some lost British palace standing firm in the midst of this nineteenth century Ontario town. The core of justice – again unbending, stolid – dispensing a truth as immitigable as the Ontario brick farmhouses.

Cobourg – and some miles on, that delicate white clapboard presence who is the Barnum House. Stopping to pay homage to this Greek Revival beauty settled here on the Ontario Front. Yankee dash at its most delicate. Just as the Cobourg

Court House was British majesty at its mightiest. Here on the old frontier. Both of them ancestors-in-common. Ours.

Taking lair in Prince Edward County – a kind of private rural keep, slung low into Lake Ontario – at Ameliasburg. And walking the country roads, see standing against the horizon, a massive farm home – at once cottage blown large, and castle writ small – some baby Blenheim this. And as I approach, realize what it is. Simply the most rotund mutation of the Honest Ontario farmhouse I have yet seen. It brings together the early rectangular and simple building (is it log underneath?) that was first home, as an outbuilding in the back; plus the gothic Victorian farmhouse with its peaked front gable (like some affronted lorgnette!); plus the High Victorian cube-shaped bulked house, added on front. All of these, partly grown out of each other, partly added on to each other – partly organic and partly mindful – all of these brought together as a single home! The absolute nineteenth century Ontario farm home. Red-and-white brick ... and all the elements bound together by a fully foliating verandah, which starts at the old back door (the gothic middle house) and comes right round the front to embrace the main block of the newer house ... culminating in a fine bay window through which I see a mass of plants in pots.

And inside are richly grain-painted cupboards and woodwork; pine, hand-painted to look like golden oak, mahogany and walnut. Full of swoop and flare. And upstairs, matching suites of monumental bed, dressers, wash-stand. With flowering violets in the windows. And – in the upstairs front hall, Victorian tassellated chairs, as deep and as square as the house itself. I walk out on to the second story verandah ... commanding a view of Roblin's lake and all the valley. Then down the front stairs, with its walnut bannister and at the foot, upright, thickset, with squared shoulders and a rounded knop -- the newel post grasps my hand.

As I leave, walking down the snake-railed road, I am saying over and over to the song of the crescent-breasted Meadowlarks, "this is the ancestral roof, this is the ancestral roof – mine and thine. This is the very flesh of a people, the way they walk, stand, talk – solidly, fully. Eyes straight ahead. No fooling ... Ontario – Ontaree-aree-areeoh."

And as I walk, I spot one, two, several of these homes – variations of each other, around the horizon.

Next day, picking up some homemade pumpkin (and gin!) jam ... and moving on:

Kingston, with its munificence of garrison greystone and Gananoque, a rural mutation of Kingston and Bath, an elegant diminutive of Gananoque to Upper Canada Village, where all of old Ontario lies to hand, our past as a manageable visual metaphor.

This was my voyage through old Ontario – not as breathless as seems. Yet every time I stopped, there was something about Ontario itself – the cumulative culture of it, all round me – which firmly kept me at once standing up and moving forward! As though this was the secret of Ontario civilization – and its very success!

* * *

At Cornwall I notice a decisive change.

The West side of the town is very respectable twentieth century Victorianate. But as I move Eastwards through it, the houses become less stern, the neon signs seem gaudier. And the names on the storefronts are French! For the next fifty miles, literally before my very eyes, I watch this remarkable visual metamorphosis: Ontario-into-Québec. British Upper Canada becoming la Nouvelle France ... No longer are the homes marching in rectilinear dialogue with the highway. But gradually they crowd in on one another – in a friendly garrulous higgledy-pigglement. Even the wood trim on the homes perceptibly changes, from a kind of wooden symmetry to something more akin to actual lace. By the time that I am twenty-five miles on into French Canada I am aware of what has happened. The British square, that rectitudinous cube (in stone or brick) that is old Ontario, has been breached – the body is beginning to undulate, from within! And I note that I am no longer driving by the line in the centre of the road – but instead from the homes or trees or buildings on each side ...

Ducking quickly through Montréal – because now it is hot July (and I have spent all Winter researching in Montréal) – with time only to enjoy the flowers sprouting all over in le Vieux Quartier (my God – it's Paris, with its kiosques and flea-markets and lounging lovers!) – on along the North Shore of the Saint Lawrence. Evading neon-lights and tourist gimcrap. Till beyond Trois Rivières, the road crosses a bridge – phooosh – right into the lap of the Church of Sainte-Anne-de-la-Pérade, this dollshouse "cathedral" which is some echo of Notre Dame in Montréal.

Deschambault – where the river banks rise high over the Sainted Lawrence, and Thomas Baillargé's glorious twin-towered church stands – *not* right-angular to either road or river, but at once set in, and riding high from, the accepting land. A majesty. Marrying river and Tiger Lilies in profusion, and fieldstone, and village. All unified in this single centre of praise. Yes ... we *can* be saved!

And with this O altitudo in my heart, settle deeper in my driving seat, and start the slow process of slowing down. In Québec there is Time still – and Time is not something to beat – but something to celebrate.

I camped outside Québec City, on the Ile d'Orleans, in a small private park – amidst the glittering Birch trees. Not seeing the Saint Lawrence, yet feeling it – in the eddying silences. And in the morning I drove down to Saint François, walking among the deep brown cattle, who – I suddenly saw – were the live, animal forms of Québec chest-of-drawers. The land and the animals in the eye of the craftsman. To the church beside the river, and feeling peace and giving thanks.

Hunting the quarry in Québec City for a few days ... finding ample – the splendorous Baroque Bed, whose very body sums up the trip from Cornwall to la Ville de Québec herself. The very way it moved. And Saint Michael slaying his friendly dragon (Catholic evil seems more graceful than Protestant).

But it was the Ile d'Orléans itself which was spiritual home. Visiting old friends, artists, farmers, judges – all living side to side, in the old homes. Seeing Jean-Charles Bonenfant, mowing his lawn ... stopping to chat, as always. "You are living an Odyssey ... back to your roots," he said. "Yes ... before they are gone," I replied.

And an evening on the East side of the island, at the home of Benoît Côté, the painter ... an eighteenth century farmhouse which he had made into his studio. Overlooking the Saint Lawrence, with the Falls of Montmorenci in the dusk distance, and the shimmer of lights from Québec City, twenty miles down to our left. Quel Bec! We sat amidst the deep Asters, and drank Chateauneuf du Pape while his bear-sized dog (un Bouvier de Flandres) romped.

Leaving Québec with sadness. Toronto is our Great City, our mod-Methodist New York. And Montréal is our gay city, our Paris. But Québec, ahh (I admit it happily) Québec is our Eternal City!

At Montmagny, stopped short, by a presence so unlike Québec – either land or people or homes. A great nineteenth century blockhouse of a building. The *form* of an Ontario brick yeoman home. But greystone – British. The British Canadian presence here, in some alien and handsome majesty. I went up – curious ... the Hôtel des Erables it is now – for dinner, which was substantial and good.

Staying at a small French Canadian trailer park, at Lac-Trois Saumons – Chez Ti-Bert. In the world of Kreighoff-for-real. Psychedelic gypsies, these old French Canadian folk. Hippies with Real Presence!

I meant to stay only a night – but I stayed three, four ... near the flowers and the tame ducks, and Ti-Bert himself walking as though in some perpetual square dance that was far from square.

And on Sunday going to the Mass at Saint-Jean-Port-Joli, remembering that this was the parish that had a solid gold Communion Service made at the end of the eighteenth century – by Ranvoyzé, I think. These poor peasants marooned in a Canadian Winter – giving thanks ... and a gold chalice.

And that afternoon I moved on, deeper into my Trek, finding signs of life and being. Following the dirt-and-gravelled roads. Amazed at the farms. Amidst rock and islands of good soil, their setting was tougher than Ontario – yet the homes were more lyrical. The verandahs more ornate. And always a rocking chair ... and someone in it.

Moving from St-Alexandre some fifty miles to the New Brunswick border, and then another fifty miles within New Brunswick to Edmundston, a strange event occurred. The French Canadian church metamorphosed before my very eyes. Those splendid grand-yet-simple stone parish churches lost some elegance, some life-slung quality – and became at once heavier and somehow more ornate. The stonework became sterner, less rhythmic. And in Edmundston, the Catholic Church was a huge, heavy stone monument. I had witnessed the passage from la Nouvelle France, to Catholicism within English-speaking Canada. Actually Edmundston is the capital of the Acadian French. And what I was seeing was the Canadian French adapting the very body of their belief to English-speaking eyes.

Something else occurred. I was not only passing from Catholicism to Protestantism. I was also passing along the U.S. border. Not two, but three cultures were mingle-mangling. On my right, across the St. John River, the stark white farm homes, all rectilinearity, and almost paperweight – in contrast with Ontario rectitudinosity. And in contrast with the enlivened substance of French Canadian homes, these white clapboard facades felt like movie-sets. It was New England, northern Maine, jutting up into the very joints of Canada. And in general contrast with these New England homes, New Brunswick farms were somewhat heavier. It was a precise example of three faiths, expressed in three different forms, fighting to claim the land.

A day and a night at a camp called Mountain View, looking up to Blue Bell Mountain – a sweet symmetry! Talking with the neighbouring farmer ... and going for dinner – on blue Scandinavian china – with home-made Aquavit. I was in the heart of an old Danish settlement. So I stayed another day, and then two, three. Going to the small white wooden church atop the hill nearby. The valley and hills rolling out beyond, like Devonshire. The church was Danish Lutheran ... and inside, the wall-panelling was that feathering I recognized from Scandinavian country homes. The pastor invited me for lunch.

When I left, a week later, I had Ontario in my bones, French Canada in my soul, and New Brunswick in my blood!

At Fredericton I knew a professor of Canadian History, Ken Windsor. And I ended up giving a "lecture" to his students – in comparative visual geography: the grid-iron flattened manscape of old Southern Ontario compared with the rumpling and rising Saint Lawrence Magnificat of Québec, and now the rolling hills and rivers of New Brunswick. How the houses were the people, were the furniture and the churches and the sounds of the voices. How Ontario voices came from without, like memos, as external affairs; and Québec voices were nasal and internal – like their deep little homes, and in New Brunswick it was a bit of both.

And later Ken and I talked of what I was *really* doing: this personal Odyssey in-to the heart of early Canadian belief ... with furniture as central evidence of an entire culture. Ken was thrilled – and said "You know – we forget how much religion was the core of early Canadian life." So I opened up and explained that in our early furniture I found the evidence of all this. How the stolid sentience of Ontario furniture, the uncompromising and straight mass of it, was the same as the early Ontario homes and people. And how these were the same as the early Presbyterian and Methodist brick and stoney churches. How – when all was said and done – Ontariana was Methodism with improved manners. *High* Methodist. A world of extrinsic emotions!

Ken laughed, and offered me a glass of Hoch – so I vouchsafed the Québec correlative: the tumescent Saint Lawrence land, austere, yet sumptuous, like the churches, like the Armchair à la Canadienne, or the Sainte-Geneviève commodes, like Sir Wilfrid Laurier ... the inner fleshed rhythms of these, a total human presence – that becomes, in the Mass, the total Presence Of Christ ... Body and Blood. So that I understood the Medieval experience of Blood running down the Altar.

And now, in the Maritimes, something else again – something "other." Oh, something in between. Some of the cubicular form of Ontario – but lighter. With some flow. Ontario is stone and brick and stolidity. The Maritimes are wood and winds. "And water," said Ken. And there is some of that inner music that is Québec; sounds are intrinsic. "The Maritimes are 'folk Whig,'" Ken offered – "the Real Presence is there if you want it."

Next morning we walked down from the University Campus ... along that street of munificent Victorian wooden homes, where Bliss Carmen and Charles Roberts spent some mutual youth. To Morning Song in the Anglican Cathedral.

We were the only ones there.

Thence I drove to Gagetown, where Sir Leonard Tilley was born ... visited his childhood home – so simple and elegant. Gagetown – where the Black Watch recently held their final parade. And grown men wept.

And on, to Saint John, Sackville, Halifax – always questing ... and the evidence growing – of our past, the reality of the furniture as the flesh and faith of our peoples. One and the same.

So that by August I was in Port aux Basques, Newfoundland. Resting for a week in the small fishing outport of Trout River. And staying five months! – assimilating all that I had been seeing. Till in January I reached Saint John's. And here I found a large version of what I had already seen in Trout River. A people and a culture as old as the Tudors, living in homes that were some fluent folk combination of medieval substance and Georgian lines. Medieval fidelity and Georgian lucidity. And – like the Mallard House at Quidi Vidi – possessed of furniture ranging in style from the Iron Age through to Victorian blown silvered glass candlesticks. Everything had been kept, everything had grown.

And when I left Saint John's a few weeks later my body and my mind and soul were at one. I wanted to sing ... I had followed the forms of our past clean across Eastern Canada – living close to them, living in them – for over a year. I had sought and found our hidden or forgotten ancestors. And I knew for certain that the furniture of the old homes was equally the furniture of the heart and mind and soul of these people. The forms of one were the forms of all the rest. Yes, I had tracked the ancient forms of our faith, from the heart of a great continent, to where they began, at the bitten edge of land and ocean. And at the very moment when it was clear that my people had to make their ultimate choice, between faith and cynicism ... I had renewed my faith – and I rejoiced ...

Pictou Portal

The overt form of this substantial pine doorway is late eighteenth century English Adamesque. The fanlight, the urns atop the side columns, the bevelled panels, the reeding, and the "sun's rays" over the fanlight: all of these are in the neo-classic tradition which was essentially (in England at least) an intellectual and cultural achievement of the aristocracy.

Yet we recognize that this vigorous doorway, so ostensibly neo-classic Enlightenment in form, is in fact something quite other. It is the very ebullience of this door which leaves us anything but "detached." We can try to flatten it out, tie it down, with our appreciative eye ... but it keeps bouncing back – and aristos just *don't* bounce! There is definitely some kind of flow and spring and ... and flesh to this door. Maybe it's those large suns, maybe it's those forms above the urns, suspiciously like fish! Maybe it's the distending deep-carved angel-wings over the fan ... The late Georgian form – the High Style Aristocrat – and the bounce and bustle of the piece, these come together and fuse. And it is this which is definitive to the door, making it unique, making it someone particular.

Who? Just Who is this "person" combining with such warm precision, such reasonable embodiment, both the bouncing bod of folk and the detached mindfull eye of the eighteenth century aristocrat?

It can't be European: there the folk did not ape their betters with such nonchalance; nor did the European bourgeois retain such pith. It isn't New England: not enough asperity and too much flesh (damnable!). Though it might be early Connecticut there is yet something too militantly massive about it, something too British. Nor is it French Canadian: it is too reasonable, too balanced – it never takes off! It is neither so garrulously folk nor so gaudily High as the best French Canadiana!

And finally, it is not early Ontario: there is something too imaginative about it, something too gusty and gutsy.

No. This doorway comes from the famous Twelve Mile House of West River – in its day the greatest hostelry east of Halifax – near Pictou, Nova Scotia.

This harmonious fusion of firm yet frolicking folk and dignified responsible squire – the blending at once of the common people and the man of quality: what Thomas Haliburton did with Sam Slick and Squire Poker; and what the Nova Scotians did as a people. Even today the Maritimers have it – a sense of sentient presence, in the flesh and mind and eye ...

Wood: pine
Date: about 1830
Place: Nova Scotia Museum, Citadel Hill, Halifax.

Armchair à la Canadienne

... remember when you first put your arms around me. In the Ile d'Orléans home of artist energumen, Claude Picher. We were in full agape, eating perdrix au chou and wild rice, with a 1951 Château Ausone. When Claude shot bolt upright and called for a "trou normand" – that intermission in a meal which is a shot-glass of Calvados drunk neat, so that the throat roasts and a hole is drilled through your stomach to accommodate more food.

I lurched happily up from the table and toppled into your undulant arms. And found my fingers wandering your rolling, turning, roiling arms, legs, seat. Fingers turning with your expanding walnut flesh, caught at the rim of yet another tip, top, knop – and a ludicrous smile of ecstasy that ...

"MAUDITS ANGLUCHES, VOUS ETES CONSTIPES ... "[57] – Claude roaring benignantly at me.

I felt some anger, consternation at Claude's taunts, and also at this way I was lolling in your arms, undignified, finger-tippling. And I extricated myself from

57 Damned English jerks, you're constipated

your arms, as though somehow I had been *had* – some part of me touched that must absolutely not ...

"THAT CHAIR, HE LIKES YOU, 'TI ANGLUCHE, 'TI CUL CARRE"[58] – Claude leering like some heavenly Mephistopheles through the added perspective of the Calvados. My wife managing a wan smile, while eyeing you as possible encroachment on our marriage. I could not understand but knew.

That was in 1959 – my core attained. My smug opacity ended.

I learned later that you are called a "Salamander Chair" for unknown reasons; in French "une chaise à la capucine," after your cowled back-rails, like a Capuchin monk's hood.

I learnt, too, that there is no chair style precisely like you in France – or anywhere else. And I began to recognize you as definitive, with your Louis Treize turning legs, and your full-embodied form virtually Louis Quatorze, and all your gaiety and elegances recalling the Régence and Watteau's Voyage to Cythera; and your arms, Louis Quinze rocaille. I realize that you were somebody unique.

I started my quest for you. And each time I found you, I knew again you were some-body – with your folk Catholic forms. And your peasant ebullience, yet your high courtliness ... till one day I accepted you as the French Canadian par excellence – you, the habitant made good! With your Medieval roots, your Renaissance and Baroque faith, and your French rococo manners – plus post-Conquest affluence. You kept everything together. Perfect case of cottage-King. I rejoiced with you.

And then, in 1964, we heard that there were a dozen of you in Montréal, available. You came dear – at a thousand dollars a head. But your vitality was necessary (my wife's dead grandfather paid). And we set you around our twelve-foot Refectory dining table, also from Québec. And watched you always alive, moving, conversing, laughing – yet serene. Quick, and not born into some still-life. We called you (in private) the Twelve Apostles.

I bought a large Crucifix, from the Gaspé, to complete you. Already you were "inadmissible evidence" – some kind of carnal rosary, confuting the Ontario Matriarch in the Mink Coat and high (sharp) heels, and Birks Blue Box.

You see, in the end, you won in me. Or, as Jacques Godbout warned me long ago – "you'll have to become a French Canadian to survive!" And I did.

Woods: walnut and maple
Date: end of the 18th century
Place: Canadiana Gallery, Royal Ontario Museum

---

58 Li'l English jerk, li'l square ass.

Adamesque Corner Cupboard

... like some great Iroquois mask, eyes aglint, mouth agape, body half-swallowed by its own mouth, this handsome cupboard comes to you as some phantas-magoric beast – if you see it in terms of its own embodiment and form – and not simply as a period piece. It comes at you strong and solid, broad in the chest, a potency

some Easter Island icon, straddling the land

which is how I see it first. As a being, some personage. Which is how it, he, she, *wants* to be seen. I know, after a dozen years evading the truth.

And this reality acknowledged, why then you are also free to see this godlike statue as a corner cupboard – of a very special kind. In his recent book, *Civilization,*

Kenneth Clark talks of "that simple, almost rustic, classicism that stretches right up the eastern seaboard of America, and lasted for one hundred years, producing a body of civilized domestic architecture equal to any in the world."

This cupboard is part of the North American classicism Lord Clark describes. It, along with an intermittent chain of fine houses across southern Ontario, and similar attractive furniture, proves that the fine sensibility of Robert Adam, and his brother James, indirectly touched Upper Canada. This particular piece was probably made about 1810, for one of the numerous Loyalist families who settled in the Kingston area. Variations of it could have been found in such homes as the Alpheus Jones house, in Prescott, or the Davey house, in Bath.

It is the very expanded, animated, cerebral quality of this cupboard – the inflated frieze, and fan-work, and paterae – which mark this piece for me as North American. Like French Canadian church carvers, the man who created this piece took European high-style elements, and blew them up, larger than life, larger than their own proportions ... to catch the eye. Hallucinogenic!

And it is the broad beam of it, the very strength and squatness of this cupboard which identifies if for me as Upper Canadian. In contrast with its English cousin, who would be more delicately self-poised; or its Yankee cousin, who would be lighter, less grand.

It has that specific combination of inflated geometric forms (neo-classic), and sheer ponderosity – some almost uneasy balance of mere-mind and sheer-mass, with some additional element of innate elegance, which makes it Yankee-Ontario Loyalist. As though the Loyalists were caught between the stolid virtues of King Billy's Whig Revolution of 1688 and the more purely intellectual assertions of the Age of Enlightenment. Plus some tincture of Stuart panache.

This is Ontario: call it ... High Methodist!

Wood: pine
Date: early 19th century
Place: Canadiana Gallery, Royal Ontario Museum

County Hepplewhite Sideboard

that we are all born in log-cabins, a slop-pail away from the chicken-sty

that snake-rail was our Crown of Thorns, opening up a new land; scraping grain from granite under a lowering (Homer Watson) sky

that we were all some kind of high-brow-hayseeds. Hayseeds with some burdensome allegiance to the respectability of Church and Crown (and some hidden deeper allegiance to future affluences!)

that we were all simple sons of the earth, with Mission explicit to build "the True North, strong and free" (McDougal of Alberta, all of us) – an improved Americaland, sans rye.

This is the myth, tacit (and Methodist at that) Canadian myth. Call it the Log-Cabin Myth. Similar in style to the tale that all Australians were progeny of penitentiaries.

But the fact is that there was always another culture in Canada. A culture of sophistications, elegances, poise and literacy. A culture which stretched from Saint John's to Niagara-on-the-Ontario-Lake, and West. Just as it stretched from

Sidney to Wellington to Bombay to rococo Philadelphia. A culture well-symbolized by those Gibbs' style Churches in each place named (Toronto's early Saint James' Cathedral was one, before the fire of 1836).

A culture represented by Frances Brooke's novel, written in 1769, in Québec City, about British Garrison life there ... *Emily Montague* – an early *Pride and Prejudice* it is.

A culture reflected in the articulate Diaries and Letters of women such as Ann Langton ... writing of the trials of a Gentlewoman in Upper Canada, like Mrs. Moodie.

No hayseeds there. But thoughtful, courteous and hard-working gentlefolk who brought their philosophy of neo-platonism, and their politics of Crown-in-Parliament, and their religion of mitigated Catholicism, Anglican ... to Canada.

This small Hepplewhitish sideboard belongs to the sophisticated English-speaking culture long domiciliated in Canada. With its finely bowed front, its delicate inlays, its oval Adamesque drawer-pulls, its arcaded centre, it is a simplified version of elaborate pieces being made in London by the world's finest craftsmen at the end of the eighteenth century.

You could have found it, in Canada, anywhere from Halifax to Windsor, around 1810. One very similar to it, larger, is at present in Rideau Hall, Ottawa. Both are in that wood distinctive of Eastern North America – Tiger Stripe Maple ... the poor man's Satinwood!

Wood: maple
Date: about 1810
Place: Canadiana Gallery, Royal Ontario Museum

Culture and Conservatism in Canada

George Grant's preface to *Heritage*

(Unpublished) Diary of Symons/Taylor/Lee visit to Grant in 1980

This section contains texts that bring together Scott Symons and George Grant. Early on in *Place d'Armes*, Symons' alter ego, Hugh Anderson, informs us that he has not yet read *Lament for a Nation*, Grant's hugely influential book of 1965. The extraordinary coincidence of the publication of Grant's work and Symons' dramatic resignation and troubled voyage to Montréal in the same year is culturally revealing evidence. Other points of convergence would follow as the two men later met and a rather careful and improbable friendship emerged. Correspondence archived at Trinity College, University of Toronto reveals that Grant was troubled by Symons' radicality, his extreme aestheticism and his sexualization of so much of human life. Yet he clearly grasped the importance of Scott Symons' gesture of refusal and dismay as part of the crisis underway. The two men kept in intermittent contact over the years and, to cite one example of the regard in which each held the other, it was evidently at Grant's suggestion that Symons was contacted by David Warren of *The Idler*, a connection which led to a number of key interviews and articles.

The Preface written by George Grant for *Heritage* is at one and the same time a concise expression of Grant's own aesthetics, his way of comprehending beautiful human objects in relation to his broader philosophical preoccupations, and a very lucid reading of what Symons uniquely brings (and very likely too late) to Canadian culture.

Symons' account of his visit to Dundas is vintage diarizing. The portrait of Grant that emerges is admiring, compassionate, fraternal. Sighting Grant, citing him and situating him, was of fundamental importance to Symons, as the piece reveals. With the presence of "minor" characters, Charles Taylor, Dennis Lee, and Sheila Grant, the extended account is in fact more like a gallery of portraits than a single image. They give us Grant, "our greatest thinker" in Symons' terms, *in situ* and crucially in relation to others.

According to Symons the diarist, the visit marked a decisive turning point in his understanding of his own mission. In an addendum to the diary extract Symons reports how Grant told Taylor that Scott Symons needed to "go deeper." He was clearly moved by this remark.

George Grant's Preface to
Heritage: A Romantic Look at Early Canadian Furniture

It is a pleasure to write some words at the beginning of this splendid book, splendid both in what is said about the furniture by Mr. Symons and in how it is photographed by Mr. de Visser. Symons shows us consummately that the furniture of any time or place cannot be understood as a set of objects, but rather as things touched, seen, used, loved, in short, simply lived with through the myriad events which are the lives of individuals, of families, of communities, of peoples. For an object is any thing (whether stone or tree or even human being) when it is held by another outside himself so that it can be organized to show its potentialities for being at the disposal of other wills, as an undifferentiated source of supply.

As our society has become objectified, we can either buy furniture in Simpsons-Sears, or distantly look at it in museums. There is a long choice of supplies for us to buy: Italianate or Swedish, Louis Quinze or Chippendale, in teak or oak or plastic, depending on our bank accounts and our fantasies. As bank accounts are always quantitative, whether in Dallas or Dusseldorf, in Twickenham or Toronto, so our fantasies move to become homogeneous. Furniture becomes the fixtures, whether in Holiday Inns or apartments. The question remains whether the heart's core can be sustained by things supplied in the same way as motor cars under the principle of organized obsolescence. Museums are needed in an age of quick change and therefore of quick destruction. This therapy has been produced by the same conditions which have produced what it would cure. Museums are not places where we can live with things. (Many of the pieces Symons describes are now in museums, but he obviously much prefers to find them elsewhere.)

Symons is telling us of furniture before it was so objectified; the furniture of three distinct societies which came together into Canada. He knows that furniture among these people was not a supply of objects, but things brought forth in the arts of those who shared a communality of existence with others who would live amidst it. He shows this about things as different as a fireplace in Halifax, a cupboard in Ontario or a communion table of a French Canadian bishop. He knows therefore that the modern distinctions between "fine" art and "craft" and between "art" and "technique," are not adequate to understand these things, because their makers assumed that beauty was not something divided from daily utility, and that "art" was in its origins the Latin translation of "techne."

The writing in this book brings the furniture before us because Symons is gifted with what I can only describe platitudinously as "the educated imagination." In our imaginative judgments we bring together the particular perceptions of our sensibilities with the universal entities. Leaving aside the hiddenness of what it would be to make Mozart's Quintet in G Minor, when we listen to its particular melodies and harmonies we may partake in a statement of what always and everywhere is. Though in listening we never leave those particular melodies and harmonies, they draw us out to the enjoyment of what can never be completely actualized in them. Symons' enjoyment of this furniture (and his help to our enjoyment) arises from the way his sensibility never loses its hold on the particular pieces before us. Yet he is led out and out from those particularities to the people who made them and lived with them, to the community they inhabited, and beyond that to the differing riches of the European civilization which lay unbroken behind them in all its surging richness of politics and religion and art. What is so satisfactory about Symons' descriptions is that he never uses the furniture as an excuse for a pedantic lecture, but rather by making us look at the furniture leads us out into the complexities of lived traditions. The man of intellect without sensibility does not bother to look at furniture; the man of sensibility without intellect cannot know fully what is given to him in his looking. In the "educated imagination" of this book we can be helped both to look and to know.

Furniture is tied closely not only to the love of the good, but to the love of our own, which may be only slightly good. It is more our own even than our clothes because it is liable to be longer lasting as jewelery or china. Of all things it is only less our own than our bodies and the bodies of those we love. "Las Meninas" is also a thing, but it attains to such universality of statement that who could dare to say that they possess it, except a king as representing a people. Perhaps a Spaniard could understand it in more detail than anybody else because of his particular awareness of what Velasquez made there; but its very universality of statement opens it to the understanding of man qua man. We can possess furniture as our own because of its very limitation. But in understanding it we need particularly an intimate knowledge of the detailed lives of those who live with it as their own. This kind of knowledge is best available to those who are of the same own. In his book Symons shows forth the knowledge of what it was to be a Canadian in the eighteenth and nineteenth centuries. To be such was precarious and even ambiguous – something so dividedly poised as that part of North America which had not broken its connection with western Europe. It was, however, something unique. Symons knows that uniqueness in its details, because he knows his fate is to be that and he has loved it. Perhaps that fate can be escaped by some who desire to be cosmopolitan and who love to be part of more powerful or fuller cultures. However, escaping a particular fate may not result in transcending it; one may enter something so general as to be almost nothingness, and therefore unsustaining. From knowledge and love of his limited fate as Canadian, Symons brings to his study of furniture an appreciation of the blood and bones of Canadian history, from which one can learn and learn. He apprehends its concrete immediacy in a way quite absent in the liberal and positivist textbooks from which our children are asked to learn about their past. If one wishes to know what was unique, ambiguous and precarious about Canada, one should read his jokes and gaieties with attention.

In writing of Canadian furniture Symons does not forget how different were the cultures of Ontario, Québec and the Maritimes; nor does he forget the differences in each, for example between Nova Scotia and New Brunswick. Ontario loyalism is Symons' own, in a way that the Maritimes or Québec are not. But it is evidence of the fact that we did in some sense come together that he can open himself to the other cultures as his own. This appears in his understanding of how greatly different were the styles of Nova Scotia and New Brunswick from those of Ontario, and how in some ways that of New Brunswick was nearer to Ontario than that of Nova Scotia. It appears even more strongly in his unequivocal recognition that the furniture of Québec shows itself as more finely beautiful than the others. He has an openness to the attainments of French North America which no citizen of the United States has yet shown. For example, it is singularly lacking in the barren comments of so rare an American artist as Henry James. What a different history Canada might have had, if more Ontario loyalists and even some Methodists had so apprehended the reality of Québec. Indeed his admiration of what Québec has been appears even more deeply in his proclamation of the sadly necessary yet impossible choice; were it inevitable that he must be either a French Canadian or part of the imperial republic, he would choose the former.

George Grant
May, 1971

Selection from Diary
on visit by Charles Taylor, Dennis Lee, & Scott Symons, to George Grant,
in his home in Dundas, Ontario, Tuesday, July 8, 1980

For several days prior, I pondered on the upcoming visit. Firstly, Grant is one of the pre-eminent thinkers in Canada in my era – in my mind (and emotions) THE pre-eminent thinker and philosopher, bar none (McLuhan is a pop-thinker, compared with Grant; and Frye is a high dry intellectual *nun*!)

Secondly, I wasn't going alone ... I was going in company with Charles Taylor (my dearest friend), and Dennis Lee (my editor). And each of these is a major Canadian figure! Chas is the finest liberal minded conservative essayist-reporter in the nation – whatever else he may be (and he is considerably *more* than just that). And Lee is (more or less) the acknowledged critical maestro of the whole of CanLit in my generation! Founder of "Rochdale College" (magnificent experiment-disaster of the '60s). Founder and maestro-editor of Anansi Press (which launched and abetted a large proportion of English CanLit of my generation ...). And a Gov-Gen's Award winner for his poetry. Etc. Not to mention the fact that more particularly for me, Lee represents, is, the one major valid voice speaking from my "rival" Canadian culture – the English Canadian Grit, Liburral, United Church, culture ... which culture I loathe and hate!

Add myself ... I can't assess me – but I certainly am a "legend in my own time" in Canada and probably what Stephen Patrick describes me as ... "the number one Tory myth-maker of my era." I am also a Canadian of formidable cultural background and education. And eloquent.

Thus ... the occasion was formidable! In my mind it brought together four of the most remarkable citizens of Canada of my time. And probably was the most remarkable literary-intellectual social encounter of the year in Canada. Of that I was pretty certain – even before it happened.

I assessed it this way – Grant, the foremost philosopher of our time; Taylor, the most enlightened "liberal" prose-writer in Canada ... our "philosopher"; Lee, King of all GritLit, posthumous representative of Egerton Ryerson and Geordie Brown; Symons, Tory Cavalier rebel-radical of his generation, posthumous representative of Bishop John Strachan and ... King Charles the First!

Add this ... ever since my interview of Dennis Lee for TV Ontario I have been feeling a low-key ire about Lee – I couldn't really (quite) get at him during the interview, because I was the interviewer ... and he got at me, using his subconscious "Moderator of the United Church" voice, stance, superior public "morality." Which enraged me (and which, of course, delighted my arch-foe, TVO Producer Michael Myers!). So I was nursing a rooted grudge.

Thirdly ... the occasion wasn't simply going to be the four (five) of us meeting somewhere for lunch or dinner, or whatever. It was all of us meeting ... right in Grant's home – right in the old badger's private lair and inner keep! In other words, there would be optimum privacy, optimum intimacy, optimum exposures of personality! And optimum chance to read Grant as a person ... in his own home and setting.

It was all of this which told me that ... the occasion was going to be, in some way, epic, seminal, possibly somewhat disastrous (some deep clashes of emotion, phrases, lurking insults, wounds ...) I was expectant, and ... wary.

Add, just for precision, some few of the areas of emotional danger.

Firstly, already referred to, a brewing feud between Lee and I (mostly on my side) ... the centuries-old feud of Roundhead v.s. Cavalier. Very real ... still very much alive in me – with Lee being rather falsely "innocent" about it all ...

Secondly – Grant's own attitude towards me – his comment a few months ago to Taylor that "I didn't want Scott Symons taking over the centre of my already crowded life ... "! – this although in the past twenty years I have met George only three times! Comments like that, returning to me indirectly – and pre-advising me that in some way I am a threat to Grant, a problem for him ... Which I cavalierly write off by saying "well, he's a suppressed closet lady." Etc.

Thirdly – always some undefined area of (potential) rivalry, competition, resentment, between Charles and myself! For example ... *he* is writing a splendid book on "the Tory tradition" in Canada, which I (variously) embody! And our very visit chez Grant is, basically, on behalf of this book ... to further scout out Grant. And part of the purpose of my presence on the visit, is to gather back-up notes for Taylor's book!

Fourthly ... Grant will have to sense some sort of spying-prying element about our visit – after all, Taylor is writing about him.

Fifthly ... I have felt a growing sense of the limits to Grant – his failure to come to grips with the passions, with life to incarnate, and also with the Eucharist – and there are some questions I want and need to put to him ...

So yes, a major difficult, wondrous visit coming up! My own resolve was to keep my mouth shut – to watch and to listen and to appraise ...

As I said to myself, the tremors, the seismic tremors will be felt all the way to Manila!

That, then, was the psychic *setting* for the occasion!

* * *

The day begins badly!

I've had a bad night's sleep ... Aaron agitated me the night before (he always manages to agitate my emotions – before my mind gets there to sort it out and understand it all). And the day before ... I wrote out a cheque for my Income Tax, for $4,000 – which simply set my Bank Loan up a further $4,000 ... to nearly $16,000! Eughhh ... upsetting, depressing.

So I get up late, bleary-eyed, in a rush. Phone Longhouse books, to make sure they've kept a soft-back cover of Grant's *Technology and Empire* for me. They haven't ... the last one was sold on Saturday. I've already spent an hour the previous week phoning bookstores to find a hard-back copy. Now I can't even get a soft-back one. I'm pissed off ... I want a copy for George to sign – for all of us to sign. Plus a copy of *Heritage* for him – after all, he wrote the Preface – and I can't even remember if, in the harum-scare-me-to-hell nature of my life from 1970 to 1975 ... if I even had the courtesy to give him a signed copy.

I phone Chas to tell him I'll be ten minutes late ... I get his answering service (so he's already left to pick me up). Shit.

Chas does arrive ... on time. As I scurry me out the door, after multiple last-minute checks on possible fire (cigarillos, ashtrays, stove etc.) – I'm a pyrophobe ... constant fear of being burnt out, final apocalypse, just as (after fifteen years, I have a new home set up).

Taylor is calm, affable. I ain't. Have to tell him we must stop off at Britnell's so I can buy Grant's books. Get there – Britnell's doesn't have a copy of *Technology and Empire* ... and only a battered copy of *Heritage*. Shit.

Finally, we're armed with *Tech and Emp*, and *Heritage* ... and me feeling stupid at my own typical inefficiencies. Taylor remains affably calm. I feel embarrassed ...

On to the Rare Wine Shop ... "OH," says Chas, "I was just going to go to the regular shop." This shocks me – we must buy fine wines for the Grant visit. So we pick up Dennis nearby ... Dennis all affable aplomb, attired in his best clean African shirt ... looking like a friendly overgrown dwarf or kewpie doll. I'm resentful of the fact he owns his own home – resentful because I feel part of his "success," his secular success, is a tacit complicitude with the Canadian Grit State which underwrites the advancement of Lee's "culture," his "background," while systematically destroying my own. Am resentful because Lee never acknowledges any of this ... simply overlooks the realities of it. And of course I feel that the result of Lee's "complicitude" is a "schizophrenia" in his prose – and a world, a life, locked in the airtight corridors of his own mind.

Well, I must behave to-day ... So I'm affable – remind Lee to bring his camera. He gets it – the size of a cigarette case (or a small cassette tape). The only camera we have between the three of us. (We're word men ... not videos!) I'm determined we should have photos of the Occasion!

Out to the car, Lee clambering in to the front seat, as we proceed to the Rare Wines Shop. As we drive down Church Street, Lee is chatting with Chas, offering his editorial services to Chas, help for the new Tory book. Which is kind ... But it isn't this which strikes me so much as the sound of Lee's voice as he does so – surprisingly high, higher than I expect from him. I listen to the sound, and the unusual speed of the words. As if Dennis rushing to get them out. Dennis curtsying to Chas, through that sound and speed, ingratiating – one dog coming up to another, offering deference, almost submission. It's all very clear – Dennis wants Chas's approval, friendship. And he is, invisibly all-but servile about it! He wants to be "friend of Charles Taylor, author, man-about-town, son of E.P. Taylor" – all of that shows in the *style* of Lee's sudden chatter, I am startled, uncomfortable. I didn't expect that from Lee.

We reach the Rare Wines Shop – Lee and I scooting in while Chas waits in the car. I know exactly what to get – a couple of German Ausleses, and a fine Calvados. Chas has mentioned that George has just discovered Calvados with immense delight. I summons the chief Wine Agent to help us ... and with Lee trailing, enter the display Cellar. There is no special Calvados on stock – so we're forced to get a Marc de Bourgogne (Hooray, that's what I *really* wanted to get in the first place!) Which Marc should we get ... I suggest the lighter Marc de Champagne, thinking of George's wife. But Lee says "let's go straight for the heavy ... " A Marc de Bourgogne de Corton Grancy. Hooray! I'm longing to introduce George to a full-bodied Marrrc – one further than any Calvados. After we've paid the bill, Lee hands me the receipt – "here, keep this for your Income Tax deductions!" Again I'm a bit startled.

As we regain the car, I reclaim the front seat – after all, Chas is my best friend. At least we're finally really on our way, nosing down towards the Gardiner Expressway. Past the Gooderham building, the fine remnants of 19th century Toronto. And towering black and gold and white above these, the sudden modern Bank Head Offices. Handsome sight – "I like the way the city rises in historic layers, gives a depth of meaning we didn't have before ... " And as we drive along the expressway we are discussing money! My Income Tax problem has reared its uncouth head. Dennis is talking about his Tax Chartered Accountant – "you should go to 'Magic Arthur,' he does wonders with Income Tax!" I can't imagine doing business with anyone called "Magic Arthur" – part of my social snobbery v.s. Dennis. But Dennis makes dear Arthur convincing ... and also makes my own Fraser & Beatty Income Tax Lawyer sound dull, hesitant, fearful ... I'm glad I haven't yet sent off my cheque and Income Tax – I'd best go talk with "Magic Arthur" indeed ... who does other writers as well.

I ask Dennis if his Income Tax was large this past year – curious about his ill-gotten returns from the world of GritLit. He mentions it was large – "because I sold my papers to the University of Toronto ... a capital gain." And again I'm envious and resentful – and want to know how much he got. He's sworn to secrecy but admits (under my probing) that $50,000 is in the neighbourhood of what he got ... Migod! And that Mordecai Richler, about five years ago, caused a stir when he got (from the University of Calgary) a sum in the neighbourhood of $125,000 ... says Dennis. I realize that I'm small potatoes – my papers not worth $10,000 ... "Keep them until two years after *Helmet One* comes out ... don't ask less than $25-$35,000 then ... " Dennis advises. I feel better. My "papers" are the only "capital" I have!

Chas has been relatively silent, driving his silent and happily air-conditioned Volvo ... miniature English Club. Finally he says with a chuckle – "do you realize that all we've been talking about is ... MONEY! We're about to visit George Grant ... and all we're discussing is ... MONEY." He laughs ... "you know, that's *all* writers *ever* discuss when they get together! I've noticed it time and time again." I feel sheepish, rebuked. Lee nods, puffs on his big cigar – " ... writers rarely discuss writing ... and only if there is only two of them present. Never more than two. And then they discuss writing indirectly, as if it were some private obscenity ... "

The factories speed by, all well-groomed, spaciously set, landscaped ... it's like broadloom carpeting, the way these post-war factories are laid out along Highway 401, Torontario's economic powerline. Miles and miles of them. That very world of engulfing technology which George Grant writes of ... But they are so cosmetically groomed and primped that it's hard to fault them – house-broken factories! Canadian – the remaining British Canadian properness about us all ...

"Going to see George now reminds of a marvellous story George told me recently, about a visit Scott made to him ... ," Charles is talking to Dennis. "Apparently Scott visited George in his home ... and, this is according to George, the first thing that Scott said was that Sheila was a Lesbian!" I start to protest, trying to recall the situation, knowing that I would never have said anything as blatant as *that*. But Charles continues – "That's what George says – ! 'Scott arrived, and he immediately congratulated me upon the fact that my wife is a Lesbian.' What's more when I told the story to Donald Creighton, Donald said 'but that's exactly what Scott said when he visited Louella and me – he announced "Louella is Lesbian ..."' Dennis is laughing. And I'm feeling very stupid. "'... Isn't that EXTRA-ORDINARY?,'" George said to me" – Charles finishes the account. And now I do remember – that was back in my high verbal heyday, late sixties, early seventies, when I was on the warpath against the Matriarchy. It is the fact that both Louella and George's wife are such strong women, which reminds me – "What I did say, to George, and on a different occasion to Donald, was quite different! In a lighter moment I congratulated them on 'having a lesbian marriage'!"

"Oh, of course, that makes it much better" – Charles laughs at the absurdity of saying any such thing at all.

"No, no – don't you see. I simply meant that Sheila and Louella are each such strong ladies, and that George and Donald are also really 'ladies.' Both men, as psychic ladies, married to these inordinately strong women, psychic dykes so to speak ... And so their marriages, by definition, are 'Lesbian' ... Don't you see? ... "

"Oh yes, it's very clear ... " Charles chortles to Dennis.

"I mean it was just humour, wit ... My comment wasn't so much about the wives as it was about George and Donald really ... And the fact that they didn't understand it at all, is part of the irony, the humour ... " But I still feel stupid. And I can see that Dennis and Charles just consider it all a part of the "impossible Scott" legend.

Hamilton looms up, and the escarpment. And that Catholic bad as Grant says ... a mod factory, gussied up ... "Cal Tech" in Canada! Eughhh ... I'm further silenced.

"This is Wentworth now ... we're getting close to Grant's ... " The shopping plazas continue, the Ponderosa Restaurants, the hamburger joints – one huge plaza ironically named "University Plaza" ... how apt! Approaching the home of George Grant indeed!

We turn off into residential streets, small homes, gradually larger, a few handsome monuments from the Victorian era ... the street coming to an end as another street crosses it in a T ... trees. A pair of grey limestone gate-pillars rising in front of the trees, solitary, almost lonely, sentinel ... I subconsciously remember – "Yes, that's Grant's driveway right there." We cross the road, enter the trees, a gravel lane, winding in ... covered by the trees, the wildflowers, a ravine falling off to the right – the lair of the badger. We are all silent. The car swallowed by this sudden woods – the sun dappling through the trees ... dappling, yes, English dapple of it ... gone the neonascent right-angle of factoryland, gone the cosmetic landscaping, the carefully chosen and kempt little trees, the pruned grass. Now it is the upsurge of foliate greens, sweet chaos of greens, warbled by woodland flowers as birdsong. The trees splurging themselves, tangled and beautifully misshapen, winding amongst themselves, the way the very driveway winds. It is so much another world, a haven, a hideaway, a remembrance ...

"Unfortunately there's a housing development right beside ... " – Charles breaks our silence. And out of my left eye I do catch the lines of modern bungalows, through the trees. But my heart has gone into the leaves. As we swing now to the right, a clutch of flowering bushes, lush, plump. And beyond them an island of lawn, and the house, a mellowed red-and-white brick home, vertical, rising to a strong central dormer ... It seems to grow there, bulwark amidst the encirclement of trees. All so right ... so Ontario, Ontar-ee-ary-ario – old Ontario. I barely have time to assimilate all of this, to wonder if this wasn't some old rectory, Anglican, or "High Methodist," when the car pulls around behind the house, comes to a stop beside a dilapidated old board-and-batten carriage shed. We begin unpacking ourselves. Charles and Dennis are already out greeting George Grant, who has hove to out of the shrubbery. For some reason I hang back, ostensibly to get the wine out of the car, and my brief case with the books in it for George to sign ... But I half-realize that I'm hiding, suddenly shy, timid of meeting Grant again. And I'm deliberately letting the others go first. Why? What have I to hide, or be ashamed of. Is it fear of Grant's scrutiny? His knowingness – one of the few men in Canada who could, can, genuinely place me, assess me, judge me, within the very terms of the culture he and I both come from? – our mutual (if vestigial) Family Compact kind of culture.

George shakes hands with Chas and Dennis (I don't see this, but the strong verbal greetings *sound* like handshakes). And then I come out of hiding, carrying wine-box and briefcase. George is standing on the path at the edge of the driveway – all I see, half-see is more correct, is his massive bearded head. For a few seconds we eye each other, silent. Finally George says ... "As for you, Symons ... " – a half-humorous, slightly rebuking greeting – echoing masters of our old schools, the Little Big Four Schools (precisely that kind of voice and phrase – a world of almost forgotten cultural complicitude).

We make our way to the back door of the home. I'm half-aware that George is walking sideways, looking at me. He gets to the door, across a dilapidated metal covering of some kind. The door is locked from the inside ... he bellows for his wife. Then backs away, still looking at me – "I don't know *why* I'm looking at you this way ... " Now *he's* self-conscious – "You are ... you are ... " He stops. Finally I ask "I am what ... ?" But he never answers, as the door opens, and we enter the house, going through the dining room, with its shuffle of antiquey furniture, and boxes, packing boxes for their move to Nova Scotia.

The living room is large, hardwood floor bare with one small Chinese rug on it. Items of furniture stranded on it. Packing boxes off in the corners. We are all standing, stranded, as I think to get the wine out of its box, present it to Sheila who has now hove to (yes, each of the Grants "hoves to" ... they don't just arrive, but "hove to," like ships, galleons). "We should put these in the fridge, to chill ... " Sheila disappears with the two wines, the Marc. George bears down on me – "*You* have a great knowledge of ... the *particular*!" ; he thrusts, almost brandishes, a large object at me. I take it before I can even see what it is, take it almost in self-defence. Finally see that it is a polychrome china statue of a parrot. "They say it's art nouveau ... " I turn the parrot over warily – "yes, it's late art nouveau ... moving towards art deco ... the sort of thing that might have been advertised in The National Geographic, say in 1923 ... "

"What's art deco?" George is still standing over me, glaring at the birds. I try to explain, badly. And pass the virulent bird back to George, like returning a truncheon which has been thrown at me. Sheila is back from the kitchen now. George has returned the parrot to its place on the mantlepiece. Charles and Dennis have backed into spectatorial seats on the sofa. Sheila takes her place to my left in an ample armchair. I have manoeuvered my way towards the only rocking chair in the room – a small, low, nineteenth century rocker. Always delighted when I can find a rocker! But George is still standing at the mantle, pointing at a varied array of china cups and saucers: "what are these?" He turns towards me, bearing one of the cups. What they are, is florid nineteenth century rococco, too gaudy for English ware, with their raised patterns, colours ... " Are they German?" Sheila asks serenely, in that firm, articulate voice of hers. "Yes, I rather think so. They're the sort of thing our grandmothers bought on their wedding trips, mementos ... display pieces." I can see that the mantlepiece is covered with these pieces, ready for packing, as George and Sheila prepare to move to Halifax in a few weeks. "They're the kind of thing that belonged in the High Victorian world of *Picturesque Canada*, back in the 1880's ... " At last I've placed the china, to my own satisfaction. And I'm free to sit down, in the calming rocker. George relinquishes the cups, subsides onto a large chaise lounge which commands the room, to the left of the fire place. His feet firmly on the floor. He looks at me ... "what's that chair you're sitting in? It came from Nova Scotia ... "

"Yes, it could easily be Nova Scotia ... "

It's a strange opening to our afternoon. This flurry of chinaware, questions. Dennis and Charles haven't been able to say anything. Spectators, perforce, to this barrage of objets d'art. And I sit silenced, feeling somewhat uncomfortable. Sheila is to my left, in an ample, deep armchair. No, she's not there merely as a spectator ... she's at once an audience, and yes, giving us all, George included, an audience, a regal rearing. George closes his eyes, his lower jaw stuck out ... opens his eyes – "I've been reading Celine – the later novels, the war novels of Celine ... He's COLOSSAL ... a colossal genius!" It's ... it's an *announcement!* It's as though some preliminary skirmish had been finished, and now ... now we are into the serious matter to hand. Now we're into ... meat. George addresses his statement directly to Dennis and Charles. Have they read much of Celine? No ... "Celine said that Europe ended with Stalingrad ... that's evil, that's an evil political statement. I don't see how such a great writer could have such politically absurd ideas ... " It's another announcement, tinctured with a question. I sit there pondering, glad to be off stage for the time being. What did Celine mean – presumably that when the Germans were stopped at Stalingrad in 1942, Europe died ... Charles and Dennis don't say much. "The Germans had no business in Stalingrad ... that's a thousand miles beyond European territory. It's nonsense ... " Another announcement, tinctured with verdict. George opens and closes his eyes, focusing on Dennis and Charles. Neither his wife nor I exist. Dennis and Charles flutter around verbally, mostly Dennis.

"He's so completely *there* when he writes ... everything is right there, *you're* there with him ... right on the train, everywhere ... " George talks by verbal fiat. Charles and Dennis look like children who have suddenly been told something by a revered and rather awesome Sunday school teacher. Dennis squirms a bit uneasily, puffs on his large cigar. Charles nods the necessary approvals. George pauses, looks at them – what does he expect them to say, to be able to say, in the face of this intellectual broadside? He clenches his fists ... "I mean Celine makes Joyce look like two cents. And Sartre ... that third-rate thinker, third-rate writer – Celine is so much greater than Sartre. And Sartre dared to attack him ... " George's voice is not loud. But when he speaks he clenches himself up, inside, drawing all his strength together, takes a deep breath ... and then his words bellow out, like a bull-bellow, a roar – that's what it feels like. Though his voice is neither very loud, nor deep. It just feels loud, and deep.

"I started to read Celine when I was feeling down. I felt I was on the edge of a nervous breakdown ... " George says this with immense candour, conviction. And Sheila snorts amiably – "oh, George is always on the verge of one nervous break-down or another. Then he goes and reads the biography of some Anglican Bishop! But this time he ended up with Celine." Her comment is affectionate, putting George in his place in a warm maternal fashion. She addresses us as a very private public audience. I chuckle inside myself ... at this revelation of George heading for a biography of an Anglican bishop, when he feels down. I would never have thought of it, yet it *feels* so right. Something of the bishop in George.

"look for something to ease my mind ... " he says. And I try to imagine read-ing Celine for ease of mind!

"What is it about Celine that attracts you, and show his genius ... ?" Dennis looks a bit puzzled.

George clenches his hands, draws several deep breaths – "he's all *there* ... it's all right there, don't you see! I mean you ride on a train with Celine, and the train is right there, and the landscape and the people, and all Celine's cranky thoughts about all of it. I hate concepts, words like 'subjective' and 'objective' – but Celine combines the subjective and the objective, *all the time.*" George is at once gleeful and awed and grateful as he says this. "What do *you* think about him?" ... George gives Dennis a verbal nudge. Dennis clears his throat a couple of times, mumbles, tentatively launches a phrase or two, as if trying to locate a complete sentence, idea. His voice seems like a whisper, and his ideas inchoate, I can't grasp what he is saying ... perhaps because he hasn't yet grasped what it is he wants to say. And whatever he is trying to say, now simply feels like fodder, for George to chew on. Curious – because in most gatherings, Dennis seems large, his voice firm, sub-stantial. Now he seems lightweight. But I know he isn't. I remember the wine, want to check and see if it's chilled yet. We need something – tea, or milk or wine ... anything. I haven't had breakfast yet. Maybe a cookie. I get out to the kitchen on pretext of the wine ... Sheila accompanying me. No, the wine's not chilled yet – but we get the tea going. Sheila says she has some sandwiches coming. I'm real-ly just glad to get a break from the living room scene, a breather. So I sit with Sheila for a few moments, while she butters some bread. Sit with her, too, because no-one has paid much attention to her; we've merely saluted her, saluted "the great man's wife." For the rest she's been a shadow. So I sit and chat awhile grateful for the breather – and very eager to see the tea and sandwiches. The kitchen is like the rest of the house (beyond the fact of packing) – it's messy, rather dirty, scattered, lived in ... rumpled. That feeling of lived in dilapidation – human, humane, real, a little unsettling ...

Then back into the living room, back into that ... arena. Because that is what it is. "I want to pay homage to Celine, great *homage!*" George is still bellowing. Charles and Dennis are still on awed duty. And as I regain my seat and look over at him, I begin to *see* him. Up till now George has been a looming physical presence (brandishing the china parrot at me, lurching over with the china teacups) – and a pent-up yet raging voice. But now I begin to see him. He is spread out on that chaise lounge, facing Charles and Dennis. Not a corpulent man – but heavy, with a precise dumpling of a belly, his body, overall, pear-shaped. That's it – basically a slender body, smallish shoulders, and then that belly. With his head massively set atop it all – his head appearing large because of his beard; and at once set in to the body, yet quite independent of it. As if the body were simply there to carry that head; to feed it and comfort it, and give it berth. A boyish face, lined but not wrinkled. The boyishness increased by a full head of hair, brushed, parted ... but somehow never quite kempt. Like a schoolboy trying to be proper, but not fully succeeding. And the whole ensemble of him, appearing massive, almost burly – some huge Socratic figure – would not be out of place in a toga. Like that portrait of George on the cover of *George Grant in Process* ... monumental, portentous, seer-like – could be one of the huge Presidential faces carved on Mount Rushmore, in the States. That kind of presence to him. There "for the ages." Yet if you look beyond that monumentality, something ineradicably boyish, and yes, slight. Generating both awe ... and some desire to help him, cuddle him (he'd hate that) nurture him.

"I want to write about Celine ... where should I try to publish it? What is there in Canada ... ?" The very thought of George Grant having to look for some place to be published strikes me as absurd – and pathetic. Our greatest thinker. "Something like the *New York Review of Books* ... " A pause ... Dennis mumbles about the Canadian quarterlies. George brightens up, clenches and unclenches his right hand, nods, burst out – "but I'd prefer the *Times Literary Supplement* ... it's bitchier! I love it, because it's bitchier ... That's what the English still have ... that marvellous bitchiness ... So full of life ... " He roars with laughter ... but it isn't laughter at all nor nor a roar – it just seems that way. It's really a squeal of delight, a huge snigger. His body clenching up, head squeezed down into his shoulders, he rages in a snigger of joy at the thought of English bitchery. Schoolboy snigger, hidden within that apparent massiveness of presence and voice. His face going red with pleasure. And as he laughs his teeth showing ... or more exactly the fact that his upper centre teeth are absent – and what we see is one yellow-ivory tusk, on the left side of the mouth. Strange contrast – massive presence, boyish face, and long in the single visible yellowing tooth. He puffs on his cigarettes – endless cigarettes, the ashes seething down the front of his shirt. Sheila has gone and returned with the tea, ready at last, and a mound of sandwiches, which she places with great dignity on the low table in front of her chair. The conversation halts, all eyes focused on the tea-table. "It isn't very much, I'm afraid, just a few sandwiches ... "

"Sheila wanted to make a cake, but I *refused* to let her do any work ... " George wheezes, clearly making a point, clearly pleased with it.

Sheila pours the tea with grace and gravity. I pass, happy to make some use of myself. And taking the chance to look around the room ... the low-keyed but eloquent gather of furniture – puritanesque New England-style armchair, a bulbous baroquish secretary-chest-of-drawers, the plump chaise lounge George is squashing, a Victorian rococo gilt screen, the low-sitting half-folt, rocking chair I'm in, Sheila's broad, low matronly armchair. Nothing the same in actual style, – an omnigatherum of pieces. But all bourgeois is Victorian in feeling, as in date. Nothing terribly fine, yet nothing merely cheap. And all agreeably, comfortably lived with and dilapidated. All adding up to some high, plump-protestant, burgher ... ahh, High Methodist, that's what it all is. No so fine as a correlative English home (a faint echo of an English vicarage – but more portly) ... yet clearly a first cousin. With an added touch of the continent to it; or of the continent imported via Victorian (and Edwardian) England ... as with that high gilt screen.

It is the pictures which give the higher tone. A Chinese picture of the eternal carp. A picture of a detail from the Parthenon – young boys cavorting in eager nude! A Madonna and Child centred above the mantlepiece ... Most of the pictures are reproductions, as carefully framed and glassed as if they were the original.

Overall it could be described as high dumpy comfortable ... with a memory of the Occident built into it all. This country family has also lived some collective variant of "The Grand Tour." It ain't just Ontario.

And as I return to the tea-table for another cup to pass, I have a good view of Sheila ... she's just like the furniture, and like George – monumental, of impressive girth, but not to appear merely fat ... at once austere, and ample. Like the armchair she presides from. An unstated antimacassar quality. Yes, she's statuesque, especially her face, a stone-carved face, like George. But regal, and there's nothing regal about George – too much little boy in him. Sheila belongs with those teacups I had to examine earlier – Victorian ironclad, with a touch of florid Europe.

Charles has made a trip to the washroom – is he making his first notes (he told me that he'd slip out to the washroom to catch important sentences, comments, on paper, before he forgot them)? George is reclining with his happy tea – "pouring tea was terribly important, you know! I remember one of those family occasions. And the tea-pourer had to leave the room for just a minute. One of the guests filled in. And was triumphant about it afterwards. 'I just couldn't *resist* pouring' she said in apology. That's what it was like in the 1940's – whoever poured tea was *very* important." George wheezes, sniggers with delight at his recollection – looks over at us to see if we've grasped that he is saying ... "I mean it's changed that *much* since then!"

The tea disappears almost as fast as the sandwiches. "Would you like a second cup George?" – Sheila asks. "Oh yes, yes ... " His eyes light up, but he refuses to allow his wife to get up and bring the tea to him. He lurches up from his chaise lounge, lumbers over to get it for himself. A major difference to his wife, and to the pourer-of-tea. Disproportionate deference, willed, but touching.

The tea consumed ... I get the first wine – a Bernkastler Auslese. George announces "wine in the afternoon – I can't drink wine in the afternoon ... I'm an

English shopkeeper! There's too much of the English shopkeeper in me for that
..." His glass sits beside him untouched as does Sheila's. But Charles and Dennis
quickly go through theirs and a second. As do I.

My courage comes back with the wine. I *know* I want to ask George some ques-
tions ... and Charles and Dennis are both pretty quiet. Charles is patiently there to
listen, for good purpose. He'll have his say on Grant in his Tory book.

"George, what is the place or meaning of the Christian Eucharist in your life,
your thinking ... ?"

He pauses ... it is pretty clear that the Eucharist has no great place for him –
"That's closer to Sheila's territory ... I mean I don't go to church ... The Christian
tradition is terribly important for us ... I want to write a book on that ... "

Somehow or other I want to close in on him ... check some things, corrobo-
rate ... "Passions are how we really learn about life ... and I think all passions lead,
finally, to Calvary, to the Eucharist ... " – I feel a little silly, I've blurted it out – some
core of me. But the issue is joined, squarely. I know that Grant places passions low
on his life list ... And I've just directly linked passions to the Eucharist!

Lee and Taylor are silent, suddenly watching. I continue – "All passions lead
to ... THE Passion, of Christ ... And that is what Canada is against – passions, and
finally THE Passion, the Eucharist. The Canadian Identity is an artefact of will,
everything is willed. The Canadian Identity is against life, all the way. It has been
a case of the Calvinists vs Christianity ... that's Canada!"

George's eyes squint – this clearly is a case of meat! He nods – "it's the whole
Western world, not just Canada. The story of the West is the story of *will*. Will gov-
erning the passions, and often ruling life against life. I agree that this is the case."
He clenches and unclenches his hands, shifts with discomfort in his chaise lounge.
Adds – "but you would be wrong to think that this society, that Canadians now
have no passion. They have a huge passion ... " he raises his arms, opening them
wide, "to make money. MONEY!" he roars the word out, in a squealing shout that
is part protest, "They stop at nothing, to make more money. Families break up.
Children are neglected. For the sake of more money. I find it AWESOME, the spec-
tacle of this passion for money. But it's there, it's a huge cold intense passion ... "
He stops, slumps back a bit in his chaise.

I am hit by George's point. I've never really thought of money as passion.
Even as I realize that his point about Canadian society to-day, is disastrously right.
And all I can do is babble my protest – "but passion for money, that's ... that's a
proxy passion. It doesn't lead to the gods. It ... it just reduces life."

George gazes at me – "when you say "the passions," you mean ... ?"

Now I just feel silly, in what I am trying to articulate. It will sound so odd.
"Well, by passion, I mean the feelings I have, say, when I go bird-watching ... the
delight, the joy, the ecstasy. I get so excited." Yes, it sounds silly. And to strength-
en my point I add – "I remember having an orgasm, when I first saw a rather rare
Warbler, a Parula Warbler ... " which only sounds sillier!

"*What* kind of Warbler? ... "

"The Parula Warbler, a blue warbler ... " The truth is that I can't really remem-
ber if it was the Parula Warbler, or another, not now – but the case stands. "I was
jumping up and down with joy, and I came ... "

Sheila shifts forwards, nods – "so *that's* what bird-watchers are really doing …" But no-one laughs. George gazes at me bemused, at once incredulous, yet with a touch of respect: "an orgasm over a *warbler* … I mean, I mean … "

"It was the joy I felt … I've had the same experience during Holy Communion …"

Sheila says "yes, it's not impossible George. Don't you remember, Goethe said he had an orgasm during the Eucharist … " George draws a deep breath, musing, somehow moved – trying to grapple with the issue.

"What I mean is that I learn through such joy … I learn about life, the birds, trees … I suddenly see the leaves more clearly, after seeing the warblers. I lived a series of such 'passions' – for birds, for wine, when I worked in the wine-harvests in France, for furniture, for early Canadian furniture. I learnt an immense amount about Canada through my love of furniture … the kind of thing that books don't teach us. That was a passion for me. I've learnt so much through the passions … " I feel that I'm talking too much, taking the centre of the floor. Yet I desperately want to raise these matters with George.

"Yes, yes … I can understand that … " George is pondering, gazing at the ceiling. His lower jaw thrust out, that lower lip determined, like a boy who has been challenged. Though it isn't so much a case of me challenging George, as of me presenting and defending something. And somehow or other I know that I must get it all out, now.

"All these passions were a discipline for me, they led me to discipline, and my art, my writing. And I only gradually learnt that they were all a part of eroticism. But Canada killed all eroticism. Reduced it to mere sex, reduced it all to the 'fun-fuck.' I only managed to fight my way to sex as eroticism in my thirties … "

" … in your thirties?" – – George explodes a gleeful protest – "I'm not sure I've come to know it yet *at all*!"

I continue, determined, a bit scared – "sex as eroticism, eroticism as the point at which the sexual and the spiritual intersect! And all *that* carried me to the Eucharist to THE Passion … "

George nods, clearly focusing himself, gathering himself together, finally pulls his eyes from the ceiling and addresses us as a group, almost as an audience – "it's a case of the Apollonian versus the Dionysian … which is more important? That's the issue. I've fought my whole life to be Apollonian – all my life! … " He pauses, starts to laugh, wheezing through his cigarette, ashes spewing down his front … " But I'm enormously Dionysian, ENORMOUSLY!" His whole body starts to quake with his laughter, a laughter that is some kind of raging giggle – I mean, don't you see … I've had to fight against being so Dionysian. I could have wasted my whole life on trivia … "

I can't resist, and blurt out – "You're a Rabelaisian masquerading as a contemplative, George … "

George waves his hand at me, shaking it – "there you are, did you see that … He always *attacks* me. He did it earlier when he referred to *Picturesque Canada* deliberately. He knew that my grand-father did that book, edited it. A cunning attack, because he knew … " George shouts it out in squealing, highish, protesting voice, like a stuck pig. Says it all half-funny, but also underneath very serious. He's gesturing at, to, Dennis and Charles, exactly like a young boy protesting to the school authorities, protesting that so-and-so has bullied him. And his tone is "there, you see, there's the evidence." And the "authorities," the jury, in this case, are Dennis and Chas, to whom he appeals directly. But Charles and Dennis don't quite know how to respond, what to say.

"Canada killed Pan ... " – I have to say something, albeit nervously.

"The whole Western World killed Pan!" George is firm, trying to regain his seriousness.

"But Pan is alive and well in Morocco ... in Fez there is a huge, a triumphal entry gate, archway, called the 'Bab Boujiloub' ... and the God of the Skins, Pan ..."

George is silent now, his whole body subsiding, as if that bout of laughter had haemorrhaged him. His lower lip jutted out, his face one step short of a petulant regret. His wine still untouched in the glass beside him. He ponders, as if there were no-one else in the room. Finally turns to Charles – "What do you think, about the passions, about emotions ... "

Charles leans forward cautiously – " I've had to fight to let my emotions go, to free them ... a long slow battle to bring them alive ... " He says it so carefully, so diffidently. Grant nods. Lee starts to comment, supporting Charles, discussing the hard road for emotional life in Canada. I note that we've finished the first bottle of wine ... and take the chance to slip out to the kitchen to get the second one. Glad too for a break – I've been talking too much, and feel selfish and exposed. When I return with the opened bottle, they are full into the Dionysian vs. The Apollonian. Lee is talking in a low voice. I pour wine for Charles, Dennis, and myself – Dennis tastes his, says how fine it is, richer than the first.

George notices that I haven't given him any ... immediately states (in a slightly aggrieved voice) ... "I want some" – then notices that his glass is still full, untouched from the first wine. He immediately settles to work to drink that, so he can get the second ...

The new wine duly presented and served, I regain my chair, and hopefully some of my composure. George says ... "Isn't it odd – I mean here I am, the Dionysian arguing in favour of the Apollonian, and you two able people with first rate minds (he nods at Charles and Dennis) ... you two Apollonians are arguing for the Dionysian." He hurriedly drinks more of the first wine ... and once again starts to ripple with laughter, his body starting to shake again, finally quaking with mirth, some huge suppressed mirth within him, with his spasms of sniggering laughter relieve, but in no way fully plumb ... " Yes, it all goes back to Apollo and Dionysus ... " He pauses and says very firmly – " And Apollo is primary!" His lower jaw protrudes again, almost sadly. "Now Nietzsche, Nietzsche wrote about.. but he's been overestimated you know. Rousseau, Rousseau was a much bigger man, original thinker ... much more ... " He finishes off his first wine glass in a determined gulp, holds the empty glass up – he wants to taste the second wine! Which I duly get up and pour. And as I return to my chair, he says quite lightly, almost an aside, an afterthought (having placed Dennis and Charles as accredited Apollonians) – "as for *him*, he's insane! ... " He sniggers again, tastes the new wine – "oh yes ... I like this ... I'm a natural Dionysian, I can't even finish my sentences, sometimes can't even start them ... " Meanwhile Sheila has worked off her glass of the first wine, and I fill hers too. Suddenly everyone, briefly, is discussing the wines – and I am trying to explain the difference between "Auslese," and "Spatslese." Dennis announces that he prefers "the Spat (sic).. it's thicker ... " George concurs.

Dennis mumbles something about the new wine. And George turns his attention to his glass. He is a remarkable sight – his head tilted into his glass ... his eyes glinting with pleasure. He coughs, sniggers, appreciates. His whole face become, yes, quite clearly become, in the past few minutes, from the time we started discussing the Dionysian, and now especially with the wine – his whole face has become ... Silenus! As if his body had undergone some change. That face and body which already today has been at once permanent little boy, and huge monumental magus ... that face and body are now some figure fallen off a Greek vase, some overwhelming Silenus, and Pan-figure, lurking with him ... taking over his body, his very being – these three utterly different realities, lurking fullscale within him – little boy, magus, Pan. It is clear enough now to be startling ...

"I want to ask a silly question, George – I suppose it really can't be answered ... When did the shift occur – I mean when did the West go awry.. turn to will, finally to a merely secular will. When did all that start ... ?"

George puts his wine glass down, ponders – " It goes way back, I don't know ... I think it really goes back to some argument between the Orthodox Church and Rome. It goes back to something in the Trinity ... "

"You mean the argument over the 'filioque clause' ... " – I remember that was the argument between Rome and the Eastern Church, and I can't resist showing my learning in this company; though I'd be hard put now to define what that argument was all about.

"Yes ... It has to do with transcendence, and mystery. The Orthodox Church kept that sense of God's transcendence, his unknowability. Rome didn't keep that ... "

"I know what you are saying. But I don't express it in cerebral terms. I experience it in my sensibility. When I enter an Orthodox Church, I can't come out still seeing merely in three-dimensional perspective. Whereas I can, from a Catholic Church built since the Renaissance ... The Orthodox Church and ritual has a resonance, an added dimension, so that I see with my ears, and hear with my eyes ... The reality you express intellectually I experience as an incarnate event." I feel somewhat silly saying these things, yet am determined they be said.

Lee adds – " I suppose the whole thing goes as far back as Saint Augustine ..." Grant nods. Taylor looks benignly mystified.

I'm startled, excited by the conversation – excited by the fact that I've met someone who relates the "crisis" of the West to the Trinity ... something I've long sensed. The huge importance of the Trinity, as a theological concept and as a metaphor for life. Obvious, presumably, for someone from the Anglican tradition, like myself. But of sufficient importance to me that if my furniture book was really about "the object as phallus," the book I had planned to do right after it, and had started doing with John ... that book, technically about early Canadian "objets d'art," about Canadian glass, silver, pottery, etc., that book was really intended to be a study on the Trinity and all life as a "Trinity" – the constant (and potent) relationship between the object, and the person viewing the object, and God! So that every action, every situation in life, has this triple relationship ... or becomes impotent. Of that I was intuitively certain. And here is Grant now, intuitively (and with massive intellectual knowledge) asserting that the Occident went awry over the Trinity. And everything in me knows he is right ... knows that modern "alienation," psychic solipsism, the advent of "black humour," and all of this is a predicate of our failure to understand and honour the reality of the "Trinity" ... But by the time I have assimilated all of this, the conversation has churned on – the question of a definition of God has been raised ... And Grant is replying "God is ... limit!" It is a startling reply – "has limits, the sea has limits ... and we learn about God through those limits. That's how we apprehend God ... " It feels so reductive, so limited. A strange contrast to George's comments about the importance of the Orthodox Church, retaining its sense of God's transcendance ...

"I'm a Protestant ... to me, thought is redemptive. I could have given way so easily to minor forms of Dionysianism ... I'm very Protestant!" George's lower jaw is thrust forward again, a kind of rueful determination to it.

Suddenly I'm struck – George must be ... "Are you of Scottish background, George ... ?"

"Am I Scottish? With a name like 'Grant'! Of course I'm Scottish." He says this with an explosive force, yet with a touch of dubiousness. He's forceful about being Scottish, yet not exactly proud of it. Certainly the Scottish tradition in Canada has, largely, undermined many of the traditions he loves. And just as certainly it is largely responsible for the willed "secular Calvinist Society" we have to-day.

"You say you're very Protestant. Yet everything in your writing tends to Catholicism, with a big or small 'c,' George" – I feel rather confused now.

"You'll have to talk to Sheila about Catholicism ... I just don't know ... " – Yes, George is now firmly back to his little-boy-plus-Magus appearance. All snigger as suppressed mirth has gone. He is silent, momentarily spent. I take the chance to pour us all some further wine. And Dennis lurches into the vacuum ... his voice muttering, mumbling. I finally realize that he is talking of "cadence" ... of cadence as source of inspiration for his writing, for poetry. Is he, following our talk about God, about apprehending God, is he saying that "cadence" or the source of that "cadence" is, for him, God. Or his definition of what God might be? Or the possibility of God coming to us through "cadence"? His voice isn't loud, as he shunts back and forth ... trying out phrases, retracting ... he isn't expressing ideas, so much as looking for what they might be. Grant has to lean forward to hear. Lee continues, on and on ... I try to find out if limit applied to cadence is Lee's definition of poetry, his way of writing poetry. The conversation has now altered radically – up to now it has been dialogue, substantially dialogue. Now it is decidedly a monologue. George conveys meanings in what he says, by the way he emphasizes words, phrases, explosively, with gestures ... It is highly dramatic, emotional, personal, human – it convokes responses and thought. It implicates the entire person, body and mind and soul ... and (insofar as it is a challenge, which conversation with George always is) balls! Now Lee is talking.. and it is a monotone monologue – it is as if Lee were talking with himself, and we are simply there to overhear that talk, and offer comments if we wish. I listen, lost in the mumble of the words. Stunned by what has occurred, been discussed up to this point ... and now startled by Lee's inarticulacy, and the relative poverty of what he is saying. As so often, I check the meaning of the words, by the sound, the flow, the voice – and it seems to me that what is really being said, what is really happening here now, is Dennis presenting Dennis ... a kind of trailer to the afternoon. Grant dominated the gathering, from our arrival, booming in on us with Celine for nearly an hour. And then the dialogue, and it was a dialogue, between Grant and myself ... an open dialogue, implicating everyone present. And now Lee is presenting his reality ... but it implicates no-one else. Certainly not in any way that the preceding conversation has. Still Dennis drones on ...

I slip out. Now is the time for me to have a closer look at the garden, the house, the setting ... which I said I would do for Charles for his book ... Step out into the green – the upslash of green. Bushes, flowers, wild-flowers, gouting up like a protective wall, around a patch of lawn. And beyond these, the trees, some memory – some rumpled echo of an old English rectory garden ... gone to seed. The wild flowers and flowering weeds growing lush amidst the bushes and some few flowers. The Tiger Lilies rampant, and the big flowering bush I always associate with John, John during our days out in the B.C. Coast, Egmont. As I stroll out towards the driveway, to get a view back to the house itself. Yes, the house is THE Ontario house, home – that red-and-white brick overgrown Hansel and Gretel cottage, Hansel and Gretel cottage with the Candy taken off. And right angles added. House that can be farm, or village home, or rectory – depending on what is added or taken away ... the basic Ontario Yeoman home – unique ... folk gone squire, yeoman gussied up for Sunday Church. I recognize and love and loathe it. Something tabby about it. Yet immense dignity – rectitude. How right that George should hold up here, take his Ontario stand here. Just like Creighton in Brooklyn. Each living in the same home, so to speak – literally the same home! And yes, off to my left, through the wall of flowers-bushes-trees, I can see the housing development, which cuts close to Grant's home here ... perhaps sixty feet away, across a road. I walk over, peer through the bushes at this encroachment – the relatively expansive, spic and spansy two-story mod bungalows. All kempt and plastic costly. One is ranch-style. Another has touches of Tudorbethan. Another is straight out of "Better Homes and Gardens," call it ice-cream Georgian. There they are – marching determinedly down the road ... nothing to be remembered by, accept their assertion. In ten years they'll start falling apart. The contrast is pungent! – this miniature palace, manorial home, so precisely Old Honest Ontario, which Grant has lived in ... still standing strong after a century, with its dilapidation somehow enriching, like moss – an extrinsic dilapidation, quick to clean. And these mod affluent bungalows, so flimsily proper on the outside ... but their dilapidation hidden, built right in, a dilapidation of the soul expressed in the glossy shabbiness of the materials used. Ontario of 1860 vs. Ontario of 1980 – yes, it hurts ... The Ontario which Mazo de la Roche made into valid romance, v.s. The Ontario ... of the CBC, and of the Gliblib Canadian Identity. The Ontario that really was "a place to stand and a place to grow," v.s. The Ontario of Technolatry and the quick buck. So much of what Grant says, in his books, expressed right here in this juxtaposition, this juxtaposition which is, in fact, a psychic debacle. On the one hand, the people living in these glossy bungalows, have no identity now, just a greedy stubbornness (at best). On the other ... there is George, badger in his lair, embodying two centuries of English-speaking Canadian culture and history – his life spent in civic isolation, he himself often crazed, as he wrestles his tortured way through the maze, trying to rescue his roots even as he bears witness to them. And as he confronts the psychic consequences of technology and its empire ...

Yes – it hurts and hurts and hurts me ... It has left me maimed, and a voyager.

I clutch my way around to the back of the house, sneak in through the kitchen, a glimpse into the dining room – its compressed grandeur of Victorian oak ... the room where John and I came, it must have been ten years ago – came to spend an afternoon with George. We were camped in our new house trailer, a few miles away, near Terracotta. And starting our furniture books ... and our trip which ended in Trout River, Newfoundland. Spring of 1969 it must have been. Came and spent a rich and ribald afternoon with George.

Yes – that day which John and I spent here, ten years ago! The memory has been lurking within me, ever since I saw those limestone gate-posts, as we entered George's keep earlier today. Memory that I've been trying to suppress, and at the same time, to locate. Memory which has made this visit today twice as difficult, emotionally dangerous for me. And now the memory rises despite me. A rich day, it was, high-minded Rabelaisian. Full of a mindful mirth. But cautious. John was on his best behaviour. And he and George got along in a fine, but covertly coy way.

I could feel George quietly appraising our situation ... testing it, weighing it – was it merely "gay"? Or was it the classical Greek love, of man and younger man? And in the end I knew that he had decided that ours was the latter ... I knew from the way he treated us throughout the day – with full honours.

And he told us, too, that day, of his discovery of God – it was during those early years in England ... he was walking in Devon. "I was going down a lane, about to go through a gate – as I went to open the gate, I knew that I didn't believe in God, but when I went through ... I suddenly knew that I did. It was just like that."

Yes – as I stand here looking into this dining room, our voices coming back to me, John's mild flirtatiousness with George.

I wrench myself away from that dining room, rife with fearful memory for me ... and note the pictures, classic Renaissance reproductions on the hall wall – must ask George what they are. And hushed and hurt inside of myself, slip back into the living room. Back to that potent tableau. George still extended on his chaise lounge – the very deployment of his body commanding the room, the very bulk of him. Charles sitting at the far end of the sofa, looking invisibly proper. And Dennis at the near end, a florid clump of Native African shirt, short legs. While Sheila remains in her arm-chair, nearest to the kitchen and any bothersome phonecalls. I slip into my low rocking chair.

The afternoon is drawing to a slow close. Dennis cadences onwards ... I remember the Marc de Bourgogne, and retreat to the kitchen to get it, open it. Returning, making a small presentation – "George has recently discovered the powers of Calvados ... "

"Through Simenon ... Maigret in Simenon ... " – George shouts out, while peering at the bottle I'm trying to flourish as caesura to Lee's cadence.

"Well for a long time I've wanted to introduce George to Marc de Bourgogne ... so we've brought this fine Corton Grancey Marc, as part of our estime for you, George ... "

The Marc is poured, explained – George peers warily at his glass. He is currently in his contemplative phase – he had lots of time to sit and contemplate while Lee was cadencing. The little boy, and the suppressed Silenic Pan, are again non-visible. He is the immobile magus. Charles gets at his Marc with a clear eagerness. Dennis with voluble gusto, George looks at the bottle – "oh, you mean MarC ... "he pronounces the 'c' strongly. "Now I know what it is – Maigret used to drink MarC as well as Calvados ... "

"You don't pronounce the 'C,' George ... " I say with grateful reproval.

"I know that ... " He still doesn't taste his Marc, just looks around it. "Now Calvados, that was a drink for a strong peasant, feet right in the earth ... Maigret was like that ... "

I want to shout out, "For God's sake just try that beautiful Marc de Corton Grancey ... " I want to know how George Grant, THE George Grant, reacts to a Marc – he'll surely out some ultimate eschatological phrase, placing my beloved Marc amidst the archangels, the dancing devils, the saints-and-sinners, immortalizing Marc for ever in Canada. I feel my suppressed glee ebbing – while George still eyes his untouched glass. Finally, the moment long since passed when he should have sipped it, he takes a cautious drop. "You'd have to be a peasant to drink that ... like Maigret ... " Fuck Maigret, I think, what do you think, feel, see, when you taste it ... He puts his glass down contemplatively, and just as the conversation is about to move on elsewhere, he points his right hand at Charles and Dennis while indicating me, and squeals – "He's been trying to debauch me for twenty years!" And with that he detonates into a screech of sniggering laughter, his arms thrown around himself, almost hugging himself. His face gone red with his own laughter. The contemplative magus instantly dissolving into a monstrous Silenic child – a Silenic boy that is boy-girl! And then as quickly as this prodigy of being, this spectacle, has surfaced, it, he, she, them, dissolve again ... and George sits tranquil, his head floating above his body, his eyes gazing at some point midway below the ceiling ...

"George, there is a further question I would like to ask ... about saints, sainthood. I mean if society is not simply a secular enterprise, if life is more than just material welfare and jobbing, then we're brought back to the old questions which confronted the saints ... "

George is silent, his head an immobile nod. Dennis puffs formidably on his cigar. And Charles has lit his pipe – presumably in part to counter Dennis's stogie smoke-screen.

"Our own culture, both French and English ... it was originally a church culture – church, religion played a huge part. You can't understand Canadian history without understanding church history – though god knows our universities don't teach much of that! But there are few saintly figures. Oh, I can easily enough find some in French Canadian history. But in English Canada ... damned few. I have to fall back on someone like McDougall of Alberta."

"Who was McDougall of Alberta ... ?" George asks, clearly chewing on my questions. His eyes appearing to read my words ... like a palpable braille floating in the air. His mind silently clanking into action – you can feel it, his process, his totally attentive mind-process.

"McDougall ... the Methodist preacher ... died in the snow ... " I've in part deliberately mentioned McDougall, to see if Lee knew of him – Lee whose two grandfathers were Methodist ministers. But Lee clearly doesn't know.

"The saints, the saints ... " George shifts in his chaise lounge, focussing deeper onto the issue. The enormous process of George grappling, physically, physiologically, as well as mentally, with a subject ... like watching some huge machine, crane, moving into position on a building site. But George is the opposite of my machine.

"Like, say the Curé d'Ars ... " I pronounce the 's' on Ars, to make doubly clear whom I mean. "Why haven't we produced people like that ... " There is something pleading, almost sad, in my question.

"The Curé d'Ars ... " Grant says the name distinctly (and correctly) without pronouncing the 's,' and looks over at me as he does so – he hasn't forgotten my reproval for pronouncing the 'c' in "Marc." He doesn't forget anything – just as he didn't forget my mention of his grand-father's *Picturesque Canada*! And I feel his counter-reproval ...

George continues – "The Curé d'Ars ... yes, it is clear that he was saintly, that he did things which we cannot easily explain ... like feeding a crowd of people from a few fish, a little bread ... " George probes the issue inside of himself ... "The saint.. the life of the mystic – seeing life as a poet, but with God present!"

It seems clear, that for George, the saint is ... the mystic. I don't quite agree, it feels reductive – or is it that for George, "saintliness" is a mystery, beyond his contemplating mind? "What *would* a modern saint be, George? What would he be doing, what *kind* of a life?" I feel an urgency in my question.

"Well ... Simone Weil ... *her* life. I mean when she says Christ visited her, came down to her, I have to believe her, I have to know that did happen ... " George pauses, muses – that lower lip of his thrust forward, determined. He has reached some line, some point beyond which he cannot move. "It has taken all my energy just to understand what virtue might be, the nature of a virtuous life ... "

Charles and Dennis are silent. Lee does mumble a line about Weil. But the dialogue, and it *is* a dialogue, is Grant and myself. Most of the words mine. But most of the "talk" is George! His resonant silence, his interspersed comments. The dialogue between my mere intent and sad questing questions ... and his booming silence. The extraordinary operation of George moving onto a question, a subject. This entire being open, receiving the question. Open in a way that no regular academic is open ... other academics receive questions through their mind, the front part of their brain – prissy reception. Like playing at love only with your fingertips. And then they, so to speak, fend the question off with a quick verbal response. But George ... George receives the question whole ... he is penetrated by the question at hand. Allows his entire body and being to be entered by the question ... so that it is his entire being which can then respond. As he contemplates and receives his answer, passed out to you as mindful words which themselves then feel palpable ...

And the real answer to my questions now, on the saint, and on what a modern saint might be ... the real answer is not Grant's words, but the immense seriousness with which he accepts the question. Which asserts yes, there is a question ... that *is* a reality! The very opposite of any quick reply, any fending off, any answer that comes merely from the front tip of the brain.

That ... and the fact, the clear fact, that George can contemplate the question of the saint, can view it through the entire being of his body then passed through his mind ... but there is then a barrier which he cannot jump. Because finally he cannot move beyond the contemplating mind. He is, as he says, a Protestant, and there is "limit" ... and he cannot transcend this. Even as he acknowledges (formidably) that transcendance is a reality, and the area in which the Occident failed itself.

Sheila is now ready to venture on to the Marc. I pour her some, George gingerly sips more of his. Charles indicates his glass eagerly, while adding (once he has received more) "this'll be my last."

I can feel one further question lurking inside of me ... risk it, expecting to be shot down – "George, when I interviewed Octavio Paz, in Mexico, I asked him what the most important thing in life is ... " – I pause briefly, then add – " and he replied, 'eroticism' ... Do you agree with that?"

George answers almost without pause – "eroticism, yes, of course, I mean I take that for granted. Eros, 'desire,' what we desire, of course that's the most important thing in life ... "

I'm startled, for me Eros isn't mere 'desire' – that feels reductive again. I lunge ahead – "And this society really knows nothing about eroticism. It reduces eroticism simply to wanting, and to sex. This society doesn't even desire, it simply 'wants,' will to want and wants to will. A reduced desiring ... "

"Wanting, wanting things ... yes, that's the desire of secular Protestants ... "

But the day is ebbing out of us now. Over four hours have passed.

"You know ... the Occidental experience may be a failure. Has it ever struck you. I mean I got up one morning recently, and was having my coffee. And it struck me that the Occidental experience may now just be a failure ... I asked Sheila what she thought ... "

George just throws the comment out, it's almost casual, a thought en passant. Dennis chortles – "imagine having that line thrown out at you over morning coffee!" And George nods and snorts appreciative laughter – "oh, Sheila was very good, she thought about it very carefully ... " We are all laughing, it's so bizarre, this comment of his, comment just dropping on us, at the end of the afternoon, almost as an afterthought, yet carrying the entire weight of our afternoon. Implicit in everything we have been discussing, yet none of us formally aware of it. George repeating – "don't you see, the Western World might well be a complete failure now ... "

We are spent now.

And Charles quickly rises, and with a surefooted elegance says, "you have been patient and kind with us today. THANK YOU." And we all rise on the merciful cue, gradually dispersing towards the door.

I have been longing to ask George and Sheila if I may have one of their varied old family teacups, my longing for "the particular," for the concrete memory, the touch ... but I quell my lust, and instead on final mission for Charles' book, ask George about the pictures, over the mantle, above the medley of cups and saucers and that flaunted china parrot – everyone was swooning over the Botticellis, but I liked this, by Fra Lippo Lipi ... " the Madonna and Child. And as we make our way out into the hall, I ask about the other two pictures – "they're from the Library at Sienna ... " – this home of all memories, the Occident gathered domestically within the Ontario experience. That great newel post of the stairs presiding.

We wend our way out to the back garden ... "we must get some photographs" – some child, and curator, and historian, in me, babbling urgently ... "Sheila, where's our camera?" Till finally we are assembled in the garden, beside a small swimming pool sheathed in bushes. Dennis in front of us brandishing his mini-camera, taking one picture. Finally persuaded to take a second! Then Sheila out with hers, another one, two ... Each of Dennis and Sheila wielding their cameras as some foreign object ... It is sunny, the day between us, some bond ... We stroll towards the car. George telling Charles that he must come to visit him in Nova Scotia. And Charles shaking hands, a courtly good-bye to Sheila and George.

I kiss Sheila good-bye ... yes, she is regal – august, I think, is the more exact word ... that kind of high dignity Canadians have so deviously eradicated in the hidden name of the Canadian res publica. The kind of dignity which can carry Sheila's weight, mass of flesh, not as obesity, but as substance, girth ... as a *title* in life! And then I turn to George, he is standing silent, smiling, half-looking at me ... as I step up quietly, holding his shoulder in my hands, and kiss him firmly on his left cheek ... He doesn't move, just stands, as I step back, and we start getting into the car, Sheila standing Rock-of-Gibraltar regal, as solid as their home, stately ... But it is George who draws my startled eye – he is standing stark in precisely the spot where I kissed him, hasn't moved an inch ... standing immobilized, his head slightly lowered, looking like a little boy, a tubby little boy ... like one of those figures I recollect from Alice in Wonderland (isn't it the Teniel drawing, of the fat boy, standing with the Walrus and the Carpenter) – George, so exactly a paunchy little boy now, and the look on his face, so quietly and precisely abashed!

I can't say anything. I've deliberately sat in the back seat for our return drive, so I can be quiet, muse, relax ... And what do I feel, oh, enormously is ... the hurt, the pain, the shock. To have been at George's, IN George's home ... IN his reality – to have felt so palpably, so intimately, so spontaneously, and in such an onflowing way, the entire rooted reality of my culture, of the culture I had grown up in as an Ontarian and as a Canadian ... a culture with roots here, yes, but insofar as it was Ontario and Canada, it was also so much more – roots back to Britain and to Europe, and (through Christianity) to the East – a millenial heritage. And it was all there, at George's ... in the house itself, in the bedraggled English garden set wild beneath the Niagara escarpment and greystone, in the very teacups and china of the home (the rampant Victorian rococco), in Sheila's messy kitchen producing homemade lumpy sandwiches, in the decor of the house (the plump and lumpy comfortability of it, the sense of generations of use), in the pictures convoking Rome and Athens and China unto Ontario ... in George's conversation and very personality – IT WAS ALL THERE!!! The world, history, reality, seen through the experience of Ontario, the experience (over two centuries) of being Ontarian! It was all there, intact, rumpling and rampaging all around us, for five whole hours – my own culture and heritage as an Ontarian, restored in me ... not just bits and pieces of it, nor some romantic novelization of it ... but the whole damned bloody wondrous thing, rich and snorting and gentle and tough and stern and affection-ate and intimate and august ... ALL THERE!!! So that I could once and for ever know, oh yes, it isn't just a memory for me, a nostalgia, a regret, a fantasy ... it was and is something huge and memorable and worthy and decent and good ... some-thing to have grown from, and to continue to grown from. Oh, to have been back inside of that, to have been back inside of it, the whole of Canadian history and being, as part of some world being ... AND THEN, to drive out of George's gates, and into this abrupt self-advertising world of kempt mod chaos, of mere plausible material self-seeking, of life seen through a looking glass, and people processed as willed meaningless "identities" ...

The factoryscape marches by. Technology and its empire alright. Oh, the rich mad multiple irony, of our visit to the Grants', and then this ... But the marvellous thing is, that after being at George's, this all looks so ephemeral, so unreal – and the reality, the rich reality, is what was at George's ... and if we have to flee to the hills to restore that reality, why then we flee to the hills.

I watch the land going by ... trying to see if there is a single gap, when the eye can't see a factory – ten, twenty miles. No, not a single gap in this mod castle, Kafka's psychic castle. And the land itself, it's gone under.

"It must be terribly hard for George. He must feel so isolated, so often alone ... as he battles for his ideas, fights to express himself against this entire society we see around us ... Charles asks Dennis. And Dennis replying "yes ... I remember phoning George at one point and George said 'sometimes I feel I'm just crazy ... plain straight CRRRRAAAZZZY' George shouted it out. It happened a couple of times when I phoned him. You could tell George really felt it." Charles nods, and clucks sympathetically.

Toronto towers on the horizon, almost beautiful, certainly impressive ... I try to remember any of George's specific comments. But few of his comments, few of the ideas as such, come back ... just a feeling of an enormous presence, grappling with an enormous reality, that enormous body receiving, as a single giant ear, every word, every nuance, every ripple ... and then that enormous child-yet-magus head processing it all in contemplation.

Dennis is puffing on one of his stogies ... I reach forward from my silence and touch him on the shoulder, massage it briefly at the neck ... feel a surge of affection for him. He gurgles in acknowledgment. And as I sit back, I wonder ... am I affectionate with him now because ... because I have so successfully, if indirectly affectionate with him now because ... because I have so successfully, if indirectly downed him at George's, so successfully put him in his place, and also, in my own mind, finally placed him? Or because I've managed to make a big fellow out of myself, in dialogue with Grant? Certainly a shift occurred at Grant's – I mean Charles, and particularly Dennis, will have to accord greater importance to the kinds of things I am, and have long been saying ... They will no longer be able to pass me off with that intermittent jocular tolerance they often reserve for me and my case. As though I were some special needy project who (through inexplicable reasons) merits assistance. After all, the axle of the afternoon was the dialogue between Grant and I – which Grant took with dread seriousness. And some major acknowledgment of me, of Scott-as-thinker, beyond Scott-merely-as-scandal, was subconsciously made by George ... through our dialogue. Some recognition that Scott is serious ... can be and has to be taken seriously. But such thoughts, if human and real, are unworthy! The fact is, that I simply do feel the surge of affection for Lee. For Dennis as Dennis ... the intellectually brilliant but inchoate Dennis – escapee from a Breughel painting ... I feel a real affection for the guy, as comrade-in-arms, and as friend.

Charles drives Dennis to his home ... we agree that there has to be a farewell dinner for Dennis, prior to his departure for a sabbatical year in Scotland in August. Dennis delighted, exits. "Thanks for an epic afternoon!" And he is gone in a swirl of his African robe.

And as Charles then drives me to my door (Charles always so courtly courteous) we muse – I mention something curious about the way George received me, initially treated me ... George so wary with me. And Charles says "Yes, he is obsessed with you in some strange way ... you represent some danger for him, some threat. It's very clear ... "

"You know, I've only seen George about three times, ever!"

"Is that so ... "

"Yes, three, maybe four times ... Once he came to see me, when I had broken away from my home, and was living in Yorkville ... He felt that my firing by the Museum was unjust, as he said, and he made a special trip down from Dundas, to visit me ... I didn't quite know why, not then. And I remember that when we were walking in Yorkville after, among all the long-hair hippies, my fellow refugees from the sixties, he stopped and burst out – 'but you challenge everyone, you challenge them, with your eyes, your walk' ... And then I saw him once with John, in his home, I just hope I took notes of that. And this time. That's all ... Three or four times in twenty years."

" Well I remember feeling that his treatment of you, that whole episode with the china parrot, and the teacups was odd. And then, later in the afternoon, when you were out in the kitchen with Sheila, he did say how relieved he was to find you in such good form, and that his initial moves, with the parrot and so on was designed to put you on the defensive – he was deliberately taking the offensive..."

"I felt that ... I mean it shut me up for about an hour! And I sensed that he really didn't want to be seen ... He did the same with you and Dennis, too – that opening salvo about Celine ... He knocked all of us out of the arena right at the start ... "

"Yes, it was clearly deliberate, a form of self-defence. And he wouldn't drink much of the wine or the Marc ... He was very wary ... didn't want to open up. But in the end he *did* ... "

We are at my door – I stumble out. "Yes, an EPIC afternoon!"

We both say it. And for about an hour after I am home, I can't say anything much at all ... just mumble apologetically to Aaron – "there was no one thing, no one phrase ... it was all so *immense* ... it'll take days for me to sort it out."

And after supper, we sit in our living room, peaceful ... I'm glad and grateful to see Aaron and to have a home ... and we quietly celebrate, me blowing Aaron to his contentment. Alleluia.

***

The next few days, especially in the mornings ... I feel a sadness, a lurking, diffuse, but deep sense of *mourning!* And I know that in considerable measure it derives from my visit with George Grant! It derives from having seen, oh, more than having merely seen, but from having *been*, once again, the full tradition from which I come. From feeling, livened within me once again, that rich, still growing, culture that is my source ... From *being* within that, chez Grant, and having it so fully and palpably corroborated AND THEN ... driving away from George's, and back to Toronto ... re-entering the world of Torontario – a world which simply seditiously and seductively deprives me of that entire reality which is mine by birth and tradition! So that my entire being naturally enters into mourning! Spontaneously ... not at all something which occurs in my mind, merely in my mind. So that I awake, in mourning ... my body, and my bodibeing, in mourning ... knowing its loss. Having witness again, so concretely, the thing lost! The tradition and reality embodied individually and together, by George, and by Sheila, and by their home.

It leaves me with a sense of outrage, and sadness ... and deprival – yes, the Great Deprival! That Deprival which affects All Canadians ... that process of losing your roots, Canadian or other, while being forced to embrace a "willed national Identity," promulgated by fiat from Ottawa! A willed identity is against being (a point I asked Grant about – and he agreed!) ... and any loss of being incurs ... mourning!

The whole day visiting Grant, and driving there and back, was such a pointed shock – there it all was, side by side: – the highway-world, of the empire of technology (technolatry) on the one side, a world that is extrinsic, of the mere mind (the airless corridors of the mind), plausible, merely material – and on the other side, the intimate, palpable, passionate, rooted, growing human and humane world of George Grant. The contrast was direct, brutal and staggering. There was no escaping the meanings of it.

And I was shattered by the "disjunction" – the fact that there simply is no connection between Grant's world, and that other extrinsic current world of Ontario (and Canada). Grant's world, his reality, has simply been "cut off," severed – willfully destroyed (except insofar as bits and pieces of it are put under glass and served up, largely for tourist purposes, as 'historic monuments' – presumably that is precisely what many academics would like to do with George and his philosophy).

I mean that to enter George's home, and to talk and be with him and Sheila, is to enter a reality that has powerful roots, can still grow ... and has so very very much still to give us – which we desperately need in exact measure as that other world of "technology and empire" takes over, takes us all over ...

And there it all was ... cut off! George and his home some *tiny beleaguered enclave* – and he himself about to retreat to Nova Scotia for the rest of his days. A terrible comment on our society ... on Torontario.

In effect, he and his home a rebuke, and a verdict ... upon all of us! Yes – *a verdict!* A verdict about what we have allowed ourselves to become. A verdict which isn't just general, something "out there" ... but which is personal – I think, for example, of Charles' desperate struggle simply to maintain any emotions at all – any deep and ongoing emotions.

And all of this sense in me, of outrage and mourning ... is only increased by my living with ... Aaron – Aaron who spontaneously, (if any willed actions can be spontaneous) practices all the tactics and strategems of the Canadian Identity, to gain his way or place or whatever. Practices the whole "willed" power trip. À la Canadien(ne). Because he knows no other ... just that harsh hidden core of Scottish-Canadian lapsed Calvinism! Which is still the hidden unstated engine of the Canadian Identity.

It is clear why I mourn. I mourn the loss of that huge (and specifically Canadian variant of) the millenial tradition Grant embodies and articulates. And at the same time, I recognize the ongoing presence of the "killer," of that which killed Grant's tradition, slow-strangling it in Canada – to wit, the Scottish-Canadian bitch. (Bitch currently embodied within my personal life, By Aaron. Though with mutation, they are *all* the same. FACT.) Yes ... that Scottish Canadian bitch, via Mackenzie King's mommy, is *still* the hidden ruling, or over-ruling force in Canada! Ruling by prevention ... the prevention of potence, to start with. And then by the plausible imposition of a willed identity on Canada.

All that – and the knowledge that this necessarily leads me to my death ... foredoomed (if not also fordamned – a very different matter) ... foredoomed to quest and find a "heroic death" as final and absolute affirmation of what I believe, and of what was lost (something truly *noble*, which was genuinely part of our birthright!)

So yes, I mourn – and inside I weep (*not* because I am any romantic – but because far from mere romance, it is all so palpably *real!*)

Quite simply, I *cannot* overcome *both* the loss (the Deprival) *and* ... the ongoing "Canadian Identity" presence of anti-being!

So yes ... my life is *pre-empted*, willy nilly ...

And thus there are only two questions of any importance for me – the meaning of saintliness, of sainthood, in this modern era – and ... the right death, the affirming (totally non-negative) death! (the search for this – and the need for be prepared for it ... to be ready on the spot, when it presents itself, instantly – to recognize it, *instantly!* With a smile that is praise and prayer and thanks-given) – YES.

How long do I have – to finish my job, my witnessing?! A few years ago, I'd have said I have not much time – a year, two, at most five. Now I feel I may have *ten years!* (Enough to finish Helmet I, II, III; and a book with Chas (our "Fiftieth Birthday Voyage to the Far East") ... *our* book of mirth. And then some further book (Saint John of the Cross's Canticle and Comments, plus St. Teresa's *Interior Castle*, but made mod, modern ... And as well some Flower Drawings, *please!* And some further witnessing (I don't yet know what). *All* of this I *can* feel within me, already there (not merely within my grasp, but actually *within me!* – nascent, pregnant in me ...)

MUST BE DONE ...

Ten years – just enough then.

Yes – the "right death" ... predicate of the understanding of sainthood ...

(Oh, I know, I ... cannot live the exemplary life, nor even *an* examplary life – but I can have lived a life which points *that way!*)

... all of this going through me, powerfully, in the two or three days after the visit with George ... and taken day by day as notes, so I can have no doubt about it ... All of this, a powerful focusing of my life, as a predicate of the visit chez George – part of his immense gift to me! Working in me ...

But I am also eager to know, sound out, the reactions of both Charles and Dennis, to that "epic visit." And two days after our return from Chez Grant, I phone Dennis on another pretext. He doesn't mention the visit! So I finally trigger his remarks by saying, "You know, after that Grant visit I just felt 'bulldozed,' hit by a bulldozer ... " To which Lee replies, "yes, I felt as high as a kite, a kind of exuberant joy. The mirth of that man, the vehemence, He's larger than life ... " To which I pugnaciously want to reply "no, it's just that Canadians are smaller than life, they reduce life." But I manage to refrain. And what strikes me is that while Dennis's comments about Grant are large, and the words he uses about Grant are exciting, yet the sound of Dennis's voice is just a matter of fact ... there is nothing excited in his voice, just a kind of cerebrally controlled, monitored awe. The very tone of Lee's voice reducing what it contemplates!

"Was there any particular remark George made which struck you, Dennis?"

"No, I can't think of any ... no. It's just the hugeness of the man, his presence ... "

Of course I speak several times with Charles on the phone in the days following the visit. Yes, Charles is pleased, pleased with the visit (his precise word – "pleased"). But at no point do I detect any excitement, much less emotional fervour. In fact, the very day after the visit, he is off to Stratford, with Jane, one of his lady friends ... for a jaunt ... And when he does write up his notes, they are three pages, and quite detached, clinical, if perceptive. None of the massiveness of the occasion is in them ... none of the rampant passion of life. And within these notes he casually mentions that he'll be getting Scott's notes on the event, which, so to speak lets him off the hook.

Which startles and worries and disappoints me. Charles is indeed the partial victim of creeping Canadensis ... that creeping inertia of emotions which threatens us all. And any doubts I may have are eliminated the Thursday following the Grant visit ... when Charles phones me at night, clearly a bit tiddley, close to tears

– he has just (once again) been thrown for a loss by his separated wife ... and asks to come for dinner the following night – something he rarely (only once before) ever done ... Clearly his margin of emotional and psychic survival is weak ...

At supper the next night, I break our rules, that business must not be discussed at any such private dinner ... and we do discuss Grant, practically nothing else. Grant as a general phenomenon ... I do this to help re-focus Charles, back into his creative work. But the discussion is mostly "therapy" for Chas – not much brilliance in it; simply the mutual recognition that some huge struggle is, and long has been, going on within Grant ... some terrible personal struggle. And Charles does mention one specific thing – "I can tell you this now that the event is over ... When I asked George if you and I could come to see him, he replied 'yes, but Lee must be there too ... ' It was clear that George felt the need of Dennis's presence, as some kind of protection against you ... "

Finally, Wednesday, July 17th, we have our first lunch together since the visit – and I give Chas the typed Diary I have already done ... twenty-two pages of it. Charles reads it through, laughs at some parts (which delights me) – and (a faster reader than I) he finishes his reading of it well before I finish my reading of the carbon copy, as I sit beside him. And as I read, for the first time, my Diary of the visit, I feel something huge welling up inside me, something I had not at all expected – and when I'm done reading, Charles says gently, a little sadly, "You *feel* it all so much more than I do, so profoundly ... it has so much more meaning for you ... " And I blurt yes, YES, ohmigod ... and am more than half in tears. Completely unaware until that enacted moment, that what was going through me as I wrote these notes the central emotion, was precisely a potent rage of tears ... rage at the realized loss, acknowledgement of the extent of The Deprival ... tears, at having seen, once again, what has been lost (for all of us) in the home and person of George Grant, and his wife.

The Spiritual Diary

It is Christ's Week! Oaxaca, Mexico

Heaven, Hell and Thanksgiving: Newfoundland

extracts compiled by Symons for *Household of God*, history of
St. Thomas's Anglican Church, Toronto.

Symons has frequently referred to his diary over the years as his
spiritual survival kit. In these selections he deals openly with heav-
en and hell, purgatory and deliverance. He attempts to treat the
manifold implications of his Christian faith which inform the most
banal and the most dramatic aspects of daily life, experienced by
Symons as a kind of lived theology.

As Symons put it in a brief addendum to his section of
Household of God: A History of St. Thomas's Church: "I have no illusion
that I am a theologian. Yet my diary notes have been of vast impor-
tance to me. It would be clear, I think, that the writings of Simone
Weil have been important to me (since 1971). Also a number of
medieval and later mystics, including Julian of Norwich, Meister
Eckhardt, St. John of the Cross and St. Teresa of Avila."

Extracts from diaries written during his Mexican sojourn in the
town of Oaxaca and others produced at the moment of his arrival
in Newfoundland in 1970 begin this section. They show Symons at
his most tortured, his most apocalyptic. It should be added that
they only begin to scratch the surface of a prodigious number of
pages archived at Trinity College.

Symons rereads himself for *Household of God*, a history of St.
Thomas's Church in Toronto, and his edited diary selections pro-
vide us with his vision of the Passion, Passion of Christ and passion
of all human life. These diaries meditate upon Eucharist, upon
communion, upon experience and concept that is central even to
the most apparently secular moments of Symons' work.

Symons' writing, here again more than a little saddening in its
isolation from the mainstream, belies his final comment in
Household of God: " I have often wondered why there has been no
tradition of such writing in English Canada, given the importance
of churches in founding this nation."

It Is Christ's Week!

Oaxaca, Mexico. April, 1968.

Oaxaca-in-the-blue-blossoming-trees-time
Tuesday, April 9, 1968.

10:45 a.m.
It is Christ's Week.
It is Christ's Week!

And I know that none of us has done so well as Christ did. None of us has lived up to Christ. Or rather none of us has lived beyond Christ, into that Redeemed Life Christ's death gave to us ... None of us has lived into the life he handed to us. The Beautiful Life in ourselves with others.

And that being so, then the best of us can but emulate, mimic, Christ. The very best of us become but De Imitatione Christi. Because we have not accepted his Gift of Life to us.

It is Tuesday already in Christ's week ... This morning I awoke to John's type-writing in the next bedroom – 7:30 a.m. ... and lay bemused, drained still – till 8. And then up, and pulling my body together did 20 pushups, 20 toe-touches, 20 kneebends. Solitary breakfast – John en route out to mail his multitude of Letters – any one of which is sufficient "legal evidence" against me, sufficient legal evidence of our full and sexual relationship, to jail me ... to crucify me. And I let the Letters go, with John. Because they are John, they are his birth, his full entry into life. And I cannot, must not stop him sending them. Even though, with the Philistines these Letters condemn me ...

and after breakfasting, walk out some little into the morning's brightsun. Fetching fresh milk at the hand dairy ... walking through the Parque, along the diagonal cobbling walks through the trees, careful to find seek the falling blue blossoms sultry on the walk underfeet. Smiling at me as my feet brush their blues. Walking through the falling flowers.

(and remembering, oh remembering that end to the Gringo Cowboy film I saw a few days ago ... in which the Hero Tough Guy dies good, and is seen – one Jimmy Ringo – riding after his death, across the Westering sunset skies. Remembering what I felt – that if I must die, fully merely die – ascared to entirely live, then this is how I want to be remembered, seen in the heart's eye of memory by those who knew who I was and knew how I did die. Want to be remembered as some sweet frightened toughguy walking through field flowers, seeing the songs of birds, the face of the coming sun, with Judith nearby happy, and John by my side – touching ... in the field of flowers and birdthrongs. Is how I want it. Only that – no other way possible to see know me. Have earned that right, that vision of myself ... my Diaries prove so. So many days through the flowersongs, the birdblossoms – Judith frightened to be with me, and I unable to touch her, faithful to our Untouchability, our Forebears, our portable lifetime Crucifixions, accepted as fidelity to Family.

Walking through the flowerstroll – Queen Anne's lace, Goldenrod ... Springtime memory of first Bloodroot. With Judith in our eye of love, and John by my thighside ... arm in arm. Always.

No other way. Need all. No other way.

poor tough little Scottieboy: yearning for the woman he loves and thus can never touch in faithfulness; and with the boy, the guy, the man, he equal loves, for the sake of life and loving – the woman and the guy each the other. His loveability. Is all. No matter what the others say, imply, accuse. Just the heart of love. And the flowers, the fieldflowers, strolling into the song of sun.

Is the only way I would be remembered – if I die, if I fail and therefore have to die

in the flowers

with Judith and my John – each for the other. Each enabling, sanctioning, permitting, blessing the other by his or her very being.

Holy Trinity. That I don't understand but know, feel ... believe and bless. Even with my dying blood, shall bless.

* * *

9:45 a.m. reach my writing table, sit, about to write – but want to oh so want to out now to Church, to that Processional of Christweek ... I'll go, pay homage, then be back – and scoot out, across the blueblossom park to find the Church of St. Thomas past the Market, ask – cannot find ... to Santo Domingo rich in golds. And ask again. Cannot. And don't even stay at St. Domingo (so heavy in gilts – too heavy is it?). But seek the Church ... It's past the Market they say ... I go. Am waylaid by market, no Church to sight. I'll market anyhow (my need acknowledged – no surge to seek the Church further ... I've paid my homage now – must be it, released by homage of my coming, seeking ... though not fulfilled – no Church servicing me).

into market, for meat, fresh meat ... along that line of stalls, meat thick stalls and fresh flies and mexifaces, find the one last night I saw refrigerated, poor little innocent Gringo I (wanting best treatment naturally) – ask for "carnes por sopa" and then two bifsteks – while the mexiwoman beside me watches slantwise, and my meat bought given I smile sheepish to her and she back, married over the need for meat I've got now ...

and on, in this overheady market barn, voice of thrumming song guitars beyond next stalls, stops me – Christ – this thrumming mexisong, this sweet descending wail as all openchested mexisongs, this full-blooded descant murmuring all this market hall – Christ: THIS IS THE CHURCH ... here is the Church I'm in ... these men, women, fresh-flied meats – IS THE CHURCH ... I know is so, I'm in the Church here. Is all I can know now, all I care want dare acknowledge know, and bow my head, my eyes down, just glance the guitarstrummer's head (should I give him a peso?) walk on dizzied, mid the stalls, buy watermelon – 4 pesos, dear, will have it as a treat with John – bananas, onions (for bone-meat soup).

and out to street, turn left from barracks where those lousy bully soldiers stole the Christian quarters from the overbearing Church long ago, turn left, pass squatting by the barrack wall that blind face of sweet singing man I saw those days ago pray aloud in the Church-beside-the-Market, pray aloud on knees I heard at other end of Church and thought it was an entire service going on it filled my gut and went quick to see what priest but found only on his knees this blind man before sidechapel altar praying fervent loud (I wanted to go to him on my knees)

is him, I pass – cannot know to peso him (but remember the man outside my Hotel Nelson, Montréal, en route to Cathedral, that Winter's day, in *Place d'Armes* ... who begged, I refused ... still inside of me)

and back to our casa with my foods – settle in, repose some little and up to write just this all ... open my Prayer Book (that one from St. James' Cemetery Chapel where they buried Dad's ashes, his Funeral Service ... took the book then for always beside me) – my Prayer Book opened, to Palm Sunday, to Monday, Tuesday now, in Holy Week ... glance, and find, of course, that Palm Sunday is (of course) Crucifixion Sunday, which I did not know, and Passion Sunday and Week, the week just passed, just passed me by. I did not openly know, never really knew, even the basics of my Christ-faith (only knew buried in my gut ... knew that somehow his Passion Week, Sunday, was mine, Thine – always so)

and put it down – Crucifixion Sunday done not coming, knowing too that Crucifixion is the High Point of my faith, not Resurrection ... as any good Heaven-fearing Protestant wills it so. So I.

Heaven, Hell and Thanksgiving: Newfoundland 1970

August

En route to Newfoundland (on the Ferry)
much, oh an infinity of pain these past days ... fleeing Ontario – geographic
Ontario. And more so, fleeing the Ontario in me ... fleeing my "Ontarioness"!
It is very simple ... I *can* say it simply – Canada has been for me a systematic trip to
Hell! A gratuitous and concerted imposition of hell in guise of the "CDN identi-
ty." THIS HAS BEEN THE ULTIMATE (NEGATIVE) NATURE OF MY LIFE WIT-
NESSING ... TO REVEAL MacCANADA AS CONCERTED CONSCIENTIOUS HELL.
(my positive witnessing has been the flowers, birds, trees: grant me this and these,
please ... "prithee" – a word I now resurrect relevantly ... "prithee" – I PRAY THEE.)

September

Let me say, for thee, that I am at least two hundred yards from any house ... on the
flank of the sea, where the last grass crisps suddenly down the earth to sand and
the sea.
I have come 3000 miles to New-found-land, for peace of body-and-being ... and
this morning I have driven a further ten miles from our Provincial Park (it is
Piccadilly Provincial Park ... on the Port-au-Port peninsula [come to this Peninsula
to be several diligent removes from the Trans-Canada Overpass. I have come here
simply to be, once again, whole-wholesome]).
...

I know all the big things in life now. The rest is sorting out ... distillation! Making
use of the harvest that is me!

October

you have to go in-to Christ
you have to enter in-to the eye of the Sun
you have bow down to be seen by the grass
you have to ssing in the Yellow Warbler
you have to acknowledge that cocks are beauteous
you have to acknowledge that all else is dust

You have to, each Morning, enter in-to the body of celebration ... or else die

There is no other way

...

You have to celebrate.
It is, truly, against Nature not to celebrate
It is a violation of self, of Firmament, not to celebrate

You have to see the sSun, you have to worship, praise, adore ... Or you do not exist.
And I know nothing of worship, praising or adoration

This I must readily confess: I KNOW NOTHING OF WORSHIPPING, NOR OF PRAISING, NOR OF ADORATION

I KNOW NOTHING OF GIVING THANKS
I KNOW NOTHING OF SSINGING, OF THE MUSIC IN LIFE

I confess that I know only how to criticize, to carp, to complain ... and all my commentary is corrosive ... ALL THAT I KNOW IS HOW TO DIMINISH

I want to add this that I suspecting have long known:
    that to give thanks is not simply to say "thank you."
    TO GIVE THANKS IS TO BE GIVEN IN THANKS

    And when you are given in thanks, what you thank is praised in the central eye of you ...
    what you are thanking locates utterly inside of you (and could kill you if it so wished)

    When you are giving thanks you are open to rape, violation, abrupt death

    When you "give thanks" it must be you, me, who is given in thanks

    It is absolute ... always

And I confess this: that I have always known all of this ... always.
And I have allowed the superimposed structure of my mere education to prevent me from Being Given In Thanks

    I HAVE TO BE GIVEN IN THANKS
    And I know when I am given in thanks, because only when I am so given in thanks do I see anything. Only if I am so given is there conjugal body of me and what I thank ... sSun, Christ, friend, warbler.

    Whereas if I am not given, then I see only "outlines," I see only detached objects. If I am not given I see the way Kodachrome sees: a world of windowless monads – or as George Grant says (Bless him, please!) I see only a "monism of meaninglessness"

    IF I AM NOT GIVEN IN THANKS AND PRAISE, THEN I SEE ONLY THE

SHADOWS ON THE WALL OF PLATO'S CAVE

and all the world is mere silhouette

I have to celebrate ... or I am still-born.
I have to celebrate each Day ... each New Morning, or I am still-life, nature-morte

AND I AM TERRIFIED OF CELEBRATION

That I have a right to be so terrified ... that every experience of my society has taught me that to celebrate is to be crucified – this does not matter.

NOT TO CELEBRATE IS TO BE (IN THE TRUE SENSE) A PERVERT

NOT TO CELEBRATE IS TO COMMIT THE ABSOLUTE CRIME AGAINST LIFE

NOT TO CELEBRATE IS THE FINAL HERESY

...

THE ONLY REASON, THE ONLY SPIRITUAL REASON, FOR MY POSITION IN LIFE, FOR MY APPARENT REBELLION À L'OUTRANCE, IS THAT MY SOCIETY IS PREDICATED UPON PERVERSITY

Said right: AS I MOVE (CLUMSILY ALBEIT) TOWARDS GRACE & CELEBRA-TION, BY DEFINITION I AM A REVOLUTION AWAY FROM MY SOCIETY

Let me confess this: that if I do not celebrate, then my "rebellion" is a heresy!

I WANT TO CELEBRATE

EVERY FIBRE OF MY BEING WANTS TO CELEBRATE

... yes – managed it, despite mere-fears of cacophony next door (wives' friendly banter of malices)

managed it,
that/this shortsweet sSong of All the Grasses
on the hillthigh, in front of me (us – thee too)
beyond the shed-shacks and ricket fence,
twenty feet from me, a sheer mat of grasses rising the hill

managed it (in so much trembling) just this truncated sSong, the way these grasses move me, as bowing down, bending me down till I am genuflection in

majesty of their prose some rich new calligraphy I understand the Chinese script
now was always the way the willows pickeral weed water-lilies swum

bending down till unafraid I bow me down (on my heart's knees)

the majesty of these mere Grasses lifting up
the heart (the language is precise. The Psalmists knew ... were just reporters of
their fact. As Praise)

LORD I HAVE SO LITTLE ... BUT WHAT I HAVE I OFFER THEE

Eucharist Diaries from Household of God

History of St. Thomas's Church (Toronto: The Church, 1993)

It was in the later 1960s that I first began attending St. Thomas's Church. I had fled my home to become a writer. And in many ways the Eucharist service became my home, certainly my inner home.

My first novel, *Place d'Armes*, set in old Montréal, had the Church of Notre-Dame de la Place on its dust jacket. And that church played an important role in the novel. Final work on my second novel, *Civic Square*, was done in a monastery, that of the SSJE in Bracebridge, with the Eucharist a daily presence. The following book, on early Canadiana, included an eighteenth-century colour plate of Notre-Dame as a major piece. And my most recent novel included a scene at commun-ion service in St.Paul's Cathedral, London (my editor at McClelland & Stewart wanted me to take it out, assuring me that modern readers weren't interested in religion of any kind). The novel I am currently working on has a deep concern for the liturgy and Communion. Indeed that remarkable book by Dom Gregory Dix, *The Shape of the Liturgy*, is central to my novel.

It is only these years later (some twenty-five years since I wrote my first novel) that I can look back and see how important the Eucharist has been to me. Central to my wrestlings with life.

And in those twenty-five years it was at St. Thomas's that I wrestled most often. Each time I returned to Toronto from a stint in Newfoundland, or the B.C. bush, or Mexico, or Morocco (places where I'd worked on my various books), I found my way to St. Thomas's. After all, Toronto was my historic home, that of my family and forebears (eight generations of them here), and I was in Toronto as much as I was away. And St. Thomas's became my parish.

I have always, since 1958, kept a diary, and carried it everywhere I went. This included church. Whatever service I attended, whichever country I was in, I kept my diary. It was my particular way of collaborating with the service, of participat-ing more deeply. Also my way of trying to understand the Eucharist more fully. So I would sit in whatever pew, jotting my notes, my reactions, my questions, as the Eucharist went on. I fear that sometimes it must have startled neighbours in the pew, though I invariably sat off to one side, as small as possible.

With the centennial of St. Thomas's looming, I went back into my diary to see what I'd written in the past twenty years while attending service there. There it all was, notes made during the sermon, or during the Communion, and marked *Sermontime*, *Eucharistime*, or *After Communion*. It was indeed the record of a man wrestling with the meanings of the Eucharist. A man certain of Holy Communion, if uncertain of himself.

Here is a selection of entries over the years. Aside from small changes in punc-tuation, or a few in wording, the entries are exactly as in the diary, and the changes are made only for clarity.

Palm Sunday, 1970:
"It, this is the Only Way ... always the sight of Christ on the Cross blows my

mere-mind. The thought, the fact of His Gift, a life absolutely given. What else matters?"

After Communion: "Back in my seat, marinating in Christ's bloodgift. And now slowly seeing them whole, as people. Real People (gift by the Real Presence). And whether it is my eyes which are whole now, or the communicants who are equally made whole, it matters little. Wholeness is back onto me."

July 22, 1979:
"I must let Holy Communion reach me today – must let myself be judged by it. The terror and tragedy of life ... the terror and tragedy of the Processional.
"All I can do is to be here, immerse myself. The only chance I have, the real renewal."

Sermon saying: "The priest is the Vehicle of forgiveness. But he is also the channel for sin." At which I wrote: "we all forget this ... a priest has a right to be a sinner; it is part of his being human."

After Communion: "The sincerity of this church, beyond understanding(?)
"Or underneath all the ritual folderol! Which is why I come. It restores triumph to life, triumph and tragedy, and both within Christ. It acknowledges and accepts the real and ongoing dimensions of life, as against the 'reality' of so-called realism which terribly truncates life and its possibilities."

The Prayer of Humble Access: "*We do not presume to come to this thy Table, O merciful Lord, trusting in our own righteousness* ...
"There it is – never have I felt this more strongly, mistrust of my own 'righteousness.' Recognition of such mistrust is essential."

"*Eucharistime: Dread, terror, hope* (and the urge to shout, scream, burst into tears as I approached the Altar – horribly powerful). This Communion is all we have ...
"It shatters me. Shatters me whole."

September 2, 1979:
"St. T's again ... wobbling my way here, never fully knowing why! But always certain that I must (and nothing to do with duty). Sensing that this (and this alone) is what stands between me and slipshod cynicism.
"Without this Service I wouldn't exist! Stupefying realization, during the Offertory Hymn ... There is my horrifying, hidden, inmost reality, that without Holy Communion I would not exist, *would not be.*
"That is the verity I cling to (and why I come fumbling, wobbling, worrying, *here*) – my only truth and my only possibility. And my recognition of this fact, the *real* margin of my survival.
"(But how can I *accept* such a fact? Everything in me resists is, side-steps it. And certainly everything in a modern society does so!)
"Without Holy Communion I would not exist – there is my terrifying reality

... It is the highest, best, most relevant thing I know. And everything else in my life depends from it (and without it, I am already destroyed!)

"The rest of my life will be spent in finding out what this means."

Sunday, November 4, 1979:
"A harrowing life, psychically in Toronto – joyless. My one real weekly respite is here ... This Service as point of departure for life as it somehow can never be lived in our era – an inner life, the palpability of the spiritual ... "

Grand Procession around the inside of the church: "One of the Sundays when they get out the whole works, *son-et-lumière* – banners and 'holy smoke' and robes and ribbons and several crucifers ... silly, pathetic, marvellous, moving. Only as the entire Procession works its way around the church do I know why it has, finally, moved me to tears ... because it convokes an ALLELUIA, as they sing 'the King of Glory passes on His way.'"

Sermontime: Yes, the fact is that I would walk into fire to affirm what this Service and that Procession are, the reality they proclaim. (And in the end I may well, literally, have to walk into fire, real actual fire, to make such affirmation.)"

Eucharistime: "*Hosanna in the highest*' – a life that does not allow us to say, to sing, to experience Hosanna, such a life is no life ... "

Right after Communion – "Once again I felt tears as 'Christ's Body' hit my tongue ... at once a caress, and a hatchet cleaving the skull; each and both at the same time.

"Yes, once again, I am one of the *'heirs through hope'*!"

Sunday, November 16, 1979
"*Unto whom all hearts be open ...* ": "What a marvellous concept (contrast to current society in which all hearts are closed, shuttered shut).

"Aperture of heart, that's what this H.C. Service does for/to me. It re-inflicts aperture of heart – prevents my heart from final foreclosure."

Sermontime: "*Our best recollection must be that we are citizens of Heaven*' – Wow (that sentence leaping out of the humdrum sermon) ... I've never thought of giving thanks for my 'citizenship in Heaven,' have barely come, now, to formally recognize and articulate the fact. I have so much trouble keeping it all in perspective, and then keeping it all going. I fumble, trip, and evade ... "

Sunday, November 25, 1979
Sermontime: "Cynicism is fear of life; masquerading as control of life!"

"Yes, cynicism is a flight from life – a whine presented as a snarl. A decided weakness presented as a strength (even as *the* strength)."

Eucharistime: "All of life as Holy Communion (or the failure to be H.C.). The world seen, and been, through (and *beyond*) H.C. – life always seen through H.C. as Monstrance."

"And each time I get to the Altar Rail is always an *approximation*, an approach, a 'sketch,' an assay ... "

Sunday, January 13, 1980
"This Service *is* ... a *horror-story*! This 'banquet' (of Holy Communion) is ... a horror story.

"Oh, nothing about this Service makes any sense to my mind! *Yet without this Service nothing makes sense at all!*"

Eucharistime: "We are *inside* it (the Eucharist) – it has happened. Just as Socrates' martyrdom happened.

"Changing the world, absolutely altering our psychic inscape. We can't escape it.

"Once my mind does accept the reality of H.C., then my mind can make sense of everything and anything."

"Yes, it is a banquet and a celebration – but first of all it is a regulation of that (ongoing) horror story (*i.e.* the Crucifixion). It confronts, enacts, then resolves that horror story. And the sense of horror is as much a part of this Service as is the sense of 'banquet.'

"Immitigable horror, and immitigable joy – these are the realities of this Service, each and both at the same time ongoing. Which is what makes it so difficult to understand or to endure or to accept.

"It is hard work, this Service, and the more you understand it, the harder it is. It is travail, at least in part, and certainly initially."

" ... at the end, on my knees for the Recessional Hymn, the Cross passing in front of me ... It was Christ passing, Christ himself ... that is the experience.

"(As it is at once bread and wine, *and* Christ's Body and Blood, so too it is the Recessional Cross *and* Christ, Christ Himself. As it is Christ en route to Calvary as much as Christ risen – the Cross is always Calvary).

"The route to the Cross is also the route to Redemption, both going on at once – horror and Holiness."

"The Holy Horror of this Service, that's what I felt today."

Sunday, January 27, 1980
"Going to the Altar, wondering 'What do I bring to the Altar? ... I know what I *receive* there' – and the answer was, 'I have to bring *everything*, everything I am or have'!

"And as I approached the Altar ... the sense of a spear going through me, a silent spear, an invisible spear ... as a ray of light.

"And the Bread, the wafer, so light in the palm of my hand, yet the weight of the world in it!"

Sunday, June 29, 1980
"an embodied contemplative act, *that's* what this Service at St. T's is, minimally ... And yes, it is the tenderness of the Service here which is striking."

Sunday, April 30, 1989
" ... made it, again! I so often feel as if it were some feat of daring and improbability, even foolhardiness ... to get to church, to Eucharist. As if it were against all odds – or even against my own survival and secular best interests.

"Something scary to it for me – daunting. Ahh, the Mass *is* ... the real critique of one's life. The real taunt and dare and test!"

"I simply come here and bask in it – the song ... and the comeliness, the ballet of the Service. It's not a war-zone. The only time I escape the secular war-zone!"

"Secularism is ... doubt.

"Spirituality is ... belief.

"Doubt is a void.

"Belief is 'insanity' in terms of the secular world! A form of epilepsy, emotional and/or psychic epilepsy. Yes, anyone with a serious spiritual life in this society would have to, variously, seem 'crazy' – *i.e.* anyone not a priest, a minister, etc."

"*Are you washed in the Blood? Have you been saved ...* ' (Sermon).

"Yes, absurd question in secular terms. Imagine in the middle of a Toronto business lunch, if you suddenly leaned forward and asked, 'Are you washed by the Blood?'

"How *does* one cope?

"Well, ongoing epilepsy – that ongoing emotional epilepsy of the secular world. (What is the Toronto media other than a form of epilepsy?!)

"One pits the secular epilepsy *vs.* what secular society would have to think of as the other epilepsy ... of the religious life!"

"Yes, I feel tears by now. The Service *has* cracked my secularity, my secular carapace. Aided by the sheer tenderness of the voices singing just behind me!"

"Yes, it's the intimacy of the Service; the intimacy it engenders (whereas our secular society is *anti*-intimacy; just as mere sex is ... anti-intimacy)."

"It's the tenderness, and the givenness (of self) this Service is and engenders ... which is (or leads to) the intimacy."

"And ... it's the Prayer of Humble Access which draws all this together, *i.e.* it's at that point in the Service that the 'mystical body of Christ' *has* ... invaded us!

"At the Prayer of Humble Access we are (within this Service) *one* ... within the Mystical Body of Christ – the Service having thus *done* what it says it's doing!

"*i.e.* there's the verbal Service (the mere words), *and* the inner Service ... of the Sacrament! The very nature of being as sacrament. The recovery of the sacral within one ... via the very movement of the Service!"

Eucharistime: " ... yes, approaching the Altar one has to *forgive everything*! One has to be empty ... utterly opened and ready. All rage voided, all resentments and hates and revenges dissolved! One has to be fused with the Service and all its meaning! And naked, emotionally naked."

After Church: "Yes, that Service is it ... hews closest to life in the deepest sense – and (alas) I keep forgetting this!

"It isn't alien to life (*e.g.* the spiritual vs. the secular). But the fundament of life itself – the deepest meaning(s) of and in life."

Sunday, July 16, 1989
"There is an absolute guarantee in life only of Calvary! Our own ... or His! Ours to choose.

"The CanLit concept of 'victim' is simply the Christian predicament sans Christ!"

"If someone asks you if you believe, you don't reply, you simply gaze at them whole!

"I don't believe so much as live within that belief. Act and react from within it. As living within a flame, a fire ... of which I am one of the flames."

The Second Trilogy

Helmet of Flesh, John of Osprey Cove

Waterwalker, Flames and Roses (unpublished)

Dracula-in-Drag, Breakfast of Champions (unpublished)

John's Letter

Two-thirds of Symons' second trilogy are still unpublished. *Helmet of Flesh*, the first, eponymous volume was published by McClelland & Stewart in 1986. The other two parts, still a work in progress, are tentatively titled *Waterwalker* and *Dracula-in-Drag*. Together, the three "novels" recount the adventures of York MacKenzie in Morocco, London, and Canada. Volume One describes the arrival of MacKenzie in Morocco and a series of wild misadventures. Constantly present through flashbacks, letters, and photographs are both London, England and Osprey Cove, Newfoundland. MacKenzie's troubled past, his largely self-provoked career difficulties, and impasse with his lover lie at the centre of the intrigue. The main thrust of the trip to Morocco is the enlightening confrontation with a civilization that lies outside the expectations of modern Western society.

"John of Osprey Cove," chapter ten of *Helmet I*, is included here. It begins in the Hôtel des Amis, Marrakech and swirls back through description of photographs to York MacKenzie's life with lover John in Newfoundland. It sets up the fundamental dramatic conflict of the trilogy and contains some marvellous description of life in isolated Atlantic Canada.

The second volume, *Waterwalker*, perhaps the finest of the three, sets up a distinctive view of London as foundational to Canadian meanings and to resolving the dilemmas of York MacKenzie. Symons'/ MacKenzie's unique critique of contemporary culture takes the main character to the Victoria and Albert Museum where he traces out "the devolution of the Occidental Orgasm" and links it to a visionary experience of a Raphael cartoon of Christ walking on the water. Theological and philosophical notions from Simone Weil and Dom Gregory Dix are interwoven with unwitting visits to S&M clubs, and encounters with militant feminists. MacKenzie plays the role of "God's Fool," *vrai-faux naif*, to the hilt.

"Flames and Roses" closes the second installment and brings the personal dilemmas of York MacKenzie to a flaming approach to final truths through the juxtaposition of a banal yet amusing dinner party with attendant tensions and a final visionary experience at the Victoria and Albert Museum.

The third volume, *Dracula-in-Drag*, is fully centred on an attempted return to Canada and reconciliation with "John of Osprey Cove," the lover so essentially present from the first volume on. It contains beautiful tableaux of Canadian seasons, lightly fictionalized commentary on the contemporary Canlit scene, and most powerful of all, a long psychoanalytic interchange with a remarkable character, the formidable Doctor Mildred.

"Breakfast of Champions," a late chapter of *Dracula in Drag*, finds York MacKenzie staying with bookseller friends Jane and Shirley and trying to comprehend a breakfast meeting with estranged lover John. The scene quickly shifts to a session with therapist Mildred who is helping York unravel the dangerous nature of his obsessive relationship with John – the Evil Eye of Morocco transposed to Canadian circumstance.

"John's Letter" concludes these selections with an extended, quasi-obsessive reading of yet another letter – in York MacKenzie's universe everything significant occurs through the missive! This completes the arc of the narrative from Moroccan recollections of Newfoundland occasioned by a letter, to a Canadian exorcism through analysis, friendship and writing.

From *Helmet of Flesh:*
John of Osprey Cove

He was awakened by knocking. Two o'clock! He jumbled the litter of pages together as Khalid set the tray on the end of the bed – "You slept past breakfast, but I've brought you lunch." York nodded. "M'sieur Claude said you received good news." Khalid grinning towards the letter. Yes, thank you, it was good news. "Very good news?" Khalid sat down. Yes, very good news. Khalid grinned delight – "M'sieur Claude hopes the news is as good as we've all been hoping for." York pondered; well yes, it was that good. "Does this mean you'll be leaving us?" Yes it did. "That's not good news, m'sieur York." Khalid laughed – "But you'll be back." Silence. "So I can tell m'sieur Claude and m'sieur Richard that you are happy?"

"Khalid – please inform messieurs Claude and Richard, also m'sieur Bertrand, in fact *le tout Hôtel*, that m'sieur York is in ecstasy!"

Khalid's eyes rotated with pleasure. And bearing the precious information, he departed. York sat abed, gazing at lunch and letter. Suddenly chuckling – this hotel was definitely preposterous. He nibbled on the lunch, cold chicken and salad. But the letter kept catching his eye. Flowers and flying zebs twinkling up from the pages. And the sound of birds: the letter, or the garden? Didn't matter. Lunch, breakfast, whatever it was would have to wait.

He picked up the letter again, skimming it. His finger tracing the signature, the wild flower surging up from "thy-John" ... surge of energy from sunflower into his finger. Like touching John's body, like touching his zeb. York's finger tracing from page to page, flowers and phalli flowing the names of Mariam and Ma Snook and all Osprey Cove, their voices singing from the letter. And suddenly he was out of bed, over to his valise for the photos. John shoving them into his luggage at the last moment – "You might want to take a peek now and then, Yo-Yo, 'cause we all loves ya!" He fished the envelope out and scurried back to bed. Pouring the photos over his knees.

There they were: the head of Farley peeping up, a giant smirk from Mariam, the sharp eyes of old Jim Snook, and a pony cantering across a beach of dories. Photos flaring an instant collage of Osprey Cove. Ma Snook at her front door, arm raised, brandishing a soup ladle like a truncheon. York chuckled, closed his eyes, not wanting to see it all at once. And heard them chattering and shouting ... waves pounding the beach, bare yards from Ma Snook's front door. Sounds and voices he had locked out these past two weeks, or that had been drowned in the din of Marrakech.

Eyes still shut, he reached for one of the pictures, opened a squint to see ... who? Outrageous flamingo pink, with yellow trim – the home of Ma and Jim Snook. Perched like a tropical bird blown off course, at the foot of a glowering grey cliff. He could hear music floating out the open window ... Ma Snook always had the radio on, fiddle and accordion music, folk songs. "I likes the accordeen," she'd say, clapping her hands in time. Daft little house, crouched amidst the armies of potato plants, tomatoes, piles of manure. The Snookery: that's what they called it. Hearth of Jim and Ma Snook, reigning elders of the clan. At once cottage and Osprey Cove manor.

York opened his eyes full. There she was, standing right at the front door of her Hansel-and-Gretel home: Ma Snook and her militant soup ladle. Standing and shouting – "I wants more space fer me flowirrrs!" Bellowing it out and waving her ladle. Must have been the morning and John and York went to borrow Jim's dory for the day. And before they got to the door there was Ma, marching out and flailing her largest soup ladle – "I wants more space fer me pretties!" And John quick snapping a photo. "Ye kin plant yer 'taties up past t'creek some!" She was storming down the front path of her home, grabbing Jim's shovel like a broadsword. And banging a hole right through the old picket fence, rootling up rows of young potatoes. Jim shaking his head, his 'taties jilted like that – "Yeeess, an she's gone plum varmint agin. Cain't do nuttin wit her whin she's loike that." As Ma Snook hurled dirt and 'taties and fence up and out, till she had her flower seeds all planted. And when done, marched back to the front gate all sweet as a daisy, as if she'd just negotiated a small adjustment in life. Standing by the white and orange and pink picket fence, patting the plastic statuette of Snow White that stood atop the fence post. And the statuettes of Donald Duck and Winston Churchill nearby seemed to nod approval. As Ma grinned a mite sheepishly, saying, "Well, an I guess it be time to sarve a spot o'tea t'the lot of ye. C'mon in."

But John was jumping with laughter, snapping another photo and was shouting, "Yer garden is a marvel, Ma Snook, sure an it's a wonder of the world!" At which Ma brandished her shovel, retorting, "An ye'll be a marvel when I fixes wit ya! I'sll jes stick ye roight up atop me fence, along wit Lard Churchill 'ere." And with that she ducked behind the fence, and came up hurling a clod of dung at the gang of them. Because by now they were six or eight, her men-folk, standing round in silent support of Jim during the destruction of his beloved potato patch. And Sammy Snook whispering to Jim – "Now look 'ere Pa, I'sll jes give ya some of me own gardin fer yer 'taties!" All of them standing bemazed; and York secretly applauding her flower-rampage, an act of genuine floral imperialism if ever there was.

"An it's *you* who's the marvel, Ma Snook!" York blurted aloud, as he lay in bed with the letter. And reached down amid the voices of Osprey Cove to pluck another picture. And taking a first glimpse saw the woebegone face, small black head bowed ... Farley, their little mongrel Labrador. Farley looking so sad there, beside John's rocking chair, as if betrayed. Whereas she was usually all cavort and affections ... adopted by the village, with food stations in all Snook homes and the butcher shop. "An 'ere comes Farlee, John an Yark will be followin' on." Oh, one day a fisherman threw a mean rock at their Farley. But Ma Snook heard about it and marched right out to hurl a good-sized rock at the fisherman. And that was the last rock ever thrown at Farley in Osprey Cove. Because the fishermen were right fearful of Ma Snook ... not of any rocks she threw but of her vibrant tongue. So Farley had the rights of the Cove, including most of the bigger male dogs who felt the little black dog was a succulent number.

But here was Farley, looking woeful and weighted down. Till York saw the white wings strung round her neck, and started to laugh: the wings were Valentine cards! It was Valentine's Day, and Farley had gone off on her daily rounds in the Cove. Gone off avisiting friends and allies, with no sense of anything out of the ordinary. But then scurried home earlier than her wont, howling to be let in. And John looked upset – "What've they done to Farley?" – as he rushed to the door to rescue her. And she scuttled in all woebegone, trailing the white objects. As if she had tin cans tied to her tail; that bad. And John angry, till he calmed Farley down and got at the things around her neck. "Come and look, Yo-Yo ... *hurry!*" John stomping his feet in glee. Showing York the envelopes tied round Farley's neck. And inside each a Valentine's card. So John had given Farley a moose bone to solace her dignity, and taken a quick photo. Then they'd sat down to read the cards.

All the rhymes and riddles and notes written in the peculiar Osprey Cove hand, nearly indecipherable. Along with hearts and wide-eyed lovers and painted bouquets of flowers. One from Ma and Jim Snook, with a note – "The two of you better git on down here for a Valintine supper, or we'll cut yor doreys off!" A command invitation.

And one from Maid Mariam, a postcard of a giant red lobster with a big heart painted on. Which York felt was mostly for John. But John laughed, saying, "We'll share it anyways, Yo-Yo!"

And one from Jed and Marie saying, "Your mitey odd neiburs and we love you, so never stop. XOXXO."

John chortling away, reading each one aloud, while Farley chomped on her windfall moose rib. And York sat between tears and laughter, sign of rare happiness. Because all the cards were addressed to "John and Yark" or "Yark and John" ... the way the kids would chant, each time they walked down along the beach to the Snookery. The kids leaning out windows or sheds or dories, singing out "John-an-Yark, 'tis Yark-an-John!" Daily chorale atop the waves, singing them home.

But most of the cards seemed to be from Ma Snook's granddaughters, Molly and Grace, a pair of bonny teenagers who played blithe tambourines each Sunday at the Citadel. Always sat right up front next to the Mercy Seat to see best. And Cove gossip said they were playing for John and York, because whenever John or York went up to the Mercy Seat to pray, Molly and Gracie would break into a special spangle of tambourine playing. And Mariam said, "Git ready fer a twin weddin' ... cause Ma Snook is plannin' t'marry off Mally an Gracie t'John an Yark!"

So that evening, when they went to Ma Snook's for the Valentine supper, John said, "But we couldn't marry both Molly and Gracie, Ma!"

"An why in tarnation couldn't ye, la?"

"Well, cause that would be too greedy like. We'sll just marry one of them between us, York and me."

"Marry jes t'one of 'em, ya say? Now that's a hard ticket!"

"Well," said John, "we'sll share her!"

There was a hush in the Snookery kitchen, as Ma pondered this special offer. The assembled members of Snookdom awaiting her word – "Naw, thet'd be lean meat fer the poor girrl!"

"But Ma Snook ... " John paused, clapping his hands – "That way she'll get twice as much, not half!" At which the Snook clan shouted in laughter, pushing

Molly and Grace towards John. The two girls shrieking in mock alarm, and fleeing Ma's kitchen as far as the door, hoping to be followed. And Ma Snook amuttering – "An youz two is a desp'rate hard ticket, an you is!" But old Jim Snook restored order, saying his "wimmin-folk was actin up agin." And it wasn't till days later they realized that all the Valentine cards purporting to be from Molly and Grace were written in different hands. Probably by Mariam, and young Sammy Snook, and Jed. Not from the girls at all. Didn't matter; York carefully kept them as joyous memory.

He gazed at the romp of photos, and felt the eyes. Warm stern eyes. Whose? His fingers moved to the photo ... old Jim Snook! Jim, alias Pa Snook, standing outside the Snookery fishing shed, working his nets. Jim in his forever leather peak cap. And forever cigarette butt dipping from his mouth. It never seemed to be lit; just there, like sweater and cap. Old Jim, caught in John's photo as final as Stonehenge.

York held by those Celtic eyes now. Jim saying something, York leaning forward to hear. "I s'pose ye'll be comin' by tonight, la. It's our bach'lir night." York nodding: yes, their bachelor evening, a custom by now. The first had been nearly a year ago, a few weeks after they'd arrived. York had dropped by the Snookery, found Jim alone – "Me wimmin-folk 'as gone out gal'vantin." Which meant that Ma Snook was out yarning with one of the family, or down at Mae Hann's store. And Jim was "bidin' home," sitting in his rocking chair by the stove, his hat still on. Did he ever take it off? And John was gone to pick up a chunk of illegal moose from Ollie Crocker. So Jim and York had sat silent awhile, listening to the surf, the howl of the village dogs. Till Jim got up to poke at the wood stove, poking up a spray of sparks and embers – "I'sll jes ginger up t'kettle a mite la. Yeeess, an we'sll 'ave a cup o'tea." Jim seemed to drink tea any time of day or night. Said coffee gave him "the blight." And padded round the kitchen, rinsing a pair of cups: special big cups with the King and Queen on them, King George V and Queen Mary. And fetched out the Gunpowder tea Ma Snook kept for special. And the sugar bowl with real cubes in it. Brushing the table clean with his huge hand, and finding a few broken cookies in the pantry.

York watched him gather the monuments, watched him nurse the kettle and brew the Gunpowder in the newest of the old teapots. And longed to give Jim something, anything, in exchange for such silent dignity. Then he remembered; he had a package of cigarillos with him – his little cheapo cigarillos.

"Would you be mindin' a cigarillo, Jim?"

"Don't know as I could. Ain't niver smoked but cig'rettes, la." Jim pushing his cap back on his head, pondering. But York got up and carried the cigarillos to Jim. Only a few feet away, he could have passed them. But he wanted to carry them over and offer one. Jim looked at the package as he might at a strange bird. But took one, and smelled it, then tucked it carefully behind his ear as if putting it politely into storage.

And when they had finished their silent tea, and York rose to leave, Jim said, "Yeeess, an I guess ye'll be comin' back on bach'lir night next week?" York said yes, he'd like to.

And the second time he went Jim just smiled, as if York had always been there.

And set up the Gunpowder special again. Then went to his cubbyhole bedroom, and came out holding the cigarillo from the week before. He held it for about half the tea. Then unwrapped its cellophane and slowly smoked it. And started talking about the early days in the Cove, before the road came in; only the boats.

After that, York went every week on bachelor night. John would go off with Ma Snook, visiting, and York would bide with old Jim. Till one night, some five months after John and York had arrived in Osprey Cove, Jim said, "Yeeess, an I reck-'n yez is livyeers now, you an John."

"An what's a livyeer, Jim?"

"Well, an ye lives 'ere now."

"Well, an I guess we does, Jim."

"Yeeess an ye duz, the pair on ye, la." Jim rolling out that elongated resonant "yes" of his ... "yeeeess." While York sat thinking that in a world of endless "no," Jim Snook had the finest "yes" he'd ever heard.

Then Jim had taken his weekly cigarillo from storage behing his ear, feeling it over, warming it with scraggy fingers. And York stood up to light it for him, feeling so proud that Jim was going to smoke it at all. And for nearly an hour he nursed that little cigarillo, and they talked of "Hospree Cuv." How wandering fiddlers and pipers had been the only entertainment in the early days, coming in by boat once or twice a year. And the whole village became a "carneeval." And the "jannies" – mummers who went about during the twelve nights after Christmas. Villagers dressed up like transvestite ghosts. Mirth and the macabre. And Jim said, "Yeeess, ye niver knows when one on 'em hain't from t'far side of yonder, la." And York asked Jim about that "la," he kept hearing it in the Cove. Hearing it at the end of sentences, like a small chirp. And Jim said he didn't rightly know, but it came from "the toime when the Frinch was about." The French? "Yeeess ... down coast a mite. Lots of them Frinch byes." York could have listened all night.

And Jim looked content – "You and John loikes Hospree Cuv some good!"

"Like ... ? We *love* the Cove, Jim!"

And that's when Jim had smiled his yearly smile. "Well, you an yer John is livyeers now, I kin tell ye that fer sartin." Then silent as he finished his cigarillo. York knew it was time to go. And ran back to find John, to tell him, "We is livyeers now!" Because he and John had been worried. Had felt the villagers sizing them up over the past months, all thousand souls. Felt a slow decision coming, as if by silent vote: would they, or wouldn't they, be welcome to remain in the Cove? The villagers were always friendly, of course. But it they didn't like you – you left! They'd seen it happen with one or two other visitors. The slow silent pressure driving them away ... But now they were livyeers. And it was only a few weeks later that they'd gotten the Valentine cards, in case the invitation to stay in the Cove wasn't clear.

York looked again at the photo. And laughed – old Jim tried to look so fierce. But always a covey of grandchildren scurrying round his rocking chair. They'd pretend to be afraid, and he'd growl, "I'se goin' t'wallop yer bottoms fer the lot o' yez!" And the kids would screech in delighted fear, and press closer to his chair. While Jim rocked more and more sternly. But his big gnarled hands would creep up and catch a child or three, and hold them tender. And York would practically fall out of his chair to glimpse Jim's eyes then ... shining velvet. And so often he wanted to tell him, but never dared. Because Jim never showed emotion.

Oh, but once he did. York picked up the photo – heard Jim's voice soft. "Ye'll be comin' back to the Cuv?" Yes, the last day, when York was leaving Osprey Cove to fly to London. He had gone to say goodbye to Snookville, and especially to old Jim. And Jim made some tea – which was strange because Ma Snook always did that when she was at home. But Jim was doing the honours that day. While Sammy Snook tried to dump York out of his chair, saying, "Well, an yer goin' t'play the swell in Londontown ... Hospree Cuv ain't grand enough fer ya!" Sammy laughing, poking his bluff affection at York, while Jed Snook chased a sheep that had stuck its stray nose in the pantry door. And little Jacob Snook was presenting John with a white kitten that John didn't want, "Cause we already got a cat, Jake, an we calls him after yer family."

Jim had carried a big cup of Gunpowder tea over to York, "fer special." And York in gratitude took a big swig – which dumped him out of his chair spluttering! The tea hoarse in his throat, and all the Snooks stomping their feet in applause. Jim must have slipped half a cup of Screech into it. And when York recovered enough to glance over, old Jim was quietly rocking, pretending to pat Farley. But as soon as York looked over he chuckled – "Jes t'tide yez over till the next time, Yark."

And suddenly the whole Snook clan was whirling all over York, and he got no further chance to speak with old Jim. Ma Snook chortling, "Give me greetins t'the Queen an Prince Philip, la!" And her sons carrying York out to the truck, right in the rocking chair. John already at the wheel, tooting the horn. But York was upset; hadn't really said goodbye to Jim. And suddenly a hush, the other Snooks making way. There he was, Jim standing right beside the truck window, chewing hard on the remains of his cigarillo. York rolled the window down as fast as he could. Jim clamped his big gnarled hand on the window ledge as if to stop the truck. And practically shouted at York – "Ye'll be comin' back then ... back t'the Cuv!"

"Yes, I'sll be comin' back, Jim."

"Yeeess, an mind ye duz! Cause yez is a livyeer now, you an yer John!" And with that Jim released the ledge and waved his boys back, because they were standing blocking the truck. And Ma was chasing grandchildren off the back, all wanting to come to the airport. John revved up with a final toot of the horn. And as the truck wheeled to leave, York saw him – saw old Jim. He was walking alone, down towards the surf, blowing hard on his nose with that big red polka-dot hankie.

"Yeeess an I'sll be back, Jim ... I'sll be back to the Cove, I promise you!" But York's voice wasn't in the truck in Osprey Cove. It was in bed, in Marrakech, as he sat amidst the photos. The babble of pictures a babble of friends, relatives, family left behind in the Cove. It felt like Christmas, or Easter at the Snookery. Or Ma Snook's birthday party: the time she wore the new dress they'd bought for her. Brand new dress from Corner Brook, with special lace collar, for high days. And Ma giving John and York a big kiss, and saying, "First time anyone iver *bought* a dress fer me. Cause I always makes me own." Ma raging with laughter, parading in her new "gown," and suddenly standing still, silent ... crying.

"Yes, I'sll be back!" And a sudden knock at the door. Khalid? Claude? York slipped over to open. It was Bertrand, appraising York's underwear with a flickering glance as he entered. And then York abed as Bertrand stood in silhouette – classic Greek today, a blouse, simple leather belt, and baggy pants. Vision over the end of the bed, limned by the sun: golden cockatoo!

"I've just been ... reading," York stammered, caught between Bertrand and Osprey Cove.

"I hear you have good news!" Bertrand swaying slightly, one arm hidden. "That's why I came."

"Oh, great news: my letter finally arrived."

Bertrand moved closer to the bed, tongue flickering his lower lip – "You've been waiting so hard for that letter."

"Yes, I suppose 'hard.' It was very important."

"I understand. Some letters *are* a matter of life or death." Bertrand smiled, bracelet jingling on his arm. "May I sit?"

York nodded as Bertrand composed himself across the end of the bed. "I hope it raised your morale, and maybe more." His arm waving time to hidden music. York still nodding to himself. "Yes ... sure death anyways, if it hadn't come." Bertrand's eyes flickered like his tongue – "I brought my flute." Producing it from behind his back. "Just for you." And putting flute to lips he lolled back, spilling a sudden serenade around the room, over the bed and each of them. Bertrand, caught in the sunlight, eyes fluttering, lips in love with his flute. Pan at the end of the bed, plying his pipes. Like John.

"I wanted to celebrate the news." Flute at his side now, eyes on York. Lips parted, leg moving closer, arm with the bracelet circling. Gold skulls dangling like little berries; Bertrand's eyes on York, smoky eyes. And suddenly York saw his own skull hanging there. And flinched.

Bertrand pulled back.

Silence.

"Those photos – he sent them to you?"

"What? ... Oh, he gave them to me before I left." York's eyes diving back to the pictures. "Osprey Cove, where I live."

"You live *there*?" Bertrand eyeing the display of Snooks, old Jim, the Citadel.

"Yes, sort of."

"Bizarre looking people, aren't they?"

"I love them."

Silence. Bertrand recoiling off the end of the bed. "I just wanted to share my music."

York nodded as Bertrand stood, gave a final flourish on his pipe. And departed ...

He dove into the photos again, hand snatching the first one it touched as if a lifesaver. Who? The Lieutenant, in full Salvation Army uniform, parading down the main lane of Osprey Cove. And Sammy Snook right behind, carrying the army flag – Blood and Fire. Mariam waddling behind Sammy with the big Bible. And *boom-ka-boom*, Sadie on the bass drum. And a scurry of kids with tambourines ... Molly and Gracie, and Jed's two. *Boom-ka-boom*, all so proud parading for Christ.

Yes, it was the very day John and York moved into the cottage next to Mariam's. In Skinner's Lane, one of the Snook lanes. Because Mariam was old Jim's sister. And Sadie next door, his daughter. And most of the others related by marriage or accident. "Snookville" it was called, some thirty various Snooks living there. The pink and yellow Snookery of Jim and Ma the headquarters. And *boom-ka-boom!* The sudden roll of a big bass drum in Skinner's Lane. A wild bugle note right off their front yard, John and York rushing to the window to see what apocalypse had struck. It was the Sally Ann, in full brigade. The Lieutenant at the head, with portable loudspeakers – "Callin' all hands fer Christ!" And John and York rushed outside agoggle, Farley following in a fit of barking. The three of them joining the parade; marching down Skinner's Lane, and on to the main road alongside Osprey Creek.

A bright and breezeless day it was, as their little band grew – more children with tambourines, several of the fishermen's wives bundling out to join up. As the Lieutenant bellowed out the word – "Callin' all soljers fer Christ!" And marching right on down to the docks, because it was the hour the fishermen came home. Loudspeaker booming as the fishermen bounced towards land in their dories – "Are ye comin' home to Christ ... or is the Divil king in yer home?" But the fishermen weren't saying too much after a hard day out on the waves. And John saw old Ned Crocker hiding a bottle of Screech under the seat of his dory. But most of them liked the young Lieutenant, because he was young and hard-working, and an outport man like themselves. Besides, some of their wives were standing right there, hollering along with the Lieutenant – "Are *you* comin' home to Christ?"

Till after much scuffling around in the boats, and Ollie Snook getting cuffed by Barney Crocker for cussin' right in front of the Salvashun Harmee like that, the first of the fishermen clambered clear of his dory and came over to stand meekly beside his wife in the brigade. And the Lieutenant announced over the speaker, "I feel a new touch o' power comin' down, Lard!" And *booom-ka-boom*. Sadie on the big drum, while the kids went wild on their tambourines. And Molly Snook rushed up and thrust a tambourine into John's hands. But he passed it to York, because he wanted some photos. John leaping round and round the group with his camera, clicking with glee. And the Lieutenant roaring, "Yesss, an we wants pictures of Hospree Cuv fer Christ!" While several local trucks rattled up, and more Covers clambered up on their backs to sing, "Glory, glory, halleloo-yaah!" Till a good portion of Osprey Cove was standing right at the docks, under the skeining gulls, the ocean rolling at their feet. "Gloree, gloree ... hallelooo-yaaa!"

And as sudden as begun, the gathered band marched jaunty back up the main lane. "Onward Christian so-o-o-ol-jers!" Back towards the Citadel at the end of Skinner's Lane. Bright white Citadel perched on a knoll; sheep grazing round, and Mariam's big ram.

" ... Gloree, gloree hallelooo-yah!" York floating amidst song and drum, abed in the Hôtel des Amis. And seeing the noisy faces of the kids he taught in Sunday School at the Citadel: little Jacob Snook, and Walt Crocker, and Susie. Eight or ten of them every Sunday afternoon. "What *happens* in t'fiery furnace, Mister Yark?" Yes, that last time it was about the fiery furnace. And Susie didn't know why Shadrach, Meshak and Abednego didn't get all burnt up quick nor a fritter.

The words booming up – "You've given the Lard yer song, yer dancin' ... will ye give Him yer life?" The Lieutenant's words. It was the final time at the Citadel, just before York left for London. And John had come, though he didn't tell York why at first. Just said he was coming along. They got to the Citadel a bit late, as everyone was singing, "I've got gloree in my soul ... gloree, gloree hallelooo-yyah!" Citadel shaking like the big bass drum, hands clapping, and all their folk and family singing to make old-time Methodists seem weak of lung. Mariam and Ma Snook right up there on the platform near the Lieutenant. And old Jim, who rarely turned up. And Aunt Glad leading the song. Aunt Glad in full regalia, Sally Ann bonnet with bulging bow and red-tabbed uniform, looking as if she was leading the Charge of the Light Brigade into a thousand certain guns ... "Gloree-gloree in my soul!" And Molly and Gracie Snook leading the jangle of tambourines right below Aunt Glad's podium, right below the sign:

J E S U S
A
V
E
S

As York stood thinking, what better way to say it than "soul-glory"? Watching the Covers celebrating God. And he and John joined in, rattling and banging their tambourines like lost gypsies.

And by the time he'd gathered his wits it was Testimony Time. The Lieutenant stepping briskly forward – "Who has a testimony t'give t'Christ?" And there was a buzz of silence, because Testimony Time was *very* serious. Even kids held silent, even Hilary Snook. And a little fuss passing through the Citadel, because Mariam Barnes was standing up. Mariam rarely gave testimony, because she said, "It scares t'pimples right onto me, iveryone lookin' at I like that." But there she was, standing foursquare, hands fidgeting. And starting in a small voice – "I ain't niver seen our Lard ... " The Lieutenant nodded, And Mariam spoke up stronger – "No, I hain't niver seen Christ. But I's watchin' fer Him, cause He'sll come back one time, I knows it!" And Aunt Glad murmured, "Haa-lay-looya!" And Mariam was shaking and sayin, "An He'sll be takin' all on us to His home – yis an He will!" And for a moment Mariam just stood there, eyes closed, the Lieutenant saying, "Yes an Christ'll take us to His home." While Mae Hann burst into voice, "An that's enough to make us sing ... " The entire Citadel jumping in to join her. And the tambourines going crazy.

And several more gave testimony. Old Art Crocker, save his soul, announcing he was "givin' up wit t'liquor like, cause Our Lard don't drink that I knows of." Drawing Mae Hann to her feet agin, in full song – "My sins are all forgiven, and I'm on my way to Heaven!" The Citadel shaking with the voices. "An that's enough to make me sing." And Mate Barnes standing so he could play the accordion stronger, while the Lieutenant clapped hands in time.

And all of a sudden Aunt Glad was up dancing. Just grabbed old Willie Hart and began stomping the platform. Old Aunt Glad skipping and hopping like a ballerina in a bonnet, face crinkled in joy. And Sammy Snook's wife onto Jess Barnes, glory-dancing! And Sadie coming in on the big Army drum so hard the plastic flowers near the Mercy Seat were bouncing in their vases. And Mollie Harris, Ma Snook's mother, was on her feet clapping her hands, all ninety-three years of her. Till John was up and over, catching Ma and pulling her out on the Platform by the Lieutenant, dancing the Glory Dance. While York sat shaking with happiness.

The dance done, Ma Snook puffed back to her seat, and John beside York again. The Lieutenant held up his hands for silence. "You've given the Lard yer song an yer dancin' ... Will ye give Him yer life?" The Covers huddled quiet under the Lieutenant's raised arms. "Will ye give Him yer life?" The question resounding the Citadel, flowing into another hymn –

Take my intellect, and use
Every power Thou shalt choose ...

And York huddled in his pew, knowing what had to be done. He put his tambourine to one side, surreptitiously checked that his fly was closed. But knowing what he must do. And was on his feet, making his way forward. Almost calm once started. And their Osprey Cove family singing the stronger as he walked forward ... under all those sharp eyes. Eyes that'd spot a partridge in the gorse at a hundred feet. Those rabbit-sharp, moose-smart, osprey-honed eyes of the Cove. Especially the kids; they could spot a fake a mile away. As York proceeded forward, kneeling just to the right of the Mercy Seat. On the plain board floor, in front of the platform. And they were all singing louder, protecting him with song –

Take my will and make it Thine,
It no longer shall be mine ...

Kneeling at the still centre of their song. Serene in his terror. And just above his head on the podium, the three blank Crosses, lace Crosses stitched by Mariam, saying all there was to say. A sudden whisper to his left, the whisked arrival of one, two other bodies beside him. He couldn't see who. And the Lieutenant's voice high overhead, on the platform – "Our brother Yark has come farward t'give himself. An now is the time fer all of us t'give 'im our prayers. He's goin' on a long trip across t'ocean. P'raps there'll be danger ... Pray he comes back t'Hospree Cuv." York hearing the words, stunned. And a voice behind him singing out – "Christ'll watch over Yark, he'sll watch over all on us, Christ will." As Mae Hann burst into song again ... Mae and Sarah Ward in duet – "He touched me, Christ touched me, an made me whole." Mae's high rolling song, and Sarah joining in. And York afraid he was going to fall over onto the floor, eyes clenched in tears suppressed for generations. He reached forward to clutch the ledge of the Mercy Seat. And touching it, felt if he but glanced up he'd see the feet of a man nailed to a tree. And did glance; saw the toes, feet with large square-head iron clouts beaten through, and blood barely congealed. Right above his head. Weight on his head ... weight of that man hanging above him, nailed. The man's words roaring soft, as down a funnel of fresh wind of two thousand years, saying –

You are beautiful, my daughter, my son, my brother ...

Voice pounding as unhurried waves into York's ears. And still the man nailed to the tree ...

All beautiful in the eyes of Heaven, if you dare know ...

York trembling in the presence of the man. Man walking so gentle between iron-studded soldiers. Walking of his own accord. Beaten, jeered at, nailed to a tree, still saying for all –

Beautiful in the eyes of Heaven, if you will but accept ...

York's knees numb on the floor, ears listening beyond the singing. The man's voice saying over and over, while the soldiers laugh and nail him. York certain that nothing remained for him but the fact of this man, and what he was saying. And what he did with his life, kept saying with his words, his blood, his nailed body.

After the service was done, John and York walked back to their trailer. York pleased John had been with him for that farewell service. Perhaps he would start coming to the Citadel again. But John just said the Lieutenant had told him beforehand that special prayers would be offered for York's trip. "When we sees you we sees Yark, and when we sees Yark we sees you ... an we wants ye t'know we likes the two on ye together!" So John had come to the service. But didn't seem very happy afterwards. Sitting brooding in the trailer. Suddenly saying, "You just want to get Christed, Yo-Yo; that's the truth." And later that night, John was eager for sex. But York couldn't.

For a while he lay quiet. The sounds of tambourines inside him ... *booom-ka-boom!* And the voices, dancing faces of Osprey Cove. And John jealous of the Sally Ann that final time – so silly, when all their friends in the Cove were Sally Ann.

But he'd already picked up the next photo. It was Mariam: Mariam with a large basket, and Ma Snook's daughter, Marie, and some of the little Snookery – all standing expectant outside their trailer. York wondering why, till he spotted the pots and pans in the hands of the little Snooks. The day of the berrying party, that's what! A few days before York left for London; he'd checked the final proofs for *Identikit*, and he and John were in the trailer, making plans for the winter. They'd follow the birds south to Mexico, where it was warm and cheap. Follow the yellow fellows for York's next book – *their* next book, because John would do the photography. Then migrate north with the birds in the spring, return to the Cove to build their home. They decided to meet in Toronto after York's holiday: promotion time for *Identikit*, then the drive to Mexico.

But suddenly an awesome war-whoop outside their window, from behind the bushes. Farley scattered under the bed, and their cat, Littlesnook, into the closet. The noise increased: tambourines, drumming, singing. Another Sally Ann parade? In the bush? John flung the trailer door open to look. There they were – Mariam and Ma Snook banging on large pots, and Marie and Gracie and Molly with tambourines, and young Gary Snook blowing on a whistle. A prance of

Snookville, whanging and banging out of the bushes around the trailer. Mariam shouting, "Out wit yez, ya pair o' friggin' jeezlies!" The whole shebang of them marching round and round the trailer, John as Pied Piper in the lead. While York sat in stupor over the remains of morning tea. And when the din-and-dance had lowered to shouting level, Ma Snook clambered in the door of the trailer, hands on hips, glaring at York – "C'mon now Mister Yark, ya cain't be warkin' an friggin' *all* o' the time. An it's a marvel of a day, no breeze like." And John standing behind Ma flipped his best wink at York, so he knew he was done for, whatever was brewing. "C'mon, ya gotta come berryin' wit us. Parfict day fer berryin'." So that's what all the pots and pans were for.

But the door had swung open, just a little. No knock, though perhaps it had been lost in the din of Osprey Cove. York looked up – Khalid's face peering round the door. Could he pick up the lunch tray? Yes. Khalid entering tentatively. And right behind him, Claude. And behind Claude, Richard. "We couldn't resist, dear friend. It's been several hours." Claude swooping past Khalid to the end of the bed. Richard scuttling for his chair. And before York could register it, all three of them established in the room, expectant. Silence. "But you haven't touched your lunch," Claude expostulated. Khalid shook his head. "That's a *good* sign," Richard piped up – "Love feeds on air!" York staring from one to the next. And Claude surveying the photos spread across the bed – "Do you, perchance, have one of John?" No, there was no picture of John there. Just Ma Snook and ... "Ha! This is very Breughel, no?" Claude reaching for the photo of Mariam. "Pure Breughel. With a soupçon of Bosch!" Claude sniffing like a connoisseur as he studied the picture while York tried to cover up the rest. And when Claude reached for another, he was suddenly out of bed, grabbing Mariam back and shoving Claude away. Claude protesting – "But Bertrand saw them. We only wanted to share!" And York spluttering, "Please, I need some time with my friends, my family." And propelling Claude Inc. towards the door. Khalid took his cue and scurried off, forgetting the tray. But Richard paused at the door long enough to wink ineffably – "Bravissimo! I can see the cure is taking."

York slammed the door, and clambered back into bed. It had all happened so quickly he could scarcely be sure they'd been there. And before he could think, was back in Osprey Cove. Back in that parfict day fer berryin'. "Okay, okay Ma Snook, we'sll go berryin' wit ye. Or ye'll never stop bellyin' at us." The fact was, Ma and Mariam had been at John and York for days to drive them up into the mountains, "T'fetch a slather o' them berries, very best kind!" After all, their truck could go way up the old lumber trails. And they could transport half the clan in the back of the truck. So yes; they'd promised. And here were all the women folk, half of Snookdom, ready to be off. Mariam clanging on her pot. "Ye dasn't need t'warry fer food, cause I made a picnic fer us – rabbit pie t'way ye likes it." Mariam knew damned well York couldn't resist her rabbit pie, best in the Cove.

And in minutes they were all swarming into, onto, and over the truck like a tidal wave. York just had time to grab his pipe, notebook and current reading, a paperback *John of the Cross*. And John already in the driver's seat, with Mariam and Ma Snook and a squad of grandchildren. The back of the truck crammed with the rest, all clattering on pots and tambourines. And just as John put the truck into gear he glanced through the back window, saw York scrunched amidst baskets and Snooklets and Farley. He stopped the truck, raced back to the trailer – coming out with camera, binoculars, and one of the collapsible rocking chairs. And proceeded to set it upright in the back of the truck – "C'mon, Yo-Yo; you can't take a scenic drive without a rocking chair!" And York found himself ensconced in the rocker, holding his binoculars and smoking his pipe, just as he had been when the first war-whoop broke out. John gave him a wink and they started off, the little Snooks chanting, "John-an-Yark ... Yark-an-John."

And John, always alert to occasion, drove the long way, slowly, so they passed smack through the length of the village. The little Snooks banging on their pots, and John honking at assorted sheep and ponies careening off the street to escape the green monster caravan. And lest the village not notice, Ma Snook leaned out the window, shouting at Una, the postmistress – "Yis, we's goin' roight up into them mountains fer the best o' the berries." Knowing that Una would waddle straight off to tell Mae Hann; and once Mae Hann knew, why all of Hospree Cuv.

York sat content, rocking and watching them wave at the startled villagers. While they rode pageant through Greater Osprey Cove, as John called it. And turned up the same steep road which had first led them to the Cove, nearly a year before ... on past the bush, where they went spying on the yellow fellows ... and out into the Gulch. That lunar rock wasteland which, Ma Snook liked to say, "Sep'rates t'rest o' the world from the Cuv!"

By the time they'd passed through the Gulch, miles of sparse spruce jabbing the eye, a solitary hawk scrutinizing the motley outing, they had fallen silent. And the fisherfolk in the next village eyed them with stern doubt – a group like that could only mean trouble. But soon they were past civilization, and on into full spruce bush. Ma Snook pointing urgently at a steep trail on their right – "That's t'one. An no one else could get up 'n ... Lots o' berries hidin' up thar, my son!" John dubiously nosed the truck up the trail in first gear, snout bulldozing through overgrown bush. And the little Snooks cowering in the back as the branches whipped past, and a lone grouse whirred irate. But the trail began to widen, and soon they were climbing steadily into the spruce forest. York back on his rocking chair, watching for grouse. And Gracie Snook standing up, leaning against the cab to see better – Gracie suddenly waving her hands wild, pointing dead ahead. York peered to see what ... about thirty yards up the trail, a giant chunk of landscape torn loose: chunk of spruce-grizzled tundra on the move. Moose! Loping with enormous elegance up the trail. John slowed the truck, and Ma Snook leaned out hollering "Git along wi ye, Mister Moose. Yer blockin' me berry crew!" Mister Moose stopped short, turning to gaze disdainfully at the racket behind. Forcing the truck to a halt. But Ma took a pan and leaned out, banging with might and main. And Hilary Snook on a tambourine. And Mister Moose gave a protesting snort and soared into the bush, like a rhino on stilts.

They lurched up the trail a few miles further, climbing steeply till the woods opened out, road dissolving into a high meadow of daisies and rocks. The Lomond River plunging off on their right – sudden vista down to Bonne Bay and the ocean. Ma Snook banging on her pot again. "Stop! Stop 'n right 'ere!" She hurtled out of the truck, sniffing the air, pawing the ground with her foot. And announced to all who would hear, "We's to the top berryin' spot o' the world, cause no one kin git 'ere save Mister Moose!" York couldn't see any berries. And Marie Barnes had started yelping about the moose, "Cause 'e might 'ave attacked us like. Y' know what 'e did t'Ollie Hart's car, jes stove Ollie's car right in." But Ma paid no attention, banging on her pot, summoning, "All hands t'berries! ... Mariam, ye wanta take the patch up past t'head of the track. An Gracie, ye best strike straight on yonder ... Molly, you an Hilary get t'where that big pine tree is, see 'n?" Ma parcelling out berry territories like a field marshal. Till she glanced up, saw York sitting in his rocking chair, laughing at the trip, the dismissal of Mister Moose, and the antics of their one and only Ma Snook. Ma wasn't having any of that – "Ay, an thar's the Lard Yark hisself, la. An I'sll wager ye doesn't pick nary a berry t'whole day through!"

"But Ma, somebody's got to guard the truck."

"Guard yer truck? Aginst what, my son? Thet moose? Ay, you an John'll be at yer friggin' soon's we gets our backs turned. That's truth! Ye runs like angels t'the Harmee on a Sunday, then ye frigs yer ... " Ma blasting up a full gale. But John jumped out of the truck, tootling on his clarinet and shouting, "Ye better be good to us, Ma, or we'sll jes drive off 'n' leave yez all here fer the night wit Mister Moose!" Which shut the young Snooks up tight as a lobster pot. But not Ma – "Ye better pluck a pot an join all hands aberryin', if y'wants t'earn yer supper!" And John said a sudden okay; he'd go with Gracie. And Ma told her brigade, "We'sll gather back at t'truck when the sun gits past that big pine, la." She pointed to the single pine standing high above the bush. "Now everyone on t'the berryin', all hands!" And various Snooks scuttled off in the indicated directions, John with Gracie, who was smiling to burst. And Commander Ma herself sped into the bush with a chortle of conquest. Leaving York sitting in his rocker on the truck. Just Farley with him, sniffing the little clearing around them.

He managed to relight his pipe, gazing down to the ocean. Long rolling view, and sudden peace as the host of Snooks receded. Sublime. But now he felt a nagging loneliness. He'd gladly have gone berrying too. But John hadn't said a word, not even a wink. So York had stayed. To guard the truck, as he said. Well, maybe he could relax, read a while. But didn't feel a bit like reading. He clambered down from the truck, strolled to the edge of the vista that tumbled down the Lomond to the sea. Pure heaven: if only John were there! He'd just presumed John would stay, and they'd chat and John play his flute, or for a time they'd both read. As they often did. Or share the dance of love. He shook his head, kee-rrist: there he went, jealous again, jealous of John's freedom. What Ma Snook said – "Ye dasna own yer John, that's truth. He belongs t'all on we!" York winced. Ma had a deadly eye for certain things. And was John's special protector against the world at large, and York in particular. "Ya kin let us have a piece o' yer John now an then, my son!" Ma really loved John. But all the Covers did, John so outgoing frisky. The first to help in their work: a fishing shed to be moved and he'd be down with the truck and pulley, hauling it to a new site. Lumber to be carted, he'd be there early morning, offering truck and a smile. Or a new dress for Ma Snook – yes, that had been John's idea too. While York stuck at home, slogging away at the book.

He picked up a stick, began doodling with it. "Yez is a mite too solumn, Yark

... that's t'word for it now, solumn." Ma's very words. But no matter! If he wasn't going to be with John, he'd rather be back at the trailer. That's why they'd moved out of the cottage, after all, at the end of the winter. Moved back into their trailer, down a ways by the lake – for privacy, more time together.

He glanced up. Farley was nosing through the rocks, taking a widdle. A pair of birds flitting a nearby tree. And the roar of silence. Farley finished her business, turned towards the truck ... and froze. Only did that when an interloper came near the trailer – someone she couldn't see or smell, the breeze going the wrong way. York looked round. Not a sound. But Farley moving wary towards the truck, hackles up. Another moose? Tricky animals, dangerous. A rock crashed behind York. He spun round – no one. But Farley barking, running at the truck. And when York looked again, there it was: the red head rising above the back of the truck. The wide smile. And the world was back – John, John of Osprey Cove! John standing on the far side of the truck, laughing. Had crept there upwind, fooling even Farley.

"Didn't really think I'd go and leave you, did you?"

"Oh, that's all right." York feeling foolish – "You just gave me a scare."

"C'mon, you old Yo-Yo!" John ambling forward, all shamble and glee. And York nodding. "Well, I still love you, you idiot." For a moment they stood quiet in the vista. Till John went to fetch York's rocker from the truck, set it on a flat moss-covered rock – "Now you can watch the world in peace." And with that spread a blanket nearby, and sat down cross-legged. Nodding in his smile.

York felt the day expand. The daisies wide-eyeing the pair of them in this improbable oasis. Like a floating inner keep, a secret rock garden. The burble of river to one side, the sound lucid and rising. "Look York – purple fellows!" John pointing at Ma Snook's big pine tree. York clapped the binoculars up, and saw the song: "Finches ... and cross-bills!" The splash of raspberry plumage. Crossbills working amid the pinecones. He passed the binoculars to John, who focused and chortled. "Hey! The ones with the big bills, crossing over – so that's crossbills! Bigger than purple fellows." John stomping his feet gleefully. "They're serenading us, Yo-Yo!" It was the song of the finches that had burbled high beside the river, giving colour to the stream. And Farley, catching their joy, was chasing a nonexistent stick, frantic to join their excitement. Till John found one and threw it for her.

They sat listening, to birds seen and unseen. And the low hum of the bush, distant churning ocean. "You know what it is, Yo-Yo? It's a welkin."

York laughed – "The world as welkin."

And John winked – "East o' the sun, and West o' the moon!" Always said that when he was happy. And suddenly up and running for his camera. Telling York not to move. "You're the one who's moving," York replied, John bouncing up and down as he focused on York and Farley – "I want a picture of my big black bear." And Farley barking because John was so excited, *snap-snap!* And John wanting another – "With your pipe this time, Yo-Yo." And York obliging as John bobbed side to side, peering through the camera. "Now try smiling, luv," John shouted. "You can do it!" And *snap-snap!* Till York laughed out loud; however the photos turned out, John was certainly a marvel taking them.

And photos done, including some of John, they settled once again in their welkin. York gazing at John, who was browsing in a book now. His red hair flaring in the sun. Always racing York's blood ... Big Red! And John glancing up to pat Farley, his eyes that sultry phosphorescent blue. York had never seen eyes like John's. Eyes that imbibed: voracious, like a tiger. Velvet – or most dangerous, smoky. He always knew John's state through his changing eyes. And now they were hot velvet.

"Hey Yo-Yo, this thing is a real sex guide – did you know that?"

"What is?"

"This book of yours; it's a first-class sex manual!" John flourishing the little paperback – the *Spiritual Canticle*. And reading a line aloud: love as fire, love burning and warming and consuming. John's own eyes burning as he looked up. And York chuckling – John could find sex in anything. John nodding, body swaying ...

At that moment, a portion of sky flustered down onto the picnic baskets. Grey, black – tails bobbing. "Giant chickadees," John whispered. Birds strutting round the baskets, pecking closer to the food. And smack! Farley plunging into the birds – who hopped monkey-like up the closest tree. Farley so protective: no one, not man, bird nor beast, was going to get her picnic food! Till the birds drifted away in a splash of beauty over some tall blue spikenards. And John ran to the truck, burbling to himself. Returning to settle on the blanket with clarinet. As York realized, those birds must have been Canada jays; never saw them up close before.

And beside him, John improvising now. Clarinet flashing up and down, splurging York's eye after catching his ear. Like the roll of the river, the song of the finches: John imitating the song of the purple fellows. His cheeks blown round, head nodding, eyes glowing up to York. As one of the jays returned and sat nearby, head cocked, curious. And York rocked in time with the music, scarcely daring to look lest it all dissolve.

Abruptly John stopped. "York, do you really believe a spiritual life can include sex?" His eyes hot velvet.

"Well, I ... " York flustered, his mind still lost in the beauty of the vista, John's tune.

"Like us, Yo-Yo. Can we really be – contemplative, and hot-rods too, like you said that time?" John looking so serious; then winking.

"Of course I do, Johno." York startled. "Like your clarinet music; that's both." Focused full on John now. And John pivoting as he sat, caressing his clarinet in a wild carol. And they would have erupted into sex on the spot, but for the realization that the Snook clan was spread all around them. So they just sat longing.

And before York knew it, John was pointing at the sun – "Look, luv, it's getting closer to the pine tree." He winked, beckoned York over to the truck. But not till he had packed rocker, blanket, and Farley into the back, leaving only the picnic baskets behind, did York realize what he was up to. They drove the truck a quarter mile down the trail, well below the dip of the mountainside, off behind some trees. Then leaving Farley locked in the cab, they crept back to the edge of their clearing, hid under some deep bushes. And just as the sun angled past the big pine tree they heard the clanging of a pot, and the first Snooklets appeared. Then Molly bundling out of the bush. Their hands and faces smeared with blue, purple, like woad. For a moment they stood bewildered. "This kin't be t'spot, ain't no truck 'ere … " "Well yis an 'tis, cause Mariam's picnic's right 'ere!" And now Gracie and Marie cast up with a pile of berries and raised a hubbub, all of them staring at the picnic baskets and the spot where the truck had been. As though the truck might pop up if they wanted it badly enough. As John and York wormed deeper under the bushes, out of sight.

"An by the Lard Jeezus, them two 'as gone on us!" Mariam trundling up with a giant pot of berries, standing quiet a moment, then bellowing. They all began piling through the brush, as if the truck might be hiding there. And the jangling of tambourines – another Snooklet, and now Ma Snook puffing up with her two pails brimming. As Mariam fumed, thrashing at a bush. Ma watching – "What's her to? … 'As she gone crazy?" Mariam wheeled in plump rage. "Well an ye kin use yer eyes, kin't ya?"

"An there ain't nuttin' wrong wit me eyes, Mariam Barnes! Jes look at them berries I plucked, two pails on 'em. More 'n you got, cause when I warks, I warks!"

"T'Lard be wit ya, Kat'rine Snook. But if thir ain't nuttin' blind wit yer eyes, p'raps ya kin tell us where t'truck be to!"

Ma set her berries down, and stood looking. "Well, an yez is right, Mariam Barnes. There ain't no truck that I kin see, la."

"Allay-looo-yaa! An what duz ya pr'pose we do – walk plum back t'Hospree Cuv?" Mariam quaking with indignation, as Ma set to howling with laughter.

"Ya might be tellin' us where t'humour be, Kat'rine Snook!"

"Well, an Mariam couldn't walk nr a hunderd yards an she couldn't, cause her's like a whale, she's that big round, la." Ma Snook laughing so hard she knocked over one of her pails. At which Maid Mariam started hiking right off, just to prove she could. That stopped Ma's laughter. And she turned to Gracie – "John an Yark is jes down t'trail a mite, sure on 't. Ya best trot down tell 'em we's back, la." Gracie jogging off with Molly, while Mariam waddled back and plumped herself puffing on a large rock, having demonstrated her hiking ability. And in moments Gracie and Molly were back, shaking their heads. No John; no Yark; no truck.

"By t'Lard, if them rangy varmins 'as gone off an left we all 'ere fer t'night wit Mister Moose … "

At which John blasted a colossal farting sound from between his cupped hands. Wally Crocker had taught him that: the sound a moose makes in the bush. And Ma Snook spun round to see where it came from. Silence … and twenty Snook eyes scouring the underbrush. Till John and York erupted from their hiding place, yodellin' and dancin' round the lot of them. As Ma stood hands on hips, chewin' on her teeth – "An I s'pose the two on yez 'as been doin' it, right there in t'bush. Friggin' soome wonderful! While we wuz gone warkin'. Well, ye ain't gettin' none o' the berry pie … Pair o' hard tickets ye is!" Ma Snook beltin it at them. While Mariam rubbed her overloaded ankles. And they only got clear by going for the truck, driving it back with the horn honking full toot to drown out the mighty Ma Snook. As Mariam spread the picnic, spewing out fresh sandwiches and tarts like first aid. And John ended taking pictures of the whole blessed lot at their mountaintop feast.

Yes, one of their "Kingdom Come" days; that's what John said. "Heaven's right here on earth, Yo-Yo. Not just in your books of religion." As he slowly undressed in front of York that night, undressed right at the supper table ... as if his naked body were theology enough. And tootling on his clarinet, drew York off to early and energetic bed.

Well, he was in bed right now – but in Marrakech. Wrong bed! Though at least he had Osprey Cove back. The bedlam band of Covers spouting laughter all round. Wondrous din ... like the Djema-el-Fna. He got out of bed, over to the bidet to pee. Imagining John in Marrakech, in this crazy little hotel. John would love it – love all the song and prance of Morocco, Marrakech, les amis. Yes, Osprey Cove in Marrakech! He clambered back into bed, seeing John parading through the market, the old covered soukh. John in a blue burnous, strolling the lanes, dropping into the antique shops ... trying a silver dagger, a Hand of Fatima. He'd dazzle all Marrakech, drive les amis voluble with lust.

And for a moment York lay in carnival. Osprey Cove mingling with Marrakech. Ma Snook taking tea with Rebecca, pluckin' them berries right off Rebecca's hat. Herbert sharing Screech with old Jim. And John would delight them all, turn the gossip of les amis into full theatre. John and Bertrand on flute duet, the pipes of Pan rollicking Khalid's garden. While Claude danced, endless houri. And Richard sat wise, his entire soul clapping time. Yes ... sure life anyways! York laughed; how John would have joshed the Colonel! And titillated James! And joined in their jaunt for the sheer lark of it, dancing highest above the flames. Singing out, "C'mon you old Yo-Yo, it's all for fun and games!" Yes, John had no need of a magic carpet; John *was* the magic carpet. Why not bring him here? Show him the Koutoubia – "As big as mine," he'd say, "and nearly as red!" Take him to Dmitri's for lunch, try to keep Dmitri's hands off him. Write the Colonel to come back, bring James. Invite Keb ...

His hand dove for another photo. It was Mariam ... standing by her sky-high mauve and red hollyhocks, just ourside her cottage-shack of a home. The yellow cottage bright as a giant goldfinch, nestled amidst fierce flowers. And as he walked past Mariam's there she was, shunting out the door, hurling a bowl of scraps into her yard. A scurry of hens from nowhere, racing into the scraps. And Mariam sighting York – "An 'tis yerself, Mister Yark. Well an I dunno as I should be seein' ya, after ye nearly left us up in them mountains yest'rday!" Mariam pulling York by the shirt-tail into her parlour – "C'mon wit yez. I'sll bile up some tea t'last ye tell London, la."

And in her parlour York went to his always chair, the apple-green rocker with the cherub wings and hearts carved into the back. Mariam poking up the stove embers – "Ye likes honey wit yer tea, dasn't ye? Jes got some frish from t'meadow. An ye won't be mindin' if we fix wit t'ram now? I'sll jes rinse some cups, la ... " Mariam prattling to herself as much as to York, waddling back and forth. Bringing out her for-special teapot, old floral English pot with daffodils and robins on it. Pear-shaped like Mariam herself. As York sat rocking and blessing Maid Mariam, feeling immemorially at home. And just as he was rocking back relaxed, saw the long white face. Face passing the front window, stuttering across the pickets of Mariam's fence, pausing beside the defiant rise of hollyhocks. Muzzle flickering, and the great rolling horns: Mariam's ram, finest in Skinner's Lane. Just standing there by fence and flowers, as if posing a question. Then tore off a float of holly-hocks. York was half out of his chair, go chase it away; Mariam's pride and joy, those flowers. How'd the ram get loose like that? And just as he was out the door, 'Arvey, Mariam's husband, came up, grabbed the ram by the horns, leading it into the backyard. A bevy of children following curious; York following with them. To a ramshackle shed set amidst a final blurt of flowers. Ram standing in front of the shed, chewing on the stolen hollyhocks, so nonchalant, lord of the lane. And 'Arvey's axe jumping from behind, high over-head, slamming down unseen by ram. Thudding between the horns with a muffled crack that spewed the holly-hocks out of its mouth. The animal slumped to its knees with a wheeze, eyes bulging. And York stumbling back into Mariam's parlour, feeling a friend had just died.

"Yer tea's jes ready, la." Mariam wading over with the pot, pouring a full cup with dainty flourish of wrist. "An 'ere's some honey." As York wheezed into the rocking chair, his own head split by that sudden axe.

"'Arvey always uses t'axe like that. 'E's some quick wit 'n; always fells 'n t'first time. Did ya see?"

York nodded. Yes, he'd seen. Saw again the ram crumpling to the edge of the hollyhocks, kneeling in abrupt sleep. And a fondness for that ram ... how often he'd seen it, king of the field, behind Mariam's. And the day it chased silly Farley.

"Yer gonna be wantin' more tea, isn't ye?"

"Oh, yes." Though he hadn't even started his cup. Mariam going over to her shelf, taking another pinch of her prize tea from the caddy with the Coronation picture on it. And York trying to rock, and feeling glad the ram had been chewing a final flourish of hollyhock. Words tumbling round inside him, threatening to tumble his chair.

"Yez is into thet thinkin' o' yers again, my son. I kin see it." Mariam stopping mid-kitchen, surveying him. "Ye be wonderin' about yer trip t'London."

"No, I was ... thinking that" – York hesitated, didn't want to say – "unless it be holy, unless it be hallowed first, then it's we who are slaughtered." Words popping out as the rocker lurched forward. York feeling absurd, and quickly adding, "That's why I was glad it had the hollyhock, like an offering ... " As if that might explain. He glanced up, expecting Mariam to laugh. But Mariam just gazing at York, her arms folded, saying – "Now thet's jes like ya. Yer always doin' somethin' ... "

"Doin' something?"

"Yer always thinkin' somethin', my son. Like what ya jes said la."

"I guess I is ... an I guess that's some bad." York sat with lips tight, wishing he'd said nothing.

"Yer not drinkin' yer tea, ya mustn't let yer tea fall cold on ya." Mariam shuffled over to the stove, warm up the pot. While York sat trying to haul himself away from that slaughtered ram. And sat gazing round the kitchen parlour, as if for the first time. The sunflowers on the floor, linoleum pattern of giant sunflowers. And the coloured print of clipper ship riding crest over the stove. And above the table the large framed verse with roses painted round –

ONLY ONE LIFE,
IT WILL SOON BE PAST.
ONLY WHAT'S DONE FOR CHRIST
WILL LAST!

Yes, all of a piece. Like the Last Supper in ornate plastic frame riding above old Jim's rocking chair. And all the bright china birds, here and at Ma Snook's. And the lace doilies in the parlour but imitation ones for the kitchen. And the curtains with crochet work – "All Hands" stitched across. As if a single Sally Ann vicarage spread through the poorer homes of Osprey Cove, all of Snookdom, because only the richer homes were Anglican. And this home ancestral to York now. As if his father's home ... father's father's home, ancestral roof, centuries back in Devon, back in the West Countrie. West Countrie croft it was, transported through the heart to bide in Newfoundland. Like the carved rocker he was sitting in; 'Arvey's hands did that, as good with knife as with axe. York reaching for his pipe, starting to rock again. And Mariam back with a "cup o' the frish" for him, and one for herself as she clucked into the other rocking chair. Peering over at York.

"My son, an I'se gonna tell ya somethin' I shouldna ... Didya know that Kat'rine lost a son, la? Yes an she did! 'Twas a wonderful lot o' years an years ago, an she lost a fine bye. 'E was jes siventeen an all that red hair, like yer John. Same flamin' hair, an t'same eyes o' fire ... " Mariam fidgeted with her cup, glancing at York. "Ya see, that son o' Kat'rine's were t'same kind as you an yer John, duz ya understand me, la?" York understood. "An Kat'rine jes took after this son o' hers, name o' Boyd. She jes took right after 'n, an 'arf beat 'im t'death, abullyin' at 'im wit her tongue. Ol' Jim paid no heed, an Kat'rine kept on drivin' at t'bye. An one day 'e was out huntin' partridge birds, up in t'Gulch. An 'e didna come back fer supper ... " Mariam got up, closed the door, plumped herself back in the rocker, the chair disappearing beneath her. "Us found young Boyd next day ... Sammy Snook found 'n. 'E had no head left. Head blowed plum off 'n. An t'Mounties said an 'twere an accidint. But Kat'rine wuddn' talk t'nobody fer months later. An one day her sez t'me – 'Tweren't no acceedint that. An ya knows I done it, I druv me own Boyd to death like that. Boyd bein' a good hunter an all. I druv me own bye like that. Didna want that kind an 'e was. An I'd niver do it agin, no matter how strange an 'e was ... niver, niver. Cause me Boyd was a wonderful bye, a right good 'n ... "

Mariam rubbing her knee, finally saying – "An then all them years later, you an John came long t'the Cuv. An Kat'rine sez t'I, 'Mariam, that John 'e's jes like me Boyd were. Looks a ringer fer me Boyd, an is jes t'same kind, la.' An thet's all Kat'rine iver said on 't. But she luvs yer John, Lard an she luvs 'im some strong."

York sat bone still. Couldn't think of anything to say. Couldn't think.

Mariam nodded – "Y'see, us thought ye was hidin' from t'Mounties. Hidin' away from t'Mainland, la. Somethin' was achasin' ya both t'hide in our Cuv. Like ye was crooks. Lets o' times crooks comes 'ere t'hide." Mariam chased a fly from her cup. "But ya wasn't no crooks. Ya was jes John-an-Yark, like us knows ya is. Come fer lovin' ... "

York managed to get some tea down.

"Yez 'as always got a 'ome in t'Cuv, my son. You an yer John! So ya mustna mind what them grum fellers like Nat Hart sez, nor Hedgar Kelt ... cause they be real hard tickets an a bust o' wind. An if they causes yez a mite o' trouble, like them words they painted across yer truck, la, why Kat'rine an me we'sll jes call out t'Snook byes, an we'sll make gooseberry pie out on t'lot of 'em." Mariam had taken up her knittin', was knittin' hard, not lookin' at York. Like maybe she wasn't sayin' what York heard her sayin'. Or maybe York didn't have to hear if he didn't want to, cause maybe she was wrong. But she wasn't wrong. She was Mariam, their Maid Mariam, an' old Jim's sister.

"An when yer over t'Londontown, remember we luvs ya. An John luvs ya somethin' fierce. Yes an I knows thet. Cause I saw him ivery day after t'two on ye quarrelled, la. An ya ran away t'Sain' John's, Yo-Yo. Ya said 'twere fer yer wark. But ya was arunnin' off an leavin' yer John. An John went 'alf looney when ya was gone. I know, cause 'e wouldna eat any o' me pie."

"Mariam, why did you tell me this?" York hesitated. "About Boyd, and ... "

Mariam plopped her knitting onto her lap and gazed out the window. "Cause yer goin' away ... an I dasn't think ye'll be back t'the Cuv, not ever. No I dasn't."

"Mariam, I'm coming back. This is my home. You're my people, my family ... I love you!"

Mariam shook her head, began knitting fiercely. "Na ... ya isn't comin' back, Yark, I knows that."

"How do you know that? I don't -"

"Cause ya is doin' somethin', yis an you is! And you is burnin', Yark ... "

"Burning from what?"

"An t'Lard Jeezus hisself be t'only one t'know that. Cause no one in t'whole Cuv knows why you's aburnin' ... Not even Kat'rine, an she's wonderful smart. But I'sll tell ya this, Yark ... " She clashed her knitting needles together like sabres, glared at York – "If ya iver leaves yer John, ye'll be dead ... One or t'other on ya, ye'll sure be dead. An I knows that, right in me bones, la. And that's why I had t'tell ya, afore ye flies off t'yer Londontown."

They were sitting back in their chairs, staring out opposite windows. Mariam, who rarely said much, saying it all. And now with that winsome smile on her face. "An ye'll 'ave some tea now, Yo-Yo ... cause ya hasn't touched nor a drop." And up again, trundling around the stove, poking and clucking. York looking round the little kitchen parlour again. No, never really seen it. Nor seen Mariam, really seen her. Nor Kat'rine either. Nor old Jim, with his great hook of a nose, wry serene smile. Never seen them as they really were, nor as deep as they saw him ... He glanced up. Mariam serving yet another round of tea, serving with a little flourish of the wrist. Like a lady, if you please. But Mariam was a lady; that was the truth.

York settled back and drank in silent toast – to Lady Mariam. Calm inside himself, just because of what Mariam had said. Her doomsday truth. When the body came shunting through the door. Body dribbling blood, chest split wide, head gone. Red and white carcass carried by two teenage Snooks and 'Arvey. The ram already flayed. And whoomph, the dripping flesh slapped onto the centre of the big kitchen table. Flesh still rippling, quivering, at the neck. Mariam turning from high tea to hand a huge curved knife to 'Arvey. And 'Arvey wielding knife with the dexterity of a giant razor. Flesh fleeing the bones at each slice. Steam pouring from the open meat as 'Arvey thrust into the barrel chest of ram, emerging with the heart, passing it wordlessly to Mariam who stood ready with a series of plastic bags. As 'Arvey sliced deeper, gut plopping onto the table ... liver, kidneys after heart. The two boys watching in silent trance, and a cat licking blood from the floor. As Mariam bundled each new item into a plastic bag.

And the ram clean done, only a scatter of bones left, 'Arvey whispered to Mariam. Mariam smiled, picked up two of the bloody bulging bags, and trundled across to York with a sort of curtsey – "'Arvey an me wants fer ye t'have the 'eart an the liver on 't. Fer John 'n' you." Mariam passing him the bundles like wedding cake. And everyone smiling, as York sat holding the warm gut of ram. The musky sweet odour of blood and intestines all through the parlour. While he sat unable to get the pipe out of his mouth because his hands were full. That sign over Mariam's table blaring his eyes:

ONLY ONE LIFE,
IT WILL SOON BE PAST.
ONLY WHAT'S DONE FOR CHRIST
WILL LAST!

And right after the final remnants of ram had been scraped from the kitchen table, and the scraps of gristle thrown to that enormous cat, there was the face in the side window. Red beard popping at the window, peering ... York wanted to shout, "John's here!" But John putting his fingers to his lips. And creeping in the door on all fours, unnoticed in the trance of children, cats, blood, packaged ram. John creeping in under the table as Mariam cleaned up. And giving her ankle a fine bite. "By the flamin' Divil, an what's it be?" – Mariam jumping back, staring under the table, staring right into John's great smile. "An it's Red Beard hisself ... an I'sll fix wit ya!" Mariam grabbing a length of gristle and walloping at John under the table. Till John crawled out – "But Mariam, I can't resist; ya's go the prettiest ankle in all the Cove!"

And after they all had final tea, John produced a big envelope. "Came special fer you, Maid Mariam!" But she said, "'Tis a mistake, I never gets no mail, la." And John winked at York, and said, "This ain't mail, and you'd best open it fer all to see." Mariam prying the envelope open as if it were a conspiracy. But it wasn't; it was a picture John had taken weeks before. Photo of Mariam with all her family, sitting here in the parlour. Mariam in the centre, in the rocker, with her knitting. And her best white blouse on. And 'Arvey beside, looking startled. And Coo Snook, Mariam's cadaverous brother who lived with 'Arvey and Mariam, because he said, "Gettin' married is jes too darned ixpensive!" And all the kids with their knit tuques on, though it was high summer.

And Mariam sat gazing at the photo; it was the finest of a series John had taken, and he'd just had it enlarged. She sat gazing, silent. Till John said, "A present fer ya, Maid Mariam, fer you an Harvey. A portrait of your whole family." And Mariam nodded – "That's what it be ... a portrait of me whole fam'ly. An I ain't niver 'ad anything like thet b'fore."

And a bit later, as John and York got up to leave, Mariam came out with another bundle of ram's meat – "Would ye like some ribs fer extra?" But York shook his head. "Mariam, you always give so much." And John gave her a big bear hug and said, "There's no price tag on the door in Newfoundland, is there Mariam?" And they strolled on back to their trailer, singing the popular song ... " There's no price tag on the door in Newfoundland."

For a moment he lay quiet, not hearing the fuss from the garden. Bertrand shouting at Claude – "Where's that old busybody gone?" And Claude replying – "She's gone to the Medina, to find a hoopoo skin. I told her hoopoo feathers were protection against ... " But York just lying, eyes open. Because now he saw the long pebble beach in front of Snookville. Saw it glowing as if by moonlight. Saw old Jim walking down to his lobster pots, and turning and smiling, waving his red hankie like a flag. And Ma Snook standing guard in her imperial garden, beside Donald Duck and Lord Churchill. And Sammy Snook painting his dory, painting it in spanking gold, "Cause I plans a big ketch o' them lobstirs this year, la." Saw them all going their daily ways in Hospree Cuv. Singing and laughing. And the spangled sound of tambourines ... " I feel a new touch o' power comin' down, Lard." And around each of them a wild bright light, around Old Jim and his Kat'rine, and Gracie and Nolly. Shimmering light ... alleluia round each and all of them. York seeing them the way he'd always felt them, but never known it. As he would see them in his heart forever ...

When he came to, the sun had long since passed his verandah. He'd slept again, John's letter and the photos of Osprey Cove strewn about his bed and onto the floor.

He got up gingerly, gathering pictures, pages of letter, that leaping sunflower of John's final page. Put them on the table beside the bed. Like a gathering of friends. And the single voice now – "If you're lonely, if you ever want me, there's the special ones." He glanced around, half-expecting a face at the door again. But the door was silent. "Special ones, just for you, Yo-Yo." And half asleep, remembered the smaller envelope, sealed. He shuffled over to his valise. There it was. And back abed, feeling silly; he's already spent most of the day in Osprey Cove. Like an all-day picnic. Despite the intrusions and solicitudes of les amis. And of course there's been no photos of John till now; John had taken them all. John the seeing eye, but always absent from his pictures.

But now John was right in his hand, right in the envelope. He felt almost smug. He'd never really left the Cove at all; just a fiction that he'd left. As he lay holding the special photos. Which would they be? John in the dory with Sammy Snook, off lobstering? Or hauling logs in the truck, all smiling lumberjack? He remembered taking a few snaps under John's instructions. Like the one of him in the kitchen, feeding their tigerstripe cat, teasing him with a fresh-fried cod's tongue.

He fondled the envelope; which photos? Which John?
John of the freckled smile, all gangly? Or John Barbarossa, Viking John in his big bush boots? Or John of the pipes, clarinet serenading the world? He tried to guess, savouring the moment. And just as he was about to reach into the envelope, it struck him again – it was John who'd found the Cove in the first place. And made

their stay there possible. When they'd been fleeing the Canadian mainland, John's mother threatening police yet again. She couldn't stop; sent the Morality Squad, the regular police, the RCMP, even Interpol, and finally in Mexico the Federales, toughest of the lot. Every time her own marriage became particularly barren, she'd send a new batch. "Mother's about due for a quarrel with Dad," John would say. "Her monthly; we'd better move on." And mostly he was right, could predict the next batch of police practically to the day. The last time they'd fled to Newfoundland; a short visit they'd thought. York would do some research in St. John's. And they'd holiday for a week or so.

After the ferry ride, they'd driven up the west coast of Newfoundland, parking truck and trailer at random every night. Small bays, forests, riverbeds. Any spot that felt "East o' the sun, and West o' the moon" – that was their haunt. And one day after they parked the trailer, John went off for a drive in the truck. Came back smiling, and wouldn't tell. But bundled York into the truck – "Something to show you, Yo-Yo." Drove him along the coast, past scattered fishing homes. And up an inland road through a lunar gulch of stones, shattered spruce. Worse than nowhere. Till the road rose steep, and they nosed into improbably green pastures, ponies cantering wild. John nodding with that inner smile, driving them over a final hummock of green. And there, several hundred feet below, was the ocean – scimitar-curve of a bay, with a giant arm of land flung into the sea on either side. And directly beneath them, a village ... like a startled gull.

John just nodded, drove down to the village, along the beach to a cluster of homes by a waterfall. Homes painted blue, pink, yellow ... And the one house, pink, with moose horns atop the door, moose horns painted bright red. And plastic statuettes on the fence: Donald Duck, Winston Churchill, Snow White.

They stopped right there, silent. And as they got out of their truck, a shadow loomed overhead: a bird, seeming as large as the bay itself, gliding over houses, beach. And a voice nearby saying, "An that's the Heagle, 'e comes over ivery day, same time, afishin'." A man standing in front of the looney pink house. And John asking, "Where are we?" The voice replying – "Yez is t'the Cuv, Hospree Cuv."

"Osprey Cove? That must've been an osprey just flew over!"

"An thet's a Sea Heagle, us calls 'n."

"But he's an Osprey, of Osprey Cove!" John jumping in glee. And the old fisherman smiling, inviting them in "fer a spot o' tea." It was old Jim Snook. And the pink house with red moose horns was the Snookery.

That was a year ago; they had never left the Cove since.

York smiled – yes, it was John who'd found the Cove. And in a special way it was John's Cove. Because if York was accepted by the Covers, John was loved by them. "Smilin' John"; he owed the Cove to John and his smile. Must tell him that, when he got back.

And suddenly his hand into the envelope for a photo. Took a quick glimpse – a china moose, statue of a moose; and a pump organ with red velvet frontal. The inner parlour of their house in Skinner's Lane. And glimpsing further spotted the lace doilies, and the wax-and-hair flowers done by Mariam's grandmother: "Remember me." And the picture of the Queen and Prince Philip, young. York grinned – typical Newfie room for best. With its ornate framed pictures of ideal farm, little boys and girls surrounded by plump geese, chickens. And of the boy Jesus working in a carpentry shop. Frames all gussied up with silver paint.

But his eyes circling further in ... to the plush Victorian sofa in the centre, its blue silk cushion. And John's head propped above ... silky red hair glistering under the flash-bulb. Hair arterial red in the light, mane of it right round to the lumber-jack beard. And eyes green jade, watching expectant. York following the line of John's head ... into the photo. Yes, one of the pictures from John's twenty-first birthday: he'd never shown them to York before. John elongated on the green sofa, right arm propping him up on the cushions, as if his red-mane head too big for him. And his body pendant from the roar of head ... skin a flickering ivory against the velvet green. Right leg extended, left leg cocked up akimbo. Body stark to the camera.

And bulls-eye centre, John's cock, distending cock dangling over his thigh. Red brush ignited in the light, like a crowing rooster ... what the Covers called a man's cock, a "bird," "How's yer bird t'day?" they'd ask in Snookville, laughing. And John's bird crowing at the core of the picture. John's rising bird a face, and his naked body frame for it. And his other face off to one side, echo of his cock-face. Lips parted, swelling in the mane of beard.

York gaped – John's body sucking him in a vortex across five thousand miles of ocean. "If you ever get lonely, Yo-Yo, if you want me, here I am." And John's wild wink as he thrust the envelope into York's valise at the last moment. Little had York guessed. This photo one of a series with their polaroid, on John's twenty-first birthday ... "'Cause we're legal now, Yo-Yo!" John bouncing into the parlour where York had been reading, yanking down the blinds, pinning blankets up over them as he always did when ready to make love. Blocking the windows against peeping Toms and Mariams.

He pushed the photo aside ... difficult taking his eyes off John, even in a photo, even thousands of miles away. Much less a picture of John flashing naked, waiting for York to walk across the parlour, claim the big red bird.

He glanced again ... John's eyes, sultry purr of eyes. Purring York's own bird now, churning his startled balls. Always like that – to see John was to churn, burn. "C'mon luve, I'll show you the wonder of the Cove!" John had finished pinning the blanket up, slowly undressing and stretching out on the sofa. And gazing at York, his cock swelling their gaze. As York set aside his book to behold another advent.

York lay, trying to think but seeing only John's eyes. Drawing him over, across the room ... across an ocean now. Grappling him. Some days they were clear, as in this picture – waiting to be filed. Some days dancing, as with clarinet – like the berry-picking day. And some days smoky. Strange hazy smoke, like the day when ... York fell back, eyes clenched shut.

A sunny day. One of those few high summer days when all the elements stood still in Osprey Cove. The wind in abeyance, the land a pool of flowers and mead-ows, and the gnarled grey carcasses of dead conifers standing eternal. And the inland lake, the pond as the Covers called it, limpid as an alpine pool. "Paradise regained," John said as they awoke in their trailer and gazed out on the morning.

York hoped they'd go for a swim. The lake and its cobbled beach was only yards away. But John had promised to help Sammy Snook with his dory. "I'll be back for lunch, Yo-Yo. We can swim then, go for a walk." John flashing his finest wink, and driving off jauntily to help Sammy. York consoled himself with the wink, and settled in to read ... Then had an idea. He'd seen Abraham Snook the night before. "I'se got a fine ketch o' trout, Yark, if ya wants some." Suddenly York was up and out the door of the trailer, cantering off to Abe's shack as fast as short legs could. Because Abe's place was nearly a mile away. Yes, Abe was home, had caught more trout that very morning – "'Ere an ye best take eight of 'em, cause John's a big 'n." Abe plopping the lake-fresh trout into a bag. And in short order York en route back to the trailer. Stopping at Sarah's to pick up some partridge-berry pie. Sarah's pies were the best in the Cove; she mixed in other berries as well, but never told the secret. Then, as he walked along the river, he plucked some field flowers, chuckling as the goldfinches skittered by. Goldfinches and warblers, always a good omen.

And as he trundled back to the trailer, was thinking of their book on the yellow fellows. Crazy idea, yet so right: not about the warblers, but *of* them, their world ... Follow their migration, stopping where they stop, seeing as they see. In pictures and words. He got back to the trailer, put the flowers in the vase. And set to, stuffing fresh tomatoes with bread crumbs and garlic; John loved stuffed tomatoes ... No more truculent tomes about culture. But a book of celebration – seeing the land, nature the way warblers do, a bird's-eye view. Then remembered the bottle of rosé they'd hidden for a special occasion, like a windless warm day in Osprey Cove. Yes, York would do the text for John's pictures: eros on the wing, John on the wing! Where was that bloody wine? – under the bed. He put it on ice. It'd cap the day. And they'd follow the warblers back to the Cove in the spring. Back to nest ... He had everything ready; was turning on their little tape-recorder to the flute music John loved, when he heard the snort of a truck. And glancing out saw it lumbering across the open field, Farley's head barking out the front window. Enough of yellow warblers – here was the real bird!

He popped everything onto the stove and tried to look nonchalant, just another lunchtime. And now John clambering through the door, saying nothing. Maybe he smelt the fish and garlic ... his eyes shooting past York, who was trying to block the view to the stove, hide the surprise a moment longer. But John's eyes darting past without even seeing York, spotting the frying pan, the fish set out to cook. And the wineglasses out. He broke into a big grin. York could never hide anything from him, not even an unexpected summer lunch. John grinning at the surprise, big flashing smile. But just as quickly the smile ceased, immobile. John suddenly remembering something, was that it? As he disappeared back outside the trailer. York looked out, saw him taking off his work-boots, socks. And hurried to cook the fish, get them onto the table, open the wine – just as John re-entered, his smile gone, and in its place a pinched grin, eyes partly closed as if slitted ... York served the trout, poured the wine with a flourish.

John sat with a grumph of fatigue, looking at the trout as at something strange, not what he'd expected. Only gradually poking at them, prodding with his fork to see – see what? And still that taut little grin, eyes hooded. At last he ate a single mouthful.

York couldn't detect anything precisely wrong in what John was doing. Yet felt the back of his neck going tight, as he started eating his own fish. John still silent. A kind of steely politeness when York glanced over, as if John were meditating on something for a moment, please. York remained silent too. But the back of his neck kinking in an odd way, as if pressure on it. While John doodled another of his fish, shoving it around the plate like an alien. And just as York was about to break the silence, a whimsical toast to their stay in Greater Osprey Cove, John pushed his wine-glass aside, abolishing it somehow, and York's toast with it.

York looked over, saw John's eyes shimmering, smoky they were. Like smoke off dry ice. Wanted to ask, was something wrong? Something upsetting at work this morning? But John's face was set in a half-smile which prevented comment, even as it denied anything could be wrong.

York sat stiff, eating bits of dead fish, sipping flat wine. Tasting neither. He still couldn't put his finger on anything really awry. Though neither Farley nor Snook had come up to the table for scraps as they usually did, especially with fish. Perhaps it was just that lunch was flowing, as it sometimes did, in a thoughtful silence. John clearly had something on his mind, that was all. And didn't want any wine at the moment ... that was all. Except that York felt his eyes hurting, and an ache starting in the back of his head. And the flowers he'd picked, and the summer day over the pond, all monochrome now.

This is insane, all in my head, York thought. And when he was done eating asked, "Would you just like a cup of tea, Johno?" But John quietly shook his head – "I really wasn't hungry at all, you know." And began rapping on the table with his fork ... *rap-a-tap-tap*. As if thinking to himself. *Tap-tappity-tap*, he dropped the fork on the table, and got up brusquely, putting on his running shoes. Then went to the cupboard, poked out a few oatmeal cookies, shoving them into his pocket. For an instant he paused in the open door: Big Red, silhouetted in the sun. Then stepped casually out of the trailer, whistling for Farley to follow. And outside stopped, glancing back at York as afterthought – "I thought I might stroll down to the beach, if you're interested in coming." York couldn't get a word out, sitting over the remains of his lunch. Shook his head. John banged the door shut, set off whistling loudly towards the beach, Farley trailing behind.

York sat numb. Nothing he'd wanted more than to wander along the pond with John. What in hell had happened? He couldn't think ... sound of that fork drumming his head ... tap-clank. Intense concentration of John, face flesh taut, as he'd tap-tapped on the table – yet elaborately casual. Still ringing in York's ears. Trivial, surely. But York's head felt severed from his body now, as by guillotine, and his body burning. As he watched John stroll off towards the beach. Strolling so casually, yet looking wooden somehow ... his back ramrod straight, that was it. And perhaps he felt York watching, knew he would be. Because he turned at the last moment, raising his arm at York, waving ... doing a funny little dance, almost a jig. That's what it looked like in the shimmering sun. Then his hand slashed the air in final wave: goodbye, Yo-Yo. As he jaunted so concertedly to the beach.

York sat burning, John's wave like a fist in his face. Entire lunch a fist in his heart. Inexplicable. Suddenly in a single leap he was out the trailer door, tears of frustration choking him as he churned barefoot over roots and rocks ... roaring like a mad thing towards John. And John turning calmly to watch, as if he'd expected him to come. John nodding in a quick little smile, watching the mad locomotive churn across the tundra. Then with an almost gleeful yodel, he started running towards the rocky beach. Running past startled children at the edge of the lake, York raging after him, catching up at the edge of the lake ... John skirting the high antlers of a driftwood log, as York hurtled through the branches. *Cra-aash* ... dropping John like a shot beast onto a scatter of fist-sized rocks. And the last thing York saw was the look in those eyes, smoky eyes wide with amazement at York's total physical abandon.

When York came to, he was lying flat on his back on the beach, weeds straggling around his face. John standing high over him, nose and mouth flowing bright with blood, staring down like a silent shout. Smoky look completely gone, and in its place a look of wild satisfaction. Eyes blaring – "Yes, that's what I want from my Yo-Yo!" But as he saw York coming to he reached down all gentle, help Yo-Yo up. Saying, "Look here, you silly Yo-Yo, you've gotta get your black bitch in hand ... you've gotta learn to handle your own hate, you know." Saying it so kindly as he helped York up, and plugged his own nosebleed with a handkerchief. Crazy words, dribbling out of John's mouth with the blood. Yet John grinning in satisfaction as he said them. "What in the world possessed you, luv? I mean, you should've just come on the walk in the first place." John blew a clot of blood from his nose and knelt down, carefully pulling a large slice of driftwood out of York's shin, blood spouting after. But York just stood numb in the wreckage of love. As John half-whispered – "Besides, you've made a fool of yourself in front of all the kids." Yes, a group of children had run up, gathering round them, wide-eyed at the spectacle.

"An what was ye doin', John 'n' Yark?"

"Oh, an we was just runnin' on a dare, Hilary" – John replying all jaunty.

"Well, an t'aint wise what ye done there, cause o' them stones."

"No an it weren't wise, Hilary!" John winked at the kids, and started helping York towards the trailer. York feeling stunned and foolish as he hobbled up the trail. And John saying, "You should really take some diary notes, Yo-Yo. You must be pretty psychically disturbed ... acting like that." And York, all rage and hope spent in that single demented crash, could only think, yes ... I must be insane. As he apologized to John "Oh don't worry, Yo-Yo. We all lose control now and then. Besides, you've been under a strain, getting the book finished. You need to get away on your holiday!" York had to agree, it was time to go.

And when they got back to the trailer, there were the remains of their festival: uneaten trout, open wine bottle, and the vase of flowers smashed to the floor as York leapt out the door. He couldn't discuss the lunch. It seemed so absurd now. And John smiling sweetly – "I'll clean up this mess." But in the middle of the night York half awoke, bed shaking. It was John, his arse lurched full towards York – John masturbating and moaning, "Fist me ... fist me!" And what the hell did that mean? York simply didn't know.

From Waterwalker:
"Flames and Roses"

When he awoke it was already past 10 a.m. His diary beside him on the bed. He stared at the last page:

"You only live from the far side of death, far side of accepted death. Only then are you truly alive. And orgasm ditto. You live, love, make love from 'the far side of orgasm.' Thus orgasm no point of arrival, but point of departure. Orgasm as the low point of life's ongoing ecstasy. Point at which life begins. At that point you touch sainthood within your loving, sharing ... "

What the hell ... ? And then remembered. Had awakened in the middle of the night. Plagued by that dinner at the Jersey Lily. A debacle, that's what? Annie in full tantrum. That final flash face of hers, a Maenad, Boadicea in heat! And the excuse she made after, driving home, that someone had snubbed her. What?

"At the country house party," she said – "I got snubbed." So she'd taken it out on the English table at the Jersey Lily.

York groaned. It was like being whipped, that's what. Whatever was going on, it was a whipping. Awake or asleep – torture.

He propped himself up in bed. Yes, they'd gone for a celebratory dinner to a place called The Jersey Lily. Stephen driving slower than usual as Annie determined to give York a nighttime tour of London. "This is Trafalgar Square, York ... "

York blinking as the Square hove to. The National Gallery, St. Martin's an entire Greek Acropolis ... the extraordinary shimmer of London at night, like ivory, shimmering ivory. And on past the Gothic pinnacles and spire – "Houses of Parliament, York. Groovy, eh?" And of course the statue of Boadicea riding wild in her chariot ...

Stephen's taking us to a very 'in' spot," Annie finally announced.

What?

"The Jersey Lily," she said.

York didn't understand.

"Name of the restaurant," Stephen said. "Edward the Seventh's mistress."

"His *Friend!*" Annie snorted.

By the time they arrived they were well beyond Belgravia and London swank. In fact an unprepossessing street, a motorcycle cluster nearby as they got out. Annie looking nervous in *her* swank outfit – small cape over a silk shirt, and full skirt. Not to mention her large earrings, silver and bloodstone.

Stephen soon had them inside, down a set of stairs to a largish room, different levels: a dias here, an alcove there, an open space. The maître d' bustled forth – "Mr. Stephen, sir! It's been a long time ... " Stephen grinned, and introduced Annie. "This is my wife!"

"A *wife*, sir?"

"No less," Stephen said.

"The maître d' bowed – "It's high time you brought her here, sir!"

"That's what I told him," Annie said.

"And this is my worst enemy," Stephen said, introducing York.

"Beg pardon, sir?"

"My oldest friend," Stephen laughed.

The maître d' escorted them across the room – "I've given you the far side, sir, more privacy." Yes, fine view of the room from a dais shared by one other table, empty as yet. And over champagne cocktails "on the house," Stephen explained this was where he brought special people to dine, before he met Annie.

"Whaddayamean?" Annie pouted.

"It was Clark Wallace tipped me off to the place."

Silence.

"There's a whole side to Clark doesn't meet the eye," Stephen said. "A Bohemian side."

And by the time they were into moules marinieres they were busy surveying the room. Annie announcing it looked like opera. Well, so it did, late Empire and Beidermeir. Lots of ormolu, a large central pedestal table upheld by gold swans. An open highboy burgeoning ruby glasses and decanters. And chairs painted gold with red tasselled cushions. Not to mention a skillful deployment of mirrors and candles which doubled it all.

"More like pocket opera," York said.

Whaddayamean?

"It's really quite intimate," York said. "It's the mirrors and opulence of the furniture which make it seem large."

"*Opera!*" Annie repeated, twitching her cape.

No matter, the moules and wine were uplifting. And their glasses soon raised – "To many more occasions together," Stephen toasted.

York heaved a sigh of relief – their evening happily launched. First evening together since his return, first private evening.

A group had arrived at the adjoining table. Three men and a woman. One of the men in dinner jacket. And the woman in expensive dress, jewelery. Annie taking a good look, pretending to eye the room but in fact appraising the new arrivals. Overhearing the maître d' saying, "Why of course, Sir Nicholas," to one of them, the tall one in the dinner jacket.

Stephen whispered he'd seen a photo of a couple of them in the papers recently.

"*Operatic!*" Annie snorted, adjusting her cape.

What?

"The way they crossed the room and took their seats," Annie said.

"Shhh," Stephen whispered.

"They don't own the place," Annie snapped.

By the time they got to smoked trout and a Swiss white wine, they were smiling again.

"So what did you do today, York?" It was Anniekins.

York didn't know what to say. That he'd heard World War I songs sung by his parents as he gazed at the statue of Eros? That he'd visited a wine shop on St. James Street and discussed connoisseurship and deprival?

"It can't be that much of a secret," Annie said.

York blinked – "I don't know what I did."

Annie stared.

Stephen laughed – "That's my York. When he can't remember you know it's important."

"I read John's letter," York blurted.

Annie sat right up – "Now that's what I want to hear about."

"That's none of your business," Stephen said quick.

"Oh yes it is." Annie said.

"Why?" Stephen asked.

"Because York's our best friend," Annie grinned. A logic hard to refute because incomprehensible.

"John's fishing for lobster," York finally said.

Lobster?

"With the fisherman in Osprey Cove," York nodded, suddenly seeing John – John out in a dory over the waves, John waving, shouting something.

Fortunately the flambé dish had arrived at their neighbouring table. Fragrance of burning brandy and flesh. Steaks flambé. Annie craning to see – "They like it rare," she reported.

"York, you should have had John join you in London!" Stephen said.

What?

"Meet you here! Return to Canada together."

York stared.

"I'd've done it for you," Stephen said, "gift ticket!"

Silence.

"Is it too late?" Stephen asked gently.

"He's en route to Toronto with truck and trailer," York replied.

"You just said he was fishing for lobster," Annie grinned.

Silence.

Annie nodded – "I'd sure like to clap eyes on your Johnnie!"

Their main course diverted Annie from John. It was marinated venison with a bone marrow sauce ardently recommended by the maître d'. The venison gained Annie's approval. But she was less certain about the bone marrow. "Makes me squeamish," she said.

Why?

"Eating the marrow of an animal," she squinted – "*Cannibalism!*"

"But what about eating its meat?" Stephen asked.

"Meat's okay," Annie stated, "but marrow, that's too *intimate!*"

York was lost in his wine, a Grands-Echezeaux. Seeing John in his wine – Big Red!

"Why doesn't York talk?" Annie finally said.

York was eyeing the room through the top half of his wine glass. Beidermeir gold through crystal and the shimmer of Burgundy.

"So what're you thinking, York?" It was Annie.

York set his glass down – "That having class, and having a society of classes, is two very separate matters. And Canada has neither."

"Weren't thinking that at all," Annie pouted.

"One of the things I was thinking," York grinned. "The other is illegal!"

"About me!" Annie snorted.

"No," York said, "wasn't thinking about you at all!"

Annie flicked her head – "Well, you should have been!"

York turned and gazed at her. Yes, both her earrings jangling.

Annie smiled – "*Why* did you flee Canada?"

"But I didn't," York said.

"You turned your back on your nation," Annie snapped.

"York lives in Newfoundland," Stephen said, "which so far as I know is part of Canada!"

"York turned his back on all of us!" Annie sniffed. "His books attack everything in Canada."

Stephen groaned.

"Say something, Archbishop!"

"Your eyes," York said, "have turned to amber."

What?

"Your eyes have changed from blue to amber," York repeated.

"Goddamned spy!" Annie sniffed, shrinking back in her chair.

A crash at the adjoining table. The waiter had stumbled with a tray of sauces, condiments. Someone's leg sticking out and waiter careening, sauces flying. Pickled onions spraying over York. Horseradish on Stephen. General mêlée as the waiter mopped himself and members of the English table.

"Dreadfully sorry," one of the Englishmen said, hoping to mop up York.

"He deserves it!" Annie said.

"Really?" the Englishman grinned. "He looks so quiet."

"Just an act," Annie snorted – "He's sly and eruptive!"

For a moment the two tables elided in fluster and chit-chat. Till sauces and onions back under control and waiter departed in an orgy of contritions.

"They seem rather civilized," Stephen said a moment later.

"Just a façade," Annie grinned. "They're high-style *lizards!*" Besides, you think everyone who's polite is civilized."

The maître d' hove to wringing his hands – "Just heard of your disaster."

"The only disaster here is York," Annie laughed. "He convokes disaster!"

The maître d' bowed – "May I offer a house specialty in apology."

"Freebies!" Annie grinned.

"On the house," the maître d' stated. "A flambé in the King's own style." And with that gone.

They finished their venison quietly. Till Annie said, "It takes a strong lady to take you two fellas on!" And winked.

Stephen gurgled into his wine.

York laughed.

"There," Annie smiled winsome, "I made York laugh!"

The maître d' and waiter were back with a trolley, trays and bottles. "A Lily Langtree special," the maître d' announced. Bottles and flames and some kind of fruit dancing by their table. "Passion fruit," the maître d' said – "Maori!"

The flames swooshing up. Like shiskebabs in Morocco. York glanced at Annie. Annie sitting tall, eyeing the flying fruit and crêpes. Maître d' with two liqueur bottles, spraying the flambé. Annie in a kind of trance over the flames, the changing flames, gold, green, red. Her eyes full amber and face surging somehow. Face under her face surging. York stared – Annie's classic profile in place and display. But underneath it another face seething, totally other.

The waiter was folding the fruit into the crêpes, flames spitting. Annie adjusted her cape.

"Do you want to take that off?" Stephen asked. "A bit warm in here."

"No, no," Annie sniffed – "*I need it!*"

Why?

Annie smiled – "To keep those snotty English in their place!"

York noticed that her profile was in command again, that surging underface gone. Or had it ever been there at all?

The crêpes were served. The neighbouring table was intrigued, asking if the crêpes as good as the fireworks. "As delicious as the Jersey Lily herself!" Stephen said. Laughter. And before they knew it a second flambé performance going on – the English table ordering the same desert. And with that the maître d' made some comment. And the tall Englishman said "but of course." And Stephen said, "why not?" And the two tables were being joined together for a "Passion fruit finale." The maître d' courtly in introductions, knowing Stephen, Sir Nicholas and two of the others. York couldn't follow it all. Except that Sir Nicholas was head of one of the big art houses. And the woman a well-known London hostess of the art world.

"We've just been to an event," Sir Nicholas was saying.

Of what?

"Bacon," the Englishman next to Annie said.

York had images of a meat-packing plant.

"Avant-garde of the Occident," Sir Nicholas stated.

What?

"Bacon, our most important painter!"

The English group had just been to an "opening" of that painter's work. The short stocky man next to Annie – his nickname was apparently "Jumbo" – was a collector of modern art, and of Bacon in particular. "What do you think of Bacon's work," he asked.

Stephen hesitated, "I don't know enough to say."

"Yes, you do," Annie sat up. "I showed you some of his work a few months ago."

Stephen nodded – "It seemed pessimistic."

"Deliquescent," the other Englishman said. His name was Peter.

Chit-chat hovered around Bacon's work. Each making a point. Except Annie and York. Annie watching askance from her profile. And York watching Annie, her earrings twitching ominously, especially after the English woman said anything. Her name, or at least nickname was "Muffy," and she seemed to have the last word on everything.

Till Annie finally she said – "It verges on the obscene!"

"Bacon's paintings?" Jumbo asked.

"Too much *porcelain*," Annie snorted.

"And what may I ask … ?" It was Mufffy.

"Too many toilet bowls," Annie stated – "His paintings stink with them!"

Stephen was endeavouring to find artistic relevance in toilet bowls.

Annie chose the moment to ask where the washroom was. It was right across the room behind a high Japanned screen. York watched her depart with bemazement. The English turned their attention to Passion Fruit crêpes and Stephen. York's eyes drawn to the room – ah, that was it, candle flames dancing in the mirrors, highlighting the gold of the furniture, the red tassels, the gilt mirrors … and the clientele along with. Operatic indeed.

A moment later one of the Englishmen saying something to York. York about to reply when he saw Annie stepping out from behind the screen over there, and pausing an instant, adjusting cape and coiffure. Then stepping out onto the floor as if toreador. Her long legs, and neck high arched, and coiffure fluffed up. As she paraded across the floor, hair ignited by candlelight, cascade of auburn with undertone of cinnamon, red-russet. York staring and pointing. And everyone looking as Anniekins stormed the floor. Pausing in the middle as if her cape caught on the edge of a passing chair. And apologizing to the client in the chair, was that it, a pirouette of Annie there in mid-floor, a flash of profile that was her entire elongated body. Certainly flash of those splendid "horns" as Stephen termed them. And Stephen staring transfixed. "Positively Viking!" one of the Englishman said as Annie finished her parade up to their little dais. Taking her seat as if nothing at all. The same Englishman – it was Sir Nicholas – saying "congratulations!" To Stephen, or to Annie? While Annie sat all wide-eyed and innocent, saying "I bet I missed some dandy conversation!"

York abruptly knew why Stephen had married Anniekins, had married that Viking who'd just paraded the floor. Stephen had always had an eye for the women, an eye for the striking, the statuesque, the dramatic – the very opposite of his own qualities.

The English group was engaged with Stephen now. Easy to talk with him, Stephen always good when meeting strangers. And Annie listening diligently, at once good little girl and Grande dame.

The maître d' appeared to ask about a cognac to follow their liqueurs. Muffy suggested an eau de vie, *une vieille prune.*

"Superb idea," Jumbo gurgled – "put us all on the porcelain!"

"I just want an ordinary brandy," Annie stated.

"There were no ordinary brandies," Muffy grinned, "just ordinary people."

A hiccup from Peter. And Annie's eyes amber again.

Yet another flambé had broken out at a table out on the floor. Flames dancing in the mirrors.

"We've started a vogue," Peter said. "Everybody's going *flambé.*"

"Auto da fé," Jumbo laughed, "like Bacon's paintings."

Next York knew they were discussing London. Peter of the opinion that it was the cultural capital of the world. And Nicholas adding, "At least the capital of the art market.

"It's the capital of connoisseurship," Peter said.

"And what's *that*?" Annie asked demurely. That innocent purr to her voice.

"Connoisseurship?" Jumbo said – "It's loving without touching!"

"Doesn't exactly define you," Muffy snapped.

"Jumbo's a carnal connoisseur," Peter added.

"Love in a toilet bowl?" Annie grinned.

Nicholas rescued the situation, asking Stephen, "What's London for you as a Canadian?"

Stephen paused – "London's a memory that belongs to all of us, not just in English."

What kind of memory?" Muffy asked.

"Roots," Stephen replied, "mutual customs, traditions ... Parliament!"

"It's a memory laid out in state," York said.

"Nostalgia," Jumbo sniffed.

"No," York said, "a case of Real Memory ... like Real Presence in Communion."

"York's a religious freak," Annie said.

"But what do *you* think of London?" Muffy asked.

"Pretension!" Annie grinned – "World capital of unearned pretension."

"Their *vieille prune* had arrived. Nicholas sniffed and tasted – "Reassuring," he stated. And Stephen declared it convincing.

"Tastes like gasoline," Annie snorted.

"An *uncut* eau de vie," Jumbo chortled.

"Behave yourself!" Muffy said.

"What does he mean?" Annie asked.

"Well, a rather ... hairy eau de vie," Peter said.

"Like this restaurant," Nicholas grinned, "Jersey Lily and friends."

"If you like this restaurant," Jumbo nodded, "you might try Le Ménage à Trois ..."

"Just exactly what I don't damned want," Annie snapped – "a ménage à trois!" And glared at York.

"Another one," Muffy said. "I've got my hands full with my own!"

Stephen tried to rescue the situation – "York has no heterosexual tendencies, dear, not since 1964!"

Laughter.

"Precisely!" Annie retorted, glaring at Stephen – "And what extra tendencies might *you* have?"

"Please show us your tendencies," Peter said.

"An inch at a time!" Muffy shouted.

The evening suddenly raunchy. Annie sitting back staring at them all, eyes slit.

"Our soirée has become very Francis Bacon!" Jumbo gurgled.

"*Toilet Bowls!*" Annie snapped.

And Muffy leaning forward to Annie – "Mustn't let these sullen sods outdo us dear!"

Annie suddenly laughing – "Amazons unite, we'll show these cocksuckers!"

If her words weren't aimed at York her eyes certainly were. And York suddenly pounding the table – "In this era of Women's Lib a good cocksucker is taboo!"

Annie lurched to her feet. Another parade to the washroom? One hand on her hip, the other dangled elegantly before her. Chin up, nose up ... slowly surveying their group. Eyes glancing down her nose in cold disdain. Her hand in a little pirouette, as if displaying rings, bracelets. And then a sniff. Excellent mime of the English women, Muffy, when they'd been introduced.

Jumbo about to protest. But Annie going sudden slack, collapsing into her own belly, and waving a flaccid wrist – Jumbo! Jumbo in effortless deliquescence. Stephen laughed nervously. As Annie drew herself up tall, languorous giraffe – Peter. Then paused as if aghast at her own performance. Yes, face aghast. And Stephen tugging at her skirt, get her to sit down. But she pulled away and began spouting ... no words, just a pell mell of sounds, syllables lolling and flopping out of her mouth – "Ahh and wash and whaaa-whaaa ... " As if an entire conversation: "Put her away, cart her away!"

Annie standing for just an instant longer, everyone staring at her. A smile creeping through her face. Smirk-smile of dark satisfaction, as she glanced down at the table. And a flick of her head, her horns. As her face surging forward, flesh of her face seething, lips swelling, rage of unleashed flesh. York leaned forward to catch it. Catch that wild Celtic Annie there. Boadicea-and-all-carnage – demonic. But already gone. Annie's perfect profile suddenly clapped back into place, mocking little smile. As she curtsied, and dropped back into her seat.

Stephen looked acutely embarrassed.

Nicholas applauded "the performance – pure Duchess of Malfi," he said.

"No," Muffy leaned forward hissing – "*scullery duchess!*"

Annie didn't seem to care. Just sat primping her hair as if she'd just eaten them all.

Yes, it had been like that, only worse. He'd already forgotten half their conversation – in self-defense? Annie blasting off against York's interest in wine, his way of tasting. "Obscene," she'd said. "It's the way he rolls his lips – illegal! And Stephen chortling – "York's been illegal for years, that's what I love about him."

"Elitism," Annie snapped.

What?

"Snobbery is a form of elitism," she'd said.

"Every society has to have an elite," Stephen replying.

"Just another form of aristocracy," Annie said. "And we've spent ages in Canada getting rid of those parasites!"

"Canada never had an aristocracy," Stephen said.

"A self-perpetuating gentry," Annie snorting – "sucks its lips over wine."

Annie at it again over class.

Well, he had the antidote to Annie-and-all-tantrum: John's letter. He surged out of bed, found the letter and reread it once, twice. Sentences he'd overlooked, entire paragraphs.

By the time he'd reread it all he could hear John's voice – "Don't forget York, we'll be returning to the Cove! We'll be back to build our home in Osprey Cove. Up by the waterfall we went that day ... " John's voice pervading the room now:

the flash of birds, sunflowers he'd drawn in the letter. And York peering around, as if John in the room, John about to appear ...

He set the letter down and lay quiet. Sounds of the London streets through the window. Throb of a metropolis. No Marrakech donkeys, no Muezzin. Nor the sheep of Osprey Cove. Just a low powerful hum, snort of distant traffic. Yes, he'd rest another few days in London, try to anchor his brain. Try to placate Annie: for precisely what? He didn't know. And see more of London. Now his fourth day in London, and he'd seen damned little. Then back to John. Yes, meet him in Toronto just before the launching of his new book. John driving their truck and trailer from the Cove to meet York in Toronto.

For a moment he tried to imagine what Toronto would look like. After their year in Newfoundland – no subways in Newfoundland. And few cars, at least in the Cove. Toronto, family home of each of John and York. Though York's family quiescent now. Father dead, and mother mellowing with age, though she didn't exactly rejoice at York's "problem" as she termed it. But his brother and sisters acquiescent, even supportive.

Remained the launching of Identikit, Stephen worried about the media reaction – "You keep goading them. One – they're bound to strike back ... " But the book wasn't about the media, it was about the whole bloody nation.

Suddenly he jumped out of bed. Had forgotten – there was a letter from his publisher, in the file Stephen had given him. Forgotten in the excitement of John's letter. he found the letter. Yes, from Mark Strachan. Ripped it open and skimmed it. No, the company hadn't folded – Mark's company always about to fold, even while it had published more best sellers than all the others put together. Or going broke over some libel suit. Or engaged in a public controversy over a new book about sex amongst penguins: Mark fascinated by all forms of sex, platonically he said – he was resolutely married. But encourage his authors to try anything.

But the news was good – Identikit was still coming out, and some advance comments favourable. Oh ... "Due to printing problems the publications date is delayed till October 24." What? Yes, a one week delay. Fine.

And one further item:

"John's parents have had their lawyer phone us. They're convinced the book deals with John and your life together. They've threatened legal action. I tried to assure them the book has nothing to do with your private life. In particular I'd be glad if you could get John's mother off my back!"

York decided it was time for breakfast. Going on eleven. He dressed and forayed down the hall. Warily. But Annie and Stephen long since gone. Stephen to Fleet Street, Annie presumably to the university. Only Thor in residence, over in Annie's retreat corner in the kitchen. "Morning, Thor! You were lucky to miss the Jersey Lily." Thor silent. And York set to making coffee, burnt toast and boiled eggs. Was soon settled at the kitchen table trying to think.

The phone began ringing. York trundled over – "Stephen, I've got the contact you need for the arms deal!"

What?

"That shipment from France to the Middle East, it's definitely illegal, going under false label ... "

Oh.

"Great story, but the contact wants money."

"Haven't got a cent!" York said.

"Who is this?"

"I don't know," York replied.

"Fucking Christ!" And the man hung up.

York returned to toast and coffee. "All I was trying to say, Thor, was that I don't know anything about it. The guy got really angry." Thor shifted slightly. "Point is, Thor, you never know what's going on in this home. Everything from arms deal to Armageddon!"

Breakfast dispatched, he proceeded to the living room. Checking the Daily Flash Board en route.

Sorry to miss you at breakfast. Tonight I've got some damn thing at the Guildhall. And Annie's got her Third World Committee Meeting. We'll catch you at breakfast tomorrow for certain.

A carefully typed note from Stephen. But right beside it one of Annie's "quickies," felt pen sketch of a group of pigs around a trough. Six pigs: two in top hats, one in a tiara, and one fondling his dick. York stared. The other two pigs with exuberant hard-ons. "Conference of Snobs at the Jersey Lily," the caption read. York made for the living room fast. Tried reading one of Stephen's many newspapers. But unable to concentrate. Annie's "quickie" kept surging up. Goddamn pigs! Including Stephen and York with erections. Had to be Stephen and himself ... the others patently the English table.

Thor paraded into the living room, taking up station on the end of the sofa. "How do you handle her, Thor?" Thor flicked his tail. "I mean you've clearly got Annie's number. She feeds you the Cat's Meow Liver paté!" Silence.

York stared round the room, up at the beams. This curious attic of a room, giant attic. As if a horn about to blow, something about to go off, fill the space. Not even all the bookcases and a piano filled it. Books! He got up, began browsing. Splendid collection of nineteenth century English novelists, up to James. Including not only Sir Walter Scott and Dickens but names only connoisseurs still read – Surtees, Bulwer-Lytton and others York had never heard of. Stephen's "litbooks" from his days at McGill. Plus a whole line of English thinkers – Carlyle, Bradley, Newman, Froude ... He paused at Acton. Yes, that was Stephen's mind – Actonian, high-minded liberal, but liberal with roots. York unable to understand how Stephen's intellect worked. But then Stephen had said, "No-one's understood how *your* mind works since Nefertiti!" York paused, photos of Stephen's mom and dad on one of the shelves. At once urbane and stern. Standing outside their home in Kingston. Yes, they looked like that old Loyalist home itself – at once gracious, genteel and ... stone. But loving, caring, still watching over Stevie from the photo.

The next bookcase was Annie. Shelves of Bloomsbury. And then a section of feminist writers, titles like *Women without Men*, *The Time of the New Amazon*, *Foul Balls*, *Women Against History* ... Those titles unnerving. Like the Annie of the Jersey Lily. A furor in the very titles. Perhaps Stephen took it for granted as part of the modern trend. But for York disturbing, and beneath whatever plausibilities, sinister somehow.

And a photo of Annie and her mother above the books. On the verandah of a Victorian home. One of those fretwork verandahs, wood scroll work like overblown angular, like the house itself, that Ontario red-and-white brick Gothic ...

Back to his chair. How had Stephen married an Annie? It was suicide, some form of immolation. Absurd, he was beginning to think of Stephen's situation the way Stephen thought of York. Besides, there were Annie's "horns" as Stephen said. And her Viking parade – no "scullery duchess" that! Presumably she was a whirling Maenad in bed ...

He stared at the room. A couple of prints by Annie's favourite English mod-artist: moons hurtling up over Stonehenge, a sun making havoc of a dead thistle – England on its lunar ear and howling. At least the sofa and chairs weren't her – big and comfy, like Stephen himself. But that Eskimo carving was Annie. Stephen hated Eskimo carvings – "caveman kitsch" he called it. And that Regency tea caddy. And the piece of mammary driftwood. All mounted on black marble for effect. That, and something he'd overlooked till now – an entire shelf of bibelots, souvenirs. A china miniature of Anne Hathaway's cottage in Stratford-upon-Avon. And an imitation black jade elephant. And a folk-carved Mountie, on a Maple Leaf wood stand. Annie's gewgaws. That, and York leaned forward, a photo of Annie as an adolescent, all dressed in a baseball kit: big smile on her face. Tomboy Annie.

York squirmed. Something about her perturbed him profoundly. Yet she was able, industrious and down-to-earth. And certainly intelligent.

"No matter Thor, I've got to like her!" And somehow did. What Annie said – "You like me despite yourself, York!"

Thor sat eyeing York. That one torn ear of his, a combative Thor, alley-cat marauder, was that it. Suddenly bent in jujitsu position, licking his own arse. York stared – Thor clearly rimming himself, effortlessly, tail twitching in the air.

Time to get out, see London.

He picked up his notebook, letter from John, and Simone Weil. Then had a thought: he still hadn't phoned the Colonel yet. He found the Colonel's number and went to the phone. And just as he reached it the phone began ringing. He turned and sped out the door.

A high London day, one of those pearly grey and gold days, clouds burnished with flickering sun.

Where to? He strolled over to the British Museum. Start there. But confronted again with the high iron fence and sheer bulk of the BM he sheered away. Stood for a moment. Then hailed a cab. "I want to go to the other place!" What other place? York leaned forward and explained. "And take your time en route."

"What's that, guv?"

"Doorways," York said, "eyes peeled for doorways."

The driver said no more, but carefully shut the window between the front seat and York. Driving slowly through the rest of Bloomsbury. Fine Georgian doors, fan lights, broken arcades. And Victorian brownstone and bulbous, reticulated rumble of façades, hairy somehow. And gargoyles. Whereas Georgian clean-shaved, silent.

Till they were sweeping past Hyde Park and into the Brompton Road. An array of high nineteenth century buildings, five, seven stories in redstone, greystone, varied brick. Mannerist passed through the Dutch seventeenth century. Gaudy parade of imperial domesticity.

Till they reached the most amazing of all – great grey Gothic cathedral belfrey set atop a giant red brick temple.

"This is it, guv, the Victoria and Albert Museum!"

York eyed the soaring entry way, statues either side. Definitely cathedral, complete with tympanum, stone carvings.

"That'll be four pounds, guv," taxi-driver staring at York gazing at the entry way. York nodded – "A secular cathedral," York said.

"What's that, guv?"

"Including tympanum!" York stepped out, paid, the driver looking at him askance. "Mind if I asks something, guv?" Fire away. "Did you find the doorway you was lookin' for back there?"

"The best," York replied "was about eight blocks back, pair of gargoyles, broken pediment and Sphinx – Stones of Venice, you know, Ruskinian." The driver stared and pulled away.

York shook his head, some taxi driver strange, that's all.

He turned to great the V & A, back at his beloved V & A. Yes, the statues of Victoria and her Albert just above the great portal, like presiding saints. And more statues stretching across the wings, artists, writers … Constable, Gainsborough, Ruskin himself. Yes, like saints, stretching out side.

He stepped back, take it all in: the neo-Gothic, neo-Romanesque, neo-Byzantine, neo-everything of the V & A – cathedral of culture! Felt at home just seeing it again. At home the way he felt in Washington when visiting the Smithsonian. Washington itself barren layout of right angles, geometric rigidities. Till one saw the Smithsonian – surge of redstone and crenellations and poetic towers. Like the old majestic railway hotel across Canada, Château Frontenac, Château Laurier, Château whatever, built in the heyday of Victorian Canada.

At home, just seeing the V & A again, and muttering as he mounted the steps, "Hello again, I'm back!"

And into the entry hall, staring as if seeing it for the first time, as if suddenly entering Raphael's *School of Athens*, it had that precise effect.

And standing inside a second foyer, great floating dome. If the entry hall was *School of Athens*, then this was St. Paul's Cathedral. For a moment he sat on one of the foyer benches.

Sat under that huge dome, high floating cupola overhead. Truly a temple …

He'd come to see something specific. Had caught his eye on his last visit just before Morocco. But what? Then suddenly standing, his feet remembering the way from last time. Up the ceramic-lined stairs like child to a secret. Soon found himself gazing at a cluster of miniature paintings. Pushing a small button beside a glass case..and the light flashing on, as if the paintings flashing. Faces igniting, floating there from four centuries ago. Lady Arabella Stuart, like a golden cat. And James First so wan white elegant. And the flames – man surrounded by flame. York fell back. Ferocious serenity of flames surround the man. And another of man holding a hand ... hand descending from the clouds, as if shaking hands with a cloud.

But the light had gone out. Only stayed on briefly. The faces abruptly gone. York leapt to light them again, faces soaring forth again. And dead centre the one he'd come for: a young man leaning against a tree, amidst roses, eglantines they were. Young man utterly insouciant as if in a trance. Yet utterly feline, virile. Completely relaxed, yet at the ready. When had a man last stood like that? So serene, elegant, poised. Well yes, some of the young men at that country house party, they had that sinuosity of line and stance. That fellow Bamber had some of it. Body almost a smile, complicit with ... With what? Some celestial carnality? The roar in the silence? Yet the people at the country house but pale echo, and this miniature the reality. Only about five inches high, three wide, yet an entire world.

The light was out again. York felt deprived. Of what? Of spring, those roses, those eyes. Eyes of all the faces, wherever you stood they were on you, like a cat.

He had the light on again – faces leaping forward again. The hand from the clouds, the man of flames. All as a single faces, feral eyes.. and flames And York suddenly seeing the heron lifting off the river, long line of white heron flashing above the river ... the Draa River down to Zagora. And Kebir pointing at the heron. Keb in flame of Moroccan sun, standing pointing. So lithe elegant in the sun. Utterly there, feline, virile. Standing at the edge of that high cliff above the river pointing. And a few yards down the road the Colonel masturbating the black shepherd boy, black spear of boy in the sun. And Keb standing pointing at the flight of herons. As the boy shot over the sky ...

York fell back from the portraits, flaming miniatures. Fell back from Kebir. Kee-rrrist, had desperately tried to forget Morocco since returning to London. Forget about Kebir, Keb's eyes, insouciance of his walk, walk that courted life and the sky: forget ... Then John's letter arriving superseding all Morocco. John's letter assuring him all was well, their love well. And York must return – siren-song of John's letter, song of John, saying "Don't fly back to Morocco, Yo-Yo – fly to me!" What York hadn't dare tell Stephen, the urge to throw everything over and return to Marrakech, to Kebir, the way Keb walked seeing the sky, the clouds. Hands coming out of the sky in Morocco. And every man a flame, aureoled in flames. Flare of life last seen in European eyes with those very miniatures. Like Shakespeare's sonnets.

Someone else now viewing the display the light flashing on again, flames ... Kebir amidst the roses! York stumbled back, fell against a visitor. Stood shielding his eyes.

"Are you alright, sir?" One of the guards approaching.

"Yes, yes." York mumbled.

"There's a restroom downstairs. A cafeteria if you need."

"I'll be fine," York nodded. "Those portraits are striking."

"Those are the Hilliard's, sir, Nicholas Hilliard. A woman here a few weeks ago fainted away complete. Said it was those pictures!"

York backed away, began strolling through the neighbouring rooms to calm down. They felt familiar, the Queen Anne chairs, Jacobean tables. And that great bed. He stood a moment in front of that giant bed, oak bed, paneled, pillared and prurient. Great Bed of Ware once again, and his cock suddenly tumescent with, cock shunting forward. Of course, he was back in his orgasm sequence again. Sequence of English rooms he'd studied when in London only weeks ago. Period rooms from Elizabethan times, time of this bed, through to the high Victorian period. And he'd noted that as he worked from the Victorian period back to the Elizabethan, and got an erection. But lost it when he worked the other way.

He thrust his hand into his pocket, push hard-on down. No further public disorder, thank you. Already a fuss over those miniature portraits. Like that lady who'd fainted. Those portraits their own insurrection, like this bed. A call to arms, each others arms. Orgasm in the glint of an eye, the flame of a rose. The way Kebir walked.

He turned back and cautiously made his way through the sequence of rooms, Elizabethan, Jacobean, Queen Anne, up to the Victorian period. And as he progressed through the Georgian period, his cock receding. No question, Georgian geometricity dampened his cock: right angles and tumescence don't agree! And Victoriana positively doused it, something to do with curlicues and gewgaws and smother loving drapes.

He heaved a sigh of relief. Deciding a visit to the cafeteria in order right now. Only stopping for the tiger en route. Tipoleo's tiger chewing a man's head off right there! One had to stop for that or admit to insanity.

Installed in the cafeteria he felt better. For one thing the cafeteria tall and spacious with a glass barrel-vault done. Part of the grandeur of the museum itself. And lest he have any doubts he had but to glance at the baroque columns rising by an exit door.

He established himself in a corner with a mug of cider, cinnamon buns, and vista onto those columns. Jotting notes: –

"Wandering around the V&A with a hard-on! Imagine Vicky being informed of a hard-on in *her* Museum ... "

He paused, took some cider.

"It was that series of rooms again, period rooms I visited last time. I'd forgotten they were located around the Hilliard portraits. Wham – by the time I hit the Great Bed of Ward had splendid hard-on! Q.E.D."

More cider. A furtive glance at the baroque pillars.

"What's Q.E.D.! Well, that there's been a decline in the Occidental orgasm since 1550. Traceable through the furniture styles. Try getting a hard-on with Victorian furniture. Try not getting one in front of the Bed of Ware. It's my V & A Syllogism, sensibility syllogism."

He spilled some of his cider in excitement.

"The murder mystery! I'm onto it all again. Our entire society an ongoing murder-mystery. Who slaughtered the Occidental orgasm? Calvin, John Knox and baseball ... "

Baseball? that was part of his theory: baseball an anti-aphrodisiac, and a diabolically clever one because it posed as phallic display. In fact gave premature prostate problems – all talk and no action! Must remember not to mention this to Stephen, would cause trouble.

"Got to get it straight. Eros displaced by sex between (say) 1550 and the 20th century. At the time of that Hilliard portrait sex was still Eros: i.e. embraced the entire person, entire ambience. Thus man a burning bush, a flame, hands form the sky. But by 20th century Eros reduced to sex and problems in Freud's mind."

He sat back. Chewed more bun, cider. Eyes wandering to a mother and child two tables over. Concentrate, Yo-Yo, concentrate! What is the difference between Eros and sex, mere sex?

"Sex always a settlement, or even a truce. But Eros a *celebration*. Sex arranges the arrangement. But Eros obviates life as arrangement."

A start. But the child over at that table getting fidgety. Was up to something.

"Sex is Eros reduced to a utility (fun or family). Eros is sex as being, whereas sex is Eros as busy doing ... "

Getting closer. York strolled over to get another mug of cider. On his way back noticed the mother slapping the child's hand. A big pout by child, aged seven maybe. One of those disturbingly pretty English boy-children. And dowdy dutiful mom.

"Sex the payoff in the world as deprival!"

The child running over to the baroque pillars. Wrapping himself around the pillars, lewd, running his arms and hands up and down those pillars. Mommie pretends not to see. But seeing it all, and furious.

He perused his notes. Excellent start for his essay on "The Devolution of the Occidental Orgasm." Just that no Toronto magazine would be eager to buy it.

"That your orgasm is exactly as large as your connection with your unconscious ... "

Now where had that come from. York didn't know. Was watching that mother drag her child out of the cafeteria.

"No wonder women on rampage for their freedom. Haven't had decent servicing since the 17th century. And even that going rancid: i.e. later Stuart period and Restoration comedy, half Eros and half sex.

Question: was Nell Gwyn that last English woman to be properly 'swived' (that Viscount's phrase about Tipoleo – "celestial swiving." Excellent.) In any case we don't even swive now, just "fuck," which is such a fuck-awful word ...

York pondered. Women's liberation a predicate of three centuries of erotic deprival. Impacted desire passed from generation unto generation, from beyond the grave in fact. Women dying in frustration and fury.

"The gay world the worst offender of all. Velocity of orgasms much greater than in the hetero world. With more bounce per ounce. But all just sex and gymnastics. Thus the Colonel and James in Morocco."

"The gays like little lost priests peddling a God who exists only in their pants. Gay bars selling 'indulgences'! The very word 'gay' proves their irrelevance."

York stooped words skidding ahead of his understanding. At least he was onto the

Big Thing again. What he'd gone to Morocco for in the first place: look orgasm in the eye. Had known that was so, yet when he got to Morocco had ducked, tried to hide behind the Colonel. But there'd been Kebir. And Keb like that Hilliard portrait upstairs, though less fey, more feline. Panther purr of Keb. Yes, Kebir was orgasm in the eye of God ... as an eye of God. And ... He paused. What the hell was John then? And why was he thinking of Kebir when he'd just received such a loving letter from John?

He stared down. Yes, John's letter with him. Along with Simone Weil. Hadn't glanced at either. Had been invaded by the V&A, that's what. Yet stronger because Weil and John with him: talismanic presences.

He cracked Weil open at random: –

"For the love of God to penetrate so low (as passional human love) it's necessary for nature to have undergone the final violence ... "

He stared at the page. Then around the cafeteria. At those tormented pillars. As if something about to happen, explode.

Enough for one day. He got up, paid for his cider and stumbled out into the maze of galleries. Following his feet, the corner of his eye. Past displays of medieval silver work, ivories, carvings, altars ... Yes, the high medieval church. Chalices and crucifixes floating by like incantations. And York feeling seen, someone watching. He looked around. A few feet away saw a tall object, like a silver sun. Sun atop a column all worked in silver, enamels, stones. And in the centre of the sun, an eye, a circle of glass. Watching him. He tiptoed up. Peering through that eye. Seeing the world of the gallery through that crystal eyes. Everything amplified, fiery.

He stepped back. A monstrance – seventeenth-century monstrance, for displaying the Host, the Body of Christ. York glancing over his shoulder – no one. Just the chant of the gallery, glancing, the accoutrements of the priests of Our Lord.

By the time he'd gathered himself together, he'd passed through several galleries. Completely lost and trying not see. Determined to find a guard for directions to the front door. He stepped into a large hall, walking across. Stopping. Someone on the ground, face stricken, grey. People gathered around in shock. A man in death agony there. People staring, faces aghast at death.

It was an enormous painting.

He proceeded to the next – an orgy of pillars, flying putti, and cherubs. And in the centre a face so serene, so beautiful that York simply gazed. In fact the faces there – beggar, lame man, maidens – so different, from another world. At once more real, more serene, yet more fleshly. World above and below. He stood back. *The Healing of the Lame Man*, it said.

And the next – group of men by the sea. Rainbow robes, Italian eye, only the Italian Renaissance saw such colour, and that blond face, young man hands in prayer. And older man, tumult of iron-gray hair, beard, on his knees. All facing the single man in white, hands outstretched – Christ. It was Christ they were facing – With His stigmata ... and his sheep.

York felt trapped. Trapped in something he hadn't expected at all. These giant paintings, hadn't seen them for years. By Raphael, the great Raphael Cartoons for the Sistine Chapel. He reeled back, turned. Saw St. Paul preaching in Athens. And the sacrifice of the Bull at Lystra ... Bull facing the final axe. And The

Blinding of Elymas. A sea of faces, flying hands ...

He groped his way to a large bench, sat down.

When he opened his eyes there it was. Diagonally across from him. the men in two small boats. Fishing, drawing nets. And the great black cranes standing in the water nearby. Other birds floating overhead. And the distant shore, smoke, turrets, men walking, the sound of gulls. And yes, that same man with the iron-grey hair, beard, kneeling, imploring. In front of the man sitting so calmly in white, his hand held up as if to say "yes." St. Peter kneeling in the boat, before Christ. Boat overloaded with fish. And the swans just beyond. *The Miraculous Draught of Fishes.* was it? But it wasn't that. It was the way those sinking boats floated. The way everything floated from Christ's hand. From the wings of the birds. From the lake, from the sky. Floating with Christ's hand. And Peter's prayer. Those boats which were meant to sink from the overload of fish, *floating!*

York caught in the silent shout of that painting. As if he would walk forward and touch those hands. James, and beautiful John, hauling up the fish.

He got up, walking slowly around the great hall. Yes, Paul at Athens exhorting. The man in the crowd right before Paul, face so innocent, an innocence that was hope absolute. And the statue of the warrior just beyond, dark rage of body of that warrior.

And the sacrifice of the bull, axe poised high over its head. And the faces so comely ... and carnal, both. Child playing the pipes. And beyond, the presiding statue of Hermes, naked messenger of other Gods. And the bull with its final crown of coloured beads. And the ram right opposite held by a man whose face was at once Pan, ram and believer.

York stood in the centre of the hall: silent shout all around him, orgy of life, colours of dawn, sunrise, the shriek of carnality ... and the calm. How was it possible? Such lips, such lusts, such prehensile hands, such riot of high horned hell. Life as opera – yet real, life as really was inside all of us.

He made his way down the hall, to the man in the boat. Stood gazing. As if the boats must move. The swans. The man in white. As if they were all walking on water, walking, walking across waves. Like the man in white, walking the face of the waters. His arms outstretched, saying "yes"!

From Dracula-in-Drag:
"Breakfast of Champions"

Jane was determined to know. Just happened to be at home for lunch when York arrived back. "So what happened this time?" she asked.

"I don't know," York said.

"Whaddaya mean you don't know?"

"I mean breakfast was like a three-ring circus," York said.

Circus?

"Complete with ring master and whip!" York moaned.

"But I thought ... " Jane said.

"So did I," York replied. "But it went the other way."

"What was his intention?" she asked.

"What would *your* intention be with a cockring and KY out on your desk?"

"I don't use a cockring," Jane snapped.

* * *

"Thursday, 15 Oct/72 – Tranta!

9:25 p.m. Spent all afternoon trying to work on my Ms. The Moroccan material. Nothing happened. Can't even read the Moroccan stuff. All I see is John! John as Superman, cracking eggs from a hundred feet above his head. *Tap-tap-tap!*

Jane says I'm impatient!

Shirley says I need an exorcist.

I literally cannot think! Brain like a fried egg."

* * *

Next morning York gathered a large chunk of his Diary together. About six inches worth, hand-written pages. And his file of John letters. What would the psych make of letters with flying phalluses all over them, flying hard-ons and sunflowers in red felt pen. He deleted the letter describing one of their sexual bouts – Dr. Mildred surely didn't need *that* intimacy! Nor a nude photo John had sent in one of his letters. Nor ...

He added pages of his novel. Moroccan pages. And put it all in a shopping bag.

Shortly after ten he was once again in Dr. Mildred's office. Sitting in that rocking chair, staring at the Angel's Wings on the windowsill. Trying not to see that carnival rocking horse.

"Well, well," Mildred said – she was padding around with her tea – "Here we are again!" Yes, in her Mildred phase. "And what've we been up to this week?" she asked.

What?

"What shenanigans?" she asked.

York closed his eyes – this woman is dotty, he thought.

"I see you've brought some of the evidence," she went on.

York opened his eyes. Mildred was pointing at the shopping bag.

"Oh," York said – "It's for you."

"I know," Mildred sniffed her tea.

Silence.

"How much did you dare bring?" she asked.

Too goddamned nosey, York thought.

"Would you please pass it to me?" she said.

York carried it over to her and she bounced it up and down on her lap. "About five pounds of it," she said.

What?

"Enough to get one's teeth into," she grinned.

York wanted to take the bag back.

"No way," she said.

What?

"This stuff'll tell the truth," she nodded. "What you really feel!" She was poking through the papers already.

Damn her, York thought.

"Been doing any writing?" she asked.

"Trying to, York said – "The Moroccan material."

"Of course," she said.

What?

"Well the Mexican material would be about John. So it's safer to work on the Moroccan ... He wasn't there as I understand."

York nodded.

"Which chapter is this one?" she pointed at the Ms. pages York had brought.

"The Sheikh scene," York said.

"Do tell," Mildred said.

"Well I'd gone up into the Atlas mountains, invited by the nephew of a Sheikh ... "

"A genuine sheikh," she grinned.

"Well, he was actually a Caid, but I always thought of him as a sheikh, he was right out of a story book. Lived in a kinduv castle up the mountains ... "

"Wonderful," Mildred nodded, jotting.

"Yes and no," York said – "I mean the dining room was magnificent. But ... "

"But what?"

York leaned forward – "It kept changing shapes!"

"That is rather special," Mildred pursed her lips.

York nodded.

"But what were you doing at the Sheikh's place?"

"I don't know. I mean I was having dinner, sheep stew, complete with head, eyes ... the Sheikh shot an eye at me."

"A stewed eye," she said, "a bit much, really. But what did you feel during your stay?"

"That I was going to be murdered. Or go screaming insane."

"And what gave you this feeling of being murdered?"

York shook his head – "It wasn't the sheikh, he was very kind, dignified. And it couldn't have been Bourhlou ... "

Who?

"The Sheikh's nephew. Kept wanting to borrow my pipe. As if by smoking my pipe he became me ... "

"Really?"

"Yes, I felt my entire personality passing into his mouth to be smoked, chewed, eaten ... "

Mildred nodded.

"Yet I felt it wasn't me there at all!"

"And who was there if not you, York?"

"I don't know. All I can do is write the story."

"And how is that going?" Mildred asked.

"Crazy," York paused, wishing he hadn't used that word. "I mean sometimes it comes like crazy then it's blocked ... "

"So even your time to yourself is focused on John."

What?

"Your novel is really about John, isn't it?"

"Well, yes, our life together ... "

"How much of the novel is actually about John?"

York pondered – "Not that much. More about Marrakech and Osprey Cove ..."

"So the novel is about John, but he isn't in it much."

"It comes down to that."

"So you don't really look directly at John that much, though the book is about him."

"That's what has happened," York said. "I mean I even had difficulty looking at photos of John in Marrakech ... "

Mildred jotted – "So John is in your novel as a kind of absence."

Silence.

"And what is John doing with his spare time these days?" Mildred asked – "apart from blocking your novel."

"Body-building, and writing his novel," York paused, glanced over at Mildred. Her eyes met his, twinkling, as in mirth, some kind of secret, nothing very difficult.

"And John is writing his novel," she said, "which I presume is largely about you and his life with you."

Yes.

"Yet John says he thinks about you less than five per cent of the time."

"That's what he said," York paused. "Yes, at that dirty bar of his."

"How did he say it?"

"Aggressively nonchalant."

"Good. It seems that unconsciously John is thinking about you all the time."

What?

"Either thinking about you, or else consciously thinking around you to avoid you, comes to the same thing."

York sat nonplussed.

"And when he's not thinking one way or another about you, he's thinking about his body. Have you ever worked with barbells, York?"

"No, not much. John got me out to a gym once or twice to work out."

Mildred jotted – "I've never done barbells at all. What's it like?"

"Hellish hard work," York said. "Punishment ... like beating oneself up."

"Oh, lovely," Mildred purred – "You are a wonderful, shall we say 'client.'"

York felt stupid. Worse, naked somehow.

"Your own words, my dear York – that's the advantage of a writer as client." What?

"You just shoot out your replies without thinking. Your mind and sensibility don't dissociate when hit with a question."

"What do you mean?" York asked.

"You said barbells felt like punishment."

"So they did."

"And John is deeply into barbells, when he isn't writing about you."

York nodded.

"So his time is nicely divided between you and self-punishment."

Silence.

"Which is what then," she asked.

"Which is his S-M."

"Brilliant," Mildred grinned. "Time for more tea."

York stared at the floor as she shuffled about, tea finally appearing in his cup from behind his shoulder. He watched her return to her chair. Imperturbable in her slippers and sweater-coat. Gramma Moses, or Whistler's mother, or ... ?

"You've seen John twice since I last saw you."

"Yes, he came ... " York gaped at the doctor – "How did you know?"

"Moreover one meeting was sweet and one quite nasty."

Yes, York gaping.

"You see, when you arrived this morning, you were nervous, fumbling with your pipe. So I surmised you'd seen him recently."

York nodded.

"And you've been partly quick, alert, and quite separately subdued and glum. So I reckoned we were dealing with two different encounters."

Silence.

"Please do tell," Dr. Mildred said.

York sank back into the rocker, relieved to tell the doctor about those damned meetings. "He came to the house," York said, "and ... "

"And what?"

"I ... " York stammered – "I can't remember any of it!"

Dr. Mildred jotted. "Yet you've been thinking of nothing but John and those meetings all week."

York nodded. Staring at the window. The Angels Wings there. Like in Osprey Cove, like ... "It was his boots!" he blurted.

"Boots?" the doctor murmured. "What kind of boots?"

"Halfway up the calf, with caribou, wildflowers, moss ... like Osprey Cove, our life there.

"I see," the doctor nodded.

"I mean they were like moccasins, but high on the leg, and all that embroidered quillwork. Osprey Cove up his legs. And John the old gentle John again. Said we could be lovers again, as if nothing had happened, as if some barbed wire fence gone ... "

Dr. Mildred nodded – "So the boots were some hidden key to John. He'd become those boots ... "

"Yes, they were the real John, the man I loved."

"And what else was he wearing?"

"Oh, sports coat, tie, portable respectability."

"With the boots hidden beneath," the doctor said.

York nodded.

"So you had two Johns there, in effect."

"Well, yes ... I mean he was all purring and gentle and ... " York paused, suppressing the advent of John's hard-on.

"And?"

"He said he wanted our love, but his mind had to go along with it."

"Splendid," the doctor said, "a lively little vignette, Mr. Mackenzie. We'll refer to it as 'Puss 'n Boots.'"

What?

"Use it for your novel. Delicious scene."

York started to chuckle – "Puss 'n Boots," but of course.

"Now," Dr. Mildred tapped her pen – "that was the 'nice encounter.' Tell me about the nasty one."

"Nasty?" York tried to light his pipe. "Well, it was breakfast ... "

"Always a perilous time," the doctor grinned.

"We discussed sado-masochism, John's need for it."

"Perilous indeed," she added.

"And afterwards I was very upset," York paused – "I was afraid I'd driven him away."

"What did you do about that, apart from stew."

"I phoned him, apologized for raising the S-M issue like that."

"What was his reaction to that?"

"Worse," York blurted – "He said, 'Oh don't worry about that York, I'm not exactly innocent, you know!'"

The doctor chuckled – And what effect did that have on you?"

"Relief ... then black."

"And you couldn't work on your novel."

York nodded.

"Tell me a mite more about the breakfast itself."

York hesitated, image of John crack-cracking eggs, like circus performer. John like some Superman conjurer. And "tap-tap-tap." And the cockring. How explain? Trivia, yet ...

"Details are telling, Mr. Mackenzie!"

York described the scene as precisely as could.

"Oh my yes," Dr. Mildred purred, "very good!"

"Good?" York protested – "It's ghastly."

"Of course," she nodded – "You were *talking* about sado-masochism, but John was *enacting* it!"

Silence.

"And knew precisely what he was doing," the doctor smiled – "As he said, he isn't exactly innocent. I particularly like the touch about the cockring ... "

What?

"Drive you crazy, my dear York!" She was purring again, jotting. "Well, well, the evidence grows. And you've passed to the offensive."

Offensive?

"Of course – you talked to John about S-and-M. And that is the hidden issue." With that the doctor stood up, puffing on her little pipe, gazing at the plants on the windowsill. Then walking over to them, fingers brushing them as she passed. She nodded – "Breakfast of Champions," she said.

What?

"Your petit déjeuner with John," she grinned, "We'll call it the Breakfast of Champions!"

York laughed. As the doctor fondled the Angel's Wings.

"It was the right time to phone him," she said. "Time to double check. Se how good your reporting is ... " She seemed to be talking to herself as much as to York. Plucking a dead leaf off the Angel's Wings. "Besides, I'm intrigued. If it's what I intuit, he'll give it away with his arms ... "

What?

"I phoned John, before you came this morning," she said, still gazing at the Angel's Wings as if the truth there.

What?

"You mentioned where he works, so I called. Said I'd appreciate a private meeting with him. He couldn't resist ... "

Why?

"I said I needed his help, insights about you ... "

Silence.

"He's the patient, after all!" The doctor flicked a dead flower off a geranium. And slowly turning facing York, gazing direct at him. For a second he caught the steel in her eyes. As at their first meeting. Just for a second, rapier out of scabbard.

Then hidden in sudden puff of pipe-smoke. And when He saw her eyes again they were Tinker Bell, twinkle ... quiet mirth. And she was fondling the leaves of the plants again.

York tried to decide if the occasion was comedy, or a seance or simply crazy.

"He was at once eager, and evasive, my dear York. What do you make of that?"

"Dunno," York said, eyeing her as she wheeled in and out amidst the plants like tweed-knit hummingbird. "I mean that's why I'm here ... "

"That's not why you're here," the doctor grinned. "No matter, what matters is your next encounter with John!"

Silence.

"I'll tell you," she said – "he was eager because he wants to tell me something. And evasive because to do so he'll have to hide something."

Hide what?

"Easy my dear York! You see, what he tells me will tell me what he's hiding."

Silence.

"What he tells me will go around the thing ... " she nodded – "Round and round the mulberry bush, the monkey chased the weasel ... " she was virtually singing now. "And d'you know what happened to that weasel, York?" She had stopped in front of a large flower, snapped her fingers and the flower soared in the air – "POP goes that weasel!" She caught the flower mid-air, stuck it in the buttonhole of her sweater-coat and returned to her chair as if never left.

York sat certain that either he was insane, or John, or his lunar psychiatrist!

"One more piece of data, York."

"Please, I'm totally lost!"

"I know. You couldn't remember what your two meetings with John were at the start. So I knew ... "

Knew what?

"That John is still succeeding."

In what?

"In what we're agreed to call 'mind fuck.' To wit ... " she jotted, "still smashing your quite excellent brain, York. Which is his intent. Moreover ... "

York sagged back in his rocker.

"Your very presence energizes him to write *his* novel.. While you ... "

"While I work like crazy on mine and get nowhere," York murmured.

"I do with you wouldn't use that word 'crazy,' York."

York nodded.

"Let's just say you're working on your novel with the manic energy of a man aware ... " she paused, pursed her lips – "aware that he's called upon to die."

York sat bolt upright in his chair.

"What does all this mean, York?"

York shook his head – "All I know is that despite everything I can do I'm being driven closer to the brink ... "

"Now that is honest," the doctor nodded approval. "John is still driving you to suicide and mind-fuck is the visible tool." She paused – "But we know that now, yet he's still driving you to ... the brink, as you put it."

Silence.

"There must be something further involved, don't you think?"

York sank deeper into his chair.

"Why do you think John is so systematically driving you ... to the bring, York?"

"I simply don't want to know," York blurted it out. "It's too late! All I see is John, when I go to write I see John ... "

"Good," she nodded – "At least you now admit you don't want to know. And why don't you want to know?"

"Because I'd lose John!" York was adamant..

"Lovely. But you haven't lost him at all."

What?

"His best energies are given to you, my dear York. He only knows he exists when you're there! Then he works on his novel ... "

"I'd lose my sense of what's beautiful in him," York said.

"Exactly," the doctor jotted – "You'd lose your innocence about him. And how would you do that?"

"By seeing what I don't want to know," York felt angry.

"And what don't you want to know?" the doctor almost cooing now.

"I said I don't know!"

"An honest reply. But," she gazing over at him – "It could cost you your life. Why is John driving you to death, York?"

"He wants to be free of me."

"I wish that were true! 'Tain't."

What?

"He knows you're writing your novel, doesn't he?"

"I told you that," York spluttered – "He keeps asking me about it."

"Dead men tell no tales, York!"

York gaped – "John is killing me so I won't tell that story?"

"That's part of it! He knows a hundred times better than you what the evidence really is. But he thinks you won't sort it through in time," she grinned. "But it isn't just that. He wants one more thing from you before the coup de grâce."

More?

"Come now, York. You're reputed to be intelligent. Your books keep telling us how very intelligent you are, in case we'd missed the point."

Shit!

"What was John's decisive comment during that 'breakfast of champions, York?"

"Decisive?" York muttered – "Dunno – all I could do was see what he was doing, photograph it so to speak."

"Exactly. John capture your inner eye once again. A kind of retinal implant he achieves – narcissistic necessity for him."

What?

"Which he requires for his 'end game' might we call it. But didn't he say something about death, York?"

"I told you, doctor! He said 'someone always has to be able to die in S-M.'"

"A serious profession of faith on John's part, don't you think?"

Faith?

"Well, if S-M is his operative life-belief. And later on the phone he said quite callously that he wasn't exactly innocent, you know."

"Doctor, I just don't know where the hell you're going with all this."

"You would scarcely be here if you did," she grinned. "A touch more tea?"

What?

"Permit me to offer you my own blend. It's fortifying." She was shuffling over to a small lacquered box on a nearby shelf. Opening it as if the treasures of the East. Sniffing. "Yes, we need the fragrance, and extra body this time."

Completely loony, York thought. And driving me loonier!

Doctor Mildred completed her tea-maneuver. And they both sat sniffing her special blend. A veritable Cognac of teas, York decided, a floral powerhouse ...

"York, did you ever feel any desire to be beaten by John?"

York almost dumped his tea.

"To perform the masochist's role for him?"

"No!" York half-shouted – "I told you that before."

Silence.

"Though ..." York pondered – "towards the end I was almost willing. *But it wasn't me ...* "

"Exactly," the doctor jotted. "But may I point out that this morning you are really quite petulant, even bitchy."

What?

"And it really isn't you. I know that." She stirred her tea.

York quelled the urge to scream.

"John admitted to a transfer of personality to you once or twice I understand."

York nodded.

"And it's really John I'm talking with now, you know."

What?

"Because John transferred a lot of his S-M into you at that delightful Breakfast of Champions."

York wished she wouldn't call it that.

"Now, revert to Morocco, my dear York."

???

"When you were at the Sheikh's place you felt you were going to be murdered."

York nodded – but what the hell did the Sheikh have to do with John?

"And you felt it wasn't you there at all."

Yes.

"Moreover, you felt that the Sheikh's nephew was stealing your persona when he stole your pipe."

"His name was Bourhlou," York said.

"Did you have any thoughts of John then?"

"Yes, that I was eager to get back to him."

"Any others?"

York pondered – "Yes, on the bus trip up, the strong feeling the trip was like our flight in Mexico, in the mountains. Flight from the police, from John's mother."

The doctor jotted for a moment – Well well," she finally said, "Maybe it was the flight from John's mom. Maybe you were at the Sheikh's place as John."

What?

"In place of John," the doctor persisted. "And maybe Bourhlou did try to steal your phallus. And if this be so ... "

"Please ... " York rubbing the back of his neck, aware of an ache there some time now.

"Back to Puss 'n Boots!"

What?

"What was John in that little scene?"

"Very pussy!" York said with rueful smile.

"Good. Your sense of humour is returning. Now, note this," she said – "So are you this morning!"

What?

"Some petulant pussy," she grinned. " And why is that?"

York closed his eyes.

"Breakfast of Champions!"

York sat a moment, fingering his neck, pain there.

"On the surface of it," the doctor said, "John is botching your capacity to think. At the same time he is completing the transfer of his personality to you ..."

Silence.

"Which means the transfer of a wad of his masochism ... "

"Wish you wouldn't use that word," York said.

"Which word?"

"Wad!" York opened his eyes.

"I see," the doctor nodded – "One of John's words?"

York nodded.

"I understand," the doctor said, jotting. "A bit gross used as John might."

"A big wad," York said – "one of his favorites!"

"As I said, a bit petulant this morning," she said as if talking to herself.

Silence.

"Now," she jotted – "the transfer of John's masochism would mean the transfer of his enormous desire to commit suicide."

York was hanging on to his neck, throbbing in his neck.

"He is completing five years of such transfer with you, York!"

What?

She nodded – "That's what all these encounters with John have been, York. Your first encounter, he was longing for your love. And what did he do?"

"Smashed me in the face," York snapped.

"On the back of the neck, if I recall," the doctor said.

York nodded.

"Next day," she studied her notes, "he enterprised fellatio ... "

What?

"He sucked your cock, to give it his blessing, as he put it."

York closed his eyes.

"But it was you he wanted! Even as he stopped before the wad," she grinned – "and what did that do?"

York couldn't follow any of it, just the pain in his neck.

"It left you further knotted," she said. "Like cutting off your testicles."

Balls!" York spluttered – "Why not just say balls."

"Exactly," she said – "balls, wad, cock ... simpler. Then the following Saturday, was it, he played Big Boss and lost. Because Big Boss he can never be."

York thought his head was going to fly right off.

"And next day he retaliated full-scale sado-masochist."

What?

"He laid an ambush in the one spot he could hope you would turn up ... "

Where?

"He certainly has fucked your brain, York – you can't even remember the sequence of encounters. Yet your life depends on it ... "

York knew his head was going to fly off – decapitated.

"Out in the country, at that antique shop."

"Yes," York said – "The Jameson's"

"The tree-pee," the doctor said.

What?

"John captured your eye with a false departure. You followed him!" she nodded. "Right out into the woods. And he flaunted his cock in your face. Triggering psychic grovel on your part."

York glared.

"The tree-pee event," she smiled. "And from that moment to the Breakfast of Champions it's been a single trajectory!"

Silence. York hanging on to his neck.

"A rapid-fire transfer of his suicide into you. The theft of your final love as energy for him!"

Silence.

"He knows someone has to die, York. Knows the death is his. Knows if you love him you'll eat his death for him. *He's simply using you this one final time.*"

York stared.

"And he's within an ace of success, York!" the doctor returned his gaze. "He knows you're innocent."

What?

"Innocent of his real methods. Knows fully what he's doing. You'll die for him. And ... "

she shook her finger at York – "he'll be free to be gay under a facade of married respectability ... "

What?

"He'll try some poor girl on. Maybe several. And the face he'll present will be yours, my dear York – earnest, sincere, naive. But he'll play Big Boss with them, sado. And be bored."

Silence.

"And his family will pay him well," she nodded – "prodigal son returned to the fold. And all that accomplished, he'll go S-M gay, York. Saying that none of it ever happened! ... "

York sat as in a trance, the doctor's words hammering right in the back of his head, right where the pain was. Words hitting, probing there. Like fingers probing down his spine, flashes of light ...

"You are committing John's suicide for him, York! Why?"

Words inside his spinal column. As York rose from his chair, standing in the midst of the room. Turning towards the window, the Angel's Wings dancing, as he went over, brushing their leaves, fingers tingling. Then turned back to the centre of the room, his two hands before him, fingers out, touching them together as if flames ... clapping his hands, stopping, laughing, listening to his first laughter in months. Laughter like spring brook cracking through ice. And head back, laughter deepening, from his belly. As he skipped a step, two, three.

Just as soon as started, he stopped. Doctor must think I'm mad. But the doctor sitting calmly puffing on her pipe, gazing at the flowers as if nothing had occurred.

York tip-toed back to his chair, sat down feeling lighter than air, talking to Osprey Cove, Ma Snook, Mariam Barnes – "Your Angel's Wings, never seen them so clearly, Mariam, dez ye hear."

"It's gone, Dr. Mildred, it's gone!"

She just nodded.

"The weight, all that weight, like a knot in my neck, back of my head. As soon as you said ... "

"Said what?" she asked.

"Said, 'You're committing John's suicide ... ' I felt airborne, that pain gone, right there." York rubbed his neck, back of his head.

The doctor was on her feet, padding over to a small cupboard, emerging with a pair of decanters – "Which?" she asked.

What?

"Olorosa or Tio Pepe, York?"

"Olorosa," York said – "touch of the sweet."

The sherry poured, the two of them returned to their chairs. The doctor held up her glass, glancing at York – "Welcome back, my friend."

"I'm so glad," York stammered – "glad to be back." And only then realizing how close his laughter had been to tears.

Silence. York finally saying – "But how did you know?"

Know what?

"That it was John's suicide I was committing?"

She shook her head – "I didn't. It wasn't till you told me about the Sheikh's place, then that S-M breakfast." She paused. "Then I felt it, right in you. It was palpable. I took the gamble. You'll have to forgive me ... "

What?

"But it was no gamble really," she said. "I mean there was nothing to lose for you. And ... there was you to win if you intuition was right."

"But you know you've won!" York stared.

"Well, yes. You rose out of your chair like a bird. And your laughter wasn't hysterical, it was lyrical, light." She grinned – And you skipped, and could caress flowers again. No need to tell that the weight had gone. I could see it gone ... "

York drank more sherry. "it's psychic voodoo, the whole thing."

Doctor Mildred pursed her lips – "It's been a murder mystery, York, pure and simple. And not done yet."

What?

"We haven't caught the thief!"

Silence.

"You see, York, I've talked to you several times now. We've been having two-hour sessions ... "

"Seances!" York blurted.

"Either way twice as intense. I can find out four times as much in two hours as one. And I've read both your books, your media novel and your recent one. I was," she hesitated – "puzzled!"

Why?

"I couldn't detect any sign of either sadism or masochism in them. Yet the evidence was that sado-masochism explained your entire predicament." She nodded. "And you haven't been hiding anything with me, other than the extent of your love for John."

York mumbled protest.

"I realized after our second meeting I wasn't dealing with you at all, but with John. He's the one should be here. But it's too late ... "

What?

"Because John has transferred his need to see a psychiatrist to you, along with everything else." She nodded – "I realized that when I phoned him. He's longing to talk to someone, get it all off his chest ... "

"So I'm here on John's behalf?"

"Just as much as you were in Marrakech and at the Sheikh's place on John's behalf. John isn't very brave, you know. He risks others for himself. Only does something after you've done it first, for him ... " She was jotting again. "Now you've come to me, he'll want to see a psychiatrist too."

"That's what he said."

"Ah, quicker than I expected. He'd really like to have me as his psych. But I can't do that ... "

Why not?

"Because I've taken an instinctive dislike to him. Besides, I'm booked up over a year ahead ... "

"Thank you for taking me."

"Now, the key is John's statement that 'someone always has to die in S-M.' His entire relationship with you, at least now, is clearly S-M, with that 'transfer of personality' as its hidden goal."

York shook his head.

"What do you feel when you think of John?"

"Pain."

"Precisely. His pain. Which in the long run amounts to his suicide. And ... " she grinned, "in the short-run his desire for sado-masochistic sex."

What?

"My dear York, do you know what John wants?"

York stared at his empty sherry glass.

"He wants you to beat him, hard ... "

York stared.

"With a belt, or your slippers, or a paddle," she nodded – "Anything will do, really. Are you aware of that, York?"

"Well, the pain, that's what he said, long ago."

"I beg your pardon," the doctor said.

"Said that his intention in life was 'to go through pain painlessly."

"Splendid," the doctor purred, jotting. "And that's precisely what he's done. And is now finalizing. Passing all his pain to his lover. And not at all innocent of what he's doing."

Silence.

"And why," she asked, "does he know he can do it?"

"Because I'm stupid," York blurted.

"It amounts to that. But more exactly he counts on your love, and your innocence. You see, the amount of pain he can sink into you is predicate of the size of your love and innocence."

Silence.

"He envies you your innocence, and lusts for it, and hates it ... "

"He said that," York blurted – "said he wants his innocence back. Several times. Yet attacks what he calls my 'criminal innocence.'"

"I'll check his innocence quotient when I meet him. With pleasure. Meanwhile, we have your mind released, now your eye, and your emotions."

"What do you mean?

"Well, in our last meeting, we spotted John's mind-fuck tactics, a kind of Catch-22 technique ... "

"You are dangerously well read," York laughed, "I mean in modern novels."

She laughed – "I can now admit I once wanted to be a writer. Then an actor. I failed at both! Ended up as a psych ... "

"Thank God," York said.

"And this time," she went on, "we've caught his emotional tactic. Your mind smashed, John has simply been dumping his emotional life into you ... "

York sat right up – "He said that. After our breakfast ... Breakfast of Champions."

Said which?

"That he didn't understand why a person like me loved a mess like him."

The doctor was jotting again – "He certainly is not innocent. I need to know how he said it, please."

"Umm, just as I was about to leave, up in his room. It just floated out rather winsomely ... "

"Well, that was the real John, the one who knows what his score is."

"But how did you release my emotions?" York asked. I mean, just now. I could feel them surge up. As soon as that knot went in my neck ... "

She laughed – "You want all my secrets. Well, I simply relaxed you, tea and chit-chat. Then I tested."

Tested?

"When you weren't expecting it, I shot my main statement at you ... " she paused – "It came as a statement, but it was really a question."

"About the suicide?"

"Yes. I knew if I was wrong your nervous system would reject it. And you'd start questioning it."

And?

"My dear York, you rose out of your chair lighter than air. So I had my proof."

Silence. York finally saying, "You're not a psychiatrist, you're a shaman."

"Better than being a 'shrink' as they call it. Besides, quite early in our meetings I sensed I wasn't dealing with a patient at all. You and I were collaborating somehow. I really didn't know what. At first I thought it was a straight suicide. But I ruled that out."

Why?

"Allow me some secrets," she grinned. "What I finally did sense was that you were being destroyed from underneath and behind – surreptitiously murdered. I knew there wasn't much time. That's why I got hold of John. When he realized who was phoning him, do you know what he did?"

No.

"He started to stammer. Then pulled his voice together. I knew he was hiding something, and afraid." She jotted – "Now I know what John was hiding."

"His murder of me."

The doctor pursed her lips – "I think we might call it a 'surrogate suicide,' York. Your suicide committed on John's behalf, with John perfectly aware."

"You've saved my life."

"I've given you a chance to save your own life. And that's far from done yet."

"Why didn't I realize what was happening?"

"Because you love John, you dolt." She nodded – "You couldn't admit to yourself that the person you love was deliberately stealing you life while covertly passing you his death!"

York sat silent, gazing at his empty sherry glass. "What were my chances, Mildred?"

"Of what?" the doctor almost fey.

"Of surviving?"

She nodded – "I don't usually discuss such matters ... with my clients."

"Now you're being evasive, Mildred."

She laughed – "You have got your mind back! And your emotions. You care again and want to know. Fine." She paused. "When we first met I thought we had less than a month to catch the thing. I mean the first thing you did when you entered my office was to check the window ... "

Silence.

"You felt like a case of terminal psychic cancer. I had a long shot to cure, using immediate and quite unorthodox tacts. "

"You've lost me again."

"I knew you wouldn't respond to my cerebral approach."

York nodded – "I mistrust the mere mind."

"So ... I ambushed you my dear York, forgive me," She glanced over. "As John so often proves, you're very ambushable."

Silence.

"By a touch of theatre, a touch of laughter ... " she paused.

York grinned – "by being a bit dotty, fey ... leprechaun."

"Thank you, you are most helpful," she grinned, yes, leprechaun. "More sherry, York. We need more sherry." And she bustled over, pouring sherry. And back to her chair – "Here's to ... 'The Case of the Surrogate Suicide'!" Yes, her voice musical, eyes twinkling like her Waterford sherry glass. And a mirth in them, shared. As if they'd been convivially unraveling some household puzzle whose solutions were obvious once done.

They drank more sherry in silence. York wondering if it had been theatre on her part. Was she fey? A fey genius. Or all for real? It didn't seem to have anything to do with psychiatry as such. More to do with being ... his being vs. John's non-being, was that it?

"One might call it Real Absence, York?"

What?

"Well, John's condition," she sniffed her sherry. "In theology one has the concept of the Real Presence ... but John feels like a case of Real Absence."

"I was just thinking of John."

"I know," she grinned – "that look on your face. As if contemplating something which constantly vanished, wasn't there."

"A mirage," York said.

"And you don't want to see him again soon!"

York stared at her.

"But this time you'll have both your mind and your eye. Your emotions are flowing again. Your eye will be disoccluded."

"Disoccluded?"

"That's how John ruled you."

What?

"Call it his 'regnancy' if you will."

York decided she was fey and wonderful and mad and a genius.

"You see, John reigned within you by implanting himself in your eye at the crucial moment. What I called a 'retinal implant' – he'd jump you inmost attention ... "

York laughed – "I sometimes called him Johny-jump-up. And his arrivals were always advents ... "

"Exactly. He'd wait till you were vulnerable, open, then jump into your expectancy, presenting himself as ... " she paused – "As Ozma, or Glinda the Good, sweetest of fairy queens."

"Bitch!" York blurted.

They both laughed. "I take it wasn't me you were referring to," she said.

Silence. York seeing Dr. Mildred as if for the first time. She always sat slightly hunched over. As if studying something. Always in her sweater-coat, hand-knit housecoat. And neat dress. With a kerchief at her throat. And slippers. A figure out of anyone's home. At home in herself. No, not dowdy, though so easily could've been so. But alert, perky ... hidden ambush. And face constant cameo, tidy comfortable wrinkles. York couldn't quite place it all. She was jotting notes. As if everyone's favorite aunt were Socrates. He finally said – "You always disarm me ... Dr. Mildred."

"No, I arm you, York. Now listen with care and stop bothering with mental notes about me. I'll give you a quick character sketch later for your novel. You're already making plans to see John again," she paused. "Now here's what you do."

What?

"You keep your mind off to one side without letting him know it. Just spectate. But keep your eye wide on him. Register every movement he makes. Let him enter your eye. Don't shield yourself from the Medusa this time. And lead him on ... all the way through."

"Dangerous!" York blurted.

"Of course. So that's my next request. Don't see him till the night before our next meeting."

"He's capable of ... " York hesitated – "of murder. Physical murder!"

"So you do know! Excellent," she was jotting again. "Anyone capable of psychic murder is capable of physical. But he's a cowardly lion."

What?

She laughed – "He'll murder someone much weaker than you, physically. If he doesn't complete his psychic murder of you now."

Silence.

"You're armed, York."

"I know."

"But still vulnerable ... "

York nodded.

"You still love him." The doctor was out of her chair padding slowly toward the door. Their meeting done. York followed silently. Just as he was leaving the doctor said, "wait ... " And passed York the flower from her buttonhole – "His head belongs to you!"

John's Letter

York returned to the country, to the home of his minister friend. It was the time of the final autumn leaves, fall fairs and 'Harvest Home.' Time of the lustiest and loudest of the Methodist hymns and the thickest 'church social' sandwiches. And pumpkin pies.

He tried to write in his novel. But nothing came. He was dead inside, inert. And remembered John's big smile as he said – "My novel's growing great now, York." Yes, part of John's 'false innocent transfer.' John saying, "What good would it do if I did take responsibility for it, York? It wouldn't change anything, anyway." John's comments surging up within him as he tried revising a chapter of his book – "You weren't worthy, York ... You don't seem to understand, I've used you, and now I'm done ... You'd make a better lover than ever, Yo-Yo ... " He stared at his manuscript, words shimmering on the page, neon shrapnel of the remains of the brain. Why do I still love him?

The Minister remonstrated – "You've got to give John time ... He still loves you, he's just afraid ... The psychiatrist has only nailed the dark side of the situation. There's God's love too, York."

But it did no good. Another few days and finally York left Ontario, fled to French Canada, to Montréal, into the Vieux Quartier, the historic and visual core of a culture other than his English Canadian culture – a Catholic and French culture, medieval and baroque in its allegiances, despite any mod overlay. There was the old Place d'Armes, with its four centuries of history, and bells in the Mass. And the Château de Ramezay by the Place Jacques Cartier. And the magnificent Beaux Arts Hôtel de Ville overtopping all, where General de Gaulle had thundered "*Vive ... Vive le Québec libre!*" York understood what those words had meant to the French Canadians. Yes, "Let my people go ... !" – a dirge in the soul. Understood because just being here now, away from Toronto's financial Canada, away from 'Torontario,' some horrible black slowly began passing from him. He was able to start writing again – at least to revise his already written chapters. An hour, two per day. A week passed, two, four. He'd reworked a lot of the Moroccan material. Some of London ... could see that, yes, he'd been in Morocco as a 'proxy-John,' certainly in part. And in London as a burnt out case, with the privilege of the seer through madness ...

Yes, it was going strong. His editor would soon have the basic book. But he noticed something that worried him greatly. Without John he tended to end up in the gay bars, places he'd have never gone before. Worse, he was being drawn to the "leather bars," as he said "to have a look." But it was more than that. One night as he was peeing in one of those "motorcycle bars," and suddenly a young man was on his knees beside him as he pissed. Young man saying "please, please," and opening his mouth. Yes, imploring York to piss in his mouth. York stared, the youngman on his knees begging York to piss in his face. Attractive young man, blond ... They ended up back in York's camper. "Master please hit my face ... my arse ... *Master*." It was York's first witting sado-masochistic experience. And as John said, he was no good at it, had no idea of what to do. Certainly wasn't excited by the event. Though the younguy said he "had the look." Of what? "A natural butch sado-Master!" It's what the little doctor had said in Marrakech – "Mephistophallic ... a butch of the brain, the best kind."

And the next day he walked the streets of the Old Quarter, muttering to himself – "What have I become? It isn't me. Yet I was in those bars ... pissing in that kid's mouth!" Was that what Doctor Mildred had wanted him to write about? He banged into a lamppost – "John, John, you've murdered me, you've cut my heart out and implanted your own."

Finally – it was the end of November – with his manuscript finished as much as could he returned to Toronto. Wanted his editor to read the material. Then go off for a break somewhere, anywhere, forget everything.

Yes, he stayed at the home of Shirley and Jane. They were glad to see him – "Your room was waiting," Jane said. "You're in much better shape now," Shirley said. They let him rest for two or three days. Meet with his editor, his publisher, one or two friends.

Then one morning they were both there over coffee as York came down. Shirley was knitting, something she rarely did early in the day. And coffee served, Jane looked at York quizzically – "guess what?"

York couldn't guess.

"I got a letter from John!"

Silence.

"He came in a couple of times when you were gone," Shirley said. "Into the bookstore, I mean."

York stared.

"Once with a girl," Jane smirked.

"Propped her up in front of us like a defensive shield," Shirley added.

"I don't know what he thought we were going to do, " Jane said.

"Eat her?" Shirley snapped.

"He was parading her," Jane went on. "Wanted us to know he was 'going out with girls now.'"

York groaned.

"Yes," Shirley nodded – "he did it so York would find out, that's what!"

"Well, I wouldn't eat a girl like that," Jane snapped.

"No-one asked you to," Shirley's knitting speeded up.

Silence.

"Then he came in by himself, about a week later," Jane said.

"I wasn't there," Shirley said.

"Just as well," Jane nodded.

What?

"He wanted to know where you were, York. And I said I didn't know."

Silence.

"He was probing," Jane went on. "I told him you were on a trip somewhere, made it as mysterious as I could."

"Which isn't very," Shirley grinned.

"Would you shut up," Jane snapped.

Shirley peered at her knitting.

"The point is," Jane said, "I had an idea ... "

"Any pain?" Shirley asked.

Jane glared, but continued – "I asked him about a former girl friend of mine ... "

"Platonic!" Shirley snapped.

"She's hetero," Jane said.

"That's her problem," Shirley grinned.

"Get serious," Jane retorted.

"Get to John's letter!" Shirley said.

"That's what I'm doing," Jane said.

Silence.

"The girl in question, Mary-Lou, happens to have many of the characteristics John has been revealing," Jane went on.

"She's a sadie-massie bitch!" Shirley snapped.

"That's what I'm saying," Jane glared.

"Well, stop beating around the bush," Shirley's knitting needles jumped.

Silence.

"What are you saying?" York finally asked.

"That Jane laid an ambush for John," Shirley said.

Jane nodded – "I realized I could find out John's attitudes to these characteristics ... "

"She means S-and-M," Shirley said.

"By asking him about Mary Lou," Jane said – "And that way I'd find out what he really feels about himself!"

"Bravo," Shirley grinned.

"You see," Jane ignored Shirley – "She's been going out with a guy we really like."

"You like," Shirley's needles rattled.

"And we want to help him ... "

"Why don't you just show York the letter?" Shirley snapped.

Jane nodded – "A few days after John's visit, I received this letter ... " She pulled the letter from her purse, held it up.

York flinched.

"We think you should read it," Jane said.

Shirley's needles went *click-clickety-click*, double time.

York sat stunned, longing to read the letter. Yet something warning him not. His spinal cord going tight, neck taut.

Jane sat holding the letter.

"What does it say?" York asked.

"I can't possibly explain," Jane said. "Best read it for yourself."

"Just skim it," Shirley tapped a needle. "Then we can discuss it."

York nodded, took the letter.

Yew Avenue
Toronto, Ontario
Sunday, Nov. 14, 1972

Dear Jane –

Just a note in apropos of our too-brief conversation last week. The conversation was too brief, our lunch too brief, but your doctored coffee made up. I enjoyed all of it. You asked me about your friend Mary-Lou. More exactly you asked my advice about Mary-Lou and her boyfriend. Said you felt they were a 'fine couple,' but that they were having difficulties. Could I help?

I have given some thought to their predicament. From what you told me the boyfriend is being much too defensive. Why should he defend himself against Mary-Lou's accusations that he's 'impractical" and 'a dreamer' etc? Any form of defensiveness is a wasted effort. One should either accept the attack levied, and levy against oneself with twice the vigor and knowledge of the accuser, or one should laugh the accuser in the face. No-one should ever feel obliged to defend themselves, least of all to oneself ... "

York groaned, thrust the letter away.

"Just skim it," Shirley said – "a bit at a time. You'll get the picture."

"Already have the picture," York said – "It's Doctor John, giving his advice to the psychiatrist."

What?

"Like he was with Doctor Mildred," York said.

"She got John's number," Jane snapped.

"Let York deal with the letter," Shirley said.

York glanced back at the letter: –

"At first I thought Mary-Lou's boyfriend had not laughed in her face because he was frightened of hurting her. And perhaps unsure of himself. It worried me that in his fear of hurting Mary-Lou he took on her charge (like electricity) of guilt. Which put him in the same position I put York into: cleansing a soul through dialogue (and in York's case, his diary). If that's what the boyfriend wants to do, okay. But I warn you that it is an adventure which – by taking on the cleansing of someone else's guilt – involved the boyfriend in a very pronounced Christ position. If you like being crucified, and I think 'in imitation of Christ' is perhaps the highest form of playing out one's masochism, then that's okay. There is nothing wrong or evil in it: only know it. If only to enjoy it more ... "

York closed his eyes.

"More coffee?" Jane asked.

York nodded – "Coffee and brandy!"

"It's only 10 a.m.," Jane said.

"Give him brandy!" Shirley snapped.

Armed with coffee and brandy York skimmed on in the letter: –

"The positive manner of describing the boyfriend's response to Mary-Lou would be 'a modest one.' The manner in which he handled Mary-Lou's accusations was certainly modest. It was also moderate and directly in the mainstream of Canadian tradition (Mainstream? It seems by the unconscious use of metaphor I really do think that there is a flow in Canadian tradition!!) This modest moderation is an admirable trait. It is perhaps even laudable. For example I think that the way you, Jane, modestly underestimate your own achievements is very beautiful. It is one of the things that make you attractive, even lovable. It leaves you approachable. It is one of the traits I like best in you, which I always marvel at, which I perhaps envy. And perhaps, therefore, be warned, want to destroy! ... "

York grabbed for his brandy.

"Don't read all of it," Shirley said, "just here and there."

"Don't drink too much brandy," Jane said.

"Shut up," Shirley snapped.

York peered back at the letter.

"Modesty is a trait that is directly in the mainstream of the Canadian tradition. And to continue the metaphor, it creates a whirlpool. The problem with modesty is that it obfuscates the fundamental exchange of sado-masochistic dynamics in the kind of relationship Mary-Lou has with her boyfriend. It is dangerous to the boyfriend if it covers over a subtly sado-masochistic relationship. And it is dangerous to Mary-Lou, for it would allow her to claim 'innocence' of any such dynamics existing between them. And after a period of several months, the boyfriend could charge her with 'destroying' him with her covert S-M. He could claim he was 'innocent' of the depth that her S-M would involve him in. And that Mary-Lou crucified him with it. The whirlpool is that his modesty would perpetrate an innocence (a false innocence, because self-perpetrated for its own conveniences) about his own desire to be Christed, that is his own masochism!"

York emptied his brandy.

"Not so quick," Jane said.

"He could be discussing me," York said.

"That's the point," Shirley flourished a needle.

Jane nodded.

York returned to the letter.

"You once said, Jane, that I had 'inverse reasoning.' York decried it as being my evil. Well, yes it is. It makes me laugh a little, in fact. The reasoning is inverse because there is an 'inversion' in every virtue. What you do about the situation with Mary-Lou and her guy I don't know. It's not in my position to make suggestions. I don't believe in it. It's not my responsibility. All I can do is give my interpretation of it. And interpretation, which, to use Nietzsche's phrase, goes 'beyond good and evil.' I wouldn't have analyzed it for you as S-M, except that 'form of analysis' – that dogma of interpretation – happens to be a form I have a certain expertise in diagnosing. And the situation of Mary-Lou and her guy, as described by you, certainly fits that dogma."

Shirley's knitting needles were click-clicking.

Jane was watching York.

York was gaping at the letter, reading parts, skipping parts.

"I think that for most people 'love is possible only through deception. The deception, which is imposed upon us by our culture, is that man – in himself –

does not want to become God. But the fact is man does want to become God – he wants to be omnipotent, omnipresent, etc. Most people leave behind this desire as 'childish,' and perhaps it is. But it is still very real, and the desire remains with us throughout life. The problem is that most people repress or sublimate this desire without ever honouring its reality. I guess that is what Nietzsche means when he talks about 'the will to power,' although I don't pretend to understand Nietzsche as much now, after reading 150 pages of him, as I did when I had only read a few of his quotes.

"But love is only successful when the will is limited ... "

York slammed the letter down.

Shirley said – "More brandy!"

Jane fetched more coffee.

" ... Love is a limiting of the will: it goes against a basic part of man's nature. Because man never accepts the reality of his will to power, he deceives himself, and his love is based on a deception. The art in life is to understand the deception, and laugh at the tension caused between the two desires. One either laughs or cries. Thus it is with a (tired) smile that I think of Mary-Lou's guy covering over his 'will to power' (All involvement in sado-masochism becomes, in the end, an expression of man's will to power)."

Silence.

York spluttered in his coffee.

Shirley's needles had come to a stop.

York skipped to the final page of the letter.

"It is with an aware chuckle that I send all this to you. I had wanted to talk about other things in this letter too. For example, Jane, your ability to work with books, and separately to read and contemplate them. I envy you that capacity. The whirlpool, or danger (if you will permit me to say so) is schizophrenia. The advantages are obvious ...

I had also wanted to talk with you a bit about my novel – how I was very aware that it was gone from my car, from my room, from my presence. You saw me bid it good-bye when I passed it to you. Well, I missed it, in its tattered grey box, after it was gone. Lots of other things are impatient to fill up the vacuum, however. I want to use the knowledge I got from it in the new areas."

"He gave it to me," Jan said – "Asked me if I'd give it an edit-reading ... " Yes, she'd been following where York was at in the letter. "And maybe find a publisher for him."

Click-clickety-click, Shirley's needles.

Crack-crackety-crash, York's brain.

"I want to repeat how much I enjoyed our conversation and lunch together. Our conversation unlocked my sense of morality, of what is 'worthy,' after almost a year-long 'freeze' of my sensibility. Not that I have been living in a moral vacuum for that time, but that I haven't had much gratuitous enjoyment of my moral sensibility: my pleasures have been more sensually obvious, like music, sun, exercise, movies. More in a word, material ...

I wanted to tell you as I was leaving your shop that I wanted to kiss you on the forehead. Obviously an urge for affection, not sex. Even if I felt a sexual desire towards you, I would never allow myself to honour it. (That's a whole other matter.) ...

Love,
John.

P.S. I'm going to hold off sending this letter to you until I check that York is still out of town. That will prevent you from being over-loaded with 'input' from both York and me.

P.P.S. I hope my comments about Mary-Lou and her guy have been helpful. If you want to talk further about it please feel free to phone me at work."

* * *

York set the letter down as if bitten by a mad dog.

"Congratulations," Shirley said.

What?

"You read quite a chunk of it," she said.

Read, skimmed, glanced, it didn't matter. From the moment he'd seen the opening paragraphs, the "Big Daddy" memo tone, and got as far as "nobody should ever feel obliged to defend themselves," York had known what the letter was. It was John defending himself, under whatever pretext.

And by the time he'd hit the phrase "brutal ruthlessness," and skated on as far as the comment about "envy" of Jane's modesty which he therefore might want to destroy ... by then York was ready to stop – which he did when he came to the piece about "inverse reasoning."

He didn't need any more. And it was only the patience and cajoling of Jane and Shirley that got him through the whole thing.

"You had to know about it," Jane said, as York set the letter down.

"And we knew we both should be here while you read it," Shirley added.

Silence.

"So what do you think," Jane asked.

York groaned – "Don't you see, for every positive assertion there's a sudden turnabout, a whirligig. It's ... it's like a backhanded confession!"

Clickety-click – Shirley's knitting needles again.

"It's the whole bloody bird," York said – "in a few pages. Anywhere you look ..."

Jane was pouring herself a brandy.

"It's what Dr. Mildred said ... "

What?

"Said John would erupt within a month ... And here it is!"

What is?

"John's confessed himself!" York said.

"It's a pile of intellectual nonsense," Jane said.

"That's not the point," York snapped – "Don't read what the goddamned letter says, it all refutes itself anyway. Read under the lines, between them, read the asides, the parentheses. That's John, what he's really presenting ... "

Clickety-click.

"I did read it with care," Jane said – "I can see it jumps, jerks, shunts ... "

"Busy smelling its own farts," Shirley snorted.

"And it's clear he took the ambush," Jane said.

What?

"Well, its clear he analyses Mary-Lou and her guy as himself and yourself, no?"

Silence.

"Reread that bit about a subtly sadomasochistic relationship," Jane said, pointing to the letter.

"I can't," York blurted – "I'll go insane!"

"Exactly," Jane said – "my ambush worked – he's describing your relationship ... "

Clickety-click.

"It's the letter of an invert," York finally said. "Not just inverse reasoning, but inverse being. Presenting itself for approval and power ... "

"It's perverse!" Shirley snapped.

"So far so good," York said.

What?

"Do you remember John's comment weeks ago, right here in this house, to you?

Jane blinked.

"He said – 'I reject York's negative analysis of me, with himself as the only solution' ... "

Jane nodded – "Yes, he seemed very proud of that statement. Repeated it several times."

"Well," York said, "how right is my negative analysis now?"

"He declares he's an invert!" Jane said.

"And then he laughs," York said – "And the laugh isn't one of joy or delight. It's hate ... "

Shirley announced it was time for some toast.

Jane got more coffee.

"That's what it is," York blurted.

What?

"It's an inner photo of John's being. A psychograph!" York said.

Jane took the letter and peered at it.

"It's in the style of it," York said. "If you pay attention to the ideas you think he may be saying something. But if you follow the style ... "

"If you follow the style," Shirley nodded, "you feel sick!"

Jane pursed her lips – "Yep, it's a smirk. An 'I'm smarter than all you put together' smirk."

"That's what I told you when it first came and you read it," Shirley snapped.

"Weel, I can see that now," Jane said.

"And the self-pity," Shirley said.

What?

"That 'tired smile' he mentions," Shirley said.

"And the weird combination," Jane said, of his 'will to power' and a pretty obvious request for my approval, my blessings."

"So you're beginning to understand," Shirley grinned.

"Now look," Jane snapped – "I was smart enough to set the ambush."

"Do you remember the night," York said, "that John wanted to give me his blessing, upstairs in bed?"

Jane nodded.

"But what he was really after was my blessing … "

"Kill York then get his blessing," Shirley said – "That was the programme."

Silence.

"The truth is that there's no relationship between mind and emotions in that letter," Shirley went on – "It's plain straight schitzy."

"But there are the ideas," Jane said.

"Uses schitziness to hold up a front of ideas," Shirley snorted.

"Willed schitziness," York blurted – "schitztrickiness."

What?

"Using schizophrenia as a toll in the will-to-power he talks of," York said.

"It isn't just split in two," Shirley said – "it's smithereens … "

The phone rang. Jane answered – "Oh, hi John – yeah, I got your letter … "

Shirley dropped her knitting.

York stared at the phone as at a rattlesnake.

"Yes," Jane said – "I think you really got the nub of it. The whole Mary-Lou thing with her guy. Yeah, it's clearly a subtly sado-masochistic thing … You think Mary-Lou knows what she's doing? Yeah … Well, of course it's for control … "

They could hear John laughing over the phone. Shirley hissed. York closed his eyes.

"Yeah," Jane said – "Shirley and I both thought you'd given a lot of thought to the letter. A week? Yeah … we're grateful … Yes, you should keep a copy … "

Shirley was about to hiss again. Jane held up her hand to prevent this.

York put his hands over his ears, and fled the room.

When he came back some minutes later Jane was just hanging up. And Shirley was … hissing!

"What in God's name did he want?" York asked.

"To be told his letter was the eighth wonder of the world," Shirley said.

"Well, it is," York said – "but not in the way he thinks."

"He wants to come and see me again," Jane said – "He presumed you were still away. I said no, you were staying with me for a few days now … "

"What did he say to that?" York asked.

"He talked on about nothing for a moment," Jane paused – "And then his whole conversation fell to pieces."

"He began to stammer," Shirley said, "I could hear it."

"He said he thought you'd gone to Mexico," Jane said.

"Now he knows you've seen the letter," Shirley grinned.

"Did he ask?" York said.

"No," Jane said, "he mumbled something, then was clearly afraid to ask."

Shirley laughed – "You two guys are on some kind of intersecting wave-length, with death as the daily double."

Silence.

"It's clear he realizes that you'll know what the letter is," Jane said.

"And it's clear he fears that," Shirley added.

"Then he knows," York said – "knows that the entire letter is a confession, a backasswards confession coming on as God-the-Father. Knows it's John defending John to you … "

Why?

"Because he couldn't defend himself to me," York said – "There was no defense, just mounting cynicism. And here, in this letter, it's a black credo … "

"Posing as candy," Shirley grinned.

"What are you going to do?" Jane asked.

York pondered – "The first thing is this letter frees me!"

What?

"It's John's psychic head on a platter," York nodded – "It confirms everything Dr. Mildred has said. Could you ever write a letter like that?"

"I'd have to be insane," Jane said.

"Is John insane?" York asked.

Shirley shook her head – "He knows too much. His own word in the letter, he's 'cogent' about it all. Using it all."

"Including using you and Jane!"

Silence.

"If he's not insane," York went on, "and he's doing what he's doing, and using everyone in the process, and peddling pain as the payoff … what is he?"

"An asshole," Jane snorted.

"Evil," Shirley said.

"Well, let me show you something," York said – "I've been reworking my novel. It's in my briefcase." He disappeared and quick back – "Here, read that … "

Jane took the pages.

"That paragraph there," York pointed.

"It's beautiful," she said, "the sense of joy, then … " she paused – "he confesses!"

"Confesses what?" Shirley snorted.

"That some deep-rooted evil in him erupts, destroys their love … "

"Exactly," York said. "It was a letter to me when I was in London."

Jane passed the letter to Shirley.

"I got three like that," York said. "All beautiful, loving … "

Jane nodded – "I read them, when I read your manuscript. They were full of love."

"He glosses over the evil in one of the lines here," Shirley pointed a knitting needle as if to impale.

"Well," York said, "there were those three letters. And now the letter to Jane …"

What?

"In effect," York said, "it is the Fourth Letter from John! The one he never wrote me ... "

Silence.

"It was the one I suspected, all through my time in Morocco. There between the lines. And his three loving letters hoodwinked me completely!"

"Siren letters," Shirley said.

What?

"His letters as a Siren song, calling you home," she nodded, "for more of the same."

"So you knew about John's evil?" Jane asked.

York nodded – "But I couldn't really believe it. But I knew, in Marrakech. And I knew on the trip into the desert ... I nearly died."

Silence.

"I nearly died John's death for him. And I knew ... I knew as James danced in the flames."

Clickety-clickety-click.

"And I knew up at Demnat, at the Sheikh's place. And as I fell down the gorge near Demnat ... I lost one of John's letters there!"

Silence.

"And I knew because of Kebir. Because of Keb's natural goodness ... "

"Who's Kebir?" Shirley asked.

"York's friend in Marrakech," Jane said.

"I knew from the way Keb walked, the flow of his pace ... "

Knew what?

"There was something blocked in John, some kind of disjunction there ... "

"And then the evil would erupt," Shirley said.

York nodded – "It all kept hitting me in the face, in Marrakech. A couple of dreams I had there. It all flooded to the surface. But I crushed it. John's letters seemed to go beyond all that. So did my love, our love ... I simply didn't want to know."

"It's weird," Jane said. "Like perfidy, I mean perfidy practiced for the pleasure of it."

"That's what Doctor Mildred said ... "

What?

"She said once you spot the perfidy you can call the sequence," York paused – "Perfidy, perjury, profligacy, debauch and depravity."

Click-clickety-click.

"He all but murdered you, York. All but ... " It was Jane.

"Voodoo," Shirley muttered. "psychic voodoo."

"I believe I've grasped that," York said, "at last!"

"John wanted me complicit in that murder," Jane said.

"Of course," Shirley said, "It all follows on beautifully!"

Silence.

"Dr. Mildred said I'd know within a month. That John would erupt within a month ... And here it is, this letter. Clear confirmation." York pointed at the letter

– "It's covert self-accusation masquerading as morality ... "

"There's more to it than that," Jane protested.

York shook his head – "It's Evil, presenting itself as a blessing. And upheld by the conventional goodness of the entire nation."

What?

"Modern Canada absolves John, you know! All Trudeauland absolves him. This letter is just his declaration of Canadian psychic citizenship. He's joined the All Canadian Club. Said so himself."

What?

"Said 'they all do it, York'!"

Jane didn't understand.

"Like Timsen," York said – "his first wife burnt herself to death ... said she was sending a message to Timsen."

Jane blinked.

"Perfidy, perjury, profligacy ... complete covert psychic debauch," York said, "over the dead body of your mate!"

Clickety-click.

"Like Madeleine Wert and her new boy-friend," York nodded – "Perfecting the national perjury, it makes a fine career."

Silence.

"It's not that they plagiarize each other, its that they plagiarize life, rendering it false, a plausibility ... "

"You're getting that look in your eye," Jane said.

What?

"Your eye is starting to whirl," she said.

"John's whirligig," Shirley snapped.

York nodded – "I read too much of the letter. It hits the head. Murders the heart. And that's the worst. I love him. And he's murdered again. Double murder. What the Minister said ... "

Who?

"A United Church Minister down near Belleville. Said John is murdering himself by murdering our love," York paused – "And I can't stop him. And a whole nation will applaud his honesty, his will to decency, and pay him well ... "

* * *

Next morning Jane and Shirley were waiting over coffee for York again.

"York, I think you should read that letter right through, calmly, with us." It was Jane.

"An act of exorcism," Shirley said.

"We'll discuss the letter to shreds," Jane said. "It's pure nonsense, you know. I studied it last night. It's bad Nietzsche and bad everything."

Shirley nodded.

York shook his head – "Little Hitler, and his will-to-power! And fifty million died. And five million were actually burnt in ovens!"

What?

"This letter is the same thing. And I'm going to deal with it – but not by reading it again. That would merely slaughter my mind."

What?

"I'd be drawn into John's nervous system again, and that's murder. I have to cope with something much more important than that letter. The evil ... Shirley's right, John glossed over it. But I remembered something last night abed. A sentence of John's, after one of his explosions of hate. He said, with immense pleasure – "It's going to get much worse, York, that's my Christmas present to you!"

Silence.

"It triggered something in my eye," York said – "Do you remember those three posters I told you about in John's bedroom here in Toronto?"

Jane nodded – "I actually saw them!"

What?

"I went to see John there. I didn't tell Shirley ... "

"There's a lot you don't tell me," Shirley snapped.

"Well, those posters are it!" York said.

What?

"They're a visual paradigm of that letter to Jane," York said.

Silence.

"Absolutely," York said. "Superman and 'the will to power.' And that motorcycle guy with his bitch-moll and her flameout ... that's the 'brutal ruthlessness.' And the butts along the beach is the whole backasswardness of John and his letter ... "

"There's a fourth one now," Jane said.

What?

"He's got a fourth poster up now – a Hell's Angel one, complete with chains, razor blades and ... "

Shirley grabbed for her knitting.

"It's all one and the same thing," York said. "And I knew the truth of it the moment I first arrived in his sweet little attic room there. All so clean and innocent, outwardly. But those posters, and his poem and ... "

Clickety-click-click.

"Do you remember my visit to London?"

Jane nodded – "It's all in your manuscript."

"Do you remember Patrick?"

"Yes," Jane said – "The S-M club guy."

"Now I know why that evening carried me to the verge of insanity."

"Patrick could be the guy in John's new poster," Jane interjected.

York nodded – "I knew it all then, that night in London. Evidence incarnate ... "

Silence.

"I haven't told you what happened to me in Montréal recently ... finding myself drawn to the gay leather bars."

"S-and-M?" Shirley asked.

York nodded.

"But that's not like you at all," Jane said. "You're a birds and garden guy ... "

Clickety-click.

"The little doctor warned me in Marrakech. Said I look so 'mephistophallic.'"

Shirley laughed – "You're our Yo-Yo, that's what you are!"

Jane glared.

"And my wife ... she was the same kind as John. Doctor Mildred yanked that recognition out of me."

"Your mind is skipping," Jane said.

"Maybe, but I've got all the data I require. I've got to write ... "

"York, you've got to rest. Go away, out of the country, and recuperate."

Silence.

"We've got the money. For your next book. And your friends ... "

Silence.

"You've got to get away from John's tentacles," Jane said.

"Hex, voodoo, exorcism and blood sacrifice," Shirley said – "isn't that enough?"

"I've got to write something first, or I'll go insane," York said. "The bedroom upstairs, it has it's own small washroom, it's own view over the park."

Jane nodded.

"And the door to it has a key, I checked."

What?

"It locks!" York said.

Yes.

"I want you to lock me in."

Clickety-click.

"From the outside. For several days. Don't let me out even if I ask.

???

"Sandwiches and milk and lots of coffee – please!"

"Look, York ... I mean how do we know what you're doing in there?" It was Jane.

"He'll be doing what he should've done long ago," Shirley said.

The Long Walk
Dear Reader –

It's been a long walk. That's what it feels like. Some forty years of it. Say since my tumultuous high society marriage (its own auto da fé) in Toronto way back in 1958.

Just a helluva long walk. Or great trek in psychic covered wagon fending off the furies, banshees and my own failings.

Have I accomplished much of what I set out to do? Yes. Often despite myself and whatever cowardice any and all of us carry. And sometimes equally (I believe I dare say it now) because of a crazy courage.

What did I set out to do? I don't fully now know. Certainly there was no plan, no blueprint, much less any academic outline for it all. But as I look back over "forty years" spent variously in desert, deep forest, psychic hurricane, or joys of garden, birds, and the eyes of others, there emerges an organic unity to my life.

In particular as I contemplate the anthology quarried by Christopher Elson out of my life's writings and witnessing I detect a pervasive common denominator, that of "God's Fool" as Nik Sheehan's recent film billed me. Or that of Socratic gadfly, to use a simpler term.

I think that "witnessing" is the right term for much of my writing. I was bearing witness as much as describing. Enacting more than merely reporting. Singing, in woe as in joy, more than talking. And not infrequently chanting, ongoing plainsong of life as murmured by a secular if thoroughly botched saint. I mean this last in the sense we are all saints, as all sinners: all willy-nilly questing the good even as we contrive to wallow in the mud.

What, you may ask, were some of the great moments of my life?

One was my Confirmation at age fourteen by Archbishop Derwyn Owen, a truly holy man and prelate in fine sense of that term. But it took me decades to realize the huge importance of that event in my life. Nor have I ever adequately lived up to it. Simply been hounded by its meanings, as I think my notes written over the years during Holy Communion at St. Thomas's Church in Toronto must show.

And seeing beauty – literally smitten by beauty in its multitude forms. Certain birds (a Quetzal while walking with my brave lover John, high in the mountains of southern Mexico in 1968). And certain objets d'art, furnishings from the past. Thus the Great Bed of Ware (group grope for Elizabethans if ever!). Or a carved eighteenth century Québec Altar by Baillargé, hosting the body of God. Or the Raphael Cartoons in the V & A in London, which quickened my faith even before I knew. Above all, certain people, faces, what I term "eyes."

I'm confident my first sighting of the Monastery of Melk, high over the Danube, enlarged what I dare call my soul.

I know some moments with my lost wife remain forever in my heart. We were "soul-mates." And will meet again in another world. It will be joy.

Some sexual and erotic moments are forever, and my life and diary speak more than enough of these.

Learning the French language constitutes a "great moment," in the prolonged sense, for me. Certainly the French language, via Québec, set me free. Liberating me from the straitjacket of Protestant English-speaking Canada.

Need I say that my own nation, Canada, gave me moments and memories of pride. Vimy, and Canadian pilots in the Battle of Britain, and the RCN in the Battle of the Atlantic, stand high! "In Flanders Fields" says much and for all of us. Dare we continue to forget?

Not least some few teachers remain always with me. I could not have survived my long trek without them. Donald Creighton who gave new voice and presence to the founder of Canada (we had forgotten him, too!). And F.R. Leavis who gave new bearings to English-speaking culture and was often pilloried for it. And the beloved Gabriel Marcel who simply called my wife "la princesse." I came to know these men much better than I deserved. But the greatest influences in my life have been, and still are, three women. St. Teresa of Avila whose Interior Château walked with me. And my adored Simone Weil (I spent an evening in 1959 with her protector, Gustave Thibon, but little knew ...). And the Emily Bronte who inhabits *Wuthering Heights*. To me her line – "I am Heathcliff" – is the most startling, staggering line in all Englit. The French have been clever enough to know (and titillate themselves with) wickedness. But with Bronte's book the English recovered rendezvous with evil.

Of what I wrote over the years, my diaries, my insatiable diaries represent the most intimate by far. Through them others will know me the way they might best have known themselves. But my letters – harvest of both trek and exile – are my greatest sharing. In particular some forty years of letters between my dearest and lifelong friend, Charles Taylor (he of the Breeders' Cup and *Six Journeys*), and myself. I remain obdurately proud of a large piece I wrote about him after his death – itself conceived and written as final letter to him. In it I portrayed the Charles I knew and loved. And in my heart set him free, presenting him to a national public.

Of my books, my favourite remains *Civic Square*. Originally entitled *The Smugly Fucklings* (my publisher demurred!), it is, as you know, truly a series of letters to ... Dear Reader. Blatantly so.

Whereas *Heritage: A Romantic Look at Early Canadian Furniture* is an unstinted song of love to a culture and a nation, at one hail and understood farewell. Irving Layton insisted on calling it "Scott's Furniture Novel." And Leonard Cohen described it as "very cunning – it masquerades as a coffee-table book." They understood ...

As for the media, my work there variously 1957 through to the 90s, it was for me a way of looking, and not a way of life. And over time I came to fear the incredible damage the media could do to a society. Responsible to no-one except their own vanity and next hurrah.

It could be said I've been a jack-of-all-trades – journalist, novelist, professor, curator, controversialist and even bad boy – and master of none. In fact I was never interested in any trade as such.

My interest was life itself.

What do I regret most?

Firstly, I assure you I have no regrets, much less any self-pity. Life is bigger, grander, more wondrous than any of my little concerns. Though like Winston Churchill I'm rather glad one only has to live it the once.

However, secondly, I can regret that I didn't do, live, all I finally did ... sooner. But I was comfortable, and selfish and afraid. I kept wondering why the hell someone else didn't do the necessary. No-one did, not in my culture. So my forty-year trek started. And my heart is glad for it.

I recently, this winter past, spent three months in my home city of Toronto. I was aware it might be my final major visit. And I took a good look. I don't conceal I was shaken by what I saw. An insensately greedy city. And with all its woes (more like endless whining and complaints), a curiously complacent, even self-congratulatory one. I decided that I was looking at a metropolis that had lost its destiny. That it had sold out in profound if surreptitious ways. Easy to say that it had gone American. But the situation went deeper than that.

Toronto was born with a mission for quality in North America, quality of life and being, as well as of doing. The lives, letters and sermons, the architecture, town plans and debates – not to mention the fury of quarrels! – of the first fifty years of York- Toronto amply indicate this. Toronto never saw itself as, nor could ever become, just another North American city – not without doing violence to itself.

But now such high mission seems to have collapsed into a grab for money and place: perqs, place, and careers gone amok is how I summed it up to myself. Everything seems perjured to that end. No-one is likely to admit this, or if did would be considered someone who had failed and was ... complaining about it!

This collapse in what I term Toronto's "mission for quality" has scarcely taken place overnight. It's long been creeping up on us. A subtle erosion of all our deeper meanings, loyalties, and beliefs. It's within many a living memory that Toronto was "the city of churches" with an avid and practiced (if sometimes staid)

Christianity. Most Torontonians had a loyalty to and affection for the Crown as fundamental to the very founding of the Province of Ontario. And Toronto's courtesy was a trademark remarked on by almost every visitor from the United States.

Now Toronto could be described as agnostic by default, republican by attrition, and smartass by defiance (its own form of envy and guilt!). Bizarre inversion of its founding values – everything inside out and upside down. De facto revolution that would never, at particular points along the way, have been endorsed by its citizens.

It is not my intention here to look for culprits – it could be said we've all variously been complicit or at least acquiescent. The deeper and more important issue is the consequences. In the bizarre and even diligent process of the erosion of our founding traditions and values, what was destroyed was nothing so debatable as "church, Crown, and courtesy" (to oversimplify), but our very capacity for allegiances, loyalties, and emotional attachments of any kind. Not to mention the forthright ability to approach a fellow citizen in a decent manner.

What we have been left with is, understandably, a vacuum, a psychic, emotional, and spiritual vacuum, showing a pervasive if covert fear.

During my time in Toronto I encountered this everywhere. People fearful for jobs, place, acquired perqs, or just the remnants of their sanity. So fearful that politeness was making a large comeback. Politeness not as presence of deep Canadian tradition, alas, but of will to survive.

Indeed one Toronto pooh-bah who made early career out of facile demolition of many of our roots and traditions had recently converted to the need for such. No-one seems to have remarked on his astonishing if wonderfully convenient volte face.

As I registered all this day by day it struck me I was looking at a new form of porn. No, not sexual porn – though God knows the new sexual frontier is currently S-and-M, predicate of the collapse of Eros, plus the surge in will to control. But psychic porn. Porn as result of emotional vacuum. Porn not as option in the current situation, but as fait accompli.

Said otherwise, the long slow betrayal of Toronto's "high mission" has led to a vacuum that is a form of impotence of life. And all new power occurs within this.

I wish this letter could have been different, Dear Reader. More of joy, less of self-evident horror. More of celebration and Alleluia. More like my best insight recently in Toronto: that prayer is something you are in, not something you do! Insight that just floated up as I was walking down Church Street one wintry afternoon.

But it is time to close.

What have I been proudest of in my life? That I have been, I believe, one of what the French term "les libérateurs de l'amour." That and the fact that I didn't settle for money, place, title (Canada boasts an elaborate system of titles, or more exactly sub-titles – honorary doctorates by the bushel, Senators with lifetime title, Honorable and Right Honorable this-and-thats, et.al.), nor mere comfort. All were more than available to me, had I just shut up. But I couldn't shut up. Too much I honoured and loved was being destroyed, covertly and consistently. So I took "the long walk," forty years of it. Often alone, but never lonely.

This year I am sixty-five. I may even receive an old-age pension for my sins – compensation for a culture destroyed? One thing is sure. It is easy to live a flaming youth. And many I know who did are long dead, violently dead. And middle age is something we endure, ultimate haven of a bourgeois society: but it is then that the hard work is done. Old age is the most difficult of all. Call it, for kindness, "sunset time." But a great sunset in life is the most wonderful exploit of all. We all know men and women who achieved this in our era. I think Morgan Forster was one. And Julien Greene. Eleanor Roosevelt was another.

Perhaps I'll manage a great sunset. I'll try. But of this I am sure – I won't die pewling in a senile bed. I quest the right death. The given death. It will find me. I'll be ready, and I'll smile ... *nunc dimittus.*

What do I hope most for you? No, not happiness, that noisy American reduction of life. But joy, life as *sursum corde* – a lifting up of your heart. Life as the thinking heart, Dear Reader. That's where the adventure lies. All the rest is income tax and footnotes.

This final letter prays for you, as I hope your very reading of it does for me.

Love,

Scott Symons
Essaouira, Morocco, summer 1998

NOTES TOWARD A CV BY SCOTT SYMONS

BORN

... in Toronto (Canada), July 13, 1933 – midway between Orangeman's Day and Bastille Day – of what was then proudly known as Loyalist stock. His mother in later years informed him he was conceived after a Tattoo ball at RMC in a room at the old Loyalist Hotel in Kingston.

Son of Major Harry Symons, author and winner of the first Stephen Leacock Award for Humour. Grandson of Wm. Limberry Symons, founder of the Ontario Society of Architects, architect of the old Union Station and many of the earlier houses of Rosedale.

Maternal grandfather, William Perkins Bull, author, chum of George V and rogue male. Member of the Mark Twain Society (the election committee included Compton MacKenzie, Stephen Leacock, Winston Churchill and Booth Tarkington).

Perforce Scott grew up with a sense of history, place and roots. And failed to understand those who didn't.

Married once (said that was enough) and one son.

EDUCATION

... at home with five brothers, one sister, one wonderful War Guest uncle. High Rosedale home with an ancient Bible in every room (some weighing up to 20 pounds) & a library of several thousand volumes – strong in Englit and poetry, the classics, & classical mythology.

Comic books were forbidden! And Scott found himself reading Plutarch by the age of twelve.

What interested him most (beyond Robin Hood & King Arthur & Grettir the Strong) was a huge copy of Dante's *Inferno* lavishly illustrated by Gustave Doré – all those voluptuous intertwined naked bodies!

At Trinity College School, Port Hope 1946-50 – an Anglican school, echoing Benedictine rule (diffusely). It was bulgingly and smugly jock. But there Scott met his lifelong friend Charles Taylor (he of *Six Journeys, Radical Tories* & The Breeder's Cup).

At U.T.S., Toronto, for Senior Matric, 1950-51 – here he encountered serious minds and his first "intellectuals": no lives were lost.

At Trinity College in the University of Toronto, 1951-55. B.A in Modern History with Frank Underhill, Donald Creighton & Maurice Careless as tutors. He represented his college on the University Student's Council, & won various scholarships including one to Cambridge University. But did not attend his own graduation day, had better things to do.

Was a member, like his father & brothers, of Zeta Psi Fraternity (this was before fraternities were sneered at). And proud that Colonel John McCrae (Toronto) & Stephen Leacock (Montréal) had been members before him.

Served in the U.N.T.D. (originally called Canadian University Naval Training programme, and the cadets thus called CUNTS, but the name was hastily changed). Had to be the worst and least pusser officer cadet they'd ever seen. Was nicknamed "horizontal Symons" because always sleeping.

At King's College, Cambridge, 1955-57. Gentleman's B.A./M.A. in Englit, with F.R. Leavis, Doris Krook (*Three Traditions of Moral Thought*), & Basil Willey (*The Seventeenth Century Mind*), as tutors. Real education in King's College Chapel at Evensong, through the choral music more than the words. And at the Fitzwilliam Museum (amazing porcelain collection and that portrait of Launcelot Andrews and Wife by Gainsborough: tutorials with Michael Jaffé there).

Informed a college don that you could know all about a culture through a period stairwell. The don was not impressed.

At the Sorbonne 1959-60. Diplôme d'Études supérieures.

Tutorials at the home of Gabriel Marcel. Strongly influenced by the Malraux of *Les Voix du Silence* & *Le Musee Imaginaire*. As by E.V. Rieu's five-volume history of iconography. As by the Paris & France of President de Gaulle.

Worked with his wife in the wine harvests at Château Palmer (Bordeaux).

JOURNALIZM (sic) & THE MEDIA

1957-58 – assistant in the editorial department of the *Toronto Telegram*. Then offered reporter's post at Queen's Park, but declined – was too busy getting married. Then asked by Editor to do a report on *Telegram*'s editorial policy since 1900. The report was declared brilliant and Scott was promptly sacked for insubordination and told he had no future in the media.

1958-59 – reporter & editorial writer, *Chronicle Telegraph*, Québec City. Started serious study of French. And noted first rumblings of the Québec Quiet Revolution (e.g. via editorials by André Laurendeau, Jean-Louis Gagnon, et al).

Took to collecting Quebec Canadiana – in particular rooster weathervanes. Was shot at by irate farmer while stealing one on a cold winter's night in St. Georges de Beauce: fortunately his wife had the getaway car ready!

1960-61 – reporter & columnist, *La Presse* of Montréal. Won National Newspaper Award & Montréal Men's Press Club Award, for series on the French Canadian Revolution. Written in French, Scott then translated it into English. It was turned down by over ten English Canadian newspapers as "irrelevant," unnewsworthy, etc. Finally taken by Gratten O'Leary's *Ottawa Journal*.

Trudeau at a party in Scott's Montréal apartment on Pine Avenue looked around & exclaimed "But you have more French Canadiana than we do!"

Laurendeau invited Scott and his wife to family Christmas réveillon. And asked Scott to join *Le Devoir*.

La Société St.-Jean Baptiste elected Scott an honorary member – first Protestant so asked.

1979 – national series on Canada for the *Globe and Mail*. The series ran simultaneously in French in *La Presse*, Montréal. The Editor of the *Globe* told Scott it was the most widely read series of the decade, and that every journalist at the *Globe* now hated him. He was right!

1980-81 – co-host and co-writer with Mary Kay Ross for 26-programme series about Ontario, for TVO. Shown many times.

Etc. (including interviews in Mexico City with Octavio Paz – he said Eros was the most important thing in life – and Lopez Portillo, President of Mexico, who said ditto.)

ACADEMICITY & CURATORIAL

1961-65 – Royal Ontario Museum (Toronto) as curatorial assistant (under George Spendlove, one of the few genuine gurus Canada has ever produced), then curator in charge of the Canadiana Collections. Came to the conclusion that Canadian history as written by most profs was a provincial version of the Whig Interpretation of history (Scott referred to this version as "barnyard Whig"). But early Canadian furniture told a very different story. Scott concluded that "furniture doesn't lie" about the meanings, intentions & aspirations of a people over time. And that Canadian history needed rewriting. He was fired for insubordination (after telling the Director he was a eunuch). The Canadiana Department itself was later abolished.

1964 – Visiting prof in the Graduate School (American Civilization courses), University of Pennsylvania, Philadelphia.

NOTES TOWARD A CV BY SCOTT SYMONS

– Research Associate, Winterthur Museum, Wilmington, Delaware.

– Visiting curator at the Smithsonian Institution (was asked to join the staff permanently but declined – said he had a rendezvous with Canada's centennial year to cope with).

1976 – Writer-in-Residence, Simon Fraser University, then taught in Creative Writing. It was then he wrote his review of Marion Engel's novel *Bear* for *The West Coast Review*. He declined writing the review several times. Finally wrote it under pressure from the *Review*'s editor. And was promptly excommunicated from CanLit.

BOOKS

Place d'Armes, 1967 (Scott's "rendezvous with Canada's Centennial"!) It won a best First Canadian novel award. Scott was hiding with his lover in the mountains of southern Mexico at the time as about five sets of police were hunting him as the author of a "pornographic novel." He finally obtained a safe conduct out of Mexico from the Canadian Embassy to return to Toronto to receive the award.

Civic Square (alias The Smugly Fucklings), 1969.

Heritage: A Romantic Look at Early Canadian Furniture (with photography by John de Visser and a preface by George Grant), 1971.

Helmet of Flesh, 1986.

(All published by what was then McClelland & Stewart.)

Helmet of Flesh was superbly translated into French by Michel Gaulin – 1997, *Québec-Amerique*
New American Library edition (with Canadian-interest elements expunged), 1988.

TREKS, WANDER YEARS, & WORK

After being fired by the R.O.M., and the noisy advent of *Place d'Armes*, Scott lived, travelled, & worked variously in:

1) the northern B.C. bush, including work in lumbercamps, oysterpicking etc. – 1968-69.

And again, 1976, lived in the bush, outside Terrace, working on his *Helmet of Flesh* trilogy. Didn't enjoy the proximity of grizzlies, but did enjoy the trumpeter swans.

2) the Newfoundland fishing village of Trout River, 1969-70, which he and his lover John adored. Wrote much of his furniture book there. And frequented the Salvation Army Citadel. Was asked to give sermons there. The Lieutenant of the Sally Ann named his new son after Scott.

3) Mexico, variously, throughout the 1970s. Mostly in San Miguel de Allende. Worked on *Helmet of Flesh*. And taught at, finally Writer-in-Residence at, the P.E.N school there. Became close friend of York Wilson, Leonard Brooks and Fred Powell. Wilson read *Place d'Armes* and said, "You write with a painter's eye."

4) Morocco. After an initial visit in 1971, he returned there in 1973 for two years. Living first in Tangiers, becoming a friend of Paul Bowles who said, "You are a strange novelist, you talk like a poet and act like a priest." Then in Marrakech. Finally in Essaouira-Mogador where he met his current lover, Aaron.

5) Toronto, 1979-81, working in the media and editing *Helmet of Flesh* which by then, under the masterly eye of Dennis Lee, had become a full trilogy of novels.

6) Rasoir from 1982 to the present, a goat hamlet 12 kilometres outside Essaouira. The peasant world of Chaucer, Rabelais and ... just a touch of Genghis Khan! Will Scarlet, Little John, and Mitch the Miller's son are visible every day. So is Loki! Home a Berber stone farmhouse, influenced by early Roman villas. It was inhabited by goats when Scott first arrived. No radio, TV, running water or electricity. But just recently a phone (which doesn't work!). Much work on trilogy, anthology, and films. Much peace ...

7) Toronto. Many returns for bread – 1983, '85, '86, '91, '96, '97 ... In 1989, in Toronto for a year. But no media jobs available for Scott (he was presumably unqualified!).

OTHER

1) A copious diary, begun in 1957-58 (the equivalent of some 50 volumes of *Helmet of Flesh*). From 1968 to the present these diaries were acquired and housed by the Trinity College Archives.

2) At one point (early 90s) he became de facto, what Jane Rule (enviously) referred to as "Writer-in-Residence" for *The Idler*, Toronto. Writing pieces that no other Canadian outlet would touch. Thus his piece on Dr. Margaret Atwood, C.C., etc.

3) In 1994, filmmaker Nik Sheehan cast up in Essaouira, with camera and crew, to film Scott for a part in *Symposium*, his update of Plato. This went on to become a film on Scott's life, *God's Fool* (premiere at Art Gallery of Ontario, 1997). Film described as more iconoclastic than Scott himself.

4) In 1995, Christopher Elson arrived in Essaouira to tape Scott. This terminated as an anthology, published by Gutter Press in 1998.

5) Hobby – trying to stay alive.

6) Favorite pipedream – that Canada should annex Greenland.

7) Secret Hope – to have known something about the chivalric.

8) Being a Beggar – at no time after *Place d'Armes* did Scott have any money, contrary to his reputation as "the boy from Rosedale." He lived by his wits and his words ... and by begging for money. Sometimes successfully, sometimes not. But he never ceased writing.

9) Honours, titles, doctorates, CanCow sponge tours, sinecures-and-tenures – none: a clean record.

10) Theology – a de facto Roman Catholic who remains within the Anglican tradition. Huge admiration for Pope John-Paul II (despite the fact that said Pope states people like Scott will burn in Hell). Hates what Cranmer did to the Anglican Prayer Book. And loves the Curé d'Ars. Church – St. Thomas's, Huron Street, Toronto, 1960s to the present.

11) Favourite suspicion – that a large part of his life was embezzled by the Canadian Identity Squad. And that writing career CV's may well be part of this.

12) Morocco – the role of Morocco in Scott's life (1971 to the present) has been large. It gave him hearth & haven. Allowing him to take his stand, hang tough, and bear witness. Armed with fluent French (Morocco is part of La Francophonie!) he could live joy (much), sustain his rooted Canadian meanings intact, and ... grow. What he loves in Moroccans is their sense of dance, music and the pipes of Pan. And their incredible smiles ...

BIBLIOGRAPHY

BOOKS BY SCOTT SYMONS :

Place d'Armes. Toronto: McClelland & Stewart 1967. (Re-issued in paperback, 1978)

Civic Square. Toronto: McClelland & Steward 1969. (Limited edition, Book in the box.)

Heritage: A Romantic Look at Early Canadian Furniture. Toronto: McClelland & Stewart, 1971.

Helmet of Flesh. Toronto: McClelland & Stewart 1986. (Also published in New American Library in hardback and paperback editions.)

IN TRANSLATION :

Marrakech. Montréal : Québec-Amérique 1996. French translation of *Helmet of Flesh* by Michel Gaulin.

SELECTED ARTICLES, ESSAYS, DIARIES, JOURNALISM:

"The Meaning of English Canada," in *Continuous Learning*, Vol.2, no. 6, Nov.-Dec. 1963.

"Rosedale ain't what it used to be" in *Toronto Life*, October 1972.

"The Canadian Bestiary: Ongoing Literary Depravity in Canada," in *The West Coast Review*, Vol. XI, January 1977.

Canada : A Loving Look. 12 part series in *Globe and Mail*, Spring, 1979.

"Glitz City" in *The Idler*, November and December 1989.

"Mazo Was Murdered" in *The Idler*, January and February 1990.

"Atwood-as-Icon" in *The Idler*, March and April, 1990.

Spiritual diaries in *Household of God: A Parish History of St. Thomas's Church.* Eds. Hugh Anson-Cartwright, Patricia Kennedy, David A. Kent. Toronto: The Church, 1993.

"The Seventh Journey" (a last letter to Charles Taylor), in *Toronto Life*, Sept. 1997

INTERVIEWS WITH SCOTT SYMONS :

Eleven Canadian Novelists, ed. Graeme Gibson. Toronto: Anansi 1973.

The Idler, no. 23 (May/June, 1989)

The Idler, no. 36 (July/August, 1992)

SECONDARY SOURCES :

Taylor, Charles. *Six Journeys : A Canadian Pattern*. Toronto: Anansi, 1977.

Buitenhuis, Peter. "Scott Symons and the Strange Case of Helmet of Flesh" in *The West Coast Review*, Vol. 21 no. 4, Spring 1987.

– Entry on Scott Symons in the *Oxford Companion to Canadian Literature*. Toronto: Oxford University Press 1997.